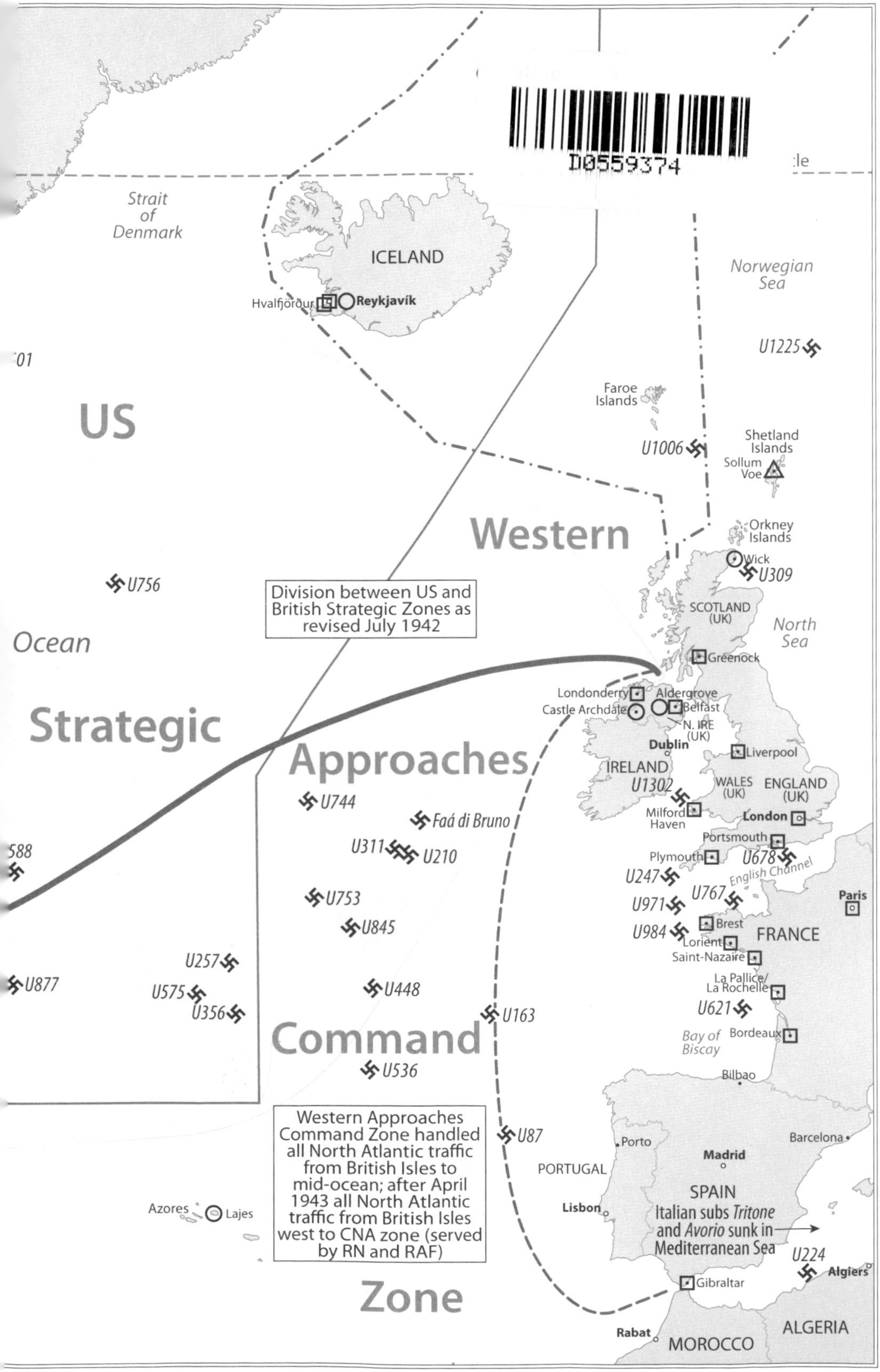

Strait of Denmark
ICELAND
Hvalfjörður
Reykjavík
Norwegian Sea
U1225
Faroe Islands
U1006
Shetland Islands
Sollum Voe
US
Western
Orkney Islands
Wick
U309
U756
Division between US and British Strategic Zones as revised July 1942
SCOTLAND (UK)
North Sea
Ocean
Greenock
Londonderry
Aldergrove
Castle Archdale
Belfast
N. IRE (UK)
Strategic
Dublin
Liverpool
Approaches
IRELAND
U1302
WALES (UK)
ENGLAND (UK)
U744
Faá di Bruno
Milford Haven
London
588
U311
U210
Portsmouth
Plymouth
U678
U247
English Channel
U767
U753
U971
Paris
U845
Brest
U984
Lorient
FRANCE
Saint-Nazaire
U257
U877
U575
U448
La Pallice/ La Rochelle
U356
U163
U621
Command
Bay of Biscay
Bordeaux
U536
Bilbao
Western Approaches Command Zone handled all North Atlantic traffic from British Isles to mid-ocean; after April 1943 all North Atlantic traffic from British Isles west to CNA zone (served by RN and RAF)
U87
Porto
Barcelona
Madrid
PORTUGAL
SPAIN
Azores
Lajes
Lisbon
Italian subs Tritone and Avorio sunk in Mediterranean Sea
U224
Algiers
Gibraltar
Zone
Rabat
MOROCCO
ALGERIA

BATTLE OF THE ATLANTIC

Also by Ted Barris

Military History

Rush to Danger: Medics in the Line of Fire

Dam Busters: Canadian Airmen and the Secret Raid against Nazi Germany

The Great Escape: A Canadian Story

Breaking the Silence: Veterans' Untold Stories from the Great War to Afghanistan

Victory at Vimy: Canada Comes of Age, April 9–12, 1917

Days of Victory: Canadians Remember, 1939–1945 (sixtieth anniversary edition, 2005)

Juno: Canadians at D-Day, June 6, 1944

Canada and Korea: Perspectives 2000 (contributor)

Deadlock in Korea: Canadians at War, 1950–1953

Days of Victory: Canadians Remember, 1939–1945 (with Alex Barris, first edition, 1995)

Behind the Glory: Canada's Role in the Allied Air War

Other Non-Fiction

101 Things Canadians Should Know about Canada (contributor)

Making Music: Profiles from a Century of Canadian Music (with Alex Barris)

Carved in Granite: 125 Years of Granite Club History

Playing Overtime: A Celebration of Oldtimers' Hockey

Spirit of the West: The Beginnings, the Land, the Life

Positive Power: The Story of the Edmonton Oilers Hockey Club

Rodeo Cowboys: The Last Heroes

Fire Canoe: Prairie Steamboat Days Revisited

BATTLE OF THE ATLANTIC

GAUNTLET TO VICTORY

TED BARRIS

PATRICK CREAN EDITIONS
An imprint of HarperCollins*PublishersLtd*

Battle of the Atlantic

Published by Patrick Crean Editions,
an imprint of HarperCollins Publishers Ltd

First edition

HarperCollins Publishers Ltd
Bay Adelaide Centre, East Tower
22 Adelaide Street West, 41st Floor
Toronto, Ontario, Canada
M5H 4E3

www.harpercollins.ca

Maps by Mark Smith of Chrismar Mapping Services.
Jacket design and photo inserts by Gordon Robertson.

Library and Archives Canada Cataloguing in Publication

Title: Battle of the Atlantic : gauntlet to victory / Ted Barris.
Names: Barris, Ted, author.
Description: Includes bibliographical references and indexes.
Identifiers: Canadiana (print) 20220269343 | Canadiana (ebook) 20220269416
ISBN 9781443460798 (hardcover) | ISBN 9781443460804 (ebook)
Subjects: LCSH: World War, 1939-1945—Naval operations, Canadian.
LCSH: World War, 1939-1945—Campaigns—Atlantic Ocean. | LCSH: Canada.
Royal Canadian Navy—History—World War, 1939-1945.
Classification: LCC D779.C2 B34 2022 | DDC 940.54/5971—dc23.

Printed and bound in the United States
LSC/H 9 8 7 6 5 4 3 2 1

To the families who sent their loved ones into the Battle of the Atlantic . . . and then grieved their loss or helped mend their bodies and minds when it was over.

List of Maps

Contents

Foreword

When Ted Barris invited me to consider writing the foreword for this book, I was honoured. I am familiar with his work, having utilized his books as a valuable resource in my own career as a military historian working in film and television. I've come to rely on his veracity and thoroughness.

Something I am proud to share with Ted Barris is a reverence for the stories of veterans. Barris's work is hallmarked by thorough research and respect for the people whose stories he retells. I have built a career guiding film and television productions and do my best to apply a similarly high ethical standard of recording faithfully what veterans tell us. Those of us who retell those stories, both filmmakers and authors, have a heavy responsibility to tell them well. It is no joke to say "I felt them looking over my shoulder." It is true; we do feel them there.

When working as naval advisor on Tom Hanks's production of *Greyhound*, a feature film based on real events during the Battle of the Atlantic, I was pleased to be part of a team whose leadership, especially Mr. Hanks himself, wanted to get it right. We truly felt those men and women looking over our shoulders as we choreographed the action sequences, explained the realities of various weapons to the CGI artists, and described how people lived and died at sea during those terrible years. Having served eleven years as an officer in the Royal Canadian Navy myself, I certainly felt my forebears watching us.

As I have done on other productions, I offered the starring actor a talisman from that era to help him feel the ethos of the time he was portraying. I told Mr. Hanks the story of a good friend, Bill, and handed him a small brass navigator's charting tool that Bill had used in the war and left to me. You'll see that small round protractor on the wheelhouse chart table whenever the chart is visible in the film. Hanks put it there purposefully as a salute to the real people whose courage and suffering we did our best to depict faithfully. After reading this book, I know, as you will, that Ted Barris understands all of this, and certainly feels it too.

I'd like to share Bill's story with you, too.

Some years ago, I was honoured to join Bill's family as they held a vigil for him near the end of his life. Bill had served in the Royal Canadian Navy over the course of a career that stretched from hard service during the war years of the Battle of the Atlantic through almost equally hard service on ice patrol duty and various Cold War assignments. Bill retired from the navy shortly after the unification of the army, navy, and air force into the Canadian Armed Forces and began a new career in Ontario's historic site service, which is where I met him.

Bill never talked about the Battle of the Atlantic during the years I knew him, except for a few funny stories and anecdotes. But when the chips were down near the end of his life, he began talking. I was deeply moved as I listened to his experiences of actions and ships whose dates and names I was already familiar with from reading, but hearing the stories from Bill, speaking from his hospital bed in his low voice, brought inescapable reality to them in a way that was quite terrible.

As a military historian, I knew the mechanics of how submarines were hunted and sometimes sunk during the Battle of the Atlantic, but one afternoon I listened to Bill describe the death by inches that was more common than the masterstroke cataclysm of which writers of fiction are so fond. He told me what the long hunt was like; the realization that the damaged submarine was no longer being careful about being quiet; how they could hear it running its motors faster, presumably as it tried to use its diving planes to resist descending as it became heavier due to the leaks. A submarine "flies" in the depths the way an airship flies in the air. It must keep near neutral buoyancy—too heavy and it can fall out of control. Bill told me they'd hear it pumping, bailing bilges that were filling from myriad small leaks into a buoyancy tank; then they'd hear the tank being blown out by compressed air, and then the motors running very hard at full speed, propellers desperately thrashing. And after more desperate loud and hard blowing, a hard crunch would be heard as the submarine was crushed by the great pressure of the sea at tremendous depth.

That particular last struggle lasted for nearly an hour—after nine hours of hunting, during which dozens of depth charges and Hedgehog projectiles had been expended on the submarine. Finally, large bubbles of air and oil would come to the surface, along with smashed woodwork and human remains. Lungs, entrails, a body.

In history books and the official record, the destruction of this particular U-boat receives only a couple of lines. But for Bill, it was an ordeal that stayed with him all his life. He wept on his pillow at the memory of it. History is more than facts and dates; it is human memory and emotion.

This book will serve to put faces and emotions on the facts and dates of the Battle of the Atlantic, the longest campaign of the Second World War. The battle was waged for nearly six years—2,074 days. In human terms, that period represents five North Atlantic winters; thousands of bleak dawns, thousands of days and nights of vigilance despite desperate fatigue; thousands of days and nights during which death might arrive unheralded.

The Royal Canadian Navy lost twenty-four warships, which took 2,000 of their people down with them. Canada's Merchant Navy service lost fifty-eight ships, which took over 1,100 of their people down with them. Despite this, the Allied navies escorted a total of 25,343 merchant ships across the wide Atlantic.

Canadians are justifiably proud that the challenge placed before us was met and surmounted. We had no choice; this fight had to be won, or the war was lost. In just six years, Canada mobilized her naval service from a tiny peacetime seed to become the third-largest Allied navy in the world in 1945. Among the Allies, Canada was the nation with proportionally the largest percentage of its population in uniform as volunteers fighting to return peace to the world.

Much has been written about the various actions and strategies of the conduct of the war, but this book will clothe those dry facts in the lived experiences of the men and women who endured those horrors and triumphs. Each of these individuals felt fear and conquered fear; they kept faith, practising astonishing resilience even during the darkest days when victory seemed terrifyingly remote.

As I think about my friend in his last days, I remember that he told me how he hated the war—how he hated it for robbing him of the carefree youth he should have enjoyed. He told me how deeply he regretted the deaths he witnessed and the killing he participated in. But he also told me how proud he felt—fulfilling his duty when Canada called, joining such a professional service, and having fought the good fight.

I read some time ago that the rate of attrition among still-living veterans of the Second World War has now surpassed their casualty rates during the hottest periods of the war. Not many are around to tell us what they saw and felt anymore. This book effectively, reverentially, and thoroughly records and passes on those memories. Perhaps one of the most powerful ways to keep peace in the world is to hold on to the memory of how hard won peace truly is. Sadly, peace does not yet come without a price.

Gordon Laco
Senior Communications Advisor, Royal Canadian Navy

Acknowledgements

In August 2020, I had reached about the halfway point in writing this—my pandemic book. Until then, I'd devoted the narrative almost entirely to the actual battles in the Atlantic: convoys of merchant ships and escort warships running the gauntlet of U-boat wolf packs between North America and Europe. However, in the midst of my writing, correspondence from an acquaintance, Jane McAllister in Athens, Ontario, suddenly changed my perspective. She thought a letter written by her aunt in Birmingham, England, to her extended family in Canada just as the Second World War began might offer some insight. The letter, a copy of which Jane enclosed, was dated September 3, 1939. It illustrated to me the plight of the average British family suddenly having to economize on everything from food to fuel, most of which was imported. The epiphany drew my attention to the life-and-death importance of those transatlantic convoys in my narrative. It reminded me why I write creative non-fiction: to put a human face on war.

Over the years, I have conducted scores of interviews with Battle of the Atlantic veterans—many of whom have since passed—but I am particularly indebted to those my father, Alex, and I interviewed in the 1980s and '90s: Dan Bordeleau, Dave Broadfoot, Harold Doig, Rodine Egan, Carman Eldridge, Alan Erson, Clyde Gilmour, Roy Harbin, Jim Hazlewood, Dave MacDonald, Don MacNeil, Terry Manuel, Margaret Los, Cliff Perry, Desmond Piers, Jerry Thornton, Murray Westgate, and Scott Young, among many. More recently, I've benefited from conversations with veterans Nan Adair Wright, Thomas Atherton, Ken Davy, Lorne Empey, Jim Hunt, Jack MacQuarrie, Ray Mecoy, and Madge Trull.

As illustrated by Jane McAllister's note, this book springs from the generosity of families who readily offered me personal letters, diaries, journals, unpublished memoirs, artifacts, and photographs that documented the experiences of many who served in the Battle of the Atlantic. Among merchant navy families, I particularly wish to thank Jane Hutchison (for her uncle John Birnie Dougall's letters), Don Rickers (for his uncle Ken Rickers's story), Steve Rae (for his father Robert Rae's video reminiscences), and Alan Bonner (for his father Harold Bonner's unpublished memoirs as a merchant sailor).

Royal Canadian Navy and Royal Canadian Air Force families contributed to my research the same way. Among them, I thank Helen Storms (for her uncle Fred Addy's service records); Geoff Mix (for his grandfather Murray Anderson's naval service); Grant Baines (for stories of his father, Gordon Baines, and mother, Hazel Le Cras, who both served); Rob Longworth and Helen McKinnon (for her father Percival Campbell's stories); George Doig and Pat MacAulay Doig (for stories and images of brothers George Sr., Harold, and John Doig); siblings Suzanne and Colin Dyke (for their father John Dyke's service saving lives); Dale Elley Bristow (for her father Lorne Elley's memories); Elaine Thorpe and Tom Franchetto (for their father Martin Franchetto's journal and photos); brothers Tim and Scott Griffin (for their father Anthony Griffin's self-published memoir); Bernice Brown Hazzard (for arranging my interview with her husband, Howard Hazzard, at his palliative-care bedside); Deanne Sky (for photos of her brother, George Jamieson); Alan Parkin and Pat English (for David Montebruno's interview of Bert Jolly); Jamie Lamb (for his father James Lamb's photos and historical accounts); Harold Mills (for his father Frank Mills's journals); Richard Norman (for background on his brother Christopher Norman); Dorothy Perry and daughter Judy (for husband/father Cliff Perry's memoirs and photos); Lee Philbrook (for her grandfather Leonard Philbrook's photos and stories), as well as fellow broadcasters George MacNabb and Jim Curran, who interviewed him; Mark Richardson (for his father Charles Richardson's info about RCAF crash boats); Mark Robertson (for loaning me the RCN sick berth staff handbook used by his father SBA Bill Robertson throughout the war); Doug Rollins (for wartime flight logs and journal of his father, Don Rollins); Davidson Tate (for memoirs and photographs of his father, Ian Tate); and Elsa-Ann Pickard (for her father Hans Sachau's photos and stories). For a unique view of wartime U-boat life, I'm grateful for time spent with Werner Hirschmann at Toronto's RCMI, and to the daughters of Walter Schmietenknop for permission to publish excerpts of his memoir, *Saved.*

As with others of my histories, I have relied on writer colleagues giving me access to their research (and permissions) for published and unpublished works, including: Ellin Bessner (*Double Threat*), Mark Bourrie (*The Fog of War*),

Carl Christie (*Truly Royal*), Sylvia Crooks (*Homefront and Battlefront*), Ken Cuthbertson (*1945: The Year That Made Modern Canada*), Anne Gafiuk (*Quietus: Last Flight*), Nathan M. Greenfield (*The Battle of the St. Lawrence*), Hugh Halliday (*Target U-Boat*), Mac Johnston (*Corvettes Canada*), Sean E. Livingston (*Oakville's Flower*), Marc Milner (*Battle of the Atlantic*), David O'Keefe (*One Day in August*), Gene Quigley (*Voices of World War II*), and Roger Sarty (*Canada and the Battle of the Atlantic*). I owe a special debt of gratitude to author David O'Brien (*HX 72: First Convoy to Die*), who sent me original research, photos, and recorded interviews of surviving crew from the motor tanker *Frederick S. Fales*.

Canadian historians have trustworthy research centres on the Battle of the Atlantic. I am grateful for their resources, and even more appreciative of their expert staffs: Xavier Parent, reference technician, and Lesley Bilton-Bravo, personnel records archivist, at Library and Archives Canada, and at Brechin Group, Jacqueline Vincent, who went above and beyond the call to find/reproduce LAC photos; Bradley Froggatt, curator of the Naval Museum of Alberta at the Military Museums in Calgary; Maggie Arbour-Doucette, collections specialist at the Canadian War Museum; Edith Cuerrier and Kayla Burry, archives technicians at The Rooms (Provincial Archives of Newfoundland and Labrador); Elena Cremonese at the Halifax Municipal Archives; Bonnie Sprack and Geraldine Hibbs, volunteers at the Bell Island Community Museum; Keith Doucette at the Halifax offices of Canadian Press for assistance retrieving Bill Mont's recounting of the Halifax riots; Terry Slobodian at the Royal Aviation Museum of Western Canada; the Naval Museum of Halifax (formerly Maritime Command Museum); and Doug Cowie, manager, Marine Museum of the Great Lakes at Kingston. I offer special thanks to the Naval Marine Archive at Picton, Ontario, and its two-person staff, Paul Adamthwaite and Betty Ann Anderson—nobody knows the length and breadth of Canadian marine history better.

Thanks to Lisha Van Nieuwenhove, editor/publisher of the *Uxbridge Cosmos* newspaper, for encouragement and antique playback equipment, and to my faithful transcriber Kate Paddison. Whenever I've asked for their help, friends have always stepped up: Rob Hart and Phil Alves for recovering lost files; John B. Kennerley for gifting me his wartime periodical library; Sean Prpick, Terry Beauchamp, Harold Beamer, Bob Mehi, and Frank Curry for supplying unexpected research; Garry Balsdon and Bill Walker for helping me track down navy contacts; Claudia McBrien, Lindy Oughtred, and Tish MacDonald for proofreading and steadfast support. And as he has for three of my previous military histories, author Malcolm Kelly (*Sprog: A Novel of Bomber Command*) provided insightful fact-checking for technical accuracy; it was *his* idea that I write this book in the first place.

As this manuscript marks my first venture into nautical material since my book about western Canadian steamboating, published in 1977, I searched for those with first-hand naval service as well as a unique skill for writing about it. Coincidentally, in the spring of 2020, Apple TV Corporation released the feature film *Greyhound*, based on C.S. Forester's 1955 novel *The Good Shepherd*. The movie featured Tom Hanks as Commander Ernest Krause, facing his first transatlantic convoy escort assignment in command of a US Navy destroyer. To ensure the film's authenticity, *Greyhound* producers hired naval history consultant and Royal Canadian

Navy officer (retired) Gordon Laco to assist the director, the cast, and Hanks himself in best capturing the atmosphere and blow-by-blow sequence on a destroyer's bridge in the heat of battle. Thus, when Gordon Laco agreed to read the original draft of my manuscript for accuracy, I was delighted. That he further agreed to write the book's introduction is indeed an honour.

For additional clarification and veracity on these pages, serving Royal Canadian Navy officer Sean E. Livingston also agreed to read the manuscript in its early drafts. An author himself (*Oakville's Flower: The History of HMCS Oakville*), Sean patiently guided my accounts of the Battle of the Atlantic through the minefield of navy constructs, process, and especially terminology. I am equally grateful that RCN(R) veteran Douglas A. McWhirter also read the work and offered his expertise. And not least among my eagle-eyed proofreaders, I wish to thank Royal Canadian Naval Volunteer Reserve veteran and friend Norman Goodspeed. Late in the Second World War, when posted to Digby, Nova Scotia, AB Goodspeed served aboard HMCS *Saguenay*. But Norman's investment in my book was not limited to his personal wartime experience. His uncle, twenty-six-year-old oiler Charles Goodspeed, died in October 1942 when his merchant steamship, *Bic Island,* was torpedoed and sunk while attempting to rescue Allied survivors of Convoy HX 212. None of *Bic Island*'s 165 officers and crew survived. Like so many military sailors, Norman wishes to honour the memory of the often-overlooked merchant sailors in the Battle of the Atlantic.

As he has with my previous books on Canadians in war, publisher/editor Patrick Crean helped inspire and shape this book from vision to final product. I cannot applaud him enough for his dedication to the idea of telling this country's people-history and my voice in that pursuit. Our partnership (cum brotherhood) has now produced eight such books over the past twenty years. Also at HarperCollins, I want to thank production editor Natalie Meditsky, editor Jim Gifford, creative services director, Alan Jones, and proofreader Gillian Watts. For the distinctive look and flow of the book, I'm indebted to two peerless pros—Gordon Robertson (jacket and photo-section design) and Linda Pruessen (copy editor). And for his unique and detailed convoy maps, my thanks to friend and life-long mapmaker Mark Smith of Chrismar Mapping Services.

Finally, I enjoy the support and affection of two families—my blood relatives, who continue to believe in my life's work, and a family of readers who care as much as I do that those who've witnessed history, such as the Battle of the Atlantic, deserve to have their experiences recorded, their voices heard, their sacrifices remembered.

Ted Barris, Uxbridge, Ontario, 2022

Royal Canadian Navy/Royal Navy Ranks and Abbreviations

Commissioned Officers

Adm—Admiral
VAdm—Vice-Admiral
RAdm—Rear-Admiral
Cmdre—Commodore
Capt—Captain
Cdr—Commander
LCdr—Lieutenant-Commander
Lt—Lieutenant
SLt—Sub-Lieutenant

Non-Commissioned Officers

CPO—Chief Petty Officer
PO—Petty Officer

Seamen

AB—Able Seaman
OS—Ordinary Seaman

Glossary of Terms and Abbreviations

AMC—armed merchant cruiser

ASDIC—Anti-Submarine Division-IC: underwater sound-ranging apparatus used to determine the range and bearing of a submerged U-boat; named after the Anti-Submarine Detection Investigation Committee, the Admiralty department that initiated research into underwater detection in the First World War

ASVR—air-to-surface vessel radar (in RAF known as AVS—aerial vessel and ship radar)

ASW—anti-submarine warfare

AVS—see ASVR, above

B-Dienst—Beobachtungsdienst: German navy radio monitoring and cryptographic service

BAMSI—British Admiralty Merchant Shipping Instructions (cards recording movements of Allied merchant ships)

BdU—Befehlshaber der Unterseeboote (or U-Boote): commander of the German U-boat service

Black Pit—portion of the mid-Atlantic over which Allied anti-submarine aircraft could not provide air cover

BR—Bomber Reconnaissance squadron

C-in-C—commander-in-chief

CAMSI—Canadian Admiralty Merchant Shipping Instructions (cards recording movements of Allied merchant ships)
CAT—Canadian Anti-Acoustic Torpedo device
COMINCH—commander-in-chief, United States Navy
DF—direction-finding
EAC—Eastern Air Command
ERA—engine room artificer
fo'c'sle—forecastle; foremost weather deck
GNAT—German Naval Acoustic Torpedo (a.k.a. T5 Zaunkönig)
Great Circle Route—shortest distance across the Atlantic between North America and the UK
Hedgehog—multi-barrel anti-submarine mortar that fired contact-fused projectiles
HF/DF—high-frequency radio direction-finding (a.k.a. "Huff-Duff")
HMCS—His Majesty's Canadian Ship
HMS—His Majesty's Ship
Kriegsmarine—German naval service
Luftwaffe—German air force
MAC—merchant aircraft carrier
mess deck—living accommodation in a ship
Metox—radar detection equipment aboard U-boats, 1942
MOEF—Mid-Ocean Escort Force
MOMP—Mid-Ocean Meeting Point
NEF—Newfoundland Escort Force
NSHQ—Naval Service Headquarters
Rüdeltaktik—wolf pack attack
RAF—Royal Air Force
RCAF—Royal Canadian Air Force

RCN—Royal Canadian Navy
RCNR—Royal Canadian Naval Reserve
RCNVR—Royal Canadian Naval Volunteer Reserve
RN—Royal Navy
SBA—sick bay/berth attendant
Schnorchel—mast for air intake and diesel exhaust in U-boats
sonar—US term for ASDIC
starshell—illumination flare descending under parachute
support group—escort group reinforcing during U-boat attack
SW1C—Surface Warning 1st Canadian
TBS—Talk Between Ships, short-range transmitter/receiver radios for sending/receiving verbal messages in a line-of-sight range between escorts
Triangle Run—convoy escort Halifax/Sydney–St. John's–Boston/New York
Type 271 radar—Royal Navy radar that could detect U-boats, though U-boats could not detect it
U-Bootwaffe—German submarine arm
Ultra—Allied code for Enigma decrypts
USAAF—United States Army Air Forces
USCGC—United States Coast Guard Cutter
USN—US Navy
VLR—very long-range patrol aircraft
WAC—Western Approaches Command
WLEF—Western Local Escort Force
work-up—training phase rehearsal for combat operation
WRCNS—Women's Royal Canadian Naval Service (a.k.a. Wrens)
WRNS—Women's Royal Naval Service (a.k.a. Wrens)

Convoy Codes

BHX—Bermuda via Halifax to UK
BX—Boston to Halifax
HG—Gibraltar to UK
HX and HXS—fast convoy, Halifax (later New York) to UK
JW—Loch Ewe, Scotland, to Russia
LN—St. Lawrence to Labrador
MKS—Mediterranean to Liverpool
OA—River Thames to Liverpool
OB—Liverpool to Atlantic
ON and ONM—Liverpool to Halifax or New York City
ONS— slow convoy, UK to North America
PQ—Reykjavik, Iceland, to White Sea, Russia
QP—White Sea, Russia, to Iceland
QS—Quebec to Sydney
RA—White Sea, Russia, to Loch Ewe, Scotland
SC— slow convoy, Sydney, Halifax, or New York to UK
SHX—Sydney to Halifax
SG—Sydney to Greenland
SQ—Sydney to Quebec
TAW—Trinidad–Aruba–Key West
TE—Gibraltar to North Africa
WS—"Winston's Specials"
XB—Halifax to Boston

BATTLE OF THE ATLANTIC

Chapter One

CALM BEFORE THE STORM

THERE WAS SOMETHING TO BE SAID FOR THEIR choice not to take sugar in their tea. Given the times, it would save them a few quid. But also, since rationing would come into effect in Britain in a few months, Alix Masheter could mix some of the sugar she was allowed—twelve ounces per person per week—into her cooking instead.[1] Just hours earlier, her prime minister had spoken on BBC Radio from his Cabinet room at 10 Downing Street. Neville Chamberlain had lamented that the British ambassador in Berlin had not received a response to Britain's ultimatum for Germany to cease its invasion of Poland and withdraw.

"Consequently, this country is at war with Germany," he had announced.[2]

That same day, September 3, 1939, the Masheter family—Alix and her husband, Ted, and their infant son, Nicholas—arrived home in Sutton, near Britain's second-largest city, Birmingham. They'd cut short a vacation in the north and driven through a hundred miles of roadway packed with lorries, buses, and cars, every one motoring to a different destination, but all heading to war. Beginning before sunrise on the previous Friday, September 1, the evacuation of hundreds of thousands of children from Britain's great cities had begun. Operation Jinmo would ultimately displace three million civilians, principally along England's south and east coasts where authorities feared German bomber attacks most. In the British capital alone on that first weekend, the famous red London buses carried 230,000 official evacuees to seventy-two London transport stations and out of town.[3] Eventually, 673,000 school-age children and 406,000 mothers were relocated to the countryside.[4]

One Ministry of Health poster promoting the evacuation program in the London Underground showed a soldier in battledress reassuring a boy dressed in shorts, wearing a toy helmet and carrying a wooden sword: "Leave Hitler to me, Sonny," the caption read. "You ought to be out of London."[5]

Alix noted that wartime blackout regulations, brought into effect the week before,* had extinguished all street lights on the family's way home. No sooner had they arrived at their Tudor Hill address when Ted ensured their automobile complied with the orders as well. He covered the car's headlamps with masks, leaving just a slit of light, and he painted its bumpers and running boards white, the sole means of visibility when travelling at night in Britain under blackout. The only sense of urgency Alex felt at this pivotal moment in her nation's history showed itself in a letter she began writing to her father and brother in Canada that night.

"I have been frantically busy making black curtains to fit over windows," she noted. And any windows left uncovered—such as those in the lavatory, pantry, and scullery, her

* Parliament passed the Emergency Powers (Defence) Act on August 24, 1939, including Defence Regulation No. 24, the blackout order.

husband simply painted over black that very night. "Not a glimmer must be seen from outside. A stressful job. But we are not afraid."[6]

The predisposition for Britons such as the Masheters to remain unafraid, unflappable, and imperturbable was a state of mind as old as the kingdom itself. Their public schools taught it. Their political leaders preached it. Their kings and queens displayed it. Their military, from the time of Alfred Tennyson's "Theirs not to reason why / Theirs but to do and die," ordered it. But what would become frighteningly clear in the days after September 3, 1939, for average British citizens—now facing a second global war in just over twenty years—was that their historic stoicism could only last as long as their stomachs remained fed. Those who'd survived the Great War and who'd lived through Germany's unrestricted submarine warfare in 1917 (which sank ships and cargoes faster than they could be replaced) saw Britain nearly brought to her knees.

As the Second World War began, there were forty-one million mouths to feed in Britain. Coincidentally, that very year, Westminster had dispatched thousands of enumerators to visit every house in England and Wales to count heads. Even King George VI and Queen Elizabeth and their staff were accounted for. Comprising 1.2 million pages in 7,000 volumes, the 1939 Register showed that the average age of a female Briton was thirty-five, the average male thirty-three.[7] But aside from painting a demographic picture of the nation, the 1939 Register was principally intended to prepare Britons for identity cards, further evacuations, allocation of wartime provisions, and ration books.

Alix Masheter had already introduced household rationing—smaller fifteen-watt electric bulbs, less coal burning at night, and, since petrol would soon be cut back for civilian vehicles, only essential use of their car. At night, Ted would fulfill his volunteer commitment for four to six hours as a warden with Air Raid Precautions (ARP) in Sutton. Then, during the day, Alix would serve two hours as a telephone operator at the local ARP office, only to return home to wage war on the kitchen front. Those among her neighbours old enough to remember rationing in the Great War suggested Alix horde her sugar and tea and "buy up kirby grips [hairpins] and elastic for knickers."[8]

Beginning on January 8, 1940, four months into the war, British homemakers had to pack patience in their shopping bags, along with their ration books and precious coupons. In the first months of the Ministry of Food's rationing program, Alix's household was restricted to four ounces of bacon or ham per person per week, twelve ounces of sugar, and four ounces of butter. Meat rationing began in March, but the July rationing got worse—only two ounces of tea, two ounces of cooking fat, four ounces of margarine, and four ounces of butter a week.[9] A nationwide shortage of sweets, however, proved the toughest deprivation of all. In place of sugar, creative homemakers turned to jam, marmalade, and syrup, but they were limited by the season.

By the end of 1940, Alix's kitchen cupboards—like most in Britain—were nearly bare. The following year, the Ministry of Food unveiled its points rationing system, which gave Alix sixteen points a month in her ration book to spend at shops that had the items she wanted. "On points," she could purchase rice, canned fruit, condensed milk, cereals, and biscuits.[10] If a product, say Spam—the American canned spiced ham import—proved too popular and stocks ran low, the ministry raised its points value, and vice versa when supply increased. The points scheme helped the ministry replenish shops with sought-after items and made Alix Masheter a discriminating shopper again, instead of a mere collector of rations.

When the Germans invaded the Channel Islands and Brittany in 1940, Alix lost her supply of fresh onions. The Ministry of Agriculture boosted production in 1941, but again the points system helped manage supply and demand. The Ministry of Food's controlled distribution system helped deliver scarce items such as oranges, lemons, and bananas to expectant mothers and under-fives;[11] unless Alix's son had encountered them before the war, Nicholas wouldn't have known what a fresh lemon or banana looked or tasted like until well after the war ended.

Meanwhile, as the U-boat war on Britain's trade lanes escalated, the consumption of fresh eggs declined rapidly; before the war Britons ate on average three eggs a week, during the war only one every two weeks.[12] That's when the Masheter household and thousands of others acquired a taste for another American invention—dried eggs. Their biscuit-like (some said cardboard-like) taste became the universal resource for homemakers unsure what to give their family at the next meal.

"Everything is topsy-turvy," Alix wrote her family in Canada that first day of the war, "but it's wonderful how calm everyone is."[13]

Britons' sense of calm masked the reality of the island nation's perilous existence, especially as the country went to war again in 1939. As the Masheters learned first-hand, a great deal of what Britons consumed came from offshore. Great Britain depended on its traditional sea lanes of trade to acquire food for sustenance, lumber for construction, steel for weapons production, and fuel to power everything on the home front and wherever British Expeditionary Force trucks, tanks, warships, aircraft fighters, and bombers might be operating. As the war began, Britons were importing twenty million tons of food per year; about 70 percent of their annual food supply came from foreign nations. Consequently, Great Britain maintained the world's largest merchant fleet—3,000 ocean-going ships and 1,000 coastal vessels.

As they had in times of peace, many of Britain's perishable and non-perishable goods arrived by sea from North America in wartime. Merchant ships from New York, Halifax and Sydney in Nova Scotia, and St. John's, Newfoundland, were literally a lifeline for people in the United Kingdom. As proof of their worth, one 10,000-ton merchant ship carried, on average, enough food to feed 225,000 Britons for a week.[14]

"Hitler must either conquer this island," Winston Churchill declared in a BBC broadcast soon after becoming prime minister in May 1940, "or he must cut the ocean lifeline."[15]

As a reaction to the threat from German surface raiders and U-boats to cut that ocean lifeline in 1939, and as it had done in April 1917 in the Great War, the British Admiralty immediately ordered all ocean-going shipping into escorted convoys. Convoys were not a new idea. They were used as a safeguard against French and American warships and privateers in the era of sailing ships, and protected troopships in the First World War, and then as this new war against Germany began. Gathering ships into a compact assembly of escorted vessels brought security in numbers and reduced the danger of U-boats targeting lone merchant ships.[16] The added firepower of light or improvised naval escort vessels flanking the convoy and long-range reconnaissance and bomber aircraft above posed an impressive deterrent against attack, at least initially.

The planning of convoys and escort strategy by the Allied navies and air forces of Britain, the United States, and Canada and their merchant navies to counter Hitler's U-boat offensive was critical. So much so that when new hostilities broke out in September 1939, an entire theatre of war—the Battle of the Atlantic—resulted and escalated into the longest sustained battle waged during the Second World War.

This 2,074-day siege, spanning the North Atlantic from the New World to the Old, triggered monumental change in Canada. As the war erupted, for example, government ministers, harbour authorities, ship designers and builders, and merchant mariners all stepped up like never before to build and operate mercantile vessels to run the North Atlantic gauntlet of Axis surface raiders and U-boat wolf packs. At the beginning of the Second World War, Canada maintained a fleet of just thirty-eight merchant ships. Its shipbuilding yards employed fewer than 4,000 workers.

Within six years, however, that number would spike upward to 126,000 skilled men and women building 410 cargo ships at shipyards in British Columbia, Ontario, Quebec, and the Maritime provinces.[17] The contracts would generate $17 million in wages and nearly $1 billion worth of merchant ships.[18] At the height of wartime shipbuilding, in 1943, Canada's production of merchant ships—150 cargo ships totalling 1,478,000 tons—was only 15 percent less than that of the United Kingdom.[19] To crew the growing merchant fleet, the Canadian Merchant Navy employed 12,000 sailors, a completely civilian service never lacking in volunteers despite the dangers they faced in the war. Despite the best efforts of military planners, however, one in eight Canadian merchant sailors would become a wartime casualty on the high seas—the highest per capita loss among Canada's wartime services.[20]

MEANTIME, the aftermath of the Great War had fostered a generation of military sailors in Germany committed to defeating the safe passage of Allied merchantmen and their military escorts, among them former First World War U-boat commander Karl Dönitz.* Just twenty-seven, eager to restore Germany's naval supremacy in warfare, and "under the spell of this unique U-boat camaraderie,"[21] he agreed to continue his service in what was then the Reichsmarine. The interwar years saw Dönitz move from torpedo boats to cruisers to commander of the quickly growing U-boat flotilla. As Chancellor Hitler renamed his navy Kriegsmarine, or "War Navy," Dönitz recommended that the Type VII U-boat—with top speed of 17.9 knots, range of 8,500 miles, and fourteen-torpedo payload—become the Reich's priority. And when war broke out and he assumed command of the Unterseebootwaffe (U-Bootwaffe), Dönitz implemented a strategy of attacking merchant convoys with specially trained packs of U-boats for greatest effect.

"If 300 boats were available," Dönitz had predicted in 1939, "the U-boat arm can achieve decisive success."[22]

As the Second World War intensified, Grossadmiral Dönitz would eventually command 830 operational U-boats and send more than 40,000 submariners into the Battle of the Atlantic. On some combat operations, his wolf packs would number up to forty and fifty U-boats, all stalking the

* Karl Dönitz's ranking will change in this narrative—from U-boat commander to admiral to grossadmiral (or grand admiral) to reichpresident just before the war ends.

same Allied merchant convoy. Despite escorts' best efforts to counter those onslaughts, the U-boats' concerted attacks against mostly unarmed merchant ships would send more than 2,000 ships (twelve million tons of shipping) to the bottom and inflict precedent-setting loss of life among merchant crews serving on the North Atlantic.[23] Crossings became most deadly when Allied convoys reached the so-called Black Pit, those mid-ocean waters beyond where Allied anti-submarine aircraft could adequately protect the shipping lanes. Repeatedly in that Black Pit, the U-boat wolf packs came close to severing Britain's ocean lifeline. And the mounting losses of ships and men would sorely test even the stoutest Allied leaders.

"The only thing that ever really frightened me was the U-boat peril," Prime Minister Winston Churchill wrote in his post-war memoirs.[24]

Frightening for a British prime minister hunkered down in his War Cabinet rooms under the streets of London, yes. But for Royal Canadian Navy (RCN) Rear-Admiral Leonard Warren Murray*—who in May 1943 would become commander-in-chief (C-in-C) Canadian Northwest Atlantic, the only Canadian to command an Allied theatre during the Second World War—it proved the greatest challenge of his navy career. It would test him to the marrow.

By the time the British Admiralty had given him that responsibility, RAdm Murray regularly attended convoy briefings at Admiralty House on Gottingen Street in Halifax. He knew most of the merchant captains preparing for each transatlantic run. He knew that despite his assurances of

* Leonard Murray's ranking will change in this narrative—from captain to commodore to rear-admiral to Commander-in-Chief Canadian Northwest Atlantic.

protection, as many as a quarter of the freighters and tankers en route to the UK wouldn't arrive safely.[25] Likewise, he understood the hardship that his Canadian escort crews regularly endured. Cold, wet, and with their crews cheek-by-jowl aboard, Canada's "sheepdog" navy of corvettes could spend weeks and weeks at sea. Tossed about like corks in vicious Atlantic gales, and fighting a nearly invisible, outnumbering force of U-boats, the rank-and-file Canadian sailors, according to Murray himself, survived on little more than "the old rations of Nelson's time,"[26] barrelled salt beef with lime or tomato juice to fight off scurvy.

The RCN went to war with exactly thirteen warships—six destroyers, five minesweepers, two training ships—and about 3,500 regular servicemen and reservists. To begin with, their attention focused on the Atlantic, but ultimately (as Japan and the Pacific came into the picture) Canadians would have to mount a "two-ocean navy." Chiefly mounting a defence of Atlantic shipping lanes, however, by 1945 the RCN had grown to become the fourth-largest navy in the world (after the US, Britain, and the Soviet Union)—with more than 400 fighting ships (900 vessels in all) and over 100,000 men and women in uniform.[27] This extraordinary output came from a nation of just over eleven million people.

At times, some said, the small ships and the fledgling crews of the RCN were all that stood between victory and defeat in the darkest days of the war. Then, by 1942, with the United States finally in the war, Allied strategists could begin a massive buildup of munitions, machinery, and troops—principally a strategic air force (Operation Bolero)—to transform Britain into the springboard for a future invasion attempt and ultimately the liberation of Europe. That would require half a million ground troops, a quarter million air force crewmen, and another quarter million personnel in supply and services. But the delivery of that eventual invasion force depended on first winning the Battle of the Atlantic. Secure the sea, military strategists said, and you may hope to win on land.

NONE of those sailors who served on the North Atlantic came from a more landlocked place than young Canadians from the Prairies. Because he'd grown up in Winnipeg, Manitoba, Able Seaman (AB) Frank Curry understood how to protect himself from biting winter winds: find shelter.[28] But on the open sea in the tiny Flower-class corvette HMCS *Kamsack*, with sixty other shipmates, there was none. Just twenty when he joined the RCN, sonar operator Curry kept a diary of his life and times aboard a Canadian escort warship.

"Very cold," Curry wrote on March 10, 1941. "A few of us huddled faithfully behind the funnel, watching our solemn convoy plunging, lunging, and rolling its way to Britain."[29]

His experience surviving Prairie whiteouts gave Curry a healthy respect for winter. Aboard a two-hundred-foot-long and thirty-three-foot-wide corvette on the North Atlantic run, however, it wasn't just the mountainous seas breaking completely over the ship that he and his shipmates endured, but the sheaths of ice—up to sixteen inches thick—that coated everything that winter. And no matter the weather on the open deck, everybody onboard *Kamsack*, including Curry, helped to bash the ice away immediately. Otherwise the ship might become top-heavy and capsize. But even when his watch ended, he found little refuge below decks.

"One's joints ache from the continuous battle trying to

remain upright," he wrote that summer. "Mess deck is a terrifying place to venture near, knee-deep in sea-water, tables smashed, clothes floating around in it, breakfast stirred in. . . . If they could only portray all this in their recruiting posters."[30]

It was this idea of portraying the nature of the war at sea that drew Lothar-Günther Buchheim to the North Atlantic. At twenty-three, he served as lieutenant and propaganda writer in the Kriegsmarine. In the autumn of 1941, he joined *U96*, with her celebrated commander Kapitänleutnant (Kptlt) Heinrich Lehmann-Willenbrock, to photograph and document the U-boat's next combat patrol.[31] After sinking a tanker in mid-ocean, *U96* altered course on the surface off the coast of Iceland, searching for convoys, recharging batteries, and heading straight into the teeth of a northeaster storm.

"It is not of this world," Buchheim wrote, but of "winds that howl steadily, of clouds that bar the horizon, of seas that look grizzled with age."[32]

"Uncommon," his commander said. "An oscillating storm front."[33]

Muffled up, clad in his work togs, a duffle coat, and rubber pants and jacket, attempting to photograph what he saw, Buchheim positioned himself in the conning tower as the U-boat bashed through wall after wall of sea water. The winds continued to rise. The breakers grew higher and gained force. The rag he used initially to dry his camera became so laden with saltwater that he had to lick the lens, using his saliva to keep it clear.

"The boat shoots up the slopes, projects its bow searchingly into the void, and dives back into the green flesh of the sea," he wrote.

The only relief from the pounding that *U96* received came when the commander gave the order to dive so his crew could eat a meal in relative peace beneath the storm.*

As a rule, Harold Pearson Bonner never came up on deck when at sea, storm or no. As a navy engineer on an Allied merchant ship, his responsibilities lay below, with the boilers and steam engines of the vessel. From a long line of merchant mariners dating back to his great-grandfather in the 1850s, Bonner, during the Second World War, worked below decks on both Great Lakes and North Atlantic merchantmen. Just before Christmas in 1944, his Imperial Oil tanker, MV *Norwood Park*, had disgorged 30,000 barrels of naval fuel at St. John's and was southbound through a storm and heading to Halifax. Fourth Engineer Bonner had just finished his four-to-midnight watch, had stopped in the galley for a cup of hot chocolate, and was visiting with his shipmate Jimmy Leboutilier, an engineer from the tanker's bridge staff.

"It's a safe night from submarines because of the weather," Leboutilier told Bonner, who was just nineteen and relatively new to the Atlantic run.[34] Leboutilier had survived the torpedoing and sinking of SS *Montrolite* by *U109* in February 1942. Instinct told him that the storm they were ploughing through would likely scare off any U-boats. He described the gale this particular night and its effect on their ship. "She's rolling nearly forty degrees. . . . She likely cannot recover from a forty-five-degree roll, or she'll go over."

Curiosity got the better of Bonner, so he donned a life jacket and greatcoat and climbed the gangways to have a look.

* While Lothar-Günther Buchheim's propaganda correspondence was first published in 1978, his more famous autobiographical novel *Das Boot* (*The Boat*) was published in 1973 and made into a movie in 1981; the film garnered six Oscar nominations.

The wind of the storm proved so powerful, he struggled to open the steel door to the upper deck. Once outside, the salt spray seemed to blot out his view of the sea. He grabbed a handrail and edged his way to the gun deck, a better vantage point.

"I was keenly aware of the horrific noise of the sea beating against our one-half-inch steel hull. When the water struck, it sounded more like metal striking metal than water. I could feel the deck twisting and rolling under my feet."

The view seemed an absolute blackout. But as his eyes adjusted, he could finally make out the ship's bow 300 feet ahead. Bonner watched as the bow seemed to rise nearly straight up. Then, as water swept over the bow and around the wheelhouse and cascaded along the upper deck, he ducked behind the funnel for protection. But the impact of all that water dragged him until he was wedged against the base of the 12-pounder gun platform. In the next climb and plunge, the tanker's propellers came out of the water, suspending the ship without forward momentum almost weightless in the air.

"As I looked forward, I was amazed we were actually corkscrewing through the water," he wrote later. "The rolls from port to starboard almost caused the wing-bridges to go under. I had seen enough. I concluded that the deck was no place for engine-room people. Better not to know what was going on up there."

VETERANS of the Battle of the Atlantic agreed that their survival depended as often on the weather as on the disposition of enemy warships. Still, at the height of the war, as many as 125 merchant ships from North America arrived at ports in the United Kingdom every week, thanks to Allied escort. Of the 2,233 merchant ships sunk on the North Atlantic during the war, only nineteen were lost from convoys with combined air and surface escort.[35] The convoys were that dependable.

As well as receiving mercantile, military, and moral support by sea from Canada, Britons at home—including the Masheter family—were encouraged to "Dig! Dig! Dig for Victory!" by cultivating gardens and growing vegetables wherever they found space. Horticultural societies, township councils, rabbit fanciers' clubs, pig clubs, and apiary clubs, plus 80,000 members of the Women's Land Army and 70,000 schoolboys, all joined the campaign to "lend a hand on the land." Over the course of the war, the number of cultivated plots—allotments—in England and Wales rose from 800,000 in 1939 to 1.45 million in 1942.[36]

Vera Lynn, who wrote and sang patriotic songs of support and longing during the war, remembered Londoners hoeing, planting, and harvesting on ground allotted for Victory Gardens in Hyde Park, in the shadow of the Albert Memorial. She noted that despite the extra effort and time required, growing their own fresh foods meant the nation as a whole was much better fed than it had been in the 1930s. Potatoes were not rationed and featured heavily in wartime British diets; by 1944 potato production had doubled compared to before the war.[37] Potatoes also served as a reminder of the sacrifice merchant mariners were making every day to keep Britons fed.

"There was even a Christmas Potato Fair held on a bomb[ed] site in Oxford Street," Vera Lynn wrote. "Each visitor signed a pledge that said, 'I promise as my Christmas gift to [merchant] sailors who have to bring our bread, that I will do all I can to eat home-grown potatoes.'"[38]

On the night of September 4, 1939, with her husband away attending to his Air Raid Precautions duties, Alix Masheter completed her letter to her father and brother in Canada behind the blackout drapes and painted-over windows of her house on the outskirts of Birmingham. Air raid sirens had blared in cities across Britain on the day before, a sound of things to come. Just twenty-four hours into the new war against Germany, Alix peeked through her curtains and wrote that the streets outside were completely unlit, quiet, and deserted. She'd written this, her first wartime letter, on onionskin paper too—her choice to economize on the weight of her letter paper and the postage required to mail it. Then, signing off, she offered a final few thoughts about her new reality as the world changed forever.

"We have to carry our gas masks with us each time we go out and keep them by us at night," she wrote. "Do not worry too much, my dears. I'm sure the stand that Britain has taken is right and just.

"Much love to you both from we three. Your loving daughter, Alix."[39]

Chapter Two

DEATH OF A CONVOY

From his vantage point, Art Silver could see every important part of his world. The crow's nest, towering about eighty feet above the main deck of this spanking new oil tanker, afforded him the best view of the convoy—merchant ships stretching for miles beside and behind him on the open North Atlantic. Keeping his vessel a safe distance from the other twenty-one ships in the convoy that had left Halifax for the United Kingdom on September 9, 1940, was his primary responsibility, although reporting anything suspicious-looking was a close second. From his lofty perspective, Silver could observe all activity forward on the 10,525-ton motor tanker, to where the bow proudly displayed the ship's name—*Frederick S. Fales*. Farther back, he could scan the superstructure amidships housing the bridge, the radio room, and the deck officers' living quarters. And aft, he could see the stern section containing the ship's diesel engine and funnel, as well as galleys, mess rooms, heads (washrooms), and cabins for thirty-six crew. On the boat deck aft he could also see a pair of lifeboats and two makeshift life rafts secured to the deck.

What really struck Silver from his bird's-eye location was that his ship was little more than a floating fuel container. Cradled within *Fales*'s 490-foot length and seventy-foot beam sat the tanker's raison d'être—130,000 barrels of Bunker C oil, collected from the fuel depots at Curaçao off the Venezuelan coast and bound for a fuel-hungry Britain.[1]

Just a year into the Second World War, merchant shipping lanes from the United States, Canada, and Newfoundland across the North Atlantic had become the most vital means of survival for Britain and the Allied war effort. And when German armies completed their occupation of most of northwest Europe in mid-1940, British reliance on the 2,700-mile-long Atlantic convoy route grew even more pronounced. Until 1939, some 20 percent of British imports had come from nearby sources—the Continent, the Mediterranean, North Africa. Twelve months later, that proportion had fallen to just 4 percent.[2]

"Unless we can establish our ability to feed this island, to import munitions of all kinds," Prime Minister Churchill had written to President Franklin D. Roosevelt, "we may fall by the way."[3]

Ordinary Seaman (OS) Art Silver was never party to missives exchanged between prime ministers and presidents. But with the war on, he'd witnessed the buzz of activity in his hometown intensifying. Born in 1915 and raised in Dartmouth, Nova Scotia, the farthest he'd ever ventured from home was wherever his employer, the Canadian Pacific Railway, sent him across the province. Not that he'd ever refused a life at sea. In 1932, when Art was seventeen, he'd joined the Royal Canadian Naval Volunteer Reserve (RCNVR), but seven years training as a weekend torpedoman did not guarantee him a front-line posting when the war broke out; in 1939, the navy had too many recruits and too few warships.[4]

Nevertheless, scuttlebutt among his pals in the North End of Halifax pointed to plenty of work in the merchant navy. Art regularly spent leisure time with his buddies Charlie Beed, Jim White, Frank Scanlon, and Gerald Scallion, who'd all grown up in St. Patrick parish, a.k.a. "Irishtown," a working-class district in the North End. If the young friends weren't buying cigarettes from the corner store at Gottingen and Gerrish Streets, they were sharing the latest news, including a classified ad that Charlie Beed had spotted in the local paper late in August 1940. Imperial Oil, one of the largest seafaring employers in eastern Canada, apparently had a tanker ship fully loaded and ready to sail to Great Britain. But it needed nearly a full crew, including firemen, oilers, pump men, a storekeeper, a cook, a baker, mess room boys, and a host of other ordinary seaman positions. Some members of Art Silver's North End gang were a bit hesitant. At twenty-nine, Jim White was among the oldest of the group; right then, he had a steady job as a plumber, but the tug of his friendship with the others brought him around.[5]

"So, we put our heads together," Silver said, "and decided to all join together."[6]

On Friday, August 30, the five North-Enders arrived at the ferry terminal building on Water Street. In an office upstairs, Beed, White, Scanlon, Scallion, and Silver presented themselves to George Findley, the Imperial Oil agent. Captain (Capt) Findley had long been Imperial Oil's shore captain, responsible for dealing with all of the company's shipping requirements—victualling (provisioning), maintaining, repairing, and, in this case, crewing its tankers.

"What do you need, Mr. Findley?" the young men asked.

"Who've we got here?" Findley said.

Each recruit described his work experience and offered references.

By all accounts Findley had a reputation for being approachable, efficient, and loyal to merchant mariners from Halifax. In quick order that day, he signed up the five young applicants: Scallion as mess room boy, Scanlon as galley boy, White as baker, and Beed and Silver as ordinary seamen. Perhaps because of his previous experience in the peacetime RCNVR, Silver would assume on-board duties as foremast lookout. Capt Findley told them they'd receive Imperial Oil's base salary for ordinary seamen—forty-five dollars a month—and instructed them to report to Earl Richards, the bosun aboard *Frederick S. Fales*, as soon as possible.

The North-Enders all went home, packed basic necessities—shirts, dungarees, overcoats, shoes, and toiletries—and returned to the waterfront, where a harbour boat would taxi them to the tanker anchored north of Halifax Harbour in Bedford Basin. All but Gerald Scallion returned quickly to the waterfront for the short ride to their new home; at age twenty-two, getting permission from home and a bit of spending money from his brother took Gerald some extra time.

The North-Enders solved only part of George Findley's crew replacement problem. Imperial Oil's onshore fixer still had key positions to fill—helmsmen for the bridge, firemen for the auxiliary steam engines, an oiler, a pump man, cooks, a victualler (the storekeeper who organized food supplies), and mess room staff, to name a few. He got on the phone and soon hired three former Great Lakes seamen: Jack Beanland from Montreal; Herbert Bonin from Penetanguishene,

Ontario; and Edward Dawn from Fort William, Ontario. Locally, he reached Clarence Cleveland from Musquodoboit Harbour, Burton Kent from Point Pleasant, Harl Morris from Advocate Harbour, and William Hart from Dartmouth. Ray Shaw, from Woodside, agreed to come aboard as the ship's victualler.

By coincidence, the day Capt Findley was looking for a mess room boy, Jack Baker, just eighteen, had decided on a whim that he was going to sea too. He wasn't inside the Imperial Oil office on Water Street but a few minutes when he ran into Halifax merchant navy veteran Sam Taylor. The experienced cook was also looking for work, but he needed a mess assistant. Taylor told young Jack to join him in the work line and to put his hand up to volunteer exactly when Jack signalled. Presently Capt Findley spoke up. "We need a skeleton crew to take the *Fales* across the pond."

"Okay with me," said Taylor, putting his hand up right away.

Findley knew Sam. He nodded, and then turned to Jack. "What about you?"

"I'm for it," said Jack, throwing his hand in the air, the same as Sam Taylor.

"Can you go up to the [Bedford] Basin right away?"

"Sure," the new cook and mess boy said together.

"Okay, now get the hell home and get permission from your mother," Findley told Jack.[7]

For a few of the positions he needed to fill, Capt Findley turned to merchant seamen who'd worked for Imperial Oil elsewhere. He convinced Simeon Rodenhizer, who'd served with the firm for eight years, to cut short his vacation in Conquerall Bank, Nova Scotia, to join *Fales*'s crew as a pump man. Findley also approached one of the youngest former employees, Bert Myers, who lived in Woodside, on the Dartmouth side of Halifax Harbour. At eighteen, Bert had dropped out of high school in the mid-1930s and worked on Imperial Oil tankers that supplied coastal communities around the Maritimes. He'd worked as an oiler and fireman on SS *Sarnolite*, and had managed to salt away enough money to take some time off. Consequently, after a first call to Bert's father, Findley knew that it would take more than a decent wage to attract young Bert to *Fales*'s crew.

On the phone from the Imperial Oil office, Findley reassured Bert that while *Fales* was powered by a modern eight-cylinder Fiat diesel engine, she still relied on two steam boilers and engines to heat crew cabins and power the electrical system. The work, he said, would be perfect for Bert.

"I don't want a job right now," Myers told Findley.

The captain made a final appeal to Myers, pointing out how important it was to get this supply of oil to Britain because people over there were facing tough times. "It's your duty," Findley said finally. "There's a war on. People are dying."[8]

The next day, Myers signed on as fireman for one trip. And over the next few days the newly signed-on crewmen all began making their way to the waterfront, where they took a motorboat taxi out to *Fales* and reported to Earl Richards.

"Once they took us on board," Art Silver said, "we weren't allowed ashore. We had to stay there for several days before we sailed."

Aboard *Fales*, the Halifax recruits quickly learned what had happened to the previous crew. According to *Fales*'s officers, the crew, principally from China, had mutinied. "They were very unhappy about the idea that war had broken out," recalled Pat O'Brien, an officer aboard *Fales*.[9] In March 1940, O'Brien had joined the merchant ship in Cardiff, Wales, as her fifth engineering officer. He'd watched the simmering discontent among the Chinese crewmen grow into disobedience and anger. On August 25, the inbound tanker cleared the submarine nets at the entrance to Halifax Harbour and arrived at her assigned berth in Bedford Basin to await convoy instructions. O'Brien solemnly watched as the thirty-six Chinese crewmen packed their belongings into empty paint drums and filed down the gangplank into the custody of the Royal Canadian Mounted Police (RCMP).

"They had fear of the [U-boat] sinkings," O'Brien said.

Fales's Chinese crewmen expressed in their "mutiny" what statisticians at the British Admiralty, the Royal Canadian Navy, and the Allied merchant navies were all witnessing in loss statistics—regularly published in major newspapers—during the first year of the war. The North Atlantic shipping lanes had become a hazardous place to work. On August 26, 1940, the day after *Fales* pulled into Bedford Basin, the *Halifax Chronicle* published a statement from the Canadian minister of defence, James L. Ralston. In an effort to reassure the public and at the same time give credit to his RCN crews, he noted that "while 2,200 ships had been convoyed [from Canada across the North Atlantic] only nine had been lost."[10]

THE broader view, had Minister Ralston chosen to characterize it, painted a less rosy picture. The very day that Britain declared war on Germany—September 3, 1939—proved to be the first day of nearly six years of war against Hitler's U-boats. That same evening, a conning tower lookout aboard

U30, which was patrolling northwest of Ireland, spotted what the U-boat's commander, Leutnant (Lt) Fritz-Julius Lemp, deduced could only be an armed merchant cruiser (AMC). He shadowed the vessel's zigzag course and eventually fired two torpedoes at it. One tore into the engine room of the 13,581-ton steamship *Athenia*, and the unarmed passenger liner, bound for Canada, came to stop in the water. She sank fourteen hours later, taking 117 of the 1,418 aboard to their deaths. It didn't matter that Nazi Germany denied the action and falsified *U30*'s records to cover it up. The attack proved to be the opening salvo in the longest battle of the Second World War—the Battle of the Atlantic.

Right after the sinking of *Athenia*, the Royal Navy (RN) instituted the convoy system to protect its merchant ships in transit, and it established a blockade against German trade by sea—harassing, sinking, or capturing German merchant vessels. In response, the Kriegsmarine deployed its surface raiders—battle cruisers and pocket battleships—to attack Allied shipping in the open seas, and its U-boats to sink merchant ships around the British Isles. At the end of September 1939—just twenty-seven days into the war—the German battle fleet had sunk fifty-three Allied ships, forty-one of them torpedoed by U-boats in territorial waters around Britain and out in the Atlantic.

Throughout the fall, however, Kriegsmarine U-boats were forced to operate from their bases on the North Sea, principally because the RN controlled the English Channel and the waters between Scotland and Norway. In addition, Germany had gone to war before its navy was fully ready. Despite promises of greater warship production, in September 1939, the U-Bootwaffe, the U-boat fleet, consisted of thirty-eight boats.[11] In effect, such a limited number of U-boats appeared to undermine Germany's ability to sever or even disrupt Britain's sea trade. But the warrior capabilities of the U-Bootwaffe's commanders and crews more than compensated for the Kriegsmarine's deficiency in boats.

Such were the circumstances when the articulate, ambitious, and ideologically driven U-boat commander Joachim Schepke arrived on the scene. Born in 1912, Schepke grew up in Flensburg, Germany, where his father's professional career as a lawyer and their upper-middle-class lifestyle helped him to realize a childhood dream of becoming an officer cadet, in 1930. Four years later, Schepke had completed service in the pocket battleship *Deutschland* and advanced to the reconstituted U-boat arm of the Reichsmarine as an instructor at torpedo school. He received his first command in 1938 in *U3*, a small Type II coastal submarine in the training flotilla, and as the war began he earned a transfer to another Type II—*U19*—in an operational flotilla.

Kptlt Schepke considered every career challenge a stepping stone to being noticed and promoted. While membership in the Nazi Party was optional for Kriegsmarine officers, for example, Schepke became an enthusiastic supporter by choice.[12] And he treated every patrol, even the menial task of laying mines in British coastal waters, with zeal and nationalist fervour. In January 1940, Schepke also proved that not only could he navigate anywhere he wished and deliver his payloads, but he could also bring his U-boat home through concerted counterattack. Overnight on January 8/9, near the Humber River estuary, he torpedoed and sank the Norwegian merchant steamer *Manx*. A responding Royal Navy destroyer drove him under with depth charges that destroyed *U19*'s rudders; he still managed to bring the U-boat home safely by steering with her propellers.

By the end of that month, Schepke stood sixth on the list of "tonnage kings," U-boat commanders with a substantial number of ships destroyed; he'd sunk seven, or nearly 13,000 tons of enemy shipping. He was just twenty-eight, but Schepke's aggressive tactics had earned him respect among his crew and raised his profile in the U-Bootwaffe.

That list of tonnage kings included more rising stars. Ahead of Kptlt Schepke in the race were other ambitious U-boat commanders with impressive totals from the first months of the war. On September 17, 1939, Otto Schuhart, the thirty-year-old captain of *U29*, searched for a convoy in the Western Approaches—waters west of Ireland that led to major shipping ports in Great Britain. Running submerged, because the Royal Navy aircraft carrier HMS *Courageous* had launched Swordfish biplanes to search for enemy warships, Schuhart tried to close on the carrier, but his eight knots submerged were no match for *Courageous*'s twenty-six, until about 7:30 that evening, when the carrier turned into the wind to launch more aircraft. Her broadside position gave Schuhart ample time and target. He fired a spread of torpedoes, then crash-dived to escape the enemy's escorting destroyers. Two of his torpedoes struck *Courageous*; she sank in less than fifteen minutes, with the loss of 518 of the ship's 1,260 crewmen.[13] In just one patrol and one attack, Schuhart had tallied 41,905 tons, and he was awarded the Iron Cross First and Second Class.

A month later, Günther Prien—a U-boat captain already awarded an Iron Cross Second Class for sinking three British merchant ships in the first week of the war—piloted his *U47* into history at the Royal Navy's Home Fleet base at Scapa Flow, in the Orkney Islands. Deemed impregnable because of its archipelago protection and added defensive works—gun batteries, searchlights, mines, anti-submarine nets, patrol boats, and block ships—Scapa Flow's natural harbour had an apparent gap of some fifty feet at its northern entrance.[14] On the moonless night of October 14, thirty-one-year-old Kptlt Prien used the illumination of aurora borealis to thread his way through the gap and into the harbour, where he spotted the battleship HMS *Royal Oak* and fired four torpedoes; one misfired, and of the remaining three, one struck *Royal Oak*'s anchor chain harmlessly. Prien turned *U47* and fired two more torpedoes from his stern tubes. Again no hits. The U-boat withdrew so his crew could reload. Just after 1 a.m., *U47* launched three more torpedoes.[15]

"After three tense minutes comes the detonation," his war diary stated. "There is a loud explosion, roar, and rumbling. Then come columns of water, followed by columns of fire."[16]

Weighing nearly 30,000 tons, *Royal Oak* rolled on her side and sank in thirteen minutes, taking 835 of her complement of 1,234 to their deaths. *U47* and Kptlt Prien returned to Wilhelmshaven to a hero's welcome. Admirals Karl Dönitz and Erich Raeder came aboard to personally congratulate the commander. Hitler sent a private plane to deliver the entire crew to victory celebrations in Berlin; then he personally decorated Prien with the Knight's Cross and hosted a lunch for the full *U47* crew. But the U-boat commander, whom German newspapers dubbed "the Bull of Scapa Flow," had only just begun. Prien went on to sink thirty Allied ships (200,000 tons of enemy shipping).

Of all the rising stars in the ranks of the U-Bootwaffe,

perhaps none had the breadth of experience that Kptlt Otto Kretschmer had. Born in 1912 in Prussian Silesia, Otto acquired a hunger for language and science from his schoolmaster father. While the young Otto also expressed interest in the navy, his father sent him to England, where he earned a degree at the University of Exeter. In 1930 Kretschmer entered the Reichsmarine as an officer cadet. He served aboard a variety of surface warships and then, in 1936, he joined the U-boat arm of the Kriegsmarine. He assumed interim command of *U35* during the Spanish Civil War, and then *U23* before the Second World War broke out.

In the first months of the war, Kptlt Kretschmer earned a reputation for mining British ports and estuaries; in one daring pre-Christmas attack on a convoy in 1939 near the Farne Islands, he sank two merchant ships in less than an hour. Rather than sending a spread of torpedo shots at his targets all at once, Kretschmer practised a "one torpedo one ship" method to conserve munitions;[17] he also recommended surface attacks rather than submerged engagement. In just five months, "Silent Otto" Kretschmer had completed nine combat patrols, spent ninety-six days at sea, and sent 30,000 tons of enemy shipping to the bottom. In August 1940, Grossadmiral Erich Raeder personally decorated him with the Knight's Cross.

The war diaries of just a handful of U-boat commanders—Schepke, Schuhart, Prien, and Kretschmer—illustrated the exponential increase in the level of competence within the Kriegsmarine's revitalized U-boat arm. By most measuring sticks, the skill and daring of these lone wolves was having an impact. Between the start of the war and March 1940, the U-Bootwaffe had sunk roughly 200 Allied ships.

The total might well have been higher if not for problems the U-boats faced with depth control of torpedoes and faulty detonators (as Prien had encountered during the attack on *Royal Oak*). Some suggest torpedo failures alone prevented the Germans from sinking another fifty to sixty Allied vessels. Nevertheless, in August 1940 the British Admiralty informed Prime Minister Churchill that Britain and her maritime allies were losing more than a quarter of a million tons of merchant shipping every month.[18]

"Dominating our power to carry on the war, or even keep ourselves alive," Churchill wrote, "[is] our mastery of the ocean routes and the free approach and entry to our ports."[19]

IT took nearly the full day to launch Convoy HX 72—the seventy-second convoy of the Second World War to depart Halifax Harbour for Britain—on September 9, 1940. As prescribed by British Admiralty edict and the RCN's Naval Control of Shipping office in Halifax, at 9 a.m. three Fundy-class minesweepers—HMCS *Comox*, *Nootka*, and *Gaspé*—and a Battle-class trawler, HMCS *Arras*, were the first to pass through the Harbour Defence Boom (anti-submarine nets) stretching from York Redoubt to McNabs Island at the entrance to Halifax Harbour. They completed a sweep at the mouth of the harbour. Next through the defence boom came River-class destroyer HMCS *Saguenay* and the former RCMP patrol boat *French*. The two warships used Anti-Submarine Division-IC (ASDIC) underwater detection equipment dating back to the First World War; ASDIC transmitted acoustical pulses of energy to reveal underwater objects, such as U-boats, as echoes returning to the transmitting ship. For ninety minutes, *Saguenay* and *French* probed sixteen miles out to sea to where Convoy HX 72 would shortly assemble.

With the Naval Control schedule calling for full readiness of all ships in Bedford Basin by 2 p.m., the Halifax section of Convoy HX 72—steamers, coal-fired tramps, and diesel-driven merchant ships—had been firing up marine engines all morning. Then, just before 1:30 p.m., the Turple Head signal station on the Dartmouth shoreline alerted the outbound traffic to commence exit from the basin, and the twenty-one merchant ships began filing through Halifax Harbour and past the Harbour Defence Boom.

Since she was a modern motor tanker, it didn't take *Frederick S. Fales* long to power up and prepare to exit the basin. However, crewmen aboard *Fales* enjoyed some last-minute excitement as their tanker got underway behind SS *Tregarthen*, with the commodore of the merchant fleet, Hugh Rogers, aboard. At that moment, Capt Frank Ramsay (deputy commodore) and officers of the afternoon watch on the bridge of *Fales* were looking intently forward, following *Tregarthen*'s lead.

Suddenly a harbour taxi appeared alongside *Fales*. Aboard, clutching his small suitcase, was Gerald Scallion. After consenting to join *Fales*'s crew as a mess room boy a few days before, the young North-Ender who'd gone home to pack his things and return hadn't. Until now. With all of his buddies—Charlie Beed, Frank Scanlon, Art Silver, and Jim White—watching the comical scene from *Fales*'s boat deck, Scallion scrambled aboard the tanker at the last possible minute. Not to be outdone, young Jim White directed his friends' attention to a gun emplacement on McNabs Island, the location of Halifax's nineteenth-century fort, off to the east side of the harbour. There, in the middle of training exercises with Halifax's 52nd Shore Battery, Jim's younger brother Ted had rushed to the fort's 9.2-inch naval gun.

"I trained the gun scopes on them at the stern," Ted White said, "and saw them all waving."

Bringing up the rear of Convoy HX 72, at just after 5 p.m., the Royal Navy's HMS *Jervis Bay*, formerly a passenger liner, passed from Halifax Harbour into the open waters off the south shore of Nova Scotia, ensuring that any and all convoy stragglers picked up the pace. *Jervis Bay*'s designation as an "armed merchant cruiser" was something of a misnomer. Even a year into the war, the Admiralty faced a shortage of warships. And so, by adding armament and White Ensign flags to former civilian vessels, the Royal Navy hoped to fill the gap until actual warships were built to provide proper convoy escort. To repurpose *Jervis Bay* as an armed cruiser, navy improvisers had removed anything on her deck that might burn, filled in gaps with sandbags, bolted eight antiquated six-inch guns to her deck, and strung telephone cable between the bridge and gun positions for communication.[20] In truth, during any potential gun battle at sea, only *Jervis Bay*'s stout-hearted crew would stand between enemy warships and disaster.

Ten hours after the first merchant ships began to move from Bedford Basin—travelling at about eight and a half knots or, in effect, the fastest speed of the slowest vessel—the last of the convoy exited Halifax Harbour. But by 6 p.m., twenty-one ships had formed the nucleus of Convoy HX 72 at sea. Three escorts—HMCS *Saguenay*, HMCS *French*, and HMS *Jervis Bay*—had all but completed what orders demanded of them. Meanwhile, as the convoy coalesced, and as a deterrent to enemy warships or U-boats, Hudson bombers from the Royal Canadian Air Force (RCAF) No. 11 Bomber Reconnaissance (BR) Squadron took turns flying patterns extending from Nova Scotia's south shore to about 250 miles out to sea, their maximum fuel distance. Once the convoy had left the extent of their air-coverage zone, the Hudsons returned to base at Dartmouth.[21] At 7:30 p.m., with her job completed, the trawler HMCS *French* also steered away from the convoy and returned to Halifax.

The next day, September 10, passed uneventfully, so after dark, HMCS *Saguenay*, with her four 4.7-inch naval guns, anti-aircraft guns, torpedo tubes, depth charges, and exceptional speed (thirty-one knots), also parted company with the formation. Convoy HX 72, or at least the Halifax section of it, was steaming into open ocean 300 miles due east of Halifax.

Over the next two days, however, HX 72 would double in size. The same day that HMCS *Saguenay* and *French* led motor tanker *Frederick S. Fales* and the rest of the Halifax section out to sea, HMS *Laurier* (a former RCMP patrol boat) and HMS *Reindeer* (a former American yacht) also escorted eleven merchant ships from Sydney Harbour on Cape Breton Island out into waters off Newfoundland's east coast to meet them. By mid-morning on September 11, the eleven ships of Convoy SHX 72 had joined the Halifax group. All of this manoeuvring, merging, realigning—indeed, all communications—had to be conducted in radio silence.

This was a tense time for lookout Art Silver. While not as seasoned as some of the old salts aboard the tanker *Fales*, during his years with the RCNVR, Art had learned the importance of a ship's lookout. He knew that a sailor standing on a ship's deck could see another ship approximately five miles away, but a lookout in a crow's nest eighty feet above the deck could spot another ship at twice that distance.*

Of course, such a powerful vantage point depended entirely on the weather between the lookout and the distant ship. On the Grand Banks, where the Labrador Current from the Arctic Ocean continuously collided with the Gulf Stream from the tropics, the resulting fog meant that nothing was certain. And even with the best seamanship and the greatest vigilance, Silver knew his ship was at the mercy of every negligent sailor in charge on the deck of a passing vessel. That's why Atlantic merchant seamen had invented fog buoys that were tethered to a thousand feet of cable and thrown astern of each ship in the convoy; in-tow, the buoy shot up a column of spray that alerted the merchant ship following behind as to what was ahead.

"We were lucky to see twenty-five feet ahead to see that buoy," Silver said. In such situations, time was critical. Even at a convoy speed of eight or nine knots, a thousand feet of cable didn't give a 10,000-ton tanker much time or distance to react. "I never took my eye off that buoy."

Fortunately, the fog abated. Then, two mornings later, on September 13, a third feeder convoy of eight freighters and seven tankers—Convoy BHX 72, led by armed merchant cruiser HMS *Voltaire* and travelling northeast from Bermuda—caught up with the first two sections and merged. But circumstances soon altered Commodore (Cmdre) Hugh Rogers's convoy size again. One ship from the original HX formation had been diverted back to Halifax, three from BHX were ordered there as well, and a fifth straggler had gone off on its own.

---

* The formula works as follows: 1.17 times the square root of elevation equals the distance in nautical miles; so, the square root of 80 is 8.94 x 1.17 = 10.46.

By six o'clock that evening, Cmdre Rogers aboard SS *Tregarthen* and Vice-Commodore Frank Ramsay aboard *Fales* were leading a convoy that now consisted of forty-two vessels spread over about twenty square miles of ocean. *Fales* led the fourth of nine columns stretching from west to east; each column consisted of either four or five ships strung out for several miles in single file. All columns, according to pre-designed plan, zigzagged in unison.

From his lookout position on the foremast of *Fales*, Art Silver could see, starboard and astern, SS *Dalcairn* (carrying 8,000 tons of Canadian prairie wheat) as well as the refrigerated SS *Canonesa* (loaded to the brim with Canadian bacon, ham, cheeses, and fish)—both ships bound for Manchester, England. Farther to the starboard and at the tail end of the ninth column of merchant ships steamed SS *Baron Blythswood* (carrying some of the richest iron ore in the world from the Wabana mines of Bell Island, Newfoundland) headed for Britain's steel foundries. Meanwhile, directly astern and of particular concern because of her cargo, sailed another British motor tanker, *Torinia*, carrying 13,800 tons of high-octane fuel for the Royal Navy and Royal Air Force (RAF). In total the convoy carried 226,661 tons of freight and fuel. Considering that the British people—the convoy's ultimate beneficiaries—needed a minimum of 40 million tons of freight and fuel each year to survive, Convoy HX 72's size was not insignificant.[22]

By the time Kptlt Joachim Schepke began his ninth patrol in the spring of 1940, much had changed in the siege at sea with Britain, including the very warship beneath his feet. His previous command, *U19*, had been a Type II design, built in 1935.

At 275 tons, its top speed was twelve knots (on the surface), with a submersible depth limit of 260 feet, a range of 1,800 nautical miles, and firepower consisting of up to five torpedoes or a dozen mines. His new command, *U100*, a Type VIIB design, was a bigger, faster, and more lethal boat. Displacing 740 tons, its speed on the surface could reach 17.9 knots; it could also dive to 750 feet and (because of its enlarged fuel capacity) cover 8,500 miles on a single patrol. Twin rudders gave the U-boat additional agility, and its armament consisted of fourteen torpedoes (triple that of the Type II), with a deck gun and an anti-aircraft gun on its superstructure for defence when surfaced. And instead of a complement of twenty-five submariners, *U100* could carry up to sixty crewmen. German shipbuilders would ultimately construct more than 700 Type VIIB U-boats throughout the war.

Their arrival would take time, and their impact wouldn't be felt until crews and boats accumulated experience under fire. Though the prototypical Type VIIA was launched in 1936, refinements took several years to complete. With other, higher priorities for the Wehrmacht (army) and the Luftwaffe (air force) to that point in the war—the invasion of Scandinavia, the Blitzkrieg into the Low Countries, the occupation of France, and the Battle of Britain, to name a few—Hitler did not signal the acceleration of U-boat construction until May 24, 1940. During the same period, the Kriegsmarine had lost twenty-three U-boats, while only thirteen new Type VIIBs had been launched. That left the U-Bootwaffe's operational strength in the spring of 1940 virtually the same as in September 1939, at about forty U-boats.

Technically, Kptlt Schepke's new commission at the Germania shipyard in Kiel should have been numbered *U70*.

But German strategists assigned their seventieth boat the number *U100* to fool the British about the overall size of the U-boat flotilla. In any event, by the end of May 1940 the new commander had met his crew and their new Type VIIB boat and had begun workups. This was normally a six-month training period, but Schepke and his crew chopped that time in half. And on her first patrol from Kiel to Lorient, France, in August, *U100* sank six ships (five of them from one outbound convoy, OA 204), adding 25,812 more tons to Schepke's ballooning tonnage statistics.

Kptlt Schepke demonstrated a different brand of leadership in the U-boat flotilla. He was aggressive and practical. He introduced a "work squad" mentality aboard his boat; between patrols, his crew received ample shore leave for recreational pursuits, but upon their return, everybody participated in the resupply work, refocusing their attention on the pending patrol.[23] When his crew partied, Schepke ensured there was plenty of schnapps to go 'round, and also the latest in music, including contemporary English jazz recordings. Schepke's distinctive approach won favour with his superiors, including Adm Karl Dönitz, who sensed that if the end result was improved morale aboard U-boats, Schepke should be encouraged.

By August 1940, Dönitz and his U-boat aces had moved their base of operations from German ports to the occupied harbours of Brest, Lorient, St. Nazaire, and La Rochelle on the west coast of France. This relocation placed most of the U-Bootwaffe's operational Type VII U-boats many hours closer to what would become Dönitz's principal target—the Atlantic sea lanes of Britain's merchant fleets. It also gathered the admiral's top "tonnage kings"—Otto Kretschmer,

Günther Prien, and Joachim Schepke—at the starting line of those operations.

By this time, each of them had sunk nearly 200,000 tons of merchant shipping. And, by coincidence, on September 1, 1940, all three happened to be in Lorient, where they found a café to celebrate their victories, well into the night, over copious amounts of wine. To mark the occasion, Kretschmer remembered, Schepke concocted a timely bet.

"Let us wager on which of us reaches 250,000 tons first," Schepke challenged his two rivals, offering "champagne for the three of us, if either of you beats me to it."[24]

Either the wine or an equal expression of bravado from Kretschmer and Prien ensured that the wager was on. It was no coincidence that the presence of three of the Kriegsmarine's most successful U-boat commanders at the occupied ports in France motivated Adm Dönitz to gamble for a breakthrough in his year-long battle with the Royal Navy convoys. The strategy of gathering U-boats into attacking formations was not new. In the last few months of the Great War, the German navy had experimented with patrol lines of U-boats fanning out across convoy routes and attacking them together. During one such operation, in 1918, two U-boats attempted a coordinated attack against Allied shipping in the Mediterranean; one U-boat was sunk, and her captain (then junior officer), Karl Dönitz, taken prisoner.

With the shift of the German navy from peacetime Reichsmarine to the war footing of the Kriegsmarine in 1936, Dönitz revisited and rehearsed his U-boat group tactics. By mid-1940, not only did he have the geographical advantage of the occupied French coastal bases (fortified by massive concrete U-boat pens beginning in 1941), but Dönitz also had Beobachtungsdienst (B-Dienst), the German Navy radio-monitoring and cryptographic service, at his disposal. As far back as 1935, German Naval Intelligence had intercepted, decoded, and analyzed Royal Navy radio communications. In fact, during the Norwegian campaign in March and April 1940, B-Dienst managed to read up to 50 percent of British naval signals; and when the British withdrew from Bergen, Norway, the Germans captured copies of enemy administrative code, Foreign Office cipher material, and merchant navy code, along with call signs and recoding tables. When radio signals from the British Admiralty to the convoys began to increase, B-Dienst was able to read and relay most of them with little delay.[25]

Despite the Royal Navy's superiority in numbers of ships on the surface and their ASDIC listening devices to detect submerged U-boats near a convoy, Dönitz felt confident that his B-Dienst intelligence and a strategy of attacking with packs of U-boats on the surface (where ASDIC could not detect them) would yield results. He called the strategy *Rüdeltaktik*, or "pack tactic." With three of his most successful U-boat commanders all on September patrols beyond the Western Approaches, and a heavily laden convoy headed their way, Dönitz instructed his U-boats to form a north-south line on the surface five miles apart across the anticipated path of the convoy.

ON paper, Cmdre Hugh Rogers expected Convoy HX 72 would complete the transatlantic crossing to the Western Approaches—a journey of 2,700 miles—in about eleven days. If all went well, by September 13 his forty-two-ship convoy would rendezvous with Royal Navy warships sent out to escort the merchantmen safely into Liverpool. But after four days of hard slogging, his convoy was only 200 miles east of Cape Race, Newfoundland. Cmdre Rogers still had nearly 2,000 miles ahead of him and things were beginning to unravel.

It quickly became clear that many of the steam-driven or coal-fired merchant ships in his convoy could not keep up to the prescribed eight-to-nine-knots mean speed. Even over the first few days, several ships had slowed, moved to the rear of the convoy, or stopped completely to deal with engine breakdowns. A series of planned evasive exercises—zigzagging in lockstep across the convoy to avoid torpedoes—that were signalled via pennants and flags from the commodore's flagship, had ended in disarray. Of necessity, communications had to happen without radio transmission.

Among *Fales* crewmen recruited for this trip, Ed Dawn was perhaps most suited to work on a North Atlantic merchant tanker. Originally a deckhand on ships of the Great Lakes and the lower St. Lawrence River canals, then a quartermaster aboard Imperial Oil tankers to Venezuela and back for three years, he'd been loyal. But he never let that blind his sense of personal survival. "They want you, body and soul," he said.[26]

Quartermaster duties aboard *Fales* meant he'd arrive on the bridge for a four-hour watch. He'd work in tandem with the first mate and often with Capt Ramsay.

"There's the board. There's the clock," the mate would tell him.

"Aye, sir," Dawn would reply. He'd look at the ship's course and, depending on the conditions and orders, take the helm. Unlike in the days of mighty windjammer wheels that towered over a man, all *Fales*'s bridge instruments were automated and hydraulic; using the small wheel, Dawn could adjust the ship's course with the easiest of grips and slightest of turns. Halfway through his watch, he and the mate moved to the wing of the bridge as lookouts for the rest of their watch.

During one such night watch, AB Dawn and the mate spotted light spilling from the side of a merchant ship in the convoy—likely an open porthole. Along with radio silence 'round the clock, at night convoys had to remain blacked out. "It was open every goddam night," Dawn said. "Talk about a dead giveaway."

If not exactly a case of "loose lips sink ships,"* it was certainly "careless light deadly at night."

Ed Dawn had survived his share of tough sailing on the Great Lakes and in the tropics, but six days into the North Atlantic crossing, on September 15, Convoy HX 72 ran into rough seas that shook even the veterans. Winds up to thirty knots whipped ordinary swells into waves "two or three times as high as the ship,"[30] making each plunge into a trough or break across a crest a bone-rattling experience. The pounding of sea and near-gale-force winds ripped down communications lines, smashed lifeboats, and shifted cargoes, rendering freighters unbalanced.

Meanwhile, tankers such as *Frederick S. Fales*, with extremely low freeboards (barely ten or eleven feet from main deck to the waterline), found their decks constantly awash with punishing breakers. The first day of the storm,

* The warning to "beware of unguarded talk" originated with the US War Advertising Council during the Second World War, but became just as popular a British idiom ("Careless Talk Costs Lives"). It eventually found its way onto a poster produced by Seagram's distillers that was displayed at drinking establishments.

two freighters dropped behind the convoy to deal with damage and engine problems. The next day, another freighter broke down completely, forcing *Jervis Bay* to slow and offer protection. The storm did not relent until the afternoon of September 18. By then, gaps in the convoy had widened, and *Jervis Bay* took hours to round up the stragglers. Then the AMC raced away from the reorganized convoy temporarily—so as not to give away an exact location with a radio signal—and dashed off a quick transmission to Admiralty that HX 72 would be late arriving at the rendezvous point to meet Royal Navy escorts from the Western Approaches. Accordingly, trying to hasten the rendezvous, Western Approaches Command (WAC) rerouted HX 72 southeasterly to the Great Circle Route, the shortest distance across the Atlantic between North America and the UK. Chopping the distance, however, did not solve Cmdre Rogers's predicament. Late on September 20, having completed her escort obligations, HMS *Jervis Bay*—the convoy's only existing protection—parted company for her return trip to Halifax. HX 72 was still a full twenty-four hours from its scheduled rendezvous with Royal Navy escorts at the Western Approaches late in the afternoon of September 21.

Those RN escorts had put to sea on September 11, two days after Cmdre Rogers and his eastbound convoy had left Halifax. Arthur Knapp, captain of the escort sloop HMS *Lowestoft* and commander of the Western Approaches escorts, faced his own challenges with this assignment. Just days before, Knapp had led an ad hoc formation of sloops, trawlers, destroyers, and corvettes assigned to escort SC 2, a convoy of fifty-four ships from Sydney, Nova Scotia, headed for the same Western Approaches. He'd suddenly faced three U-boats patrolling to the limit of their endurance, about 600 miles west of Britain, all three lying in wait for the UK-bound convoy. Over the next three days and nights, the U-boats sank five merchant ships. Knapp had apparently faced one of the first ever "wolf pack" attacks of the war in the Atlantic. Since his new assignment—to escort HX 72 to the North Channel—presented the same conditions, he feared the same result.

As the darkness of September 20 closed in on Convoy HX 72, 500 miles from Bloody Foreland off the coast of Ireland, so too did a threat greater than any Atlantic gale, any debilitating mechanical breakdown at sea, or even a telltale lit porthole in the night.

THE first U-boat torpedo fired at a ship of Convoy HX 72 failed to hit its mark. Just after dusk on September 20, Kptlt Günther Prien brought *U47* to the surface to reconnoitre what appeared to be an armed merchant ship cruising alone. Since *U47* had been on patrol for a number of days beyond the Western Approaches, Prien had but one remaining torpedo, which he launched from an aft torpedo tube. The weapon veered into a harmless circle, and the intended target, HMS *Jervis Bay*, continued westbound for Halifax without a hint she had been attacked. Nevertheless, *Jervis Bay*'s presence told Prien a convoy was near. Now carrying out his role as convoy spotter, he immediately transmitted an encrypted message with his location and sighting to German Naval Command at Lorient. Dönitz ordered radio silence for all but *U47*, and a pack of five additional U-boats altered course to intercept the convoy.

Kptlt Otto Kretschmer, whose Type VIIB *U99* had already sunk three small steamers on this patrol, responded first. He raced directly to Prien's position. Arriving at 25°W longitude on the fifty-fifth parallel, Kretschmer found the seas calm and plenty of moonlight. Initially, he saw no sign of the convoy. He submerged to deploy his hydrophone listening device, heard the distinctive sound of ship propellers to the south, and pursued. Back on the surface, north of the convoy, he took advantage of cloud covering the moon, closed on the tanker in the No. 15 position on the port side of the convoy—the very end of the first column of ships—and launched an electric torpedo. It was twenty minutes to midnight.

The British motor tanker *Invershannon* shuddered with an explosion in the forepeak (the bow) of the ship; this hold was typically kept dry for extra buoyancy and to help maintain stability when the tanker was fully loaded with 13,000 tons of fuel oil in rough seas.[27] But with the forepeak flooding, the water pulled the bow under quickly. There wasn't time to send a distress signal, but most of the crew abandoned ship safely. Meanwhile, *U99* swung across the back end of the convoy, heading for its far starboard corner. There Kretschmer fired a torpedo into the freighter *Baron Blythswood*, her holds filled to the brim with more than 5,000 tons of iron ore.

"Single torpedo at heavily-laden freighter from 580 metres," Kretschmer noted in his diary. "Direct hit amidships. Ship breaks in two and sinks in forty seconds," taking half the ship's crew under before they knew what had hit them.[28]

Charging up the starboard flank of HX 72 twenty-five minutes later, Kretschmer found the British motor merchant *Elmbank*, also low in the water with 5,156 tons of timber and steel loaded in Cowichan, British Columbia, carried through the Panama Canal, and now headed for Belfast. *U99* put a single torpedo into her starboard side and Kretschmer immediately learned the ship's identity when her radio operator transmitted "SOS. *Elmbank*" as she veered away from the convoy and began to take on water. Kptlt Prien arrived on the scene and joined Kretschmer as crews from both U-boats loaded shells into their 88mm deck guns and directed their fire at *Elmbank*'s waterline, trying to sink what was left of the freighter. The attack was nearly an hour old, and, with no escort present, there had been no response.

Only when *Elmbank*'s radio operator flashed his distress signal, about forty-five minutes into the attack, did Cmdre Rogers (aboard *Tregarthen* at the head of the fifth column) and the masters of the other forty merchant ships recognize that the convoy was under attack. Tanker *Frederick S. Fales* still led the fourth column of ships, and her off-duty crewmen began gathering on the boat deck, peering into the night astern, and wondering who would be next.

The carnage continued as other members of the U-boat pack arrived on the scene, among them *U48*, commanded by Heinrich Bleichrodt.* Kptlt Bleichrodt was fresh from similar wolf pack attacks on the eastbound Convoy SC 3 and the westbound Convoy OB 213. Like *U99*, *U48* approached HX 72 from the rear, using moments of obscured moonlight to pick targets. He chose the steam merchant *Blairangus*, loaded with 4,409 tons of pit props for the British mining industry. No sooner had the water settled from the torpedo explosion than Bleichrodt saw lifeboats lowered and the ship

* While his first Kriegsmarine service was aboard surface raiders such as the heavy cruiser *Admiral Hipper*, by the end of 1940 Bleichrodt had become a U-boat commander, sinking twenty-five ships and receiving the Knight's Cross of the Iron Cross with Oak Leaves.

disappeared into a rain squall; that was the last he saw of it. Meantime, Kptlt Kretschmer had expended his remaining ammunition, sinking both *Invershannon* and *Elmbank*.

With that, *U99* withdrew and set a course for Lorient.

At first light, Cmdre Rogers took stock. Four ships at the extremities of HX 72 were gone. He ordered freighter *Pacific Grove*, roughly in the middle of the convoy, to release a smoke float to provide a temporary screen over the adjacent merchant ships. With no other means of defence, save the convoy's forward momentum, Cmdre Rogers signalled his remaining ships to commence further zigzagging and coaxed as much increased speed as he thought the convoy could muster—maybe ten and a half knots—hoping against hope he could hasten his rendezvous with the Royal Navy escort. At about 2 p.m., two hours earlier than expected, the escorts came into sight. Still leading the fourth column of the convoy, Capt Frank Ramsay and the crew aboard *Frederick S. Fales* sensed some relief—Art Silver, in the crow's nest, first among them.

"We figured everything was all right now," he said.

Capt Arthur Knapp, commander of the Western Approaches escorts, began assessing damage. He had no choice but to send his most powerful weapon, destroyer HMS *Shikari*, miles to the west, where the first attack had occurred, in search of survivors. Then he positioned flagship sloop HMS *Lowestoft* at the port bow of the convoy, and his three Flower-class corvettes, HMS *La Malouine*, *Calendula*, and *Heartsease*, clockwise around the convoy. *Shikari* would bring up the rear after retrieving merchant sailors from life rafts or floating debris. Five warships and the remaining thirty-seven merchant vessels ploughed on, desperate to reach the North Channel.

Throughout the daylight hours of September 21, the U-boat status changed too. Kretschmer and *U99* had departed the scene, but both Kptlt Prien in *U47* and Kptlt Bleichrodt in *U48* continued to shadow the convoy. Well to the east, several other U-boat commanders considered their options. Kptlt Wilhelm Ambrosius, in command of *U43* and completing a long patrol, chose to head to Bergen. Kptlt Hans-Gerrit von Stockhausen in *U65* was also at the end of a three-week patrol. But the remaining U-boat in the pack—*U100* under Kptlt Schepke—wasted no time. He advanced with all possible speed. Despite heavy rain and the potential for being spotted by enemy aircraft, Schepke chose to stay on the surface and spent the day closing from about 100 miles.

The daytime watches aboard *Frederick S. Fales* had tripped into evening ones without incident, according to fifth engineering officer Pat O'Brien. Twelve hours had passed since the last torpedo attack, six hours since the escort had set up a defensive screen. Erring on the side of caution, the officers ordered a lifeboat drill. *Fales* was just over a year old, and the safety equipment on board seemed more than adequate. The ship carried four lifeboats—one on either side of both the bridge and aft deckhouses—secured with davits and fall ropes (small cranes for lowering each boat to the water). With thirty-six crew and a dozen officers (forty-eight in all), the lifeboats had capacity, if needed, to carry all aboard to safety.

But the ship's former crew had additionally installed a pair of Board of Trade rafts, each comprising empty drums lashed together in a couple of rows and connected by planks. In an emergency, each raft could comfortably carry fifteen or twenty men. During the lifeboat drill, one *Fales* crewman wondered aloud why, under such threatening conditions, the lifeboats remained so tightly lashed to the ship.

Meanwhile, the convoy had picked up speed, which Pat O'Brien considered a blessing. During the merging of the three separate convoys from Halifax, Sydney, and Bermuda, O'Brien's watches below in the engine room had been unnerving. One moment, responding to the bridge, the engineers would open up *Fales*'s 4,350-horsepower engine, the next cut it back. Slowing those massive eight-cylinders felt awkward and created unwelcome tension among the crew. But with *Fales* closer to her top speed, tensions had eased. O'Brien came off his watch and retired to his cabin, one level below the boat deck.

By 8 p.m. on September 21, with darkness descending, quartermaster Ed Dawn had completed his second four-hour shift at *Fales*'s helm as well as providing lookout on the wing of the bridge. He'd handed the watch to Harl Morris. When the RCN had refused Harl's application earlier in the year because they were swamped with volunteers, Morris had joined *Fales*'s crew along with former fishermen Burton Kent and Simeon Rodenhizer. They'd all signed on as able seamen at sixty-five dollars a month plus 25 percent danger pay. Off-watch, Dawn joined a gathering of crew on the boat deck at the stern. One of the officers came along.

"Next one that lights a cigarette's gonna buy it from the bridge with a gun," he said.

Everybody knew that any light—even the glow of a match or cigarette embers—could be seen for miles. Nobody lit up. All eyes were glued to the horizons. Below decks, the cigarettes were being consumed another way. Cook Sam Taylor and mess boy Jack Baker had cleaned up after the evening meal and started a game of poker, with packs and cartons of cigarettes as poker chips. Baker had already won a few games and had several cartons of winnings piled in front of him. Crewmen Jack Canning and Bill Kearley joined the game. Bert Myers had also completed his watch in the boiler room, so he'd entered the game too. The previous night's attack on the convoy had triggered Bert's sense of self-preservation. He wasn't taking any chances. So, seated at the poker table, Myers wore a forty-two-dollar tailormade overcoat with his Mae West life jacket underneath.

"Word had come down from the bridge," Myers said. "There were still U-boats in the area."

About five miles from the poker game aboard *Fales*, just before nine o'clock, the final member of the U-boat wolf pack stalking Convoy HX 72 surfaced astern of the remaining merchant ships. Joachim Schepke and *U100* had covered more than 100 miles of the North Atlantic in less than seven hours. Trimming his U-boat on the surface, so that just her conning tower was visible, the newcomer surveyed the scene ahead.

"About twenty shadows are sighted," Schepke entered in his war diary. "My boat is between row two and three [of the convoy]." He recognized that HX 72's escorts lay outside the nine columns of merchant ships. So, by penetrating the escort defences and positioning *U100* within the columns, he calculated his odds for inflicting damage would be greater. From a mile and a half distance, facing an apparent wall of three ships in a cluster, he concluded, "To get into the convoy, I decide to shoot my way in."[29]

In rapid succession, Schepke called for torpedoes to be fired from three bow tubes. Just as quickly, he turned the U-boat sufficiently to fire a fourth torpedo from a stern tube.

The four "eels" took just over two minutes to reach their targets—all hits—ploughing into *Dalcairn* in the sixth column, *Canonesa* in the fifth column, and *Torinia* in the fourth. Kptlt Schepke quickly swung *U100* around again to keep pace with the convoy, taking a position in the gap he had created.

Amid the explosions, distress signals, and confusion that followed, ships burst into flame, sirens sounded, distress starshells were fired, and escort vessels raced "pell-mell to the scenes of action and dropped their depth charges."[30] On the bridge of the flagship, Cmdre Rogers witnessed fire and distress signals across three columns of ships behind him; fearing that an order for a sudden convoy course change could jeopardize the escorts, he increased *Tregarthen*'s speed but maintained course. The master aboard *Empire Airman,* leading the ninth column, however, panicked and steered out of the convoy; as he did, he exposed his ship to a perfect stern-tube shot from *U100*. Less than a minute later the torpedo struck and the merchantman went down quickly by the bow. In less than fifteen minutes, Schepke had mortally struck four vessels. And in the darkness and chaos, nobody knew where the attacker was.

Aboard *Fredrick S. Fales*, helmsman Harl Morris had just moved from the wheel to the bridge wing with the second mate for the latter half of their watch. "Look!" he called out, jabbing the mate's shoulder. "Look what's going on back there!"[31] Just then, the sound of explosions from the fuel oil aboard *Torinia*, a half-mile behind in the column, caught up with them at the head of the convoy.

"Look at that one," Ed Dawn called out to his buddies on *Fales*'s boat deck. "Over there!"

But just as quickly, the distant fires and thunder of

explosions were eclipsed by a new sight and sound ahead of them. Aboard the HX 72 flagship *Tregarthen*, lights began to flash on the foremast. Then a series of red and green flares appeared overhead. It was a universally understood signal. Cmdre Rogers had ordered the convoy to disperse immediately.

"It's everybody for himself," one of Dawn's shipmates called out. Immediately, everyone aboard felt the surge of *Fales*'s reserve power. Capt Ramsay had called for ahead full speed and the ship lurched forward. Dawn recalled that the acceleration caused sparks to fly from the funnel as the ship's diesel engine ignited excess carbon in the system. If nothing else, the additional speed and freedom to zigzag at will provided some sense of security. Bert Myers remembered an officer reassuring the crew that *Fales*'s twelve knots could outrun any U-boat.

Actually, the dispersal of the convoy gave Kptlt Schepke's U-boat additional space and time to choose her next targets. Off to *Fales*'s port side and now some distance behind, the British merchantman *Scholar*, with 5,484 tons of steel, arsenic, lumber, and cotton for Manchester, became Schepke's fifth target; the U-boat set her on fire amidships with just one torpedo hit. Schepke had now used eight of the dozen torpedoes in his U-boat arsenal; however, with a new vessel rising before him against the horizon in the moonlight, Schepke ordered two torpedoes readied for firing for the first time that night. He called for straight-line shots at a depth of ten feet.

"Double shot at tanker," his war diary read, with the first G7e (electric) torpedo at 11:53 p.m. and a second moments later. In just over a minute, Schepke in the conning tower and crewmen below on hydrophone listening devices heard and felt the impact of the first torpedo striking and exploding into *Frederick S. Fales*'s forward holds on the port side. "Two violent explosions, massive tongues of flame and the deck completely splits open," noted his diary.[32]

In the crew's mess aboard *Fales*, the cartons of Camel and Lucky Strike cigarettes suddenly flew off the poker table. Players and spectators tumbled like bowling pins. Some of the auxiliary lights came on. But then the second *U100* torpedo exploded into *Fales*'s engine room, below the mess. The tanker seemed to jump with the more lethal hit. "Then it was panic, everybody trying to get through the door to the deck," Myers said. And everybody in the crew mess—Taylor, Canning, Kearley, and Baker, leaving all his cigarette winnings behind—grappled through the darkness toward the hatch that led to the boat deck. "One on top of another, like animals."

With the second explosion, Art Silver, the ship's lookout, found himself covered in Bunker C oil from *Fales*'s shattered fuel tanks. He couldn't see. Fires had broken out near the torpedo impact points, but because Bunker C has a higher ignition temperature than petroleum or refined fuel, the crew coped with spewing oil, not burning oil. Temporarily blinded, Silver groped along a companionway to the boat deck, finally getting to his abandon-ship station—the lifeboat on the port side—but the second explosion had blown that boat to pieces. There was nothing there. Wiping the oil from his eyes, he dashed to where the other lifeboat was secured in its davits on the starboard side of the ship; he found other crewmen—Herb Bonin, Ray Hansen, Harl Morris, Earl Richards, and Bert Myers—all trying to guide the lifeboat, suspended by its davit falls (ropes), down to the water.

But with the ship sinking to port by the stern and the bow rising, this remaining lifeboat was dragging precariously across the starboard side of the ship. Eventually they got the lifeboat into the water and began hatcheting the davit falls that kept the lifeboat tethered to the ship. *Fales*'s bow began to rise. The lifeboat davit falls were still intact. If the ship suddenly plunged, the lifeboat would go down with them in it.

"We'd better jump for it," Bonin called out to his shipmates. "She's going down!" And those in the lifeboat jumped overboard into water coated with Bunker C oil gushing from *Fales*'s broken hull.

Another frantic scene unfolded at the starboard Board of Trade life raft. Unlike the lifeboats, the rafts were not supposed to be tethered to the ship; the idea was that they would float free and provide immediate refuge if *Fales* went down. But when Ed Dawn arrived on the aft boat deck, he found the Board of Trade raft securely lashed, and he yelled to Charlie Beed for a knife. Dressed only in a shirt and pants and covered in oil that was spraying "like rain" everywhere, Dawn kept hacking at the lashing on the life raft.

"I'd just cut the last rope and lost the knife when the raft floated free," Dawn said. "Eventually there were eleven of us on the raft."

Fales's bow steadily rose in the tanker's death throes. The captain and officers from the bridge—by order of the Admiralty—could not leave the ship before they'd met certain protocols: the radio officer had to send a position distress signal and the senior officers had to gather up the ship's vital papers, including the British Admiralty Merchant Shipping Instructions, for disposal overboard in weighted canvas bags (to keep them from enemy hands). Fulfilling those duties, however, left the bridge crew precious few minutes to abandon the ship safely. At the bridge lifeboat position, those in the launched boat held on to the fall tackles, waiting for the master and first officer to arrive. Capt Ramsay tried to slide down the fall tackles but fell into the water. As those in the lifeboat attempted to rescue him, the fo'c'sle of the sinking ship plunged down onto the lifeboat, pitching everyone into the water. In all, twenty of *Fales*'s crew died in the explosions and sinking. The ship had gone down in less than five minutes.

The carving of Convoy HX 72 continued. Just past midnight, on the beginning of the third day of U-boat attacks on the same convoy, *U100* found Norwegian merchant ship *Simla*, carrying 8,000 tons of scrap metal, steaming as fast as she could away from the main body of the convoy. One torpedo shot into her bow and the vessel went down almost as if she were submerging like the U-boat that sank her. Earlier, Kptlt Bleichrodt had torpedoed the British merchantman *Broompark* at the same corner of the convoy as its first casualty, *Invershannon*. In just under forty-eight hours, U-boats attacking in a pack had sunk eleven merchant ships (73,000 tons of ships with 100,000 tons of freight and 45,000 tons of fuel aboard).* They'd killed 116 merchant seamen outright.[33]

That left sixteen *Fales* crewmen now on rafts in the North Atlantic, as well as nearly 100 additional merchant sailors who'd abandoned ten other sunken ships, all struggling to survive. Drenched, freezing, and coughing up oil, they were adrift several hundred miles from the closest coast of the British Isles.

"We started swimming," Bert Myers said, "but we only got out a few hundred yards and I realized I can't swim to Ireland." Buoyed by his Mae West life preserver under his overcoat, he stopped and watched *Fales* sink behind him.

* Thirty-one merchant ships survived the attack on Convoy HX 72 in September 1940; of those, seventeen would be sunk by the end of the war.

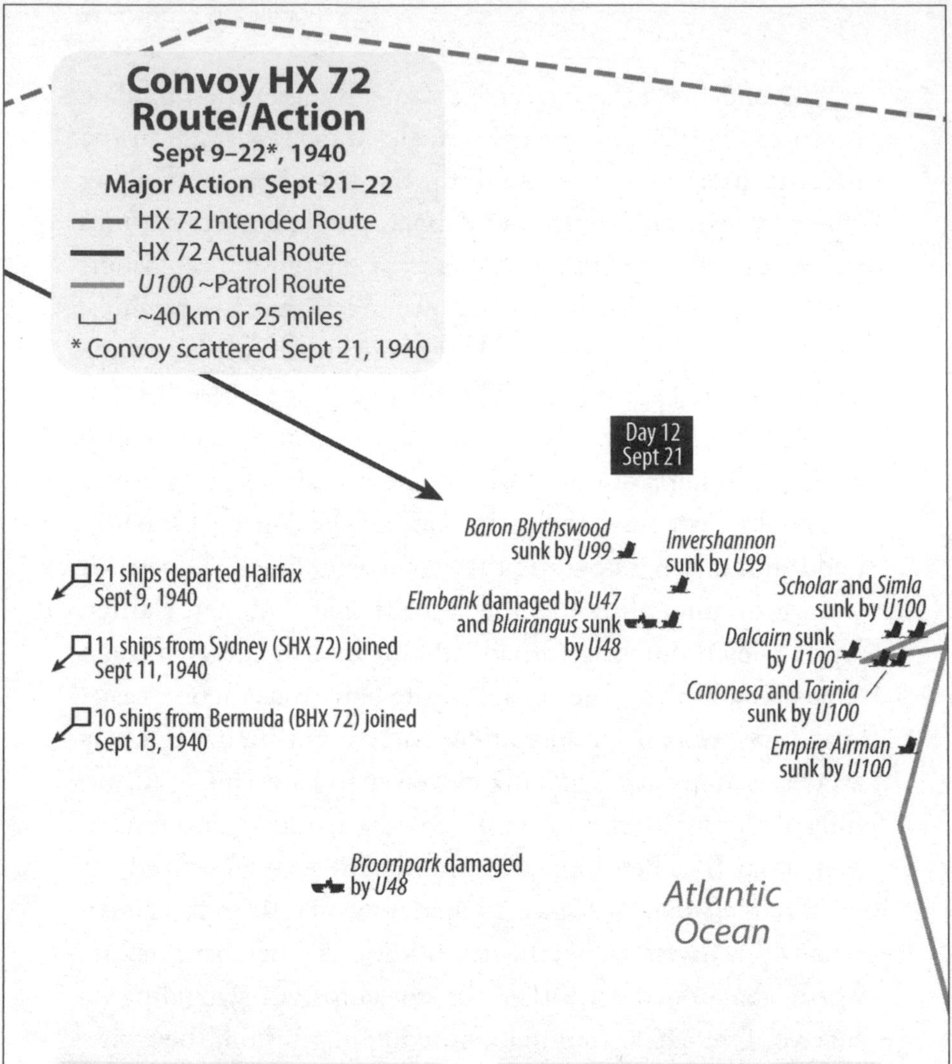

HX 72: U-boat, Ship Attacked, Tonnage			
Sept 21	*U99*	*Invershannon*	9,154
Sept 21	*U99*	*Baron Blythswood*	3,668
Sept 21	*U47*	*Elmbank*	5,156 (d.)
Sept 21	*U48*	*Blairangus*	4,409
Sept 21	*U99*	*Elmbank*	5,156
Sept 21	*U100*	*Canonesa*	8,286
Sept 21	*U100*	*Torinia*	10,364
Sept 21	*U100*	*Dalcairn*	4,608
Sept 21	*U48*	*Broompark*	5,136 (d.)
Sept 22	*U100*	*Empire Airman*	6,586
Sept 22	*U100*	*Scholar*	3,940
Sept 22	*U100*	*Frederick S. Fales*	10,525
Sept 22	*U100*	*Simla*	6,031
Sept 22	*U32*	*Collegian*	7,886 (d.)
Total Sunk & Damaged (d.)			**85,749**

HX 72: Escorts, Type, Dates Attached		
HMCS *Comox*	Minesweeper	Sept 9
HMCS *Nootka*	Minesweeper	Sept 9
HMCS *Gaspé*	Minesweeper	Sept 9
HMCS *Arras*	Battle Trawler	Sept 9
HMCS *Saguenay*	Destroyer	Sept 9–10
HMCS *French*	Patrol	Sept 9
HMS *Jervis Bay*	Liner/AMC	Sept 9–21
HMCS *Laurier*	Patrol	Sept 10
HMCS *Reindeer*	Yacht	Sept 10
HMS *Voltaire*	AMC	Sept 13
HMS *Lowestoft*	Sloop	Sept ??
HMS *Shikari*	Destroyer	Sept 21
HMS *La Malouine*	Corvette	Sept 21–25
HMS *Calendula*	Corvette	Sept 21
HMS *Heartsease*	Corvette	Sept 21

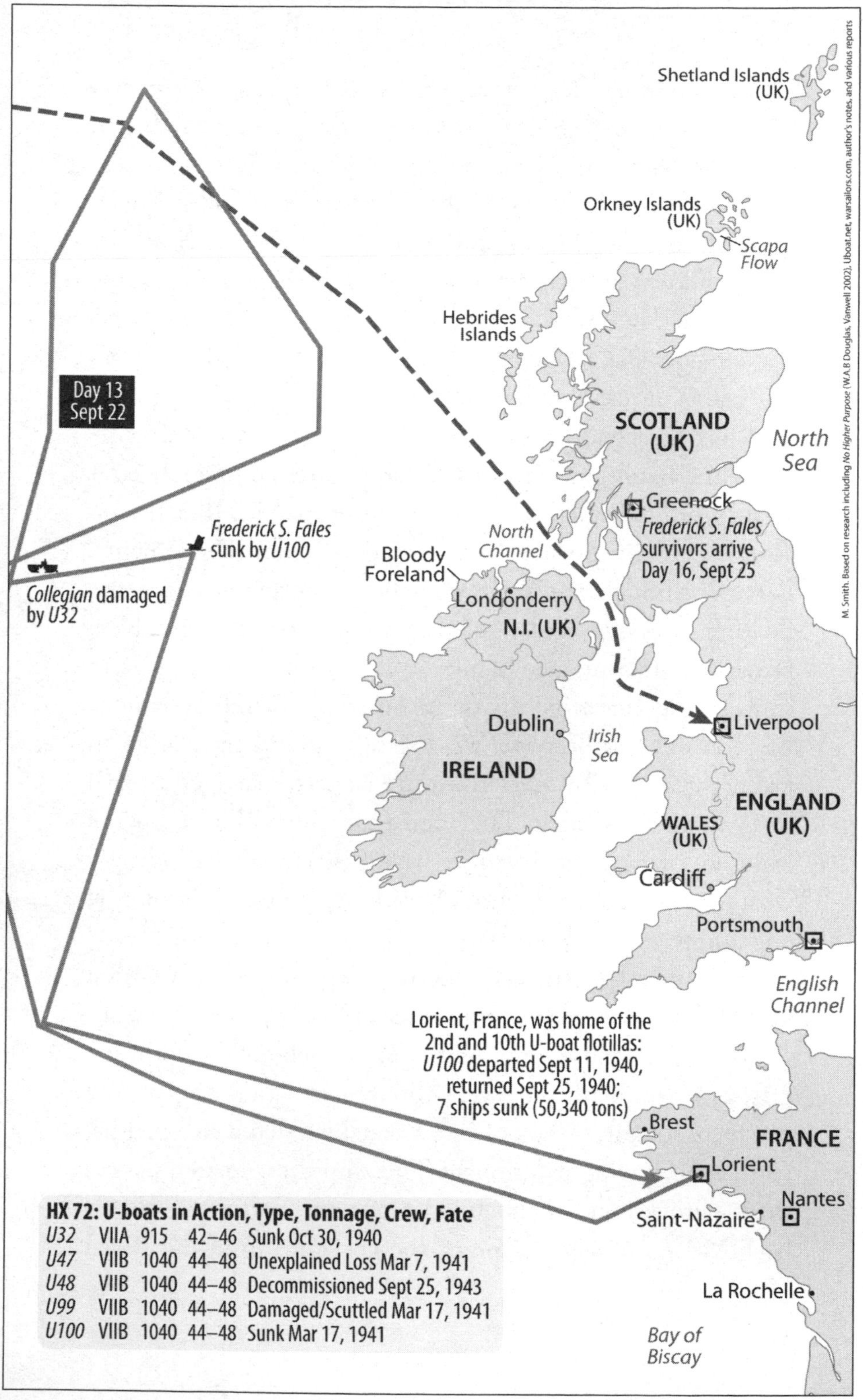

HX 72: U-boats in Action, Type, Tonnage, Crew, Fate

U32	VIIA	915	42–46	Sunk Oct 30, 1940
U47	VIIB	1040	44–48	Unexplained Loss Mar 7, 1941
U48	VIIB	1040	44–48	Decommissioned Sept 25, 1943
U99	VIIB	1040	44–48	Damaged/Scuttled Mar 17, 1941
U100	VIIB	1040	44–48	Sunk Mar 17, 1941

The night went silent. Myers worried that if he swam too far, he might be overlooked if rescuers came along. He began shouting. Shipmate Jack Canning called back in the darkness and guided Myers to one of the Board of Trade rafts. There, Canning and Ray Hansen pulled him over the barrels of the raft and down onto the adjoining planks, where he collapsed, exhausted. The raft did not protect or provide for its occupants—no walls, no gunwales, no sails, not a rudder, and no provisions. It just kept them afloat.

On the second Board of Trade raft, Pat O'Brien remembered the hands and faces of his shipmates completely covered in heavy Bunker C oil. It occurred to him that the oil covering might provide some protection from the elements. Partway through the night, somebody spotted a bag in the floating wreckage and hauled it in, hoping it might have provisions. It contained blankets, which would at least cover some of the men from the ocean spray and wind. Somehow, those awake on the two *Fales* life rafts found each other in the night and, with ropes from life jackets, managed to lash the two rafts together. The men took shifts. Those on the exposed planks, partly underwater, switched periodically with those up on the flotation barrels, sharing the discomfort and a hope they'd be rescued.

"Any praying that was done was done privately," O'Brien said. "No songs were sung. I don't recall any conversation at all."

Just past noon on September 22, somebody on O'Brien's raft, as it rose with the swell, thought he saw a ship in the distance. Art Silver took off his sweatshirt, tied it to a paddle, and began waving it furiously. The ship drew nearer, passed them, circled, and then pulled alongside. It turned out to be HMS *La Malouine*, one of the corvettes from the Royal

Navy escort. Quickly the corvette crew threw down scramble nets and brought the *Fales* survivors aboard. Bert Myers tried climbing up the nets but faltered near the top; somebody grabbed him by his hair and pulled him the rest of the way. He peeled off his new forty-five-dollar overcoat and pants, expecting he'd retrieve and clean them later, but a crewman threw them over the side.

"I thought I was pretty strong," Harl Morris said. "I went up the scramble net, but when I went to jump on deck my knees buckled and I couldn't stand up." Somebody steadied him as he took in the scene around him—scores of crewmen of different nationalities, many coughing and vomiting oil and sea water.

"I pissed oil for four days," Jack Baker remembered.

On deck, where 114 survivors sat or stood crowded together on the corvette's outside main deck,[34] Art Silver appreciated the generosity of *La Malouine*'s crew, who gave them each a shot of rum, offered showers, and provided fresh clothes from their own lockers. Then he went looking for his pals from the North End of Halifax, but Charlie Beed, Frank Scanlon, Jim White, and Gerald Scallion, who'd rushed aboard *Fales* from that taxi at the last minute, were nowhere to be found. Such was Silver's first life-and-death experience at sea. It wouldn't be his last.

With *La Malouine* now underway and bound for Scotland, the corvette's Royal Navy captain, Lieutenant-Commander (LCdr) Ronald W. Keymer, walked among *Fales*'s survivors offering words of encouragement. Helmsman Ed Dawn thanked the captain for stopping to rescue them.

But Keymer protested. "You see that fellow there," the captain said, pointing to *La Malouine*'s lookout. Keymer told

Dawn and the others within earshot that escort commander Knapp had sent his corvette to find survivors of the U-boat attack the previous two nights. They'd been looking for hours when *La Malouine*'s engineer told Keymer that the ship was at the point of no return on fuel. The captain had set a course for home. "Our lookout happened to look back with his binoculars and shouted, 'Wait! There's a raft!' There's the guy you can thank. There's not another ship within a hundred miles of here."

SHATTERINGLY simple and perceptive, LCdr Keymer's observation that his was the only ship on that part of the ocean summed up the dilemma of Allied navies on the North Atlantic during the first year of the war. Too many convoys, too much territory to defend, and insufficient means to do so. The plight of Convoy HX 72 was not unique, although it became the first Allied convoy of the war to lose six or more ships in the Battle of the Atlantic. In his diaries, Winston Churchill noted that the week ending September 22, 1940, "showed the highest rate of loss since the beginning of the war . . . in fact greater than any we had suffered in a similar period in 1917."[35]

On the other side, Karl Dönitz had only just begun his campaign of Rüdeltaktik, an offensive the admiral expected would inflict great damage on his enemy. He customarily took careful note of what he called the "effective U-boat quotient," or the average tonnage sunk per U-boat per day. Dönitz had every reason to be pleased when the effective quotient went from 541 tons per day in June 1940 to 758 tons per day in September—thanks to HX 72 and other pack attacks.[36] As Dönitz had hoped, his U-boat aces had ratcheted up their tonnage scores: Kretschmer sank three ships for a total of 17,978 tons; Bleichrodt sank one, taking with it 5,136 tons of freight; and Schepke sank seven ships, or 61,300 tons of cargo and fuel. He would go on to sink thirty-seven Allied ships, or 160,000 tons of freight.

Two days later, when he'd docked *U100* back at the U-boat pens in Lorient, Kptlt Schepke received a hero's welcome; he was awarded the Knight's Cross and, in November 1940, the Oak Leaves. Meanwhile, the Propaganda Ministry took full advantage of his notoriety. Schepke met Adolf Hitler, spoke at rallies espousing Nazi ideology, and promoted a new book about his exploits, entreating young Germans to join the U-boat flotilla "to face their vilest enemy on the high seas."[37]

The decimation of Convoy HX 72 made it clear to the British Admiralty that things would have to change. Confronting and defeating Dönitz's Rüdeltaktik would require as much inspired leadership, internal fortitude, technological innovation, and stealth as the Allies could muster. Escorts and escorting had to improve exponentially. The number of ships and more experienced crews—actual warships and trained sub-hunters—would have to grow, acquire more sophisticated technologies and techniques, and apply them farther out into the North Atlantic than ever before. Allied planners had to address the Black Pit—that vast stretch of undefended North Atlantic Ocean—that lay beyond the reach of land-based warplanes. Old rules of engagement no longer applied. New ones for tracking, chasing, and destroying U-boats, while still rescuing crews of abandoned ships, were needed. And weapons—those aboard warships and those crafted by Allied intelligence and counter-intelligence—would have to anticipate and become more lethal than those developed and delivered from the other side. To survive Germany's U-boat gauntlet in the North Atlantic would require, if you will, an Allied sea change.

But the Admiralty could not blame the death of Convoy HX 72 solely on inadequate defence against wolf pack tactics. While Britain had always placed a high priority on the safe passage of its bread-and-butter merchant shipments, simultaneously crises elsewhere had bled away much of her military capacity.

In June 1940, during Operation Dynamo, every available Royal Navy warship (aided by thousands of citizen vessels) had converged on the English Channel to withdraw 340,000 British, French, and Belgian troops from Dunkirk. From July to September that year, the RAF had dispatched nearly all of Fighter Command into defending British airfields, cities, and war munitions factories in the Battle of Britain. Indeed, during the very weeks that Convoy HX 72 assembled in Halifax, Sydney, and Bermuda and merged off Nova Scotia, Fighter Command experienced some of its heaviest aircraft losses—421 Spitfires and Hurricanes destroyed or damaged.[38] At the same time, RAF Bomber Command had completed hundreds of sorties against occupied seaports in the Netherlands, Belgium, and France, where German barges were preparing for Operation Sea Lion, Hitler's planned amphibious invasion of Britain. Clearly, the attention of British air and navy crews was focused east on occupied Europe, not west on convoys exposed to the Kriegsmarine's new pack-attack weapon.

Just how vulnerable those Western Approaches remained to enemy incursion became clear, at least to the surviving Canadians of the British tanker *Frederick S. Fales*, on

September 25, 1940. Just three days after the sinking of their ship and the decimation of their convoy 500 miles off Ireland, their rescue ship, HMS *La Malouine*, plied up the Firth of Clyde to deliver 114 survivors of HX 72 to the Scottish port of Greenock. In addition to the merchant sailors on her decks, *La Malouine* was escorting into port the British steam freighter *Broompark*, partly submerged but miraculously still afloat after the U-boat attacks the previous week.

"It was a helluva nice day. Sun and a bit of cloud," said Ed Dawn, rescued helmsman from *Fales*. "All of a sudden, this [Dornier] bomber comes down and drops two bombs."

The bombs exploded in the sea just ahead of the crippled *Broompark*. But by this time everybody on the crowded decks of *La Malouine*, including Dawn, was looking skyward as the German bomber circled for a second run at the two ships. LCdr Keymer brought *La Malouine* around hard to present a broadside in front of the merchantman, the corvette's pom-pom gun firing, as another two bombs plummeted toward the ships. This time, one of the Dornier's bombs fell into the sea and exploded harmlessly. The second scored a direct hit on *Broompark*, but bounced off the deck and overboard without exploding.

"Holy Jesus," Dawn said, "I thought we're going to get it again."

Either that was the last of the Dornier's bomb load or the return fire had scared the Germans off. Soon after, the freighter, her escort, and their shaken crews pulled into Greenock Harbour. They would live to fight another day. By the skin of their teeth.

Chapter Three

"WHAT THE FATES HELD IN STORE"

THEY LOOKED LIKE THE FLOTSAM AND JETSAM they'd survived.[1] Their coats, pants, and shoes were ill-fitting because most were borrowed. The hats they wore had come from the Sailors' Home facility that had housed and fed them in Liverpool; the facility had also arranged passage home to Canada for them in November 1940. Some of the men leaned on suitcases that had seen better days. So had everybody in the page-three photograph published in the November 27, 1940, edition of the *Halifax Daily Star*. The picture's caption read: "Survivors of Frederick S. Fales Arrive." Indeed, for ten of the eighteen men depicted in the photograph, this was their first time stepping back onto the streets of home—either Halifax or Dartmouth, Nova Scotia. The others, from across Atlantic Canada, would also soon be reunited with loved ones for the first time since their merchant tanker was torpedoed two months earlier.

Coming home to the Bay of Fundy coast in Nova Scotia, helmsman Harl Morris was paid $2,200 for his promised one-way-trip wages on *Fales* to Britain and for his lost property.

He gave all his compensation money to his mother to help her survive, and within a month he got a call-up for armed service. The Royal Canadian Navy was about to launch its second Flower-class corvette, HMCS *Sackville*, from Saint John, New Brunswick, and when it did, Morris was in her ship's company. For thirty-eight months he returned to the North Atlantic escorting merchant ships, not serving in them. The navy also recruited Jack Baker, former mess boy aboard *Fales*; he too returned to the North Atlantic run for the rest of the war, this time aboard destroyers and corvettes.

Art Silver, who'd served as *Fales*'s lookout, was a little surprised that reporters fussed over his surviving the sinking at sea. Instead of returning to the merchant navy, he presented the credentials from his Royal Canadian Naval Volunteer Reserve days; the navy snapped him up and posted him to HMCS *Ottawa*. Fortunately, they transferred him away from the River-class destroyer to train gunners before *Ottawa* was sunk in September 1942, with the loss of 119 lives. Still, the loss of his North-End friends Charlie Beed, Jim White, Gerald Scallion, and Frank Scanlon in *Fales*'s sinking "stuck with me, and I never got over it."[2]

Frank Scanlon's mother explained to those remembering her son that when Frank hurried to join *Fales* for Convoy HX 72, he'd told her she was losing her baby. He'd likely meant that he'd chosen a life at sea on his own, not that he expected to die in the sinking of the tanker. Frank's father seemed more disturbed, even at that early stage of the war, that the world hardly acknowledged what merchant navy volunteers contributed to the war effort.

"He may not have been in uniform," Scanlon's father said, "but . . . he died for his country just the same."[3]

Frank Scanlon's death in the *Fales* sinking, while nearly invisible, as his father suggested, was not unique. Of 12,000 Canadians who served aboard merchant navy ships during the Second World War, 1,344 became casualties—1,146 killed (including eight women) and 198 taken prisoner. From *Erik Boye*, the first Canadian merchantman torpedoed, on June 15, 1940, to the last, *Avondale Park*, sunk on May 7, 1945, a total of fifty-eight Canadian-registered merchant ships were lost to enemy action[4] (overall, Allied merchant navies lost 2,233 ships[5]). It was little compensation to Frank Scanlon and his father, but merchant navy deaths at sea did not go completely unnoticed. Canada's wartime minister of transport, Joseph-Enoil Michaud, called his country's merchant seamen "the fourth arm of the fighting forces."[6]

By global standards, that fighting force emerged almost overnight. From a disparate array of tankers, steamships, motor vessels, trawlers, sloops, and borrowed lake ships—just thirty-seven merchant ships in all—at the beginning of the war, Canada's merchant navy grew to a fleet of 180 ships by 1945. Indeed, Canada's merchant shipbuilding programs propelled its mercantile fleet to become the fourth-largest in the world by the war's end. Canadian Merchant Navy men and women served aboard 25,343 voyages, carrying 165 million tons of military and civilian supplies from North America to Britain.[7] But the cost in lives of that transatlantic passage was dear. Canada's merchant navy mortality rate in the Battle of the Atlantic—one in eight—proved to be higher per capita than for any of the country's other fighting forces.[8]

Even if he'd known them, such dismal odds for survival in the wartime merchant navy could never have dissuaded John Birnie Dougall from going to sea. Born in March 1920 in Timmins, Ontario, John excelled in everything at school, racking up hundredth-percentile grades in arithmetic, spelling, composition, and geography. When his family moved to Cornwall, on the St. Lawrence River, John continued to excel in scholastics, led his high-school band on the bugle, and in 1937 joined the RCN as a cadet. After completing his senior matriculation (high school) the following year, he listened to the advice of his uncle in Scotland and chose to go to sea as an apprentice in the merchant navy. First he worked aboard an American tanker. Then, as the war broke out, his uncle helped him land a position on the British-owned tanker SS *San Felix*, carrying 10,000 tons of fuel oil, each trip, from ports in South America to Liverpool. He wrote to his mother, Rachel Dougall, regularly about training and studying for his mate's certificate, as well as the restrictions that the war had begun imposing on him at sea.

"Since the war has broken out, all my letters should be sent to England," he wrote on September 23, 1939. "We are now under the Admiralty [authority]. Our ports are not known. Everything pertaining to the ship is to be omitted in our correspondence."[9]

J.B. Dougall complied grudgingly, but he also deduced that enemy strategists wouldn't have to look too far to intercept *San Felix* along her regular shipping route. Once clear of her British ports, the ballasted tanker took three weeks to cover the 4,600 miles westbound across the equator to one of her South American fuel-oil destinations. Whether the Shell Oil storage tanks were at Curaçao, Dutch West Indies, or across the Tropic of Capricorn in Montevideo, Uruguay, or in Buenos Aires, Argentina, taking on the crude oil took another few weeks. Then, fully loaded, *San Felix* and her crew would begin the weeks-long return trip—travelling no faster than ten knots—up the eastern seaboard of North America to join other ships bound for Britain.

"The convoy system is in full swing," he wrote to his mother. "I hear losses inflicted on our shipping is [*sic*] very small. . . . Don't you worry about this son of yours. After all, this is much better than the trenches."[10]

As one of two apprentices aboard *San Felix*, Dougall had to pay full attention to orders from the ship's officers—running errands for the captain, washing and painting the ship's superstructure, and taking his turn on deck watch. On his own time, John continued studying mathematics, navigation, engineering, ship construction, logarithms, and seamanship so that when the captain decided it was time, he would be ready to write a first-year exam for his mate's certificate. Beyond that, he took every spare moment to write home, sometimes testing the attentiveness and patience of navy censors.

"I shall write from next port-of-call, giving you some news, which would be best left out, as I hear censors are as thick as flies in Halifax," he wrote his mother that fall.[11]

The censors clearly had no sense of humour; one had written in pencil on the same page of his letter, for Rachel to see, "Would advise against this in interests of his own safety."

In spite of his devil-may-care attitude about security—John was still just nineteen—as a dutiful son to his mother and model for his younger brother James, he wrote letters home nearly every other day; they got posted each time *San Felix* docked. He boasted to Rachel about high marks on his mate's certificate exams in core subjects, such as navigation and engineering, and promised to do better in his second year on seamanship tests. Meanwhile, in April 1940, he made sure he got a letter home to James for his eleventh birthday, applauding his sibling's achievements in music, with Cubs, and skating with his Cornwall minor hockey team. But he also offered brotherly advice on school work, reminding James, "It's what you have in your head that counts in this world."[12] Completing a round trip to Britain, *San Felix* went into drydock at Cardiff, Wales, but that same spring, when the tanker resumed its transatlantic circuit, bringing vital oil to Britain, ship's apprentice J.B. Dougall would find himself closer to the war than he'd ever thought possible.

WITH three oceans at its gates, Canada in 1939 (plus the Dominion of Newfoundland) enjoyed the peacetime expanse of 150,000 miles of coastline. In war, however, with the threat of attack by Kriegsmarine warships initially along its Atlantic coast, and later from the Japanese Imperial Navy on the Pacific, its peacetime natural asset became a wartime logistical nightmare. The Royal Canadian Navy had gone to war with a permanent force numbering fewer than 1,800 servicemen and 1,700 reservists. Its naval arsenal consisted of exactly six destroyers, five minesweepers, and two training ships, divided more or less equally between its east and west coasts.[13] Canadians serving in the Royal Navy often heard the RCN ridiculed as the "two-ocean navy."[14]

As the war began, Jeffry Brock found himself on the Pacific side of Canada's schizophrenic naval deployment, playing a vital role. Having joined the Winnipeg Half Division of the Royal Canadian Naval Volunteer Reserve, the first such unit in the country in the 1920s, he rose to full lieutenant by the 1930s. Brock had earned his watchkeeping certificate, passed courses in gunnery and signals, and by 1937 had moved to Vancouver. By day he worked at a market research company in the city, and by night as commander of HMCS *Discovery*, the RCNVR recruitment and training facility ashore in the Stanley Park barracks. Britain's September 3 declaration of war against Germany did not immediately include Canada. But sensing the inevitable, Brock mobilized at *Discovery*—posting guards and securing army cots, blankets, stoves, and food—while waiting for the other shoe to drop. On September 4, Brock received orders to deliver lists of reserve officers' names to the RCN's Pacific dockyard in Esquimalt, next to Victoria on Vancouver Island.

The passenger ferry was the only means by which to deliver those lists personally. But she had already departed on her last trip of the day from the mainland to the island. So Brock jumped aboard a smaller ferry in the West Vancouver harbour. As luck would have it, the harbour taxi was operated by friend and fellow volunteer reserve officer Ron Jackson.

"Ron, you know the war has changed things," Brock blurted out to Jackson. "Follow the Victoria ferry out of the harbour. I have an important message to pass on to her captain."

"Good heavens, Jeff! She has a great turn of speed," Jackson returned, "and I'm not sure I can intercept her, [but] let's have a go at it."[15]

And so, off the pair went, chasing the huge passenger ferry, hoisting the "K" flag on Jackson's mast while sounding dash-dot-dash for "K" on the boat's siren. It's the internationally accepted signal meaning "Stop instantly."

The passenger ferry skipper slowed and stopped in the Strait of Georgia, where Brock shouted on a megaphone: "There are confidential papers to pass to the captain . . . to be delivered personally to the Naval Dockyard at Esquimalt. Would the captain send a line aboard to receive them?" Which he did.

When Jeff Brock got back to Vancouver that day, a newsboy selling his papers shouted that the British Admiralty had assumed control of all merchant shipping in the Commonwealth—using the codename "Funnel"—including Canada. Brock had anticipated such wartime orders affecting Canadian navy and merchant navy personnel. He'd gambled that a fellow reservist running a smaller ferry would recognize the serious nature of the moment, and so would the ferry captain. Brock had gone with his gut.

"I was relieved [that my] daring and unusual peacetime initiative had turned out to be just the sort of thing the captain of the Victoria ferry [might] expect," Brock wrote.[16]

Six days later, on September 10, 1939, Canada declared war on Germany, and the Royal Canadian Navy's thirteen warships and roughly 3,500 sailors were fully activated. Two months after that, Brock moved to the very naval base that had received those Admiralty orders, HMCS *Naden*, as assistant staff signals officer. It was the beginning of the "Phony War," and while skirmishes between Royal Navy warships and Germany's surface raiders and U-boats ramped up on the North Atlantic, at Esquimalt the war seemed a long way away. At *Naden*, Brock greeted a unique crop of recruits, retired RN and RCN officers who wanted back into uniform and into the new war, as well as a brand-new crop of volunteers. Then Brock received and decoded another Admiralty message: Britain was suffering from a maldistribution of wartime resources—in other words, it had more ships than qualified officers for command.

"We in Canada had more officers qualified for command than we had ships," Brock noted. So, using his gut instinct again, he sought permission and joined twenty-four other young officers rushing across the country to get passage from Halifax to England. "We had at last entered the war zone and were itching to find out what the fates held in store for us."[17]

Margaret Los felt that same urge to step up and do her part, but not until she was pushed. A teenager during the Great Depression in Toronto, she sensed that everybody in her community was poor. She also felt that her first obligation—helping her widowed mother make ends meet—trumped everything. But during the first couple of years of the war, the streets of her neighbourhood became devoid of men; they were all enlisting in the forces. She hinted to her mother that she wanted to join the war effort too.

"I don't know what's the matter with my children," her mother told her. "I've got wimps for daughters."[18]

Margaret was dumbfounded.

"If it had been me," her mother continued, "I would have joined the first day they announced [the war]. I don't know what I did wrong."

"Do you want me to go away from home?" Margaret asked.

"I want you to have a life," her mother said.

In July 1942, when the Canadian government formed the Women's Royal Canadian Naval Service (WRCNS), informally known as the Wrens, Margaret knew it was her time. But she decided it had to be done properly. Enlisting was like a job interview, she reasoned, so she put on a chiffon dress, a white hat, white gloves, hose, and white shoes. It was a hot summer day when she boarded the Queen Street trolley in the west end and headed to downtown Toronto. But when she exited the streetcar, the sky opened up. It poured rain, and by the time she'd reached the sea cadet building on Lake Shore Boulevard, the chiffon had wrinkled, her shoes were muddy, and her hair was "straight as a pin, which wasn't stylish then." Nevertheless, she had the attitude the newly formed women's naval service was looking for. Recruiters shipped her to HMCS *Conestoga* in Galt, Ontario, for basic training. She was twenty.

After a few weeks, the navy hustled her along to the huge signals school at HMCS *St. Hyacinthe*, east of Montreal on the south shore of the St. Lawrence River. Spread across twenty-five acres, *St. Hyacinthe*'s classrooms and barracks housed up to 3,200 officers, ratings, and Wrens.[19] During three months of instruction, recruits became visual signallers, wireless telegraphists, coders, radar operators, and radio artificers. Initially Margaret studied Morse code and the basics of wireless radio. It was intense work, but she'd excelled in math and science at school, so the concepts didn't faze her.

Margaret loved the gender ratio at the school too—thousands of men to twenty-five Wrens—but she wasn't fond of those administering the Wrens' social activities, the town's Catholic nuns. Periodically, when she got time off, Margaret enjoyed the chance to go cycling; however, the nuns wouldn't permit the Wrens to cycle in shorts, only long, navy-issue skirts. It got worse when she wanted to go swimming.

"The nuns were always looking to make sure we wore a brassiere under our bathing suits," she said. "If we didn't, we couldn't go swimming."

Following eight months of intensive training, and dodging the nuns, Petty Officer (PO) Margaret Los had become proficient in high-frequency radio direction-finding. HF/DF, or

"Huff-Duff,"* intercepted enemy radio transmissions, allowing Allied operators to locate enemy units—in this case, U-boats. As a Huff-Duff operator, Los would serve in the secret radio facility at HMCS *Coverdale*, just across the Petitcodiac River from Moncton, New Brunswick. Hers was a case of being in the right place at the right time. She would become one of the so-called listeners—Wren radio operators monitoring U-boat wireless transmissions throughout the Battle of the Atlantic.

Leonard Warren Murray's experience and responsibilities at the beginning of the war—as a captain and director of naval operations and training for the Royal Canadian Navy—positioned him ideally too. At almost every turn in his life and career, Leonard Murray had landed on his feet. Born in 1896 in Granton, on Nova Scotia's Northumberland Strait, Leonard was clearly attracted to the sea even as a boy. And when he saw his first warship, the Royal Navy cruiser HMS *Berwick*, she seemed to grab his heart and his head. In 1911 he went to Halifax to enrol in the first-ever class of the Royal Naval College of Canada (RNCC); he graduated third of nineteen cadets.

At the outbreak of the Great War, as a midshipman in the RCN, he was posted to Ottawa as a cipher officer, while four of his RNCC classmates served aboard HMS *Good Hope*, which was sunk with all hands lost in the Battle of Coronel, off Chile, in November 1914. His wartime service aboard RN

* Before the Second World War, British meteorologist Robert Watson-Watt built a device that could determine a direction bearing of the source of radio emission from a lightning bolt; several devices could locate positions, and he could calculate the movement of storms. During the war, he considered that such a direction-finder could be useful in catching brief enemy transmissions. High-frequency direction-finding (HF/DF, or "Huff-Duff") listening posts on land and aboard ships at sea assisted Royal Navy ships in making cross-bearings on short U-boat transmissions, thus fixing the location of the sender. The Kriegsmarine never learned how the enemy located its U-boats.

and RCN warships broadened his skills as a gunnery officer and navigating officer. Then, between the wars, his service aboard British ships opened the way to enrolling in the Naval Staff College at Greenwich, England. There, during an amphibious exercise as naval commander, he organized a thirty-six-ship convoy and escort. Not normal practice, the exercise raised eyebrows at the college. Back in Canada in the 1930s, Murray lectured on the convoy concept, suggesting modifications.

"Instead of patrolling the focal areas [near ports or narrow passages]," he observed, "the group of ships forming the convoy is escorted by an armed escort capable of dealing with any possible scale of attack. . . . In the convoy method it is not possible for an enemy to attack without laying herself open to attack and possible destruction."[20]

Leonard Murray also commanded the RCN destroyer HMCS *Saguenay* for two years, and then served another stint overseas at the Admiralty Operations Division. Late in 1938, he took the lead in training and naval operations at Naval Service Headquarters (NSHQ) in Ottawa.[21] The very day that the Admiralty mobilized Britain for war—August 21, 1939—Capt Murray initiated RCN mobilization, nearly two weeks ahead of Parliament's official declaration of war, although he did admit that he'd drafted an organizational chart of the naval service "on the back of an envelope, one day."[22] Add to that the physical premises of the NSHQ in Ottawa—located between a downtown delicatessen and several floors of Department of Agriculture offices—and one gets a sense of the ad hoc nature of Canada's preparations for war.[23]

Such were the times that a graduate of the first-ever class of the Royal Naval College of Canada, who'd worked out theoretical convoy and escort manoeuvres at a British naval staff college, who'd mobilized Canada's wartime navy before a formal declaration of war, and who could envision an org chart of Navy Service Headquarters on a scrap piece of paper, could lead Canada's naval forces against the U-boat threat. Capt Murray appeared to have all the right credentials for the job of naval operations and training. Further, on September 3, 1939, when *U30* sank the passenger steamship *Athenia* northwest of Ireland, causing Britain's first casualties of the war,* the act confirmed in Murray's mind that Nazi Germany fully intended to unleash a no-holds-barred U-boat campaign against British merchant and naval shipping. It also provoked Capt Murray and his NSHQ colleagues to present a calculated response to William Lyon Mackenzie King.

"We were able to impress upon [the Prime Minister,]" Murray explained, "that this kind of anti-submarine war was one that our small Canadian navy was best fitted to compete in."[24]

Not only did the RCN administrators receive approval from Ottawa for their planned response to the U-boat threat, but within a year—on May 23, 1941—the British would call on their Commonwealth sister navy to go even further. The RCN would assume responsibility for anti-submarine escort between thirty-five degrees west (the farthest extremity of the Western Approaches to UK destination ports) and the Grand Banks of Newfoundland (the eastern limit of escorts operating from Canadian ports). A newly christened Newfoundland Escort

---

* SS *Athenia* sailed September 1, 1939, from Glasgow for Montreal with 1,667 aboard (500 Jewish refugees, 469 Canadians, 311 US citizens, 72 UK subjects, and 315 crew); 98 passengers and 19 crew were killed in the torpedo attack. Lt Fritz-Julius Lemp in *U30* saw a darkened ship zigzagging and concluded she was a troopship.

Force (NEF) would attempt to shepherd convoys across the most treacherous waters of the North Atlantic. And Leonard Warren Murray would command that force.

IN a world war, even during its preliminary stages, no corner of the Commonwealth could be overlooked as a potential target. Not even a tiny, oval-shaped island nestled in Conception Bay, along the eastern coastline of the Dominion of Newfoundland. Just six miles long and two miles wide, Bell Island was home to about 6,000 people as the war began. At that time, its inhabitants thrived as fishers and farmers, but mostly as miners at the site known as Wabana, the Abenaki People's word for "place where daylight first appears."

Prospectors reported rich iron-ore deposits at Wabana as early as the sixteenth century, but industrial mining didn't begin there until outside interests from eastern Canada developed the site in the 1890s. As the miners exploited the seams of ore on the island, surface mining soon gave way to excavation that eventually created a network of tunnels and shafts stretching across thirty-two square miles underground. In the 1940s, Wabana miners were working as far as three miles out under the sea; in other words, the sea floor now formed the roof of what was then one of the most extensive subterranean iron-ore mines in the world.

The proximity of the Wabana mine to the coal fields of Cape Breton and the steel plants of Sydney made Nova Scotia industries among the mine's principal customers. By the 1930s, as much as 30 percent of Canada's steel was smelted at Sydney from ore imported from Bell Island, Newfoundland.[25] The reputation of Wabana ore also attracted buyers from the United States and Germany. Particularly following the Great War, when France occupied Germany's industrial Ruhr Valley, ocean-going carriers from Germany arrived at Bell Island regularly—beginning in 1936—to load thousands of tons of ore bound for German smelters producing steel for ships, planes, and tanks. But with Britain's declaration of war against Germany in 1939, what had been a peacetime port of call for Germany's merchant ships suddenly became a potential military target for its Kriegsmarine warships.

The threat was not lost on Newfoundland's commissioner of defence, Lewis E. Emerson, who convened a meeting with members of Canada's Department of External Affairs in February 1940. At the top of the agenda, Emerson led a discussion about ways and means to protect Bell Island—its people and industry—from U-boat attacks.[26] The commissioner recommended that the RCAF build an aerodrome near St. John's to dispatch bomber reconnaissance aircraft. Next, the commissioner met with Major-General Thomas V. Anderson, head of the Canadian Army, Rear-Admiral Percy Nelles, head of the RCN, and Chief Air Vice Marshal George M. Croil of the RCAF. Emerson emphasized that Canada's armed forces needed to recognize Newfoundland's strategic importance to Canada, and he urged air protection for the Dominion's Atlantic coast.

"No planes to spare," came the answer from the RCAF.[27]

Canadian External Affairs did manage to scare up some protection for the Bell Island mines. From the Canadians came two 4.7-inch artillery pieces to be positioned above the docks where ore carriers were loaded, and searchlights on cliffs overlooking the Tickle, the stretch of water between the island and the mainland village of Portugal Cove. Meantime, the

Newfoundland Militia recruited about 120 men and erected barracks, an officers' mess, and a parade ground for the men stationed there. Dominion Steel and Coal Corporation, which operated the mines, agreed to house and feed the First Coastal Command, a military unit dispatched to stand guard on Bell Island against an as yet unseen enemy. Commissioner Emerson's greatest fear had left a couple of platoons of riflemen and a battery of gunners with, apparently, nothing to shoot at.

Controlling the surface sea lanes of the North Atlantic was clearly vital for the survival of Britain; protecting the supply lines to the Soviet Union and, by extension, its survival in the Allied war effort was equally important. But so too was command of the air space above those lanes. The routes that Allied convoys travelled to maintain the flow of food, fuel, and munitions to ports in the British Isles, and from there to the war's Eastern Front, the war in the Mediterranean, and any potential invasion of Nazi-occupied Europe, demanded powerful, sustained, and far-reaching air cover. The presence of even a single aircraft overhead often frustrated the intentions of U-boat wolf packs.[28] However, as convoys such as HX 72 learned in September 1940, that undefended 600-mile stretch of the North Atlantic beyond the reach of land-based RAF and RCAF Coastal Command anti-submarine aircraft—the Black Pit—proved deadly. It would take the Allied air forces months to acquire the aircraft, tactics, technologies, and crews to fill that mid-Atlantic gap.

Facing challenges in the cockpit had never fazed Squadron Leader (S/L) Norville Everett Small* in either a civilian or a military aircraft, so he had no reason to think

* Norville Everett "Molly" Small's ranking will change in this narrative—from flight sergeant to flying officer to squadron leader.

he couldn't deal with the Black Pit. And with thousands of hours in the air to back him up, he would even offer some workable solutions when the time came. But that wouldn't happen until his commanders seconded him for service in the Battle of the Atlantic.

Norville Small was born in Allandale, Ontario, in 1908 and joined the fledgling RCAF between the wars, in 1928. He got a taste of every military aircraft the air force had in its arsenal at the time, particularly those with pontoons or boat bottoms on Canada's Pacific Coast. But by 1937, commercial aviation had lured Flight Sergeant (F/Sgt) Small away from the military and into civilian bush flying. He learned to pilot, navigate, and maintain aircraft that hauled food supplies, mail, exploration equipment, prospectors, and industrial workers into northern Canada. He flew Fairchild, Junkers, and Norseman bush planes with legendary partners and competitors Clennell Haggerston "Punch" Dickins, Grant McConachie, and Wilfred Reid "Wop" May. Together in the late 1930s, the "pilots of the purple twilight" opened up outposts in the far North. Their hours were long, the rewards slim, and the conditions often deadly.

"We had bad weather . . . to Fort St. James" was a typical message in Small's files when he flew Canadian Airways bush operations into northern British Columbia. "All passes north plugged tight . . . was fortunate to land at Bear Lake."[29]

The outbreak of war in 1939 pulled Norville Small back into the RCAF, and as soon as his superiors examined his pilot's log—hundreds of hours flying in all conditions to all points of the compass—his fate was sealed. The Air Force posted him to Eastern Air Command (EAC) and No. 10 (BR) Squadron at Dartmouth, Nova Scotia. Flying Officer (F/O) Small, "Molly" to his flying comrades, began flying anti-submarine sorties providing air cover for convoys along the East Coast. He also conducted advanced flying instruction and, in 1941, because he was familiar with flying boats, helped deliver US-built PBYs (Catalinas) to Britain.[30] Such Ferry Command flights required their crews to depart Bermuda and fly unaccompanied across the Atlantic—over, under, and through periodic storms—to deliver the fifteen-ton Catalina, as many as thirty hours later, safely at moorings in Greenock, Scotland.[31]

"A pilot of outstanding ability and sound judgment," read one of many endorsements in F/O Small's flight log from that period.

In March 1942, RCAF National Headquarters in Ottawa not only recognized Small's aptitude in flying anything the Air Force threw at him, they also noted his leadership and problem-solving skills. They gave him command of No. 113 (BR) Squadron at Yarmouth, Nova Scotia, just as U-boats began to threaten shipping within Canada's territorial waters all the way up the St. Lawrence River to Quebec City. But it was in the cause of shrinking that Black Pit in the mid-Atlantic that S/L Small brought all his unique talents to the fore.

NELSON Shead presented a wide array of valuable skills to the Royal Canadian Navy recruiting office when the war broke out. He had no military experience, but Nelson and his two brothers—Bill and Harry—had all grown up around Selkirk, Manitoba, at the southern entrance to Lake Winnipeg. With their ancestry in the Fisher River Cree Nation, all members of the Shead family had traditionally fished for food on the lake, or they had worked aboard boats in the lake's thriving fishing industry. Deceivingly shallow and instantly tempestuous, Lake Winnipeg made everyone who worked the fishery wise to the ways of precarious seafaring.

"Lake Winnipeg is much shorter with more vicious chop," explained one Shead family member. "And the ships are smaller and narrower, so they rock like hell."[32]

First Nations enlistment during the Great War had surprised Canadian government officials, particularly when regulations for military service initially stipulated that all applicants "be a British born subject of a white Race."[33] Nevertheless, about 4,000 Indigenous men from Canada served overseas between 1914 and 1918. Roughly half the eligible Mi'kmaq and Maliseet men from New Brunswick and Nova Scotia signed up. Practically all of the Saskatchewan File Hills band and BC's Head of the Lake (Nk'maplqs) band enlisted.[34] A Winnipeg newspaper reported that "thirty descendants of Métis who fought at the side of Louis Riel in 1869–70 have just enlisted at Qu'Appelle."[35]

That trend continued when Canada put the call out for able-bodied men to volunteer for service in 1939. Six months into the Second World War, a hundred First Nations men had joined the Canadian armed services; by war's end 3,090 were in the army, air force, and navy. All three Shead brothers joined the Royal Canadian Naval Reserve (RCNR), applying the skills they'd honed on Lake Winnipeg fishing boats to survival on the North Atlantic run.

George Edward Jamieson grew up near the water as well—the Grand River that ran through the Six Nations reserve in southwestern Ontario. But his experience as a youth came from the family's ninety-acre farm near Ohsweken, Ontario. His father (Mohawk) and his mother (Cayuga), both of the Six

Nations of the Grand River First Nation, sent young George to school in Toronto. He soon joined the Royal Canadian Sea Cadets and was taken on by the navy's Volunteer Reserve as a boy bugler. When Canada declared war on Germany in September 1939, George was among those 100 Indigenous men from Canada to sign up right away. After his basic training at HMCS *Stadacona*, Jamieson was streamed into gunnery; when he joined convoy escorts he would specialize in anti-submarine warfare (ASW).[36] Aboard the minesweeper HMCS *Drummondville*, Chief Petty Officer (CPO) Jamieson would serve in the defence of Halifax Harbour, in the Gulf of St. Lawrence, and along the coast of Newfoundland.

Working the land had preoccupied three generations of the Mills family of Grey County in west-central Ontario. But the Depression drove the youngest members off the land. In 1939, son Frank, at twenty-three, had enough money for tuition to train as a machinist at Standard Engineering in Toronto. With war work suddenly available, he landed a job machining parts for the Tiger Moth trainer at De Havilland Aircraft of Canada in Downsview, Ontario.

But as handsomely as he was paid at the plant, Mills became trapped in the "war worker required" category, a fact that frustrated him in 1940, when he considered enlisting in the armed forces. Eventually he convinced his foreman at De Havilland to endorse his plans to join up. The resulting letter acknowledged Frank's "desire to join some branch of His Majesty's Forces," and noted that "though reluctant to lose his services, this firm is prepared to grant him his release."[37] Frank Mills chose the Royal Canadian Naval Volunteer Reserve and enlisted at HMCS *York*, on the Canadian National Exhibition grounds in Toronto. Sent to

HMCS *Naden*, Canada's west coast naval base in Esquimalt, Frank Mills began basic training as a stoker. There AB Mills acquired armed-service toughness through drills and exercises, learned discipline by following the orders of his superiors, and became accustomed to teamwork by facing onboard challenges with his shipmates. But from the outset, he knew how he could serve best.

"I didn't join the navy to shovel coal," he told his trainers. "I'm a qualified machinist."

The navy was desperate for machinists in both its Atlantic and Pacific fleets, so Mills's instructors hustled him up the ladder to train as an engine room artificer (ERA) at HMCS *Comox*, on Vancouver Island. Literally from the inside out, he learned the operation and maintenance of marine boilers, steam engines, condensers, pumps, and gauges. He learned different fuel types (wood, coal, and oil) and how to measure the energy (BTUs) each generated. He immersed himself in the running of vertical triple-expansion steam engines, which were the main powerplants inside RCN minesweepers, corvettes, and frigates at that time.

By the time Mills got to Vancouver Island, three new corvettes were under construction. Each triple-expansion steam engine stood twenty feet high, was twenty feet long, weighed 120 tons, and generated up to 2,750 horsepower. Both in port and at sea, Mills learned how to bring a dead-cold boiler up to maximum steam production inside eight hours, and how to generate enough constant steam to get his ship underway within an hour. The efficient running of boilers and engines—the heart and lifeblood of any steam-driven warship—became second nature to him. In just under eleven months, he'd graduated to ERA Petty Officer 2nd class.

Then, suddenly, PO Mills's expertise was required at Port Arthur on Lake Superior, where he was sent to observe the installation of boilers and engines in a brand-new minesweeper, HMCS *Sault Ste. Marie*. Once again Frank Mills's sense of pride and purpose altered his military career. On Lake Superior, the freshly launched minesweeper went through sea trials with her new captain and crew aboard, including PO Mills. But things got tense soon after the work-up began.

"All ahead full," the commanding officer (CO) ordered. He wanted to push the sweeper's powerplant to her limit immediately.

"No, sir," returned Mills, knowing the sweeper's system wasn't up to full temperature or pressure yet. "You don't know how these engines work."

His insubordination could have resulted in a court martial, but the CO delivered a more immediate judgment. "You needn't worry about the engines," he told Mills. "You won't be on this ship once it gets to Halifax."

PO Mills had made the correct deduction but the wrong decision by defying the CO's direct order. HMCS *Sault Ste. Marie* survived the sea trial and the transit to Halifax. But just as the captain had threatened, Mills was promptly posted off the minesweeper and back to the Halifax machine shops, repairing battle-damaged convoy escorts. Still, PO Mills would get his chance, not just overseas but as an ERA aboard the frigate HMCS *Outremont*, on active convoy duty across the North Atlantic and up the perilous run to Murmansk, Russia.

Much the same way conditions in the Great Depression sparked Frank Mills's determination to leave an Ontario farm to become an RCNVR machinist, so did the state of the German economy in the 1930s serve as catalyst for a civil servant's son to leave home for the Kriegsmarine. Born in 1925, the fourth of eight children, Walter Schmietenknop first apprenticed as a blacksmith to help his family survive the times. But even as a journeyman in Kleefeld, Germany, working daily from early morning to 7 p.m., his meagre wages proved insufficient. Meantime, the war had begun. Rather than wait to be drafted into the army at seventeen, Walter told his father he'd like to join the navy.

Basic training led him to submarine school in East Prussia, and eventually to Kriegsmarinewerft, the naval shipyard in Wilhelmshaven, where the warship on which he would serve—*U767*—was under construction. Walter became an orderly for the U-boat's captain, Oberleutnant (Oblt) Walter Dankleff. But soon his immediate superior arrived at the yard, and Lt Helmut Schuster was an officer to be feared, obeyed, and trusted.

"Leutnant Schuster turned out to be one of the best officers on our sub," Schmietenknop wrote. "The crew treated each other like a family. An officer might even act like an indulgent father with mischievous boys."[38]

At Schuster's insistence, Walter studied submarine manuals diligently as shipyard workers installed each internal component of his Type VIIC U-boat. Then, suddenly, Schuster led his recruits through a drill on a new training device. The apparatus had an upper diving tank about ten feet deep—it represented the ocean. Another tank, situated below the first, contained air—it represented the U-boat. The lower tank could be flooded with water. A vertical shaft ran between the lower and upper tanks with a hatch on top, simulating a U-boat's hatch—it represented an escape route.

One by one, the sub trainees entered the bottom tank of air. Once each was sealed inside, that lower tank was flooded with water, and the sailor had to make his way into the shaft, up through the hatch, and through the upper tank of water to the surface. Mastering the drill prepared a submariner for escaping from a sinking U-boat.

"At first, it was frightening," Schmietenknop wrote, "but we got used to it, and I enjoyed these diving sessions. Two or three of us practised this for about an hour every afternoon."

The final stage of training—ten days of tactical manoeuvres—took *U767* and her crew out into the Baltic Sea. The simulated war game included four merchant ships, with escorts and aircraft cover on one side and ten U-boats in pursuit on the other.

"It was like real war," Walter wrote. "The freighters had destroyer escorts, just like the enemy's in the Atlantic."

The U-boat flotilla commander sent the U-boats in different directions to find the convoy; after a day's search, when a U-boat found the convoy, the others converged. Using the advantage of a moonlit night, *U767* approached a freighter from the dark side. No torpedoes were fired; instead, each U-boat surfaced and flashed Morse code lights at the target ship, signalling a strike. All went well until one of the escorting destroyers caught up with *U767* as she submerged and nearly rammed her during the dive. The German submariners also had to contend with another realistic simulation—reacting to attacks from enemy aircraft.

"The idea of this sort of realistic training," Walter wrote, "was that if we couldn't make it here in these maneuvers, we wouldn't make it in a real battle situation either."

The time for training, simulated escapes from a sinking

U-boat, and war games on the Baltic was over. Electrical engineer Walter Schmietenknop and *U767* would soon be tested in actual combat on the Atlantic.

In marked contrast to the Royal Canadian Navy's dozen or so warships, 3,500 permanent and reservist sailors, and a modest headquarters next to an Ottawa delicatessen, the Royal Navy's strength and headquarters in London, England, reflected its motto "*Si vis pacem, para bellum*"—"If you wish for peace, prepare for war." In the summer of 1939, His Majesty's Royal Navy boasted 129,000 officers and men, 73,000 reservists, and 317 warships.[39] Its administrative headquarters lay just off Whitehall in the heart of Westminster. The Board of Admiralty, Naval Intelligence Division (NID), and all their support staff resided in the stately Old Admiralty Building, just steps from the prime minister's residence at 10 Downing Street.

Initially, the Admiralty's response to the U-boat threat came from Room 38 inside the Old Admiralty Building, which served as the office of Rear-Admiral (RAdm) John Godfrey. A veteran of Great War campaigns at sea in the Dardanelles and the Mediterranean, Godfrey adopted the practice of taking his staff and subordinates into his confidence and giving them responsibility without interference. He also placed high value on intelligence and bold actions, having learned this under the wing of Adm William "Blinker" Hall, the director of Naval Intelligence (DNI) from 1914 to 1919.

"Mistakes may be forgiven," Hall preached. "But even God himself cannot forgive the hanger-back."[40]

In 1939, when RAdm Godfrey took over from Hall,

the Royal Navy, despite its dominating size, faced numerous challenges. It was hamstrung by diplomatic agreements. The Washington Naval Conference of 1921–22 had restricted the British from building new warships so that the United States could maintain parity. Then the London Naval Treaty of 1930 saw the number of capital ships (battleships and battlecruisers) reduced. And finally, the 1935 Anglo-German Naval Agreement allowed Germany to rebuild its fleet, as long as it remained 35 percent the size of the RN. One clause in that agreement, however, allowed the Kriegsmarine to possess submarine tonnage equal to that of the entire British Commonwealth of Nations. Thus, when the Second World War began, Nazi Germany's shipyards had already built sixty-five U-boats and put twenty-one of them to sea. Consequently, anti-submarine warfare would quickly become a new priority for Britain's director of Naval Intelligence.

RAdm Godfrey considered intelligence as "evaluated information," which would consist of "estimates and warnings based on fully documented analysis" that could provide Royal Navy strategists with day-to-day operational intelligence. He and his staff would be "scientific in their approach, establishing hypotheses and testing them against raw data"[41] before delivering them to the Admiralty's Plans and Operations Division. And so as not to become a "hanger-back," the new DNI, just like his predecessor, chose to recruit civilians—including scholars, bankers, corporate heads, and lawyers.[42] He chose them not for their oath to King and Empire, but for their initiative, imagination, and desire to win the war. Among others, Godfrey approached banker Charles Hambro (later in the British secret service), solicitor Edward Merrett

(Godfrey's private secretary), and stockbroker Ian Fleming* to join his intelligence team.[43]

Another of his civilian choices was a lawyer who was working at the time as an interrogator of German prisoners. Rodger Winn's boyhood ambition had been to join the Royal Navy, but an acute attack of polio in his youth had left him with a twisted spine. Despite the physical disability, he had earned degrees from Cambridge and from Harvard in the United States. And his ability to aggregate and distill information fit perfectly with Godfrey's priority for evaluated information. Winn applied what he'd learned as an interrogator. He read battle reports, studied air reconnaissance data, and began to understand U-boat tactics better than anybody at NID. Both Godfrey and Winn operated on the principle that intelligence had to stand on its own.

"[Our job is] to resist the temptation of allowing the truth to be bent by what people would like to hear," Godfrey said.[44]

RAdm Godfrey quickly posted Winn to the Tracking Room, part of the Operational Intelligence Centre inside the Old Admiralty Building. The room featured wall charts and maps and a large table on which staff pinpointed U-boat and surface raider locations. Winn deduced that certain types of U-boat signals represented predictable situations—short signals might reveal the U-boat had sustained damage or indicate its intention to end a patrol and return to base. Successful prediction of U-boat action just 51 percent of the time, Winn suggested, could mean lives or ships saved and U-boats sunk.[45]

One time, the tracking table showed two homebound tankers close together, and a direction-finding (DF) fix showed a

* At the time, Ian Fleming worked as a junior partner at Rowe & Pitman; he would become Godfrey's second-in-command at NID, and after the war would author the James Bond 007 spy thrillers.

U-boat a short distance away. The director of the Operations Division asked Winn if he could predict the U-boat's movements and whether it would endanger the tankers. Winn's reading of the U-boat's signal gave him sufficient sense that, yes, the tankers were in danger. To definitively determine if Winn's readings were correct, one tanker was diverted to a course Winn calculated would steer it clear of the U-boat. The other was left on its existing course. The next morning, Operations learned that the diverted tanker had passed that stretch of the Atlantic unmolested; the other had been sunk.

One result of Winn's accurate intelligence was a changing of the guard in the Tracking Room. Toward the end of 1940, when the existing Tracking Room director was transferred, RAdm Godfrey campaigned to have Winn, a civilian, appointed as its new director. The proposal went all the way to the First Sea Lord himself, and so Winn was thus appointed as Temporary Commander RNVR Special Branch (and head of Tracking Room staff) without a single day's experience at sea or previous naval service. Nevertheless, his expertise soon won rave reviews from those at sea in battle. Royal Navy Adm Andrew Cunningham, returning from his command in the Mediterranean, couldn't praise Winn's results enough.

"His knowledge of U-boats, their commanders, and almost what they were thinking about was uncanny," Cunningham said. "Every submarine leaving an enemy harbour was tracked and plotted, and at any moment Capt Winn could give numbers, likely positions, and movements of all the U-boats at sea. His prescience was amazing."[46]

In the fall of 1940, at the height of the Blitz, work began on a massive block at the northwest corner of the Old Admiralty Building. Known as the Citadel, the stone and concrete enclosures would soon house the Operational Intelligence Centre, including the Tracking Room. Presumably bombproof, the Citadel (cynically referred to as "Lenin's Tomb") offered Capt Winn more room in which to work and the authority to deal with the looming U-boat war. In time, the Tracking Room (later, more specifically, the Submarine Tracking Room) and Winn's intelligence regimen would become a model for both of Britain's naval allies in the Battle of the Atlantic—the Canadians and the Americans.

ALL of the Royal Canadian Navy's eventual strengths—its continuous flow of trained volunteers, its brain trust of experienced officers, its growing array of anti-submarine technologies, and its escort prowess at sea—depended, at the beginning of the war, on one important but as yet missing component: efficient and rapid warship production in Canada. In part, that missing component was eventually provided by an unlikely source, an American-born engineer who didn't just build things but also built and exploited opportunities. As an industrialist, Clarence Decatur Howe had a knack for bringing together people with both business savvy and a knack for problem-solving. This allowed him to become very successful in the private sector, but also—inside government—to spearhead the delivery of ships to both Canada's armed forces and its merchant navy in a time of war.

With a family tree that dated back to the original Puritan settlers of Massachusetts, C.D. Howe was born in 1886. On his father's side, he was related to the author of "The Battle Hymn of the Republic," and on his mother's to American naval hero Stephen Decatur, after whom he was named.

Graduating near the top of his class at the Massachusetts Institute of Technology at age twenty in 1907, he accepted a professorship at Dalhousie University in Halifax. In 1913, he left academia, became a British subject, and entered the federal civil service, taking a position with the Board of Grain Commissioners in Fort William, Ontario. That led to a thriving enterprise building a network of massive grain storage elevators across western Canada.

Though the Great Depression hit his business as severely as any in Canada, Howe weathered the economic storm, while also criticizing federal governments of all stripes for not charting a path through the economic malaise. His views attracted both Liberal and Conservative Party strategists, but he wasn't interested in running unless his election automatically delivered a Cabinet post. In the 1935 election, when Howe won the Port Arthur seat for Mackenzie King's Liberals, the prime minister gave him the Ministries of Marine, Railways, and Canals, which soon amalgamated as the Ministry of Transport.

As war loomed, Howe considered how Canada should prepare for the worst. On September 13, 1939, three days after declaring war on Nazi Germany, the King government created a department of supply, later the Department of Munitions and Supply. With Howe as minister, the department functioned more like a large corporation than a government ministry, as Howe recruited and appointed business executives, not civil servants, to help shape Canada's wartime supply policy. They were paid a nominal fee of a dollar, thus becoming known as "dollar-a-year men," and were given nearly free rein to seize private property, divert materials from civilian use, and generate war supplies by whatever means they deemed necessary. It was said that C.D. Howe viewed the war as if it were a kind of megaproject and that money wasn't an issue, only production was.[47]

As an indication of just how rapidly and apparently unilaterally the Ministry of Munitions and Supply was prepared to move, Minister Howe announced on January 24, 1940, the government's intention to build forty-six whale-catcher-type anti-submarine vessels (corvettes), twenty-eight minesweepers, and forty-one boats for various tasks: ammunition and provision lighters, refuelling scows, aircraft-salvage boats, tenders, and bomb tenders. Two weeks later, King's Cabinet approved a more ambitious program to build ninety corvettes and minesweepers (forty-six corvettes had ballooned to sixty-four) for an anticipated cost of $54.2 million.[48] Work began at fourteen Canadian shipyards, including Saint John, New Brunswick; Sorel and Lauzon, in Quebec; Port Arthur, Midland, and Collingwood, in Ontario; and Prince Rupert and Victoria, in British Columbia.

Canada's war effort at sea needed ships. It would get them. "Before the war is over, everything will be needed, so let's go ahead anyway," Howe said. "If we lose the war, nothing will matter . . . If we win the war, the cost will still have been of no consequence and will have been forgotten."[49]

C.D. Howe's eventual control and direction of Canada's munitions and supply made him a target of both Opposition politicians and press editorialists. It earned him the moniker "Minister of Everything." However, the slings and arrows of Conservative Party critics in Parliament and commentary in the newspapers paled by comparison to the near-death experience he faced late in 1940. On December 6, Minister Howe stepped aboard the British motor passenger ship *Western Prince* in New York. Travelling with him were several of his dollar-a-year men—financier E.P. Taylor, department store owner W.C. Woodward, and Montreal accountant and former Quebec Cabinet minister Gordon W. Scott. The four men, among the wealthiest and most influential in the country, planned to attend meetings in Britain about furthering Canada's contributions to the war effort. They joined 164 passengers and crew bound for Liverpool. The captain of *Western Prince* chose to sail the Atlantic without escort.

Eight days into their journey, and about 500 miles west of the Irish coast, the crew of *U96* intercepted the passenger ship. It was just past 7 a.m. on December 14 when the U-boat fired a G7e torpedo at the eastbound ship. It missed. But the second torpedo struck the liner forward. C.D. Howe was just awakening in his berth and felt the shudder of the torpedo explosion. *Western Prince* came to a stop in the water and began sinking by the bow. Typical of the time of year and the ship's location, seas were heavy and winds chilling. Nevertheless, the captain ordered passengers to the lifeboats. By the time ninety-eight crew members and fifty-five passengers had floated clear of their ship, *U96* had reloaded and fired a *coup de grâce* into her victim. *Western Prince* went down with the ship's master, eight crew, and six passengers in less than two minutes.

Fortunately for the survivors, *Western Prince*'s radio operator had managed to transmit a distress signal before abandoning ship.[50] But that didn't guarantee rescue. British Admiralty Merchant Shipping Instructions (BAMSI) forbad any merchant or navy vessel—unless ordered to do so—from stopping to rescue survivors at sea, particularly if a U-boat was known to be in the vicinity. Despite the standing order, however, having heard the SOS call, the master of the merchant steamer *Baron Kinnaird* raced to the scene. Eight hours later, the merchantman arrived to haul the nearly frozen survivors aboard, including Taylor, Woodward, and Howe. In the rough seas, however, the lifeboat carrying Gordon Scott smashed into the *Kinnaird*, and he was killed.

The experience shook C.D. Howe deeply. "[I] considered every hour that [I've] lived from that day onwards to be borrowed time," he later told a British interviewer.[51]

What also might have crossed Howe's mind—if not then, soon after—is the fact that had German naval intelligence known or understood the stature of Howe, Taylor, Woodward, and Scott as powerhouses of Canadian industry and key players in the country's war supply decision-making, the sinking of *Western Prince* could have become an even more substantial German victory. The deaths or even capture of Howe and several of his key "dollar men" might have delivered the Nazi propaganda machine one of its greatest early coups of the war.

Instead, Howe and the dollar men had survived almost unnoticed. What's more, the news of *Western Prince*'s torpedoing was, for a time, successfully suppressed by the Canadian government's wartime censorship system—the Directorate of Censorship. If not for MacKay Radio, a New York–based news-gathering agency, which intercepted *Prince*'s SOS call and relayed it to American news outlets, then to the *Ottawa Citizen*, Canadians wouldn't have immediately known about C.D. Howe's plight.[52] The control of such sensitive (and often bad) news would emerge regularly as U-boat operations drew closer to Canada's Atlantic coast.

However, on December 18, Howe and the surviving members of his entourage carried on with their mission to meet British business and government leaders about the status of the Commonwealth war effort. And if the pleas from Britons didn't put every aspect of C.D. Howe's work at Munitions and Supply into even sharper focus, certainly his ordeal in an open lifeboat on the North Atlantic did.

Despite a year's worth of experience and attempts to respond to the threat, Allied sea lanes remained critically vulnerable to U-boat attack; in 1940, U-boats had sunk 2.6 million tons of cargo. In the first six months of the war, Canada emerged as Britain's sole supplier. But if Canadian merchant convoys and escorting RCN warships couldn't guarantee continuous and reliable supplies for the UK's civilian population and war industries, then certainly Canada's supporting role in the war effort would be thrown into doubt.

Chapter Four

CEMETERY OF SHIPPING

Britain's declaration of war against Nazi Germany interrupted the party that the Canadian Pacific Exhibition (CPE) threw late that summer of 1939 in the port of Vancouver. On August 31, the CPE was honouring the officers and crew of two Royal Canadian Navy destroyers—HMCS *Fraser* and *St. Laurent*—stationed at Esquimalt naval base on Vancouver Island.[1] In the middle of the celebrations, however, naval headquarters in Ottawa ordered the two destroyers to sea, to proceed with speed down the Pacific coast, through the Panama Canal, and to commence service in the Atlantic war.

That's when the life of RCN Lt Desmond Piers changed too. Through the winter of 1939–40, the destroyer in which he served, HMCS *Restigouche*, had joined her sister ships *Fraser* and *St. Laurent* escorting the first troopships with Canadian soldiers aboard overseas to England. But by the spring of 1940, with Hitler's Blitzkrieg ("lightning war") consuming northwestern Europe, and expeditionary forces withdrawing in chaos, the Royal Canadian Navy received a distress call on May 23 from the Admiralty in Britain. Piers remembered that the message was simple and direct: "Send ships! We desperately need every ship you can provide . . . to pull troops out of Europe."[2]

Several years earlier, when Desmond W. "Debby" Piers announced to his family his intention to join the navy, recruiters told him the two quickest ways into the regular navy were via the Royal Naval College of Canada in Dartmouth, Nova Scotia, or by gaining special entry through the public-school system in England. Piers chose the latter and spent five years aboard the RN's heavy cruiser HMS *Frobisher*, earning a wage of twenty-five cents a day but gaining valuable credits and experience.[3]

When he returned to Canada, he passed all of his exams—navigation, gunnery, and anti-sub signals—for entry to the Royal Canadian Navy, and he joined the crew of the newly christened RCN destroyer HMCS *Saguenay*, based at Esquimalt. In 1939, as the war began, Piers was transferred to *Restigouche* (commissioned in 1938). With HMCS *Skeena* and *Saguenay* (commissioned in 1931), *Restigouche* was the sixth River-class destroyer built in British shipyards for the Canadian government; the other three were HMCS *St. Laurent*, *Fraser* (commissioned in 1937), and *Ottawa* (1938).

With British forces withdrawing from France, Piers suddenly found himself on the firing line. Operation Dynamo had dispatched as many Allied naval ships and civilian vessels as could sail the English Channel to retrieve hundreds of thousands of British Expeditionary Force troops stranded in towns and on beaches along the French coast. As they reached England during the first week of June 1940, the Canadian destroyers received orders to race on to the town of Saint-Valery-en-Caux, west of Calais. When *St. Laurent* and *Restigouche* arrived offshore, Piers saw smoke and flames everywhere. The Germans were positioned on high cliffs around the town, pounding the retreating 51st (Highland) Division on the shore.

The scene spurred Cdr Horatio Nelson Lay, on the bridge of *Restigouche*, into action. "Piers, get an officer," Lay shouted. "Send him ashore and find out what's happening!"[4]

The Canadians learned that Scottish troops were trapped in the town; they apparently had abandoned all their armour in the rush to the sea and were just waiting to be taken prisoner.

Piers recalled going directly to his cabin, where he looked in the mirror and said aloud, "Piers, you're it!" He grabbed a bag, put a set of binoculars, an Aldis lamp (for signalling), and a bottle of whiskey inside, and returned to the bridge. "Ready to go, sir," he told Cdr Lay.

"I didn't mean it to be you, Piers, but go ahead anyway," the captain said.

Piers took the ship's whaler, motored to the shore, loaded as many men into the boat as he could, and began the return trip to *Restigouche*.

"I got about a mile out," Piers said, "and *St. Laurent* and *Restigouche* came dashing in, firing at the top of the cliffs where the German guns were firing at us. . . . These were the first shots fired in anger at the enemy during the war by the Royal Canadian Navy."

But the RCN would soon count its first casualties too. Later in June, Royal Navy cruiser HMS *Calcutta* led a flotilla to rescue another pocket of retreating Allied troops, at Saint-Jean-de-Luz, on the French border with Spain. HMCS *Fraser* picked up forty-four French and British Expeditionary Force troops, while HMCS *Restigouche* evacuated the Polish

Army general staff and about 200 refugees, and all headed back to England. As night fell on June 25, the three warships made their way toward Plymouth at twenty knots, with *Fraser* in the lead, *Calcutta* second, and *Restigouche* astern, all three zigzagging to avoid enemy fire. In the course of manoeuvring, however, two of the warships were suddenly on collision course in the dark, causing "*Calcutta* to cut *Fraser* exactly in half in the middle of the night," Piers said.

When *Restigouche* arrived at the collision site, Piers said, the entire stern of *Fraser*, including two funnels, was adrift but still floating. Capt Lay manoeuvred his quarter deck alongside *Fraser*'s stern section to pluck stranded sailors from the wreck. *Restigouche*'s crew launched a whaler to retrieve others in the water, and then searched for the other half of the ship, even defying protocol by turning on searchlights to look for more of their comrades. Piers said they finally found the forward half of *Fraser* at a sixty-degree angle in the water, with more than sixty survivors aboard singing "Roll Out the Barrel."

"We were alarmed," he said. "We'd found no captain, no officers; all apparently lost."

By 6 a.m., *Restigouche* had docked back at Plymouth with crew, military evacuees from Saint-Jean-de-Luz, and *Fraser*'s survivors all safe and sound. Everybody wondered, what next?

"What should we see coming up the harbour about 7 a.m.," Piers continued, "but a ship with a great big box on its bow. It was the cruiser *Calcutta*. And what's on front? She had gone through *Fraser* so exactly that the whole of the bridge of *Fraser* was deposited on the bow of *Calcutta*—captain, navigator, and officers of the watch. Nobody lost."

Given the general chaos and loss that Allied forces experienced during the hasty withdrawal from France in May and June 1940, the sight of *Fraser*'s officers safe aboard *Calcutta* gave the Canadian contingent overseas some sense of relief. But this was a Pyrrhic victory, not a proud moment for either the RN or the RCN. Recriminations, a bitter investigation, and grief at the loss of fifty-eight RCN personnel followed. The Canadian navy, in mid-1940, still had relatively few regular-force sailors, so the loss of so many aboard *Fraser* hit the service hard.* And losing a precious destroyer, in the face of Hitler's likely launch of a summer amphibious invasion of England, didn't help either.

In correspondence via the UK ambassador in America in July 1940, Prime Minister Churchill wanted President Roosevelt to know that German bombing attacks had sunk four Royal Navy destroyers and damaged seven more. He hoped Britain's dwindling supply of warships might prompt Roosevelt to loan or lease to Britain a number of older American destroyers as a stopgap.

"I am confident . . . that you will leave nothing undone to ensure that fifty or sixty of your oldest destroyers are sent to me at once," Churchill wrote. "Mr. President . . . in the long history of the world, this is a thing to do *now*."[5]

CHURCHILL was far too busy to notice—dealing with the fall of France, the deliverance from Dunkirk, the loss of the

* Just four months later, many of *Fraser*'s survivors had been reassigned to her replacement destroyer, the newly renamed HMCS *Margaree* (formerly HMS *Diana*). On October 22, just as *Margaree* began a transatlantic crossing back home to Canada, she collided with merchant ship *Port Fairy*. Eighty-six of those killed in the *Port Fairy* collision had survived the *Calcutta–Fraser* collision.

French fleet, the Battle of Britain, and Home Defence preparations for an expected German invasion—but an expatriate filmmaker was hard at work in Canada that summer, generating moral support for Britain's besieged Atlantic convoys. In 1939, Prime Minister Mackenzie King was searching for ways to give the country's war effort a higher profile. The government hired Scottish filmmaker John Grierson to study the Canadian government's use of motion pictures. And as general manager of Canada's Wartime Information Board, Grierson recommended formation of the National Film Board (NFB) to produce nontheatrical films, in this case documentaries about Canada's wartime mobilization. The series *Canada Carries On* was born, and episode number one was titled *Atlantic Patrol*, to showcase the Royal Canadian Navy's escort operations on the North Atlantic.

Over a stirring fanfare with clear strains of "O Canada" intertwined, a point-of-view sequence of massive RCN destroyer guns swivelling to their forward position directed the viewer to the open sea ahead.

"The broad Atlantic, vital highway for men and munitions passing from the New World to the Old," boomed the voice of narrator Lorne Greene.[6] A regular reader of the evening news on the then three-year-old Canadian Broadcasting Corporation radio network, Greene was nicknamed "the Voice of Doom."

With equal authority on the film soundtrack, Greene next stated the challenge that wartime navies of the British Commonwealth faced—particularly the Royal Canadian Navy—to deliver war supplies that Britain required to achieve victory. Grierson had a specific vision for *Atlantic Patrol* and the eleven other documentaries of the *Canada Carries On* series. "[It was to] get Canadians to focus on their collective energies . . . understand the strategy of war in a Canadian context," explained Albert Ohayon, NFB collections curator, "and to unite in a collective purpose to crush tyranny and fascism."[7]

To make his point on film, Grierson scavenged from US movie libraries, borrowed British archival footage, and somehow acquired confiscated Nazi propaganda film showing young German submariners learning battle strategy and Kriegsmarine shipyards launching new U-boats. But in the most compelling sequences, the documentary took the viewer aboard an RCN destroyer on patrol. There, Grierson's film crews captured the call to action, navigation orders being carried out by bridge crew, and weapons crews at gun positions and depth-charge throwers.

"It may be a false alarm," announcer Greene continued, "but the destroyer crews take no chances. In a trice, the guns are manned, loaded, and bearing down on their target."[8]

"Visibility, one-double-O," called a gunnery crewman.

The crew had swung her dual 4.7-inch guns into position.

"Salvo ready to fire," the gunner leader called out.

"Open fire!"

Next, the perspective from the bridge.

"Full speed," came the call from the bridge. "Stand by depth charge . . ."

"The throttles are opened full out," Greene boomed next. "The ship quivers from stem to stern as the mighty turbines drive her forward at thirty-seven knots. Screws lash the seas as the destroyer tears . . . toward her objective."

Depth-charge crews released their explosives from stern positions, and explosions sent plumes of water skyward.

"No submarine can survive within twenty feet of an

exploding depth charge," Greene explained. "And at far greater distances, an explosion will start leaks in the hull, shatter the electrical gear, and demoralize the crew."

As the undersea explosions subsided, Lorne Greene added an exclamation point to the destroyer's impact. "So, under the protection of Canada's navy, another convoy with its precious load of war supplies for Britain passes safely . . . In their keeping is one of the most vital lifelines of the British Commonwealth. . . . They are on Atlantic Patrol, fulfilling the great traditions of those who serve beneath the White Ensign."

Grierson and his fledgling National Film Board made quite a splash with their first piece of wartime propaganda. Despite their nontheatrical film designation, *Atlantic Patrol* and subsequent installments of *Canada Carries On* were welcomed in sixty Canadian movie theatres as well as screening venues in the United States, India, the West Indies, and the United Kingdom, for Prime Minister Churchill to enjoy.[9]

As he waited for Franklin D. Roosevelt's answer to his desperate plea for those old American destroyers, Winston Churchill received no good news from the sea lanes to and from Britain. The latest statistics were the worst of the war so far. U-boats and German surface warships had sunk 101 Allied and neutral merchant ships in the month of May 1940 alone, and another 140 in June.[10] That summer brought more losses at sea reminiscent of the 1939 sinking of SS *Athenia*, adding to the civilian death toll. The British passenger steamship *Arandora Star*, converted to a troopship, had just completed a series of successful round trips rescuing Allied troops from Norway and France, including the joint Royal Navy–Royal Canadian Navy operation bringing expeditionary troops out of Saint-Jean-de-Luz.

During the first week of July, however, the former luxury liner became a floating prison. At Liverpool, the vessel embarked 200 British military personnel, who brought aboard—under guard—nearly 1,300 "aliens" and prisoners of war (POWs). The previous month, the British War Cabinet had decreed that some 8,000 Germans, Austrians, and Italians between the ages of sixteen and seventy living in Britain posed a threat to the nation's security. Cabinet had them herded into internment camps. But as the war arrived on Britain's doorstep, the government feared fifth-column (Nazi and Fascist sympathizers) espionage, and ordered the aliens interned abroad for the duration.

Among them was German-born Hans Moeller, a twenty-eight-year-old Jewish refugee who had fled Bremen for England and then enrolled in school. Ernesto Moruzzi had been born in Italy, and following emigration to Britain just after 1900, he had established a sweets shop in the Welsh town of Neath. Neither man had any rights in wartime Britain, so both were taken from their homes that spring of 1940. Each thought he was headed for further internment on the Isle of Man, in the Irish Sea.[11] Instead, Moruzzi was one of 734 Italians and Moeller one of 479 Germans, as well as 86 German POWs, put aboard *Arandora Star* at Liverpool on the last day of June 1940. Their British guards had instructions to supervise their passage to St. John's, Newfoundland, and thence to internment in Canada. They would never get there.

Arandora Star had steamed just seventy-five miles west of Ireland, where Kptlt Günther Prien, commander of *U47*, found the former passenger liner unescorted. It was just past 6 a.m., July 2, when he fired a single torpedo that exploded on *Star*'s starboard side aft. The ship's engine room immediately began to flood; the incoming water crippled her turbines and generators and snuffed out her lights and communications. The radio room managed to get a distress signal transmitted. Then, in the scramble to escape a sinking ship, 1,300 internees, POWs, and guards began the rush to fourteen lifeboats and ninety life rafts—sufficient to carry only 500 passengers away from the ship. Among those in the water, Sgt Norman Price, a member of the Worcestershire Regiment guarding the internees, watched *Arandora Star*'s final moments. Many of the internees were afraid to leave the ship, he wrote, but at 6:40 a.m., as the bow rose for its final plunge, many leapt from the ship, injuring themselves on wreckage in the water.

"I could see hundreds of men clinging to the ship," Sgt Price said. "They were like ants and then the ship went up at one end and slid rapidly down, taking the men with her."[12]

Inbound that morning, escorting the British battleship HMS *Nelson* to the Western Approaches, HMCS *St. Laurent* received *Arandora Star*'s SOS and responded. It took the Canadian destroyer seven hours to reach the location of the sinking, but there began one of the most remarkable rescues of the war. LCdr Harry DeWolf ordered the ship's whalers over the side to retrieve individuals bobbing amid wreckage and fuel oil; for hours, Canadian sailors threw themselves into the water to assist exhausted survivors aboard *St. Laurent*.

"Lying frequently with engines stopped and with no protection from U-boat attacks," one report described, "the destroyer waited while this work went on."[13]

Only when *St. Laurent*'s crew had pulled all lifeboat passengers to safety did LCdr DeWolf call for full ahead. Below decks, the rescue crew made every possible bunk or hammock available to the survivors. But very quickly, the destroyer's crew began to recognize that those they'd rescued came from nations Canada had declared her enemy.

"Most of these people are Germans and Italians," *St. Laurent* signalled the Admiralty.

Nevertheless, saving some 861 passengers from *Arandora Star* proved to be one of the largest individual rescues of the war. Thc Italian government went to some lengths, via the Brazilian embassy, to express its appreciation for the saving of Italian nationals. And LCdr DeWolf was cited for his heroism. The sinking of *Arandora Star* killed more than 500, including a dozen of the ship's officers, forty-two crewmen, and thirty-seven military guards. Between July and the end of December 1940, 213 bodies washed up on the Irish coast, among them internees Hans Moeller and Ernesto Moruzzi, who were buried at civilian cemeteries in County Donegal, in Northern Ireland.

"To turn upon people originating from Germany and Austria," wrote François Lafitte, a landed immigrant from France, "seemed . . . to be a betrayal of all the values for which we were fighting."[14]

CARNAGE on the North Atlantic proved relentless that summer. At the end of August, authorities in the Western Approaches organized an outbound assembly of merchant ships. Besides thirty-two ships ballasted for the westbound trip, Convoy OB 205 included SS *Volendam*, a former Holland America ocean liner that had managed to escape the Netherlands before the Germans overran the country in May 1940. Then in June, serving the British Ministry of War Transport, the ship was assigned to the Children's Overseas

Reception Board (CORB), formed to evacuate British children from the UK across the North Atlantic to Canada. On August 29, 1940, *Volendam* welcomed 320 such children and their guardians aboard at Liverpool. The next night, at about eleven o'clock, with the convoy heading out to sea about 230 miles west of Ireland, *U60* spotted the liner and fired two torpedoes that penetrated *Volendam*'s forward hold. The captain issued an abandon-ship order and, in spite of rough seas, every one of the eighteen lifeboats got away safely.

"I saw British pluck at the age of five," one British seaman noted. "One would have thought that boys and girls, roused from their beds, rushed up on deck and passed into lifeboats would have been afraid. They sang *Roll Out the Barrel* until they were safely onboard rescue ships."[15]

The merchant ships in the convoy rallied around *Volendam*, which didn't sink but was towed (with one of the two torpedoes, unexploded, still embedded in her bow) and beached at the Isle of Bute on the west coast of Scotland. All the children were saved. The directors of the CORB reviewed *Volendam*'s sinking and recommended to the Admiralty that faster transports be contracted to carry the children to Canada. A week later, SS *Nerissa* sailed for Canada and delivered thirty-four children safely to Halifax, although a passenger later reported that a torpedo was launched at *Nerissa* during rough seas and only "our bucking ship, bow to the heavens one minute and waving its screws the next, rose at the right time to let the torpedo pass below our stern."[16*]

But by mid-September, when SS *City of Benares* made the transatlantic crossing, the CORB's good luck had run out.

* SS *Nerissa* crossed the Atlantic thirty-nine times carrying freight and passengers mostly on her own. On April 30, 1941, *U552* found her unescorted eastbound, fired four torpedoes, and sank her; 207 of 291 aboard were lost, the third-largest loss of life of the British Isles in the war.

Convoy OB 213 left Liverpool on Friday, September 13. Four days out, *City of Benares* steamed west at the head of the centre column; bad weather had prompted the convoy to stop zigzagging. Just after 10 p.m. Kptlt Heinrich Bleichrodt and *U48* caught up with the convoy and fired two torpedoes at *Benares*.* They both missed. But a third, released just after midnight, slammed into the passenger liner's stern, and the ship began sinking right away. Derek Bech, aged nine, had booked passage with his mother and two sisters as private passengers, not part of the CORB group. He recalled that the ship sank in less than thirty minutes.

"Some of the children were killed in the explosion," he said later. "Some were trapped in their cabins. The rest died when lifeboats were launched incorrectly and children were tipped into the sea. All I can remember were the screams and cries for help."[17]

A number of heroic acts stood out amid the confusion and death that night. Some of the children who survived recalled the ship's crew racing back and forth from cabins to lifeboat stations, ensuring that unaccompanied children got into lifeboats. Meanwhile, John Lazarus, a Jewish-Canadian who'd made an eastbound crossing on a merchant ship to the UK earlier in 1940, and then upgraded his skills in England to become a wireless radio operator, served in *City of Benares*'s radio office. He stayed at his post, repeatedly transmitting distress calls; later, when the *Montreal Gazette* learned of his loyalty, it remembered him as one of the "knights of the key."[18] Of the 100 children aboard that night, eighty-one died in the sinking or from exposure in

* Kptlt Bleichrodt and *U48* had set out from the U-boat flotilla headquarters at Lorient on September 5. That night they attacked Convoy SC 3 and sank four ships. On September 17, they sank *City of Benares* and two other freighters, and on September 20, they joined the pack attack on Convoy HX 72.

the lifeboats. Several of the children lost on September 17 had survived *Volendam*'s sinking on August 30.

Winston Churchill, who had opposed "any stampede" of children or anyone else from Britain,[19] promptly cancelled all CORB programs evacuating children to Commonwealth countries. He had always considered such action as a public admission to the enemy that Britain was losing the war. The deaths of child evacuees brought unnecessary grief to an already battered home front.

That summer, the War Cabinet consented to a different type of export—not of Britain's children but of another national resource. And had the Nazis known about or intercepted this export, it would have delivered a lethal propaganda blow to Britain's war effort. From the moment the war began, the British government had demanded that all UK subjects make known their securities with the Treasury. Using the Emergency Powers Act, the government had then confiscated those registered securities to underwrite its wartime purchase or production of armament.

In June, however, with the very real threat of Nazi invasion, Churchill had also hatched a plan to install his government in Montreal and, should it be necessary, to lead the Commonwealth from Canada. As part of the transition, the Bank of England had prepared for the worst, planning to run a "shadow bank" with its headquarters in Ottawa. The challenge was to move England's entire reserve—about £1,800 million worth of securities and gold[20]—across the U-boat-infested North Atlantic to Canada. The secret plan was code-named Operation Fish.[21]

On June 24, 1940, Alexander Craig and an entourage of Bank of England specialists arrived at the docks in Greenock,

Scotland. There they were welcomed aboard the Royal Navy cruiser HMS *Emerald* by Capt Francis Cyril Flynn. About the same time, heavily guarded train cars were guided into sidings adjacent, and crews transferred 2,229 bullion boxes, each containing four bars of gold, into the warship's magazines. The boxes were so heavy they bent the angle irons beneath *Emerald*'s magazine floors. In addition, crews packed 488 boxes of securities into other nooks and crannies aboard. In total, the so-called treasure ship now housed £130 million from the Bank of England.[22] Operation Fish would be the largest transport of wealth in history, provided *Emerald* and her escorts arrived safely in Canada. But that night, when they sailed from Greenock, Capt Flynn had to consider not only his nemeses, the Kriegsmarine U-boats, but also the North Atlantic weather.

"The seas whipped up as soon as we rounded the north coast of Ireland, next morning," he said. "When we turned out into the Atlantic, we were punching into a heavy sea and a rising gale."[23]

At first, the escorting destroyers led the convoy sailing in a straight line, while *Emerald* zigzagged behind. That allowed the cruiser to alter course, travelling at a higher and safer speed during the crossing. But the seas rose even more, and Capt Flynn chose to send the destroyers back to port while he carried on alone.

"I put *Emerald*'s speed up to twenty-two knots," he said, considering it was ample to outrun any U-boats. "Those first three days, the going was such that many of our crew became seasick."

On the fourth day, the weather began to clear, and on the morning of July 1, Canada's Dominion Day, *Emerald*'s lookouts spotted the Nova Scotia coastline. By 7:35 a.m., the ship and her cargo were moving through the Halifax Harbour Defence Boom en route to safe moorings. Capt Flynn's mission was complete. Waiting ashore, a dozen railway luggage coaches were lined up at quayside. As the boxes of bullion and securities came ashore, Bank of Canada officials checked each one off. Twelve hours later, the loaded and guarded train sped off to Montreal, delivering the securities into the underground vaults of the Sun Life Assurance Company building under RCMP surveillance. Meanwhile, the gold bars continued their journey to Ottawa to take up residence in the vaults of the Bank of Canada.

Less than a week later, another shipment—£192 million in gold bullion and 299 boxes of securities, with a total value of £442 million—repeated the circuit. Again the ocean's elements—fog, ice floes, and gales—posed a greater threat to the gold-bearing liner *Batory* and her escorts than enemy warships. But by summer's end, the Admiralty reported to Prime Minister Churchill that Operation Fish convoys of British, Canadian, Polish, and American ships had delivered more than £637 million in gold safely to Canada. Miraculously, while German U-boats and surface raiders had sunk 134 Allied and neutral ships on the Atlantic during those same three months, not a single gold-carrying ship had been lost.[24]

Autumn brought another flotilla of ships to the British war effort. On September 1, the UK and US governments finally signed the "destroyers for bases" agreement that would deliver fifty aging 1,200-ton American destroyers to Britain. In return, the US would gain access to land in various British possessions where the US Navy (USN) and US Army Air Forces (USAAF) could establish bases rent-free for ninety-nine years. While he faced political criticism from an isolationist Congress for violating the US Neutrality Act, President Roosevelt had made the case that the leases would enhance national security, particularly along the US East Coast. To make his argument, Roosevelt used an analogy of the house next door catching fire; the neighbour considers that he has a hose he can hook to a hydrant to help put out the fire.

"I don't say to him before that operation, 'Neighbor, my garden hose cost me fifteen dollars; you have to pay me fifteen dollars for it.' No! I don't want fifteen dollars—I want my garden hose back after the fire is out.'"[25]

Within a week of the lend-lease signings, the first six US destroyers had quietly sailed into Halifax Harbour, docking side by side. At 10 a.m. on September 9, 1940, there was little or no fuss as the Stars and Stripes were lowered aboard the "four-stackers." Then the US crews filed down the gangplanks, making their way to the train station for home. Ninety minutes later, Royal Navy crews, recently arrived from Britain, marched aboard all six destroyers and raised Union Jacks. As a bonus, when the British sailors settled in, they found luxury items (which they'd likely not seen for several years) left behind by the Americans—coffee, ice cream, and tinned pineapple.[26]

WORD of the handover of the Town-class destroyers to the Royal Navy no doubt gave the War Cabinet and its prime minister some welcome respite. But it was short-lived. The convoy battles of October 1940 would not only illustrate the wisdom of Operation Fish but would also severely test the mettle of Allied naval crews, merchant navy sailors, the

Admiralty, and Churchill himself. In a series of journal entries he categorized as "ocean peril," the prime minster assessed his country's challenges at sea.[27] German surface warships and Luftwaffe reconnaissance aircraft regularly escaped detection by RN or RAF patrols and attacked Allied trade routes at will. WS convoys* of troopships to the Middle East, India, and from Canada to Britain had left naval resources at home very thin. He even admitted that success delivering such convoys was not the result of overpowering the enemy but merely relying on evasive routing and the vastness of the oceans.

"A far graver danger [is] added to these problems," Churchill confided. "The only thing that ever really frighten[s] me [is] the U-boat peril."[28] During the summer, he continued to predict that he and the population could fight and win the battles in the skies over Britain, and that Hitler's invasion plans would fail. "But now our life-line, even across the broad oceans and especially in the entrances to the island [is] endangered."[29]

The experience of inbound Convoy SC 7, a slow convoy travelling no faster than about seven knots from Sydney, Nova Scotia, to Liverpool, illustrated the prime minister's fears. On October 5, thirty-five merchant ships emerged from the Cape Breton harbour and formed up with experienced RN Capt Lachlan Donald Ian Mackinnon as convoy commodore aboard SS *Assyrian*. The sea freighters carried a wide array of supplies vital to Britain—steel ingots from Sydney, grain from Great Lakes elevators, and iron ore from Newfoundland—and was configured in the traditional nine columns of a convoy.

* The prime minister later learned such convoys received the initials *WS* to signify "Winston's Specials."

What Convoy SC 7 did not have, however, was adequate escort. HMS *Scarborough*, a Royal Navy sloop, was the only warship available. Formerly assigned yacht duty in Newfoundland, ferrying the governor to outports around the Dominion, in 1939 the sloop had been fitted with a four-inch gun for use against surface raiders, plus fifteen depth charges.

Four days out, the eastbound ships ran into a southerly gale that scattered the vessels, reducing the convoy's overall speed to six knots. After a week, still heading east, *Scarborough* had managed to wrangle the convoy back together, and two more escorts—the sloop HMS *Forney* and the corvette HMS *Bluebell*—arrived, lifting the spirits of the merchant crews. In truth, however, the three warships had not worked together before. There was no common tactical doctrine or prepared plan of action in case of attack. The warships had little or no radio linkage, and visual communication at night, especially with the freighters spread across six miles of open North Atlantic, was non-existent.[30]

On the night of October 16, *U48* found the convoy, silhouetted against a clear moonlit sky. Korvettenkapitän (KK) Hans-Rudolf Rösing reported the ships' position to others in the wolf pack and commenced his own attack, hitting two ships on the port flank of the convoy. Capt Mackinnon instinctively ordered an emergency turn to starboard while the two sloops chased the diving U-boat. *Scarborough* continued her pursuit of *U48* for a full day, but found neither the U-boat nor her way back to rejoin the convoy, thus reducing the convoy's escort defence. Meantime, a third sloop, HMS *Leith*, and a corvette, HMS *Heartsease*, arrived. But the U-boat pack numbers were now overwhelming. By 10 p.m. on October 18, seven more had joined the pursuit—

U28, *U38*, *U46*, *U101*, *U123*, *U100*, and *U99*—the latter two commanded by experienced aces Kptlt Joachim Schepke and Kptlt Otto Kretschmer, respectively. Kretschmer's log reflects the U-boat commander's confidence and the fate of the convoy:

"October 18, 2124 . . . Convoy . . . in sight. . . . 2202. Weather, visibility moderate, bright moonlight.

"2206. Fire stern tube . . . At 700 metres, hit forward of amidships. Vessel of some 6,500 tons sinks within 20 seconds. I now proceed head-on into the convoy.

"October 19, 0015. Three [escorts] approach and search area in line abreast. I make off at full speed to the southwest. . . . Torpedoes from other boats are constantly heard exploding. The [escorts] do not know how to help and occupy themselves by constantly firing starshells which are of little effect in the bright moonlight."[31]

Kptlt Kretschmer and *U99* alone had sunk seven merchant ships; he fired his final torpedo at four in the morning of October 19. During the three-day ordeal, Cmdre Mackinnon spotted one of the U-boats from the bridge of SS *Assyrian*. Since the merchantman's only gun was mounted at the stern, Mackinnon accelerated his flagship to ten knots in an attempt to ram the fleeing U-boat, which also accelerated and pulled away. Forty minutes later, with no results, *Assyrian* was separated from the safety of the convoy and suddenly under torpedo attack herself. Two missed, but a third crashed into her starboard side, flooding engines and destroying lifeboats. Surviving crew managed to launch life rafts, but Mackinnon ended up in the water, clinging to wreckage until HMS *Leith* found him and hoisted him aboard in a net. As well as *Assyrian*, Convoy SC 7 lost seventeen of its thirty-five merchant ships. In response, no U-boats were damaged or lost.

The slaughter continued the next night, when U-boats from the same pack crossed paths with another inbound convoy. Like Convoy HX 72, which had been attacked a month earlier, HX 79 consisted of forty-nine merchant vessels sailing eastbound at roughly fifteen knots into the same Western Approaches for Liverpool. It too had escorts—two destroyers, four corvettes, three trawlers, and a minesweeper. But again, the navy escort commanders had thrown the warships together at random. The corvettes and their crews had little or no experience at sea. And none of the naval officers aboard the escorts had met prior to the convoy to work out a plan of attack. U-boats sank fourteen ships in Convoy HX 79, and seven more in a third convoy, HX 79A, bringing total losses in three days to thirty-eight ships.

The unorganized, untrained, and under-gunned state of convoy defences was creating a cemetery of shipping across the North Atlantic.

While the Admiralty could temporarily suppress specifics of the tonnage and crew losses sustained by Convoys SC 7 and HX 79, it could not hide what some felt was the final insult to Britain's once global supremacy at sea. On October 26, the Canadian Pacific liner RMS *Empress of Britain* raced—at some twenty-four knots—toward Liverpool with 223 British servicemen and 419 crew members aboard. Spotted by a Focke-Wulf 200 (Condor), the Luftwaffe's most effective long-range bomber, *Empress* came under attack about seventy miles off the northwest coast of Ireland. The Condor made three bombing runs, igniting fires the length of the ship, but the liner remained afloat.

Almost immediately, Royal Navy communications dispatched two destroyers to pick up survivors and escort *Empress* to safety. But Adm Karl Dönitz got word of the attack—reinforced by B-Dienst, the Kriegsmarine's radio interception service—and relayed the location to *U32*. Kptlt Hans Jenisch* shadowed the liner through October 27, eventually firing three torpedoes, two of which struck either her boilers or fuel tanks, causing a massive final explosion. Ten minutes later *Empress of Britain* went under. Most of the liner's crew and servicemen survived.

For the Allies, the three devastating attacks on inbound convoys and the sinking of *Empress* made October 1940 the blackest month of the war at sea. The U-Bootwaffe had managed to sink an astonishing 352,407 tons of merchant navy freight; in terms of Adm Dönitz's "effective U-boat quotient," that was 920 tons sunk per operating U-boat per day.[32] Such losses represented the nadir of Allied fortunes in the Battle of the Atlantic. But the events that Winston Churchill had labelled "ocean peril" in his private journals were seen through a different lens by Karl Dönitz and the Kriegsmarine command, who described them as "*die glückliche Zeit*"—"the Happy Time."

THE war didn't seem to have any room for Nancy Adair—especially in the middle of 1940, when the Phony War descended into the real thing, Nan's life was a constant reminder that she didn't fit in. Although she had been born in England in 1920, she didn't speak with an English accent. That's because, after

* German newspapers proclaimed "Plutocrats' Liner Sails No More!" The pilot of the Condor received the Knight's Cross of the Iron Cross; but three days after sinking *Empress of Britain, U32* was sunk off Ireland, and Kptlt Jenisch was captured. He returned to Germany in 1947.

the Great War, doctors told her father, a veteran who'd been gassed, to move to the country; he promptly relocated the family to a fruit farm in the Niagara Peninsula of southwestern Ontario. So Nan got her education, her accent, and her exposure to a casteless society at school in St. Catharines, until 1938, when her parents moved the family back to England. But at her new home in Leighton Buzzard, Bedfordshire, Nan felt like an outsider. The girls she met formed cliques, attended cocktail parties, and made fun of her Canadian accent.

"In Niagara, nobody cared very much who you were. There was no class distinction of any kind," she said. "Back in England, I felt very foreign, like I didn't belong."[33]

While the war was the great leveller, bringing all Britons together, every time Nan tried to find a place to serve, something seemed to block her way. Her parents connected her with a recruiter for the Women's Royal Naval Service (WRNS), known as the Wrens. But on the day she'd planned to take the train to London for an interview, the tracks on the Euston line were bombed by the Luftwaffe and she missed her appointment. She felt disheartened and lost. Things brightened, however, when Nan met a family acquaintance, John Moore, who suggested she consider a job opportunity nine miles from her home, in the town of Milton Keynes. When she arrived at the address, an old English mansion on the edge of a fifty-eight-acre estate, she was welcomed by a well-dressed man named Alistair Denniston.

"Good morning, Miss Adair," he said. "We understand that you would like to join us here. We call it 'the family.'" He began to explain that the "family" was looking for well-educated people who had majored in perhaps mathematics or linguistics. "We're looking for the cream of great minds."

"What's this little Canadian girl from the farm back in Ontario doing in a place like this?" Nan thought. Then she asked Denniston a question: "What will I have to do? I might not be up to it. I've never been to university."

"No, no, it's quite all right," he said, and then turned to asking her a series of questions designed to determine whether or not she was "trainable." Having ascertained that she was, Denniston explained the terms of her employment: she'd have to work shifts for a minimum wage, and she'd have to sign a statement swearing to uphold the Official Secrets Act. None of that bothered Nan at all. Finally he asked, "Miss Adair, would you like a little time to think about it?"

"That would be very nice," Nan said, suddenly feeling a bit less stressed.

Denniston invited her to stay seated, went to the door, and said, "How about five minutes?"

He returned after the allotted time.

"Yes," Nan said, "I think I'll do this."

"Welcome," said Alistair Denniston, deputy director of the British Government Code and Cypher School (GC&CS). "Welcome to the family."

As a member of the GC&CS, Nancy Adair had officially joined the secret agency to "advise as to the security of codes and ciphers used by all [British] government departments and to assist in their provision." But in addition, GC&CS was also tasked with studying "the methods of cipher communication used by foreign powers."[34] Nan agreed to work at a wartime wage of eight shillings and sixpence a week (six days a week with one day off, or twelve days straight with two days off) in the facility housed at Bletchley Park. She had finally fit in. She was officially doing war work, but, having signed a pledge to uphold the Official Secrets Act, she could tell no one what she was doing. Not even her own family.

Each day on the job, an unmarked station wagon, operated by a Mechanised Transport Corps driver in civilian clothes, arrived at Nan's home in Leighton Buzzard to pick her up for the ride to work. If she worked the 9 a.m. to 4 p.m. day shift, the station wagon picked her up an hour before she started; likewise for the evening or overnight shifts. Her only identification was a pass into Bletchley Park.

To start, Nan Adair worked in a large room with other women, sorting messages with no apparent objective. On her short breaks, she noticed others entering and exiting a room at the end of a busy corridor. She considered that Bletchley hadn't hired her just to sort messages. She went with her instinct and complained to Hugh Alexander, the administrator of Hut 8, which handled all Kriegsmarine intercepts. Two weeks later, when she arrived for her shift, Nan was escorted to the room at the end of the corridor. It turned out to be the "crib room," or linguistics section.

There, for the first time in her life, she saw what looked like a typewriter contained in a wooden box. In addition to a keyboard, the machine had a plugboard with cables, and wheels embedded in its facing. This was Enigma, the encryption device used by Nazi Germany to protect military communications. Its electro-mechanical rotors scrambled or unscrambled the twenty-six letters of the German alphabet, based on the settings of the rotors. There was more than one Enigma in the room. Nan learned that the wizards in her new workspace had built several replicas to try to break the enemy's military codes.

Among her new associates were British cryptographers Joan Clarke and Shaun Wylie, as well as codebreaking specialist Rolf Noskwith and Cambridge mathematician Gordon Welchman. Eventually Nan met the man everyone called "Prof." And bit by bit, she learned why Bletchley considered him so vital. Alan Turing had always shown signs he was a genius—enrolled in a day school at six, independent school at thirteen, and at sixteen solving advanced mathematical problems without benefit of calculus. He graduated with first-class honours in math from King's College, Cambridge, and published a paper on computable numbers in 1936. Soon after, he published his plans for a "Universal Machine"—not a computer, but one that mimicked the behaviour of another machine. While completing his PhD in mathematics at Princeton (where he studied under Einstein) in 1938, he worked at the Foreign Office as assistant to Alfred Dillwyn Knox, exploring cryptology, and began working part-time at the GC&CS.

In 1939, Turing and Dilly Knox, then the senior code-breaker at GC&CS, met with Polish Cipher Bureau crypt-analysts who had been working at cracking German codes since 1932. Turing and Knox saw the replicas—Enigma doubles—the Poles had built. At Bletchley full-time when the war broke out, Turing worked exclusively at developing his "bombe" system (similar to the Poles' *bomba kryptologiczna*, or cryptologic bomb),* an electro-mechanical machine—his Universal Machine—that could imitate Enigma, its rotors, its ring settings, and its plugboard, and break the German military codes. At age twenty-six, Alan Turing was head of the naval cryptographers at Bletchley, working in that room at the

* Polish cryptologists Marian Rejewski, Henryk Zygalski, and Jerzy Różycki developed the *bomba kryptologiczna*, or cryptologic bomb, in October 1938; it was an electrically powered aggregate of six Enigmas and took the place of some one hundred workers.

end of the corridor with other members of the Hut 8 family, including newcomer Nan Adair.

"This was where they told me what this was all about," Nan said. "They had procured an Enigma, made a replica of one . . . and others were pinched."

ONE of the first "pinches," or hostile captures of secret Enigma equipment, occurred about the time newly recruited Nan Adair joined the cryptography team at Bletchley. It happened unexpectedly, in the busy channel of the Firth of Clyde, on the west coast of Scotland.

At thirty-two, Hans-Wilhelm von Dresky had devoted half his life to the Kriegsmarine, almost exclusively aboard U-boats. When the war began, he'd already been in command of *U33*, a Type VIIA U-boat, for a year. On his first two patrols, he and his crew sank ten small ships in the Bristol Channel, for which he'd been awarded two Iron Crosses. In early February 1940, *U33* received orders to lay mines in the busy Firth of Clyde waterway, near the port of Glasgow. Inexplicably, Kriegsmarine commanders had not enforced a regulation preventing mine-laying U-boats from carrying the Enigma machines and code books, which were usually restricted for use aboard long-distance patrolling U-boats.[35] Nevertheless, during his third cruise, on February 12, 1940, von Dresky nosed *U33* (with an Enigma machine aboard) into the Clyde estuary, preparing to lay eight mines near the entrance to the Royal Navy base. It was the middle of the night when lookouts in *U33*'s conning tower spotted an oncoming minesweeper.

LCdr Hugh Price, captain of HMS *Gleaner*, received reports of a strong hydrophone effect—mechanical noises underwater—a mile off his starboard bow.[36] His ASDIC operator confirmed contact of the vessel ahead. Price ordered searchlights turned on, and *Gleaner*'s lookouts spotted the last of *U33*'s periscope cutting through the water as the U-boat dived. LCdr Price had his crew prepare depth charges for a shallow pattern, since the Firth was barely a hundred feet deep at that point. It was just before 4 a.m.

The first four explosions around the U-boat, which was resting on the bottom, sent *U33*'s submariners tumbling throughout the vessel. More critically, the blasts damaged her delicate instruments, triggered leaks all along the hull, and cut the boat's main lighting system. When the dimmer emergency lights came on, von Dresky consulted with his long-serving shipmate Kptlt Fritz Schilling; the chief engineer recommended applying some pressurized air to remove water from the diving tanks, enough to lift *U33* off the bottom to make a dash for deeper water.

However, Price forced von Dresky's hand with another depth-charge attack, which accelerated flooding inside the U-boat. Von Dresky panicked and ordered all tanks blown, to surface the U-boat and allow his crewmen to save themselves and prepare the boat for scuttling. Kptlt von Dresky gave one last order to his crew. Once outside the U-boat, those directed by an officer to remove the eight critical metal or plastic rotors from *U33*'s Enigma machine were to toss those rotors into the sea to prevent them falling into enemy hands.

U33 broke the surface at 5:22 a.m. Gunners aboard *Gleaner* opened fire, and then realized the U-boat crewmen leaping into the sea were surrendering. During the short time when the minesweeper was pulling alongside *U33* to rescue the German submariners in the water, engineer Schilling, still inside the U-boat, opened all vents to the torpedo tubes and set scuttling charges to further shatter the hull and sink the U-boat. He tried to outrun the water and explosions but died in the attempt. The same blasts ultimately overcame the captain as well. Von Dresky's body was one of twenty recovered later. So too was some valuable intelligence. One Royal Navy sailor, searching the clothing of rescued German submariner Friedrich Kumpf, found something in his pockets.

"They look like the gear wheels off a bicycle," he told his superior officer.[37]

The bicycle-like parts turned out to be the alphabetic Enigma rotors, or *Walzen*, that von Dresky had told his men to toss away. German Navy Enigma machines, as Nan Adair had learned, contained rotors numbered I to VIII. The cogged wheels of metal and black plastic looked similar on the outside, but the Roman numerals signified that each had quite different internal wiring. By accident or good fortune, sailor Kumpf's pocket contents had delivered two previously unknown Enigma rotors—VI and VII—to Bletchley Park cryptanalysts.[38]

Enigma was a "poly-alphabetical substitution cipher," meaning that each letter typed into the machine became "permuted," or altered, to emerge as a different letter, making the possible variations seemingly endless.[39] Each Enigma machine's rotors, ring settings, and plugboards turned a plaintext message into apparently random nonsense. The German army and air force used Enigmas with three rotors, which meant letters typed on the machine had 17,576 × 263 possible outcomes. The German navy used eight rotors, which multiplied the number of possible outcomes by 150 million million. The challenge that cryptanalysts in Hut 8 at Bletchley Park faced, therefore, was reducing 150 million million possible combinations to a more manageable number to break the code, determine the message, and send it to the Admiralty. The pinch of *U33*'s rotors helped make that possible.

As the war entered its second year in the fall of 1940, neither the capture of Enigma rotors nor the Bletchley cryptanalysts' replica Enigma machines had been able to solve Churchill's immediate problem—getting vital supplies from North American ports safely across the North Atlantic to the Western Approaches. Nor could those early inroads into German naval intelligence give Canada's flotilla of escorting warships an edge over U-boat stealth or the Kriegsmarine surface raiders. October's grim tally, almost 350,000 tons of lost cargo, gave way to even bleaker events the next month.

Until the fall of 1940, the Admiralty had relied heavily on the skills and firepower of armed merchant cruisers and crews serving Britain's Merchant Navy to protect convoys. HMS *Jervis Bay*, for example, had provided eighteen years of peacetime service as a passenger ship with the Commonwealth Line. But when the war broke out, armament specialists in Halifax had installed Victorian-era guns fore and aft, and overnight, HMS *Jervis Bay* became a pseudo-warship for convoys such as HX 72 in September 1940. In truth, *Jervis Bay* was no match for the likes of German surface warships or U-boats. Like most in Halifax, *Jervis Bay*'s commander, Capt Edward Fegen, had no forewarning that the German heavy cruiser *Admiral Scheer* had recently slipped through Royal Navy blockades around the British Isles to intercept and destroy Allied shipping in the mid-Atlantic.

The Admiralty's first inkling of *Admiral Scheer*'s presence came just before 5 p.m. on November 5, when *Jervis Bay*'s lookouts spotted an unfamiliar profile ten miles off.[40] Capt Fegen quickly recognized that he was now facing the firepower of a German heavy cruiser—alone. Eight days into the eastbound voyage of Convoy HX 84, off the coast of Iceland, *Jervis Bay* was the sole ocean escort for thirty-seven merchantmen. Fegen's radio shack dashed off messages that the AMC was under attack and his convoy was to scatter. As the merchant ships dispersed, Fegen piloted *Jervis Bay* straight for the cruiser. Over the course of the next twenty-two minutes, unable to range any of her six-inch guns against the eleven-inch guns of *Admiral Scheer*, *Jervis Bay* was reduced to a flaming wreck. Three-quarters of the AMC crew, including the captain, died in the headlong attack. But the crew's selfless act allowed most of HX 84 to escape; Capt Edward Fegen received a posthumous Victoria Cross.[41] Meanwhile, *Admiral Scheer* pursued and sank five merchantmen.

On November 20, Western Approaches HQ ordered the four available Royal Canadian Navy destroyers—HMCS *Skeena*, *Ottawa*, *St. Laurent*, and *Saguenay*—to rendezvous with Convoy SC 11, an assembly of twenty-four ships en route from Sydney, Nova Scotia, to Britain. November gales played havoc with the rendezvous, not to mention any orderly progress of the eastbound convoy. Among many inherent issues that the RCN's four escorts faced in such conditions was the River-class destroyer's notoriously narrow hull; in steep swells, the destroyers couldn't keep station in a convoy or manoeuvre the customary sweeps around the convoy at dusk.[42] Then, to make the matters worse, at eleven o'clock on November 22, when the convoy altered course to evade a suspected U-boat in pursuit, some of the merchant ships fell out of the formation. To prevent collisions in the dark, they turned on their navigation lights.

Kptlt Joachim Schepke, in *U100*, pounced, sinking seven merchant ships overnight and killing more than a hundred merchant mariners in the attack.[43]

A week later, HMCS *Saguenay* picked up Convoy HG 47 about 400 miles west of Ireland, on its way from Gibraltar to the Western Approaches. The destroyer, positioned astern of the convoy, had been outfitted with radar, but her crew had difficulty differentiating between harmless echoes and actual enemy contact. Early in the morning on the second day of the escort duty, *Saguenay* responded to a flare in the distance. As the Canadian warship altered course away from the convoy, a torpedo struck her forward, ripping apart thirty feet of the bow back to the "A" gun position. At that moment *Saguenay* gunnery lieutenant Louis Audette was about to begin his watch, making his way from the starboard aft of the ship.

"There was a strange hush about the ship," Audette said.[44] Born in Ottawa in 1907, he'd already been called to the bar and was running a law practice in Montreal when he chose to join the Royal Canadian Naval Voluntary Supplementary Reserve in 1938; he was commissioned the next year. At thirty-four, Audette was among the oldest of *Saguenay*'s crew and regularly called "Uncle Louis."

Since the torpedo had blown most of the ship's fo'c'sle away and left her two forward guns ablaze, LCdr Gus Miles ordered Audette to take charge of the aft guns. Lookouts had spotted the profile of *Argo*, an enemy Italian submarine, 800 yards away. In the confusion to man, load, and fire the aft guns, some non-gunnery crew volunteered, including a young rating named Clifford McNaught. Lt Audette assigned McNaught to supply the gun positions—lifting fifty-pound 4.7-inch shells and placing them in the gun tray—as the gunners opened fire on the Italian sub. When there was a pause, Audette approached McNaught in the dark.

"I know you're not familiar with the shells," Audette began. Then, for McNaught's benefit, the officer went down on one knee and pointed out which shells were armour-piercing and which were starshells. When he looked back up at McNaught, the youngster was holding his hands in the air. In the dim light, Audette realized the man's face and hands had been severely burned by the fire around them.

"Go below!" he ordered the rating. "Go to the doctor in the wardroom and get medical care!"

Moments later, Audette found McNaught sobbing on the open deck. "I told you to go below," he said.

"I can't," McNaught moaned. "My hands! I can't go down the ladder."

Audette realized the man—responding to the ship's emergency—had managed to lift and place heavy gun shells in trays despite his horribly burned hands, but he couldn't guide himself down a ladder to safety. Audette put a line around McNaught, lowered him to the main deck, and had him taken to sick bay.

Meanwhile, the explosion of the torpedo had thrown Lt Harold Wright, the engineer officer, out of his bunk. He'd threaded his way past wreckage and sailors to the forward mess decks, where a fire had broken out. He tried pulling a man from the fire, but a further explosion went off in the ship's paint shop.

"I saw there was not much chance of getting anybody else out," Wright said, "until we had the fire under control."[45] He ordered what was left of the ship's forward gun magazines flooded, and reported to the bridge.

By this time, LCdr Miles had closed watertight doors forward to prevent further flooding deeper into the hull. But as crews attempted to extinguish the fires, smoke and flames began to threaten the bridge. Engineer Wright let LCdr Miles know the ship was not going to sink. But with his destroyer clearly ablaze in the night, the captain ordered his crew to prepare to abandon ship should the submarine close for a second attack. *Saguenay*, normally able to top thirty-one knots, was limping along at about four. By midday, Royal Navy destroyer HMS *Highlander* had arrived and received five of *Saguenay*'s officers and eighty-five other men not needed in the attempt to keep the destroyer afloat and moving. The explosion and fire aboard *Saguenay* had killed twenty-one and wounded eighteen. By December 5, tugs had towed the bow-less *Saguenay* to safety at the Isle of Man. Damage to the destroyer would take until May 1941 to repair.

Damage to the reputation of Canada's escort ships and crews was another matter. The Board of Inquiry investigating *Saguenay*'s procedures and responses during the escort of Convoy HG 47 interviewed LCdr Miles and the commander of HMS *Highlander*, Cdr W.A. Dallmeyer.[46] The board queried why *Saguenay*'s speed when torpedoed had only been twelve knots, making her an easy target for the Italian sub. Miles contended that as an escort he needed to conserve fuel. When questioned, Cdr Dallmeyer noted that the Canadian destroyer had her ASDIC running, but only passively (using only the hydrophone component of the set); Miles said that was Western Approaches protocol. The board criticized *Saguenay* for having so many men sleeping in the forward mess decks, where the majority of the casualties had occurred. Miles noted that Canadian NSHQ policy demanded that the ship carry trainees as well as the ship's complement, so there was nowhere to house those extra sailors but in the mess decks.

When the Board of Inquiry toured the damaged *Saguenay* in drydock, its members did note "that the steaming of this ship safely back to harbour . . . represent[ed] a very considerable feat of seamanship and endurance."[47] The board also commended the crew for attempting to engage the enemy sub, despite *Saguenay*'s crippled state. For salvaging of the destroyer, LCdr Miles was awarded the Order of the British Empire.

At the root of the grilling that LCdr Miles and *Saguenay* endured in that December inquiry, however, were the systemic problems that RCN ships, RN ships, and merchant navy vessels needed to fix on the North Atlantic run. Among other things, the depth charges aboard Allied warships had proven inadequate, and the escorts had little consistency in establishing effective screens around convoys at night. Distance was a growing hazard. As the U-boat threat moved farther west, so did dispersal points—where escorts left outbound convoys or met inbound ones; as a consequence, short-range escorts regularly ran short of fuel. The old design of corvettes posed more problems the farther across the Atlantic they were expected to sail; their short forecastles, intended for inshore work, proved inadequate on the high seas. Generally, space for men and munitions on long-distance operations always seemed inadequate.[48]

The bigger picture left a lot to be desired as well. By the end of 1940, the Admiralty understood that escort forces needed overhauling to become more organized with more warships assigned to each convoy. Ad hoc arrangements of ships—throwing together escorts that hadn't previously worked as a group—left too many holes in the protective screen. The escort system needed better leadership and more thorough training in both convoy defence and anti-submarine warfare. Escorts needed higher-quality detection equipment; the Royal Navy began affixing Type 286 (metric wavelength radar) to escorts' mastheads; these became the first escort radar employed in the Atlantic war. And to give escorts eyes at night, "snowflake" illuminants became standard.[49]

Over the same period, the German U-boat flotilla was also adapting to warfare and conditions farther west, deeper into the North Atlantic shipping lanes. Having established his new headquarters on the occupied coast of France, Adm Dönitz, as Befehlshaber der Unterseeboote (commander of the U-boat service, or BdU), could now send and receive hourly reports of convoy locations and velocities from U-boats shadowing them well out into the Atlantic. BdU Dönitz understood that enemy direction-finding could often intercept such transmissions, but the benefit was worth the risk; the Germans assumed as well that the British had not miniaturized their DF technology for shipboard use.[50] Kriegsmarine's command centres also believed their transmission interception service, B-Dienst, could continue to organize U-boat patrol lines to intercept convoys. Finally, with Dönitz's Rüdeltaktik now tried and proven, a shadowing U-boat could lead the others to their prey and, once engaged, each U-boat commander could rely on his own instincts to complete the job.

In 1940, Britain had lost four million tons of shipping, principally because of U-boats.[51] The coming year would reveal who had learned the most from past mistakes, and which way the tide of the Atlantic battle would flow.

Chapter Five

SEA WOLVES AND SHEEPDOGS

As Christmas 1940 approached, Ordinary Seaman Gordon William Baines had a lot on his plate. Since he'd enlisted in the Royal Canadian Naval Volunteer Reserve the previous August, and then completed his basic training at HMCS *Stadacona*, the land-based naval station in Halifax, Gordon had decided to focus on signals. He was a details kind of person. In 1927, when he'd turned fourteen, he successfully completed a semaphore course offered by the local cadet corps in Montreal, where he grew up. Later, in the 1930s, he taught himself Morse code. It made sense, with the war on, and as an RCNVR recruit, to build on his strengths. So, late in 1940 he was reading, writing, studying, and advancing quickly through the navy's nine-month signals training, among the toughest trade courses at *Stadacona*.[1]

Not surprisingly, as a young man of twenty-six, OS Baines had a number of other things on his mind. With his family living in Montreal, he wrote letters diligently to his parents and three surviving brothers (a fourth had died of influenza after the Great War). But he especially made time for letters to his girlfriend, Hazel Le Cras, back in Notre-Dame-de-

Grâce in west-end Montreal. Gordon and Hazel had been a couple since 1937, and with Gordon so far away, they made up for the distance by writing each other regularly.

"I've a question I want to ask you," Gordon wrote from Halifax on November 21, "but before you reply, I want you to consider it very carefully."[2]

Gordon cared deeply for Hazel, but he had a pretty clear-headed understanding of the hardships that wartime relationships faced. In his letter, he asked her to remember the kind of work he'd been doing before joining the navy; he'd worked for Canadian National Railways as a messenger in their land department during the 1930s, but tough economic times had forced the CNR to lay him off. He'd shared with her his hope to one day complete his high-school education and perhaps become an architect.

"Prospects ahead are very uncertain," his letter continued. "There may be some very dark times in store for me." But despite the uncertainty, despite the war, Gordon felt it was time to make things permanent. "I want to see you at Christmas, Bright Eyes . . . to slip a ring on your finger. Will you make me the happiest man in the world and marry me?"

Four days later, Hazel Le Cras posted her answer. She told him that she'd tried a number of times to put her response into words. She considered his warnings about the realities of serving in the war and the uncertainty of work prospects after it was over. He'd suggested they not actually marry until the war ended, and she agreed with that idea. But whatever the circumstances, she wrote, "It has been my one hope . . . I might be your wife and share your joys and sorrows.

"Don't stay away too long, Boy Blue," Hazel wrote finally. "And the Christmas season can't come too soon."[3]

They went ahead with the engagement at year's end, but the demands of Gordon's service in Halifax pushed their relationship to the back burner for a time. Not only was the regimen for wireless-radio training intensifying, but so were his responsibilities at the base. He continued to score eighties and nineties on his practical courses in procedure and organization, coding, flashing, semaphore, and buzzer (telegraphy). But he'd also signed on as duty messenger in the *Stadacona* signal school where he was training. As such, he was at the beck and call of the school's chief telegraphist. His predecessor, Hugh O'Hare, actually left Gordon a list of "house rules," and all fifteen—delivered somewhat tongue-in-cheek—required respect, promptness, and precision.

"You may have to, like Johnnie the Call-Boy, go forth and in a loud, clear voice, lustily page some fortunate, or misfortunate being, to report to the Reg[ulating Office]," O'Hare wrote. "If you work conscientiously at this, some lucky day you may rise to fame at the Michigan State Fair Hog-Calling Contest."[4]

Despite the added responsibilities of duty messenger, and the original weight of signals training, Gordon Baines earned leave to attend his own engagement party back home that Christmas. And about the time he was placing a ring on Hazel Le Cras's finger in Montreal, the Saint John Dry Dock and Shipbuilding Co. in New Brunswick launched HMCS *Amherst*, one of fifty-four Canadian-built corvettes.[5] During the following summer, the corvette arrived at Halifax Harbour. In August 1941, the newly christened *Amherst* received her first crew, including qualified telegraphist OS Gordon Baines. His fiancée wouldn't see her "Boy Blue" for a while. After work-ups and anti-submarine-warfare training,

Amherst assumed her role as escorting corvette in the hectic shipping lanes of the North Atlantic.

NEARLY as precious to the British prime minister and the Admiralty as the fifty American lend-lease destroyers at this point in the war, the Flower-class corvettes began emerging from Canadian shipbuilding yards as ice went out on the St. Lawrence River and the Great Lakes. The first, *Trillium*, slipped down the ways at the Canadian Vickers yard in Montreal even as France fell to the Germans in June 1940. The remaining nine in that contract—*Arrowhead*, *Bittersweet*, *Eyebright*, *Fennel*, *Hepatica*, *Mayflower*, *Snowberry*, *Spikenard*, and *Windflower*—came from Vickers in Montreal; Marine Industries in Sorel, Quebec; or Davie Shipbuilding in Lauzon, Quebec. They were all completed and commissioned by February 1941,* then sailed directly overseas to augment the Royal Navy's escort strength in the coastal waters of the British Isles.

The name "corvette" originated in the 1700s, when the French built a speedy three-masted, barque-rigged man-o'-war with one tier of guns on a single deck. Steam engines and steel ships made the French corvette obsolete. But in 1915, a designer with a shipbuilding company in Yorkshire, England, presented a modified whale-hunting vessel as a sub-chaser. It took the Admiralty twenty-four years, but in 1939 they invited William Reed to Whitehall to discuss his concept for a warship larger than a trawler but smaller than a destroyer—a ship that British yards could build quickly and inexpensively.[6]

* The first Britain-bound corvettes lacked important warship accessories—deck guns. In their place, to give the impression of armament, crews fashioned gun barrels out of wooden posts for the transatlantic crossing.

Winston Churchill (then First Lord of the Admiralty) didn't like the name *whaler*, so he chose *corvette* instead. Churchill referred to his new sub-chasers as "cheap and nasties," and their price tag for construction in Canada—around $530,000 per ship—reflected their economy.

As well as being economical, corvettes had a simple design—length of 205 feet, breadth of 33 feet, and a draught of about 15 feet. Their four-cylinder, triple-expansion steam engines below decks delivered about 2,750 horsepower and an economical cruising speed of twelve knots; their range was 3,500 miles (1,000 less if running at their top speed of sixteen knots). Once Canadian shipyards had delivered the first ten corvettes to Britain by February, they continued with the construction of C.D. Howe's remaining fifty-four corvettes for delivery to the Royal Canadian Navy during the remainder of 1941. Those corvettes came from shipbuilding yards on the upper St. Lawrence River, around the Great Lakes, at Saint John, New Brunswick, and along the Pacific Coast.

The corvette's crew complement consisted of about fifty men—a lieutenant or lieutenant commander as captain, four additional officers, three leading seamen, twelve able and ordinary seamen, four telegraphist/signalmen, a chief engine room artificer, and three additional ERAs, nineteen stokers, two cooks, and two stewards.[7] In addition to their regular duties, some crewmen doubled as coders, gunners, torpedomen, and detection operators. But as escort operations demanded longer patrols at sea over greater distances, and more escorts per convoy, the crews aboard corvettes ballooned to as many as seventy-five or 100 men per ship.

"Think of it," RCN stoker Morley Barnes recalled, "about a hundred men all cooped up in this little tin can."[8]

War wasn't supposed to be comfortable. On the other hand, even the corvettes' original British design intended these small warships to provide better than average seaworthiness, quick acceleration, speed, manoeuvrability, ASDIC (sonar) capability, watertight subdivision, and durability. Like their whale-catcher predecessors, the new-generation corvettes were built to be agile—with an almost cork-like reaction to rough seas, and responsive handling. Even under such adverse conditions as those dispensed by the North Atlantic, corvettes should be able to turn a complete circle in 100 seconds; in other words, out-manoeuvre any surfaced or submerged U-boat.[9]

The rough-and-tumble conditions aboard a corvette might explain why James Douglas Prentice, recently enticed from his retirement as a rancher in the interior of British Columbia, seemed right at home on board one of Churchill's "nasties." Born in Victoria, BC, in 1899, by age thirteen James had decided he would join the navy. Family persuaded him to choose not the Royal Canadian Navy but the Royal Navy instead. In the Great War he was at the Battle of Jutland and later served as first lieutenant aboard the battleship HMS *Rodney*. In 1934 his RN career seemed to stall, so he took early retirement and returned to the family's Gang Ranch* in BC's Cariboo Country. Most knew him as "the monocled cowboy," since he was regularly seen wearing a Stetson, riding breeches, and a monocle.[10]

When the RCN mobilized for war in 1939, Prentice accepted a position as staff officer at the base in Sydney, Nova Scotia. But he quickly grew restless with his shore job. The

* The Gang Ranch originated in 1863, during the Cariboo Gold Rush, when American ranchers Thaddeus and Jerome Harper came to the area, negotiated for land with the Chilcotin First Nation, and herded cattle along the Fraser River. Originally the Canadian Ranching Company, the Gang Ranch became the largest ranch in North America.

next summer, the navy transferred him to Halifax in command of the recently commissioned corvette HMCS *Lévis*, and there he might have stayed but for a reunion with the officer commanding Halifax Force, Cmdre Leonard Murray. The two had known each other at the Royal Navy's staff college. Murray immediately assigned Prentice the position of Senior Officer, Canadian Corvettes.* But with many of those corvettes still under construction or not yet commissioned, it was the navy equivalent of waiting in a corral for unbroken horses to arrive. So lifelong rancher and now navy planning officer Prentice made sure he knew what to do when the unbroken corvettes arrived.

Assigned to supervise and prepare the growing corvette flotilla, Commanding Officer Prentice, or "Chummy," as he was known, understood that the best combat education did not happen in classrooms; it happened during sea training. However, even on manoeuvres, he quickly recognized that commanding officers in the RCN fleet had insufficient background in convoy work. "Ships are seldom in station," he said. "Even on wonderful nights, [escorts] are continually losing their convoys. [They] cease zigzagging for fear of collision under conditions of weather or visibility,"[11] even though, Prentice sensed, their COs should be honing those skills under such adverse conditions. In other words, any success at convoy escort or, more critically anti-submarine warfare, depended on the competence and adaptability of the corvette crews on operations at sea.

"The enemy is not destroyed in war by untrained ships," he often told the officers he trained.[12]

* James Prentice's ranking will change in this narrative—from captain to senior officer to commander.

As the war began, Royal Canadian Navy facilities were training 2,673 officers and ratings from the RCN, the RCNR, and the RCNVR. Eight months later, those same training depots—at HMCS *Stone Frigate* (borrowed space at the Royal Military College) in Kingston, Ontario, and HMCS *Stadacona*, in Halifax—had 6,528 officers and men enlisted. The reserves alone had experienced a tenfold expansion. Very quickly, accommodations at *Stadacona* were bulging at the seams. By April 1940, for example, the Halifax shore establishments and training programs had 1,394 ratings on the base; the barracks could only house 556.[13] The trainees learned basic navigation, pilotage, seamanship, gunnery, minesweeping, "a smattering of torpedo,"[14] and they experienced a couple of weeks of sea training.

RCN volunteer James B. Lamb came through HMCS *Stone Frigate* at that time. He valued the instruction in the basics that he received there. But once at sea aboard his first escort corvette, HMCS *Trail*, Lamb recognized a new reality. "When you joined a ship in the corvette navy," Lamb wrote, "you passed from one world into another."[15]

Corvette crews, Lamb learned, looked nothing like the classics he'd studied back at *Stone Frigate*. They were young. The officers and men were mostly right out of high school or were former blue-collar workers from construction sites, farms, food-processing plants, logging companies, or railway yards; anybody over the age of thirty got stuck with the nickname "Pappy." Consequently, corvette people were all junior in rank and rate. Most of the upper-deck crews were ordinary seamen and leading seamen who'd stepped into jobs normally assigned to petty officers. Meanwhile, the corvette engine room was often filled with young men who'd enlisted directly from mechanical training schools. Lamb remembered that aboard one of his earliest corvette postings, the captain was a former merchant navy lieutenant, with a volunteer reserve lieutenant as his executive officer and a couple of sub-lieutenants as officers of the watch.

"You left behind the Big Navy, where you had done your training . . . and you joined an outfit that was run along the lines of a small corner store," Lamb wrote. "These were chummy ships, whose destinies seemed always to be bound up with yours. . . . For most of us, the corvettes . . . became home."[16]

Cdr James Prentice appeared to present a unique blend of old navy and new. Aboard his newly commissioned corvette, HMCS *Chambly*, the commander spoke with a pronounced English accent, smoked cigars, and sported that monocle. He ran his ship with ample Royal Navy rigour, but with a sense of fairness that found favour with crewmen on the lower decks.* On one occasion, a number of *Chambly*'s crew decided to wear monocles too, while on parade. Prentice noted the mimicry, finished his rounds, stopped in front of the ship's company—all of them expecting a full rebuke.

Instead, in full view of the assembly, Prentice tossed his head back, which flipped the monocle into the air, and when it fell, it landed perfectly whence it came. "When you can do that," he said defiantly, "you can all wear monocles."[17]

Above all, Cdr Prentice respected the responsibility Cmdre Murray had given him to whip Canada's growing flotilla of corvettes into shape. And Prentice intended to deliver.

* RCN volunteer Clyde Gilmour recalled that his warship commander allowed crews to grow beards at sea, but the practice changed when experience showed that the whiskers of too many shipwrecked sailors soaked up fuel oil on the ocean surface and rendered victims unconscious from the fumes (interview by Alex Barris, June 24, 1993, Toronto).

Even if the corvettes' hunting grounds were limited to the waters in and around Halifax Harbour, he would ensure that RCN corvettes became the equivalent of a striking force while defending Nova Scotia's south shore. And even if RN and RCN strategists dismissed corvettes as less-than-essential warships, he intended to show that, to the contrary, corvettes could prove themselves as lethal sub-killers.[18]

Prentice quickly assessed the corvette's strengths and weaknesses. While he understood that its top speed was only sixteen knots, he also recognized that its piston engines meant each corvette enjoyed the quick acceleration its engineers promised. In addition, the larger corvette rudder and sleek hull configuration would deliver on the designer's guarantee of agility and responsive handling at sea. If life on the ranch had taught him anything, it might have been his realistic approach to survival. The corvette, Prentice deduced, was less expensive to replace than its U-boat adversary, so if it came to that, the trade-off might be worth the risk in a battle, even in coastal waters. What's more, the corvette commander had worked out alternative methods of attack that would make his escorts less defensive and more offensive.

Royal Navy experience demonstrated that a small warship attack against a submerged U-boat began at 1,200 yards, within range of the surface ship's sonar. The hunter then closed on the submarine using its best sonar search speed—about twelve knots—to reach a point of depth-charge throw-off directly above the sub. The RN method had the hunter accelerate to an attacking speed before deploying depth-charges, which allowed the charges to descend to the target while putting sufficient distance between the corvette and the resulting underwater explosions.

The problem, as Prentice saw it, was that the U-boat could detect the change in propeller noise of the hunter as it accelerated to its depth-charge throw-off point. The sub could then react by rapidly changing course or depth. The hunter's acceleration also drowned out its ASDIC contact with the sub on its final approach, thus removing the advantage of the corvette's agility to react if the sub took evasive action. Consequently, Prentice instructed his corvette crews to attack at a constant speed from first contact to throw-off, thus allowing continuous sonar contact throughout the attack. He recognized that such tactics could leave the corvette relatively close to the concussion of the exploding depth charges, and the potential for some self-inflicted damage; there was a real possibility the blast could lift the stern of the corvette right out of the water, putting additional strain on its machinery and crews. But if the tactic gave the hunter a better chance of sinking the U-boat, he thought the gamble was worth taking.

The British called Prentice's quick-attack tactics "cowboy convoy defence." He didn't care. He preferred any approach that would keep the enemy "well stirred up."[19]

CANADIAN shipbuilders had delivered Churchill's "cheap and nasties" to Britain in early 1941; shortly after, those same shipbuilders were set to ease another of the prime minister's headaches. As early as the summer of 1940, C.D. Howe, Canada's minister of munitions and supply, had mused about expanding Canada's shipbuilding capacity into cargo-ship construction. He learned that numerous berths—on both the east and west coasts—had space enough to build merchant ships as large as 9,000 tons, and his department proposed construction of sixty-eight of them.[20] Temporarily, contracts to build navy warships overtook that availability. But later that year, when a government mission from the UK arrived in North America, searching for ways to offset the British Merchant Navy's losses, the Canadian government offered a solution: it would form Wartime Merchant Shipping Limited (WMSL), initially to build ten cargo ships.

The only problem was funding. But when the US and UK signed the lend-lease agreement in March 1941, it opened the US market to Canadian war production—in particular, the construction of 10,000-ton cargo ships. Canada could build and sell the ships to America for transfer to Britain under the lend-lease deal. The impact was immediate. Over the next two years, the US purchased ninety Canadian-built merchant ships for transfer to the UK. E.P. Taylor, one of Howe's dollar-a-year men, optimistically suggested WMSL could build seventy-five to a hundred merchant ships a year that way. But even Taylor's prediction underestimated the true output. Canadian merchant shipbuilding would in fact exceed one million tons in 1943 and 1944. By the end of the war, Canadian shipbuilders had produced 400 merchant ships for the war effort.[21]

Howe had succeeded in transforming the Canadian economy to an industrial mindset. "Never again will there be any doubt," he said in 1943, "that Canada can manufacture anything that can be manufactured elsewhere."[22]

But all of that was still a year or two into the future. Meantime, Churchill agonized over the mounting merchant navy losses—a total of 2,314,000 tons from April 1940 to March 1941 in the Western Approaches alone. He wrote privately that "this mortal danger to our lifelines gnawed my bowels." Publicly, to his War Cabinet, he said, "we have got to lift this business to the highest plane, over everything else. I am going to proclaim 'the Battle of the Atlantic.'" On March 6, 1941, his government issued a lengthy directive that boiled down to one objective: "the U-boat at sea must be hunted."[23] Churchill acknowledged the impact of Dönitz's wolf pack tactics, the U-boats' unchecked surface attacks at night, and the Royal Navy's need for faster escorts and more effective radar. Most of all, he urged the unsparing efforts of scientists, airmen, and sailors to win "the U-boat war."

As the British prime minister was giving the eighteen-month-old siege in the North Atlantic an official name, Canadian merchant sailor Jerry Thornton joined the crew of *Black Condor*, a steam freighter departing Halifax Harbour. It was his very first convoy to England. On March 1, 1941, HX 112, an assembly of forty-one merchant ships—including thirteen tankers laden with fuel oil for Britain—left Halifax bound for Liverpool. Just eighteen, Thornton had earned his radio certificate at the Radio College of Canada in Toronto and was eager to contribute to the war effort. The British Marconi wireless company had then hired him and assigned him to the radio shack aboard *Black Condor*, a former American steam freighter transferred to the British merchant fleet for wartime service.[24]

For two-thirds of the crossing, the only adversities facing Convoy HX 112 were high winds and turbulent seas. During one storm, Thornton recalled, lines securing the cargo on and below decks began to break as the ship battled the mid-Atlantic tempest. The ship spent the remainder of the trip with a ten-degree list. Eventually the 5th Escort Group of six warships rendezvoused with the convoy to shepherd it through the Western Approaches to Liverpool.

Radio operator Thornton and *Black Condor* didn't know it, but Convoy HX 112 was about to make history. In the vanguard of escorting destroyers was Cdr Donald Macintyre, aboard HMS *Walker*. To his first action as senior officer escort in the North Atlantic, Macintyre brought Royal Navy experience dating back sixteen years, including service as a pilot with Fleet Air Arm, anti-submarine patrols off the British coast, and destroyer postings in the Far East. Macintyre, leading an escort of five destroyers and two corvettes, was nonetheless relieved to find his appointed convoy steaming eastward 200 miles off the coast of Iceland.

"Early on the 15th March, 1941, my searching eyes saw the forest of topmasts rise over the western horizon," he wrote, "and I knew our rendezvous was well made."[25] Most of that first day, Macintyre and the escorts conducted housekeeping around the convoy—sweeping the track of the convoy, tightening its columns, corralling straggling merchantmen, and positioning escorts to screen the convoy. Not shared with any of the merchant navy crews, Macintyre fought a nagging doubt: "how ill-equipped their escort really was. . . . I couldn't prevent the enemy from attacking, [but] I would do everything humanly possible to avenge the victims."[26]

He didn't have to wait long. About midnight, *U100* intercepted the convoy and surfaced. Unseen, the U-boat closed quickly on the first merchantman in the outer port column of ships. As Kptlt Joachim Schepke had so often done, he ordered a fan of four torpedoes—three fired from bow tubes and a fourth from a stern tube—in succession. Less than two minutes later, the first of his shots struck the motor tanker *Erodona*, which was carrying 6,000 tons of benzine oil and a crew of fifty-seven.

Aboard *Black Condor*, in the column of ships adjacent to *Erodona*, Jerry Thornton was on his way to the radio shack to begin his watch. He heard the thud of the torpedo striking home, looked to the horizon and witnessed the resulting holocaust. "The bonfire from it just lit up the whole sky," he said. "You could see the whole convoy. The ship disappeared in a little over thirty seconds."

"I had never before seen this most appalling of all night disasters," Cdr Macintyre wrote. "And on the bridge of *Walker* we were shocked into silence by the horror of it. . . . No one could possibly have survived."[27]

Nonetheless, as alarm bells clanged throughout HMS *Walker*, sending men to action stations, every eye on the bridge scanned the horizon for any sign of a U-boat pulling away. Schepke and *U100* had crash-dived, but the ASDIC ping aboard *Walker* brought no responding echo. It was the same aboard the other escorts. No sounding reports. No sightings. But then, at dusk the next evening, March 17, as *Walker* continued to lead Convoy HX 112 closer to the Western Approaches, Macintyre received a welcome signal. Escorting destroyer HMS *Vanoc* had made contact with a U-boat six miles distant and was giving chase. What gave the Royal Navy hunters a sudden advantage was a piece of equipment recently installed aboard *Vanoc*. For the first time, a primitive Type 271 seaborne radar set had given a surface ship a confirmed radar sighting of a U-boat, where traditional ASDIC had detected nothing.[28] In pitch darkness, the radar gave *Vanoc* an accurate range-and-speed reading of *U100*.

Schepke had chosen to surface to confront his destroyer pursuer, hoping he could launch a torpedo before being spotted. But within half a minute *Vanoc* had homed on the

U-boat, and moments later the bow of the RN destroyer collided with the superstructure of *U100* at ramming speed, pinning Schepke against her periscope standards. Only six of the crew below managed to escape the plunging U-boat. The other thirty-eight died, including Kptlt Schepke.

But Schepke's fellow sea wolf Kptlt Otto Kretschmer carried on where *U100* had left off. At 10 p.m., just minutes after *Walker* had returned to her station outside Convoy HX 112, *U99* infiltrated the columns and, protected by the merchant navy ships themselves, began firing at will. Within an hour *U99* had torpedoed six merchantmen and sunk five. Macintyre directed *Walker* through a gentle curving course, putting every point of the compass under surveillance. Then he spotted a thin line of white water—the unmistakable sign of *U99*'s periscope slicing through the surface. Kretschmer put the U-boat into a crash dive. But Macintyre was on top of the U-boat's turbulence immediately and unloaded a pattern of ten depth charges. The charges exploded with a crack, throwing waterspouts as high as mastheads astern of *Walker*. In response, the pattern yielded a second series of explosions.

As certain as Macintyre was of a kill, there was no wreckage or oil on the surface to verify. *Walker* began the task of rescuing men in the water from the sunken merchant ships. Then *Vanoc* rejoined the convoy (with news that she had sunk *U100*) and the two destroyers worked in tandem to reach the location of ASDIC contact with *U99*. This time a pattern of six depth charges flew through the air, followed by the detonations. This forced the U-boat to the surface, where a gun battle ensued, even as *U99* was sinking. In minutes the U-boat was gone and *Walker*'s crew began a rescue operation of the exhausted submariner survivors, among them Kptlt

Otto Kretschmer, still wearing a pair of Zeiss binoculars around his neck. The tonnage king had sunk forty-six Allied ships, more than 270,000 tons of freight.

By daybreak the escorts had gathered as many merchant ship survivors as they could find and resumed their stations around Convoy HX 112. Aboard *Black Condor*, Jerry Thornton heard that the U-boats had sunk six merchant ships that night, but found some solace in the news that their escorts in return had sunk two enemy subs.

"I considered escorts useless in rough weather," Thornton said. "We'd get such rough seas that the blame things would disappear in valleys of the waves. We wondered if they'd ever come up again. But I still marvelled at what those sheepdogs did."

Thornton and the rest of the surviving HX 112 merchantmen and escorts soon learned that "those sheepdogs" had not only put two of Dönitz's three famous U-Bootwaffe commanders and their U-boats out of the war, but just five nights earlier, a sister destroyer, HMS *Wolverine*, escorting Convoy OB 293, had caught the third notorious sea wolf, Kptlt Günther Prien, and his *U47* on the surface. Following a short pursuit, *Wolverine* had successfully depth-charged and sunk *U47*. All the U-boat's forty-seven submariners were killed, including Kptlt Prien, the "Bull of Scapa Flow."

ADM Karl Dönitz dismissed "the loss of three most experienced commanders at one and the same time [as] purely fortuitous."[29] But even if he felt little remorse over the deaths of his top tonnage kings, the U-boat admiral experienced some discomfort at the sinking of three Type VII U-boats in less than a week. At the beginning of 1941, his Unterseebootewaffe had twenty-two of its ninety commissioned U-boats on active duty in the North Atlantic. In January they had accounted for the torpedoing of fifty-nine Allied merchantmen without losing a single U-boat. During a dismal March, however, while the U-boats sank sixty-three merchant ships, overall the U-Bootwaffe had lost five boats.[30] The Kriegsmarine could not sustain that poor ratio for very long.*

When he heard about the deaths of Prien and Schepke and the capture of Kretschmer, Herbert Werner, a submariner aboard *U557*, wrote that their loss "stunned and baffled the country." More important, he couldn't fathom why it had happened. "Our losses were negligible compared with the casualties U-boats had inflicted upon our adversaries," he wrote. "[But] we were without explanation. Had the British introduced new weapons or techniques of anti-submarine warfare?"[31]

New weapons and techniques? Perhaps not. *U99* was nearly captured by HMS *Walker* because Cdr Macintyre had resorted to a commonsensical, methodical circuit using visual observation. He'd also switched from a five- to a ten-charge pattern of depth charges (delivered by hand when more sophisticated technology broke down[32]). Meanwhile, HMS *Vanoc*'s successful attack on *U100* resulted from a last-minute addition to the small ship's detection equipment, the Type 271 seaborne radar. And as discouraging as Convoy HX 112 losses had been, the escorting destroyers and corvettes were buoyed by their successful team approach to combat operations; they had tracked and attacked in pairs—one ship

* Prien, Kretschmer, and Schepke represented the thirty-sixth, thirty-seventh, and thirty-eighth of thirty-nine U-boats sunk in the first eighteen months of the war; from April to the end of 1941, a further thirty U-boats would be lost.

maintaining contact via ASDIC, the other launching depth charges. Making the best of what they had, the First World War–vintage destroyers and sheepdog corvettes had minimized the sea wolves' bite. The U-boats' so-called Happy Time was, for the moment, over.

If momentum in the Battle of the Atlantic had shifted away from the Kriegsmarine, so too had the battlefield itself shifted. Through the second year of the war, the Germans had moved the headquarters of most U-boat operations bound for the Atlantic to the occupied French seaport of Lorient. Adm Dönitz had set up a command post nearby, in a château at Kernével, at the mouth of the River Blavet. Now his U-boats could rely on new facilities at Lorient for fuel, supplies, and repair, and (instead of returning to German ports) effectively eliminate a fortnight of travel time plying the waters to and from the Atlantic shipping lanes.[33] On the Allied side, in February 1941 Royal Navy Adm Percy Noble and all of Western Approaches Command (WAC) had relocated to Liverpool; by April they had organized Western Approaches Convoy Instructions (WACIs), allowing closer co-operation between command staff and the crews at sea.

Meanwhile, to pre-empt the Kriegsmarine from using Iceland as a refuge or future base of operations, in 1940 the British had sent expeditionary troops to occupy the island's coastal areas, calling on the Cameron Highlanders of Ottawa to share garrison duties there through the winter of 1940–41.[34] As a follow-up, by April 1941 the RAF had posted bomber reconnaissance aircraft from Coastal Command to protect Hvalfjord, the naval base just north of Reykjavík. The toehold in Iceland provided some refuge, a relay point for anti-submarine escorts, and an extension of air cover with short- and long-range U-boat-hunting aircraft.* These adjustments also extended the escort protection of WAC farther west.

On the North American side of the Atlantic, Canadian escorts operated northeast from Halifax to the fringe of the Grand Banks. By May 1941, what remained between the limits of British anti-submarine escorts operating from Iceland and escorts from Canada was a gap of about 1,000 miles where convoys travelled with little or no protection. It was within that unprotected stretch of ocean—the Black Pit—that U-boats continued to operate with impunity. On May 20, 1941, the Royal Navy brass asked their sister navy in Canada to fill that gap.

LATE that spring, with no fanfare or fuss, seven Royal Canadian Navy corvettes—HMCS *Alberni*, *Agassiz*, *Chambly*, *Collingwood*, *Orillia*, *Pictou*, and *Wetaskiwin*—had made their way from Halifax to the Narrows at the entrance to St. John's Harbour. Led by Cdr James Prentice—senior officer, Canadian corvettes—the RCN warships represented the latest Admiralty initiative to bridge the mid-Atlantic Black Pit and forcibly deter U-boats from harassing North Atlantic merchant shipping there.

Just a year before, nobody—neither the British nor the Canadians—had seemed willing to help protect the Dominion of Newfoundland with either military aircraft or warships at sea. In 1941, however, the Admiralty suddenly needed a base

* By the middle of 1941, RAF bases in Britain and Iceland could dispatch some 200 long-range maritime patrol aircraft—eighty Hudsons, thirty-six Catalinas, and ten Liberators (built in the US)—as well as Whitleys, Wellingtons, and Sunderlands (built in the UK).

in North America that could extend convoy coverage 600 miles farther east of Nova Scotia into the Atlantic. St. John's seemed the natural choice. Admiralty also communicated with the RCN's Naval Service Headquarters in Ottawa about how many corvettes it could contribute to the base. NSHQ said seven right away, fifteen in a month, and forty-eight in six months.[35] The deal was done. In that moment, Admiralty designated the Newfoundland Escort Force as the western extension of Western Approaches Command. And with RCN Capt Leonard W. Murray coincidentally in the UK at that moment, Admiralty named him officer commanding.

"This is what comes of being in the right place at the right time," Murray said.[36]

Nobody felt more in the right place than Chummy Prentice. This posting to lead the corvettes into active escort duty was the opportunity he'd been waiting for ever since Murray had assigned him to be the RCN's master of corvette training.

Prentice's navigating officer aboard *Chambly* captured the excitement leaving Halifax in his diary. "A general rush all round to-day," Mate Anthony Pickard wrote. "The afternoon was spent in a general panic. Our charts finally arrived at 7:30 p.m. Additional ammunition came. A.A. armament (2 Twin Colts .5-inch) were mounted." Then, arriving at St. John's and passing through the Narrows, which were just a third of a mile wide, he took in the 500-foot cliffs encircling the harbour. "There is a brooding, ominous look," he concluded, "as if they waited only upon a signal to pour down the pent-up power of frowning centuries upon us in one huge cascade of wrath."[37]

While significant, the arrival of the NEF's warships and personnel in St. John's Harbour nearly got lost in the bigger picture of the war at that moment. Cdr Prentice and the corvettes had arrived almost simultaneously with news that the German battleship *Bismarck* and her consort, the heavy cruiser *Prinz Eugen*, had suddenly left moorings at Bergen, Norway, and were headed through the Denmark Strait to hunt down Allied convoys. In response, British Home Fleet warships had departed Scapa Flow in the Orkney Islands. The battleship HMS *King George V* sailed wide to the southwest, while her brand-new sister, *Prince of Wales*, joined the older battle cruiser HMS *Hood* in the chase, steaming for a direct interception between Iceland and Greenland. On May 24, aboard *Prince of Wales*, Sub-Lieutenant (SLt) Stuart Paddon (one of forty Canadian radar officers in the Royal Navy) reported radar blips identifying the enemy warships.

In the first exchange of salvos, shells from *Bismarck* pierced *Hood*'s aft magazine and exploded, tearing the ship apart. In mere minutes, the Mighty *Hood*, flagship of the Royal Navy, had vanished; all but three of *Hood*'s 1,418 crewmen were killed, including three Canadian midshipmen—Thomas Beard, Francis Jones, and Christopher Norman.* But some RN shells had found their mark against *Bismarck*, flooding forward compartments and contaminating some of her fuel. The two German warships separated, *Bismarck* attempting a dash to safety at the occupied port of St. Nazaire, France. But by May 27, Allied ships had overtaken and shelled *Bismarck* until the wreck sank, killing more than 2,100 of the battleship's complement; only 114 survived.

But for James Prentice and his band of escorting corvettes, just landed in St. John's, the sinking of *Bismarck* was half an

* The only tribute to HMS *Hood* and her war dead (including Canadians Beard, Jones, and Norman) can be found in St. John the Baptist Church near the village of Boldre in England. The painting and book of remembrance were paid for and installed by Phyllis Holland, widow of *Hood*'s captain Lancelot Holland.

ocean away, a problem on somebody else's watch. Days after arriving in Newfoundland, Cdr Prentice and HMCS *Chambly* responded to orders to meet and screen HMS *Repulse*, the Royal Navy battle cruiser that had participated in the hunt for *Bismarck*. To some, the contradiction of tiny *Chambly* protecting massive *Repulse* in Conception Bay, Newfoundland, would have seemed laughable. To Cdr Prentice and his immediate superior—Cmdre Leonard Murray, taking command of the newly christened NEF in St. John's—the moment signalled a critical changing of the guard.

For a generation, war at sea had consisted of colossal clashes between fleets of fire-breathing behemoths that continued until one side or the other withdrew. But in 1941, war in the Atlantic shipping lanes, at least, had become a battle of wits. On one side were nimble corvette crews protecting virtually unarmed merchantmen; on the other, a nearly invisible U-boat enemy attacking at night and from beneath the surface of hundreds of miles of the cruellest waters on the globe. The Battle of the Atlantic had become a war of attrition.

FOR a few days in August 1941, the two most important decision-makers in the Battle of the Atlantic disappeared. On August 3, a nondescript passenger train arrived at the US Navy submarine base in New London, Connecticut. A few newspaper reporters who'd sniffed out the VIP passenger onboard discovered that US president Franklin D. Roosevelt had come to the base to rendezvous with *Potomac*, a former Coast Guard cutter he had renovated as his "Floating White House." After a couple of photos and quotes, the reporters were told there would be no further press coverage; the president was going on vacation. For a day *Potomac* cruised off the south coast of Massachusetts. Figures seen at railing of the Floating White House and thought to be the president's party, however, were in fact imposters. By then the president had secretly boarded heavy cruiser USS *Augusta*, which immediately set a course north out of US territorial waters.[38] The real FDR would disappear for two weeks.

Those same first days of August, a different train departed Chequers, the country home in Buckinghamshire of the British prime minister, and carried Winston Churchill along with key aides and a large ciphering staff to Thurso, on Scotland's north coast. A small boat named *Morning Glory* carried the entourage out to the destroyer HMS *Oribi*, which whisked them to the Royal Navy base at Scapa Flow. That night, Churchill and company boarded the battle cruiser HMS *Prince of Wales* and put to sea with a large convoy outbound through the Western Approaches.[39] The prime minister seemed to vanish too.

Canadian telegraphist Jerry Thornton knew where the prime minister was. His merchant ship, *Black Condor* had narrowly escaped devastating U-boat attacks the previous March and was now part of the westbound convoy that included *Prince of Wales*. In fact, he saw the message flashed from the prime minister's ship requesting permission to enter the convoy.

"It was the largest convoy [to date] to cross the North Atlantic, about eighty ships," Thornton said. "*Prince of Wales* asked if she could go right through the middle of the convoy. Then we got a signal back that [Churchill] congratulated us on our station keeping."

The prime minister, then sixty-six, took advantage of some time to himself, resting in the Admiral's sea cabin on the bridge.

He contemplated the previous year's successes and setbacks, composed correspondence for chiefs of staff, and contemplated his impending first meeting with President Roosevelt. The lull in the action gave him "a strange sense of leisure,"[40] and he read his copy of *Captain Hornblower R.N.* and took in a screening of *Lady Hamilton* purely for distraction.

Lt Desmond Piers also discovered he was in the company of Prime Minister Churchill in the middle of the Atlantic. For the previous year, Piers had been in command aboard HMCS *Restigouche*, on dozens of escort assignments between Halifax and Iceland. In early August, his ship was refuelling at Hvalfjord when he received orders to join the westbound convoy 250 miles south of Iceland. *Restigouche* caught up with *Prince of Wales* and joined the escort screening the cruiser to the US naval base at Argentia, Newfoundland. Awaiting their arrival were the battleship USS *Arkansas* and cruiser *Tuscaloosa*, alongside the cruiser *Augusta* with the president aboard.

At 9 a.m. on Saturday, August 9, 1941, Churchill's delegation was ready to meet Roosevelt's. American naval officials had neglected to take into account the ninety-minute time difference, however, so Prime Minister Churchill and his entourage had to cool their heels while the president and company finished breakfast and got ready for the 10:30 meeting. With steel will, President Roosevelt, at age fifty-nine and still coping with lifelong effects of polio, stood to welcome Churchill aboard *Augusta*.

"At long last, we meet, Mr. President," Churchill said, shaking his hand briskly.[41] Then, as the navy band played the two national anthems, Churchill stood to attention on one side of the president as Roosevelt leaned on the arm of his son Elliott on the other. Churchill then presented Roosevelt with a letter from King George, and the two leaders introduced each other's delegations before commencing their first talks.

Churchill had hoped to get Roosevelt to bring the United States into the war. He was disappointed when the president explained that his limited powers and the strength of isolationist sentiment in the US prevented any such commitment. Nevertheless, the two leaders crafted the wording for a military alliance crucial to the defence of the free world and laid out what would follow an Allied victory. It was titled "Atlantic Charter." Meanwhile, another warship arrived at the historic Argentia meetings—HMCS *Trail*, the RCN corvette escorting the Shell Oil tanker *Clam* with fuel for *Prince of Wales*. Initially, RCN SLt James Lamb recalled, the proceedings took place in the distance. All he wanted was a chance to see HMS *Prince of Wales* up close. He got more than that when one of the cruiser's radar officers invited fellow Canadians aboard for an informal tour.

"For simple country boys, fresh from a corvette," Lamb wrote, "the *Prince* was strictly Buck Rogers stuff."[42]

It also proved to be a ticket for crews of several of the RCN escort ships to join the reciprocal ceremony that Churchill staged for the president aboard *Prince of Wales* the next day—Sunday morning church service. Lamb recalled the shuffling among the luminaries on *Prince*'s quarterdeck to get themselves into a position befitting rank and status. He remained awestruck at witnessing the meeting of powers determining the future course of world events. Lamb recalled that the church service seemed interminable, but that its redeeming moment proved to be the singing of "Onward, Christian

Soldiers," with Churchill waving his hand in tempo like an orchestra conductor. Thinking he'd seen everything, Lamb found himself corralled among other RCN officers and crew and led by Lt Piers into *Prince of Wales*'s cavernous wardroom. There the president and prime minister held court amid a circle of admirals, generals, and air marshals.

"Elbowing his way through all the heavy brass, Debby [Piers] approached the Great Man, interrupting Winston in mid-sentence," Lamb wrote. "Would they like to meet the officers of their escort, the men who'd brought them here?"[43]

Once again, all present were lined up to be introduced, one by one, to the two leaders of the free world. Lt Piers did the honours as each man, including Lamb, was treated to a handshake and bright smile.

"After that, all was anticlimax," Lamb continued. "All of us could hardly wait to get a letter off home or draw all eyes at the bar when we began a conversation with: 'The last time I chatted with Winston . . .' or 'Franklin told me himself . . .'"[44]

On August 15, two weeks after both Churchill and Roosevelt had virtually vanished, the made public the fruits of their talks. They agreed that neither the UK nor the US would seek land gains from the war, and that any territorial changes would have to respect the wishes of the affected people. They stated that self-determination is a human right, and that they would advance the causes of social welfare and global economic co-operation. They declared the need for freedom of the seas. They called for steps toward postwar disarmament.

While the president could not commit to direct American involvement in the war, his delegation made clear it would defend a "neutrality zone" and would therefore protect convoys west of Iceland.* Specifically, USN destroyers, called Task Force 4 (after January 1942 known as Task Force 24) and stationed at Argentia, would take over escort of fast (HX and ON) convoys between Newfoundland and Iceland, under the command of Adm Ernest J. King, commander-in-chief of the US Atlantic Fleet. By process of elimination, that left the slow (SC and ONS) convoys to the Royal Canadian Navy. In other words, the NEF, commanded by Cmdre Leonard Murray, was handed the tougher task of sheepdogging older, less agile, more vulnerable merchant ships, which then became easier prey for U-boat wolf packs. And the Canadians had no say in this realignment of Allied resources.

Within twenty-four hours of the charter's publication, the president and the prime minister were en route home to opposite sides of the Atlantic. By August 16, *Augusta* had delivered Roosevelt's party back to his holiday yacht waiting off the coast of Maine, and the president travelled by motorcade to a waiting train for the trip back to Washington. By August 18, *Prince of Wales* had carried Churchill, via Iceland and a seventy-three-ship convoy, back to Scapa Flow and his return train to London. He considered the significance of their meeting: that "the United States still technically neutral, joining with a belligerent Power in making such a declaration, was astonishing."[45]

DURING the week that warships transported President Roosevelt and Prime Minister Churchill to their secret meetings in Newfoundland, a state-of-the-art U-boat, the 740-ton

* FDR permitted US Navy ships of Task Force 4 to escort all fast convoys west of Iceland, except in the approaches to Canadian shores, supporting the fiction that these were American merchantmen with other friendly nationalities attached. The US had entered the war at sea.

U501, received some final alterations in the German-occupied port of Horten, up the Oslo Fjord in Norway: removal of deck torpedo containers and repairs to a projecting rod that protected the U-boat's hydroplane. The Deutsche Werft shipbuilders had launched *U501*, a Type IXC U-boat, from Hamburg in December 1940, with plans to have her new crew conduct acceptance trials the following spring.

The design, production, and rollout of Germany's older Type VII U-boats had translated to much success for the U-Bootwaffe and its supreme commander, Adm Karl Dönitz. Between 1939 and 1941, more than 700 of the Type VIIs had proven their worth, particularly when commanded by such skillful U-boat warriors as Günther Prien, Otto Kretschmer, and Joachim Schepke. The commissioning of the larger, more powerful, and more heavily armed Type IX, however, offered the prospect of even greater returns. At 252 feet in length and 1,200 tons displacement, the Type IX was 52 feet longer and 460 tons heavier than the Type VII. Its top speed on the surface was 18.3 knots, and 7.3 knots submerged, slightly faster than the earlier model. As armament, the newer U-boat operated with six torpedo tubes (one more than its predecessor) and twenty-two-torpedo capacity (eight more than the Type VII). Perhaps its greatest asset was its range—as much as 14,000 miles (compared to 8,500 miles). One important drawback existed, however, as the Type IX took ten seconds longer to dive.

Dönitz had planned to assign these new, more lethal Type IXs to his star tonnage kings—Prien, Schepke, and Kretschmer—but by March 1941 they'd all been killed or captured. Instead, one of U-Bootwaffe's younger commanders, Korvettenkapitän Hugo Förster, approached the

Admiral "on bended knee" to be given command of *U501*.[46] Although Dönitz approved the promotion, there was perhaps one flaw in his decision. While KK Förster had served as a commander in the Kriegsmarine since 1936, he had left a German torpedo-boat flotilla as recently as 1939 to train in U-boat command and had trained in U-boats only since 1940. Submarine warfare was very new to Förster. And *U501*'s new crew was also inexperienced. Of the six officers, fifteen petty officers, and twenty-six men onboard, only the engineer, several petty officers, and two ratings had ever served in combat conditions.[47] In fact, in the summer of 1941, as *U501*'s crew practised torpedo firing and diving procedure off the Norwegian coast, KK Förster was, in effect, learning combat procedure and tactics at the same time as his crew.

Nevertheless, *U501* joined Adm Dönitz's new mid-1941 initiative against Allied convoy routes south of Iceland. On August 7, fully loaded with food supplies and armed with both electric and air torpedo types, *U501* and crew left the pens at Horten, Norway, to patrol the Denmark Strait, between Iceland and Greenland. Tensions and inexperience were further complicated when Förster ordered a dive to test recently completed repair work. Submerged almost two hundred feet, the U-boat hull seemed to groan irregularly under the pressure. The captain had second thoughts about the manoeuvre. "The integrity of the hull is paramount," Förster told his chief engineer, "particularly if attacked."[48]

Oblt Ing Gerhard Schiemann, who'd served previously aboard *U16* and *U22*, disagreed, claiming that *U501* was designed to take it. The two argued.

"I refuse to go deeper," Förster insisted. And that ended the discussion.

Survivors Of Frederick S. Fales Arrive

The day the war broke out, September 3, 1939, Alix Masheter (1), a Canadian living in Birmingham, UK, wrote relatives back in Ontario that her family's survival in Britain was now dependent on imports delivered by North American merchant convoys. Like most convoys departing Halifax, HX 72 began with a pre-departure conference (2) at Admiralty House in Halifax plotting the safest route. Its fate would be determined by U-boat commander Joachim Schepke (3) and his crew. The nineteen merchant sailors of tanker *Frederick S. Fales* interviewed by the *Halifax Daily Star* (4) on November 27, 1940, were among the few alive to tell the tale.

1

2

3

In 1938, John Birnie Dougall (1), age eighteen, left his home in Canada to serve in the merchant navy; even as the war overtook his ship and transatlantic trips, he wrote his mother Rachel Dougall (2) nearly every other day. Margaret Los (3) joined the navy in 1942; she worked among "the listeners" at HMCS *Coverdale* in New Brunswick, eavesdropping on U-boat transmissions (4). George Jamieson (5), from the Six Nations reserve in Ontario, served as an anti-submarine warfare officer in HMCS *Drummondville*, escorting convoys on the Triangle Run. Hours of bush and military flying inspired Norville "Molly" Small (7) to test his ideas for extending the range of his anti-submarine flying-boat patrols over North Atlantic convoys (6).

4

5

6

7

1

2

3

4

At the start of the war, Admiral Karl Dönitz (2) claimed all he needed were 300 U-boats (1) to bring Britain's merchant shipping to its knees; he'd eventually command 830 subs. In response to the threat, in August 1941, Allied leaders (3) Franklin D. Roosevelt and Winston Churchill met secretly at Argentia, Newfoundland, and co-authored the Atlantic Charter, which among other things sealed a lend-lease deal delivering the first of fifty US destroyers (4) to the Royal Navy via Halifax to Britain. Meanwhile, in 1939, the Royal Canadian Navy had just a handful of warships, but by war's end had become the fourth-largest navy in the world, thanks in part to the domestic shipbuilding initiatives of C.D. Howe (6), so-called minister of everything. In six war years, his program launched 543 warships, including 122 corvettes such as HMCS *Orillia* (5) from the yards at Collingwood, Ontario, in 1940.

5

6

1

2

3

When James Prentice (2) took over training of the Newfoundland Escort Force of RCN corvettes (1) protecting convoys, he believed the best defence was an effective offence. Gordon Baines (3) took up that challenge as telegraphist aboard HMCS *Amherst*, but he never lost touch with his family or his fiancée Hazel Le Cras, seen here (4) at their engagement in 1940.

4

5

6

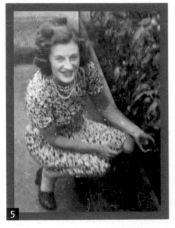

Nan Adair (5) grew up in Canada, but in UK in 1939, she wanted to serve; she couldn't find her niche until interviewed at a mansion in Milton Keynes, UK. There, at Bletchley Park, she was invited to join Alan Turing (inset) and his team of experts breaking German navy Enigma codes with devices known as bombes (6), which mimicked Enigma's rotors, ring settings, and plugboards.

Early in the war, U-boat commanders Günther Prien (2) and Otto Kretschmer (3) quickly gained reputations as "tonnage kings," sinking thousands of tons of Allied shipping. Initially, RCN warship commanders lacked experience; Anthony Griffin (1), commanding HMCS *Pictou*, said it was "the blind leading the blind," and in November 1942, Desmond Piers (4) in HMCS *Restigouche* said he was "three years a lieutenant leading a convoy crossing the Atlantic." Among Canada's secret weapons, however, was a rapidly growing shipbuilding force—including 4,000 women workers, here on lunch break in a lifeboat (5) at a yard in Burrard, BC.

1

2

3

4

5

6

In May 1942, the RCN posted telegraphist Murray Westgate (1) and cipher officer Ian Tate (2), pictured at left with senior officer Paul Belanger, to Gaspé, Quebec, just as the base HMCS *Fort Ramsay* officially opened (3); they felt as if they'd been sent to the wilderness of wartime service. But on May 11, when civilians began rescuing merchant seamen (4) from torpedoed merchant ship SS *Nicoya* in the Gulf of St. Lawrence, Westgate and Tate suddenly found themselves in a new Atlantic battlefield, right on Canada's doorstep. The earliest defences against U-boats off Gaspé were high-speed Fairmile motor launches (5) constructed by shipbuilders such as Hans Sachau (6) at his yard near Humber Bay on Lake Ontario.

1

2

In September 1942, when a U-boat attacked a merchant ship in the gulf, the torpedo instead wound up on the Saint-Yvon, Quebec, waterfront (1). Ian Tate photographed civilians curious to see the inadvertent first German naval attack on mainland Canada. Meanwhile, James Lamb (3) and his shipmates in HMCS *Trail* rescued oil-soaked survivors (2) of the torpedoed USS *Chatham*, the first American troopship sunk by enemy action in the war.

3

4

The Battle of the Gulf came to a climax in October 1942 when *U69* torpedoed and sank passenger ferry SS *Caribou* (4); nursing sisters Margaret Brooke and Agnes Wilkie (5), returning to Newfoundland, were among 191 passengers and crew thrown into frigid Gulf waters that night.

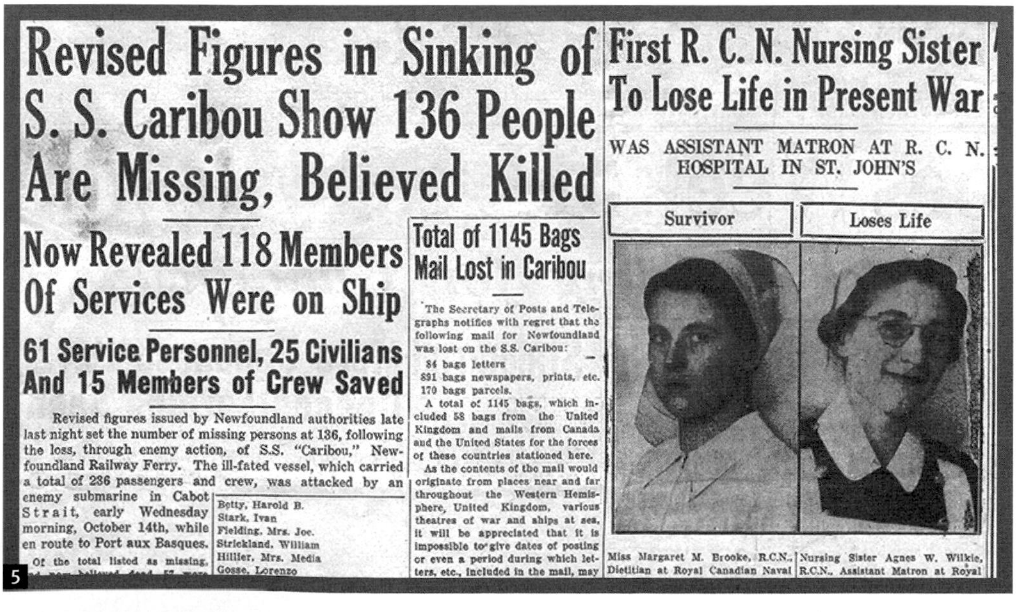

Revised Figures in Sinking of S. S. Caribou Show 136 People Are Missing, Believed Killed

Now Revealed 118 Members Of Services Were on Ship

61 Service Personnel, 25 Civilians And 15 Members of Crew Saved

Revised figures issued by Newfoundland authorities late last night set the number of missing persons at 136, following the loss, through enemy action, of S.S. "Caribou," Newfoundland Railway Ferry. The ill-fated vessel, which carried a total of 236 passengers and crew, was attacked by an enemy submarine in Cabot Strait, early Wednesday morning, October 14th, while en route to Port aux Basques.

Of the total listed as missing,

Betty, Harold B.
Stark, Ivan
Fielding, Mrs. Joe.
Strickland, William
Hillier, Mrs. Media
Gosse, Lorenzo

Total of 1145 Bags Mail Lost in Caribou

The Secretary of Posts and Telegraphs notifies with regret that the following mail for Newfoundland was lost on the S.S. Caribou:

84 bags letters
891 bags newspapers, prints, etc.
170 bags parcels.

A total of 1145 bags, which included 58 bags from the United Kingdom and mails from Canada and the United States for the forces of these countries stationed here.

As the contents of the mail would originate from places near and far throughout the Western Hemisphere, United Kingdom, various theatres of war and ships at sea, it will be appreciated that it is impossible to give dates of posting or even a period during which letters, etc., included in the mail, may

First R. C. N. Nursing Sister To Lose Life in Present War

WAS ASSISTANT MATRON AT R. C. N. HOSPITAL IN ST. JOHN'S

Survivor | Loses Life

Miss Margaret M. Brooke, R.C.N., Dietitian at Royal Canadian Naval

Nursing Sister Agnes W. Wilkie, R.C.N., Assistant Matron at Royal

5

Adm Percy Nelles and Navy minister Angus L. Macdonald (1) (third person unknown) examine a model of an RCN corvette, soon to carry the bulk of the responsibility for shepherding transatlantic convoys. Known as Winston Churchill's "cheap and nasties," corvettes such as HMCS *Battleford* (2) looked more submersed than afloat, which required crews to take extra care securing depth charges (3) and below decks coping with life in the cramped crew's mess (4).

The saving grace for some was assembling for "up spirits" (5), the navy's traditional daily tot of rum to each member of a crew. When Leonard Philbrook (6), the food provisioner aboard corvette HMCS *Sorel*, took the job of dispensing the rum, he suddenly became very popular.

Late that same week in August, on the twenty-fourth, sixty-one merchant ships left the port of Sydney, Cape Breton Island, as eastbound Convoy SC 41. Simultaneously, seven other merchant ships sailed from their Wabana berths on Bell Island to rendezvous with the Sydney convoy by September 1, just beyond Newfoundland's Strait of Belle Isle. By then, the escorting warships had corralled the merchant ships into a pre-arranged configuration of twelve columns with eight escorts—destroyer HMS *Ranpura* and seven RCN corvettes—forming a screen around the convoy. The rhythm of launching, organizing, and escorting such large convoys was commonplace at Sydney and Halifax by that time. Just days after SC 41 departed in early September, the Naval Control of Shipping Office at Sydney organized SC 42, consisting of sixty-seven more merchant ships and four escorts. SC 42 would follow the same course as SC 41, travelling northeast toward the Arctic Circle, just south of Greenland, and through the Denmark Strait to Britain.

On September 3, Adm Dönitz communicated new orders to KK Förster and *U501* to join an attack pack gathering south of Greenland. Dönitz hoped his U-boats could intercept an unsuspecting eastbound convoy before it reached the Western Approaches. The next day, *U501* encountered *Einvik*, a Norwegian steamer straggling behind Convoy SC 41. Förster torpedoed and sank it, but the radio operator aboard *Einvik* managed to dash off a distress signal. The Admiralty quickly diverted two other convoys—ON 12, heading west from the UK, and HX 148, heading east from Halifax—around the probable U-boat patrols in the North Atlantic.

But without realizing it, Convoy SC 42 was coursing northeast from Newfoundland straight into a waiting wolf pack. What had begun as a trio of U-boats, attempting unsuccessfully to track down a slow-moving convoy from Halifax, had grown. Then, on September 9, just east of Cape Farewell on the south coast of Greenland, Oberleutnant-zur-See (Oblt zS) Eberhard Greger and *U85* sighted funnel smoke on the horizon and closed on the sixty-seven ships of SC 42, all drawn up into twelve neatly organized columns of freighters and tankers. He fired a series of torpedoes, but none connected; then, following standard U-Bootwaffe procedure, he shadowed the convoy at a distance and communicated his discovery to the growing wolf pack, now numbering fifteen U-boats.

Evident from Eberhard Greger's failed attack was the relative inexperience among some of the latest members of Adm Dönitz's 2nd U-Boat Flotilla. This was Greger's first patrol in *U85*.[49] Likewise for Heinz-Otto Schultze aboard *U432* as well as Hans Ey and his crew aboard *U433*. Hans-Heinz Linder, commanding *U202*, would eventually complete six patrols (236 days at sea), but he was also early in his U-boat career. Friedrich Guggenberger would later famously sink the Royal Navy aircraft carrier HMS *Ark Royal* in the Mediterranean, but in September 1941 he too was new to patrolling. Similarly, Horst Uphoff, commanding *U84*, was on his first patrol. Fritz Meyer and *U207*, also on their first combat mission, would not survive it; they were sunk in the Denmark Strait on September 11. Heinrich Schuch and *U38* had sunk one ship in August 1941, but this was just their second patrol. And fresh from training, Heinz-Joachim Neumann and *U372* were on their first patrol, just like Förster and *U501*. Most were unproven in war, but they would learn the hard way—in battle.

Inexperience had been Cdr James Prentice's mortal enemy during his first year with the Royal Canadian Navy—not *his* inexperience, but that of his charges. In August 1941, as newly appointed senior officer, Canadian corvettes, with the Newfoundland Escort Force, Prentice had faced the greatest challenge of his navy career—taking a growing fleet of tiny corvettes intended for harbour patrol, manning them with inexperienced volunteers from across Canada, and transforming ships and crews into deep-sea sub-killers.

Their baptism of fire arrived during those early days of September 1941. In the darkness of early-morning September 5, Prentice's corvette, HMCS *Chambly*, and her sister ship, HMCS *Moose Jaw*, had just put to sea from St. John's. Never letting them stay long enough in port to get dry, Prentice had ordered *Chambly* and *Moose Jaw* into work-ups—practising convoy screening, U-boat detection, and assault tactics—off the coast of Newfoundland. Not one to sit and wait for trouble, but more likely to go find it, Prentice had decided to stage his advanced exercises farther out to sea, closer to the shipping lanes off Greenland where U-boats and convoys were likely to tangle. And if called upon for assistance, Prentice knew exactly what he'd do.

"When we get there, we'll not have to worry about the convoy," he told Edward Simmons, his first lieutenant onboard *Chambly*. "Our job will be to find the enemy and kill him."[50]

Cdr Prentice didn't know that the Canadian 24th Escort Group—destroyer HMCS *Skeena* and her Flower-class corvettes HMCS *Alberni*, *Kenogami*, and *Orillia*—escorting SC 42, were about to meet a growing wolf pack head on, near Cape Farewell, Greenland. Much like some of the novices on the German side, crews aboard the three Canadian corvettes escorting SC 42 were experiencing their first ocean convoy. NEF had tasked the four escorts to screen a convoy of twelve columns of freighters and tanker ships three miles wide and a mile and a quarter from front to back.[51] Suddenly, on the morning of September 9, Prentice received new orders from Cmdre Murray at NEF HQ in St. John's. He was to steam with all possible speed northeast to reinforce *Skeena* and the other warships escorting Convoy SC 42.

That night, the wolf pack struck. Just before midnight, *U432* approached the convoy along its port wing. Seas were moderate, and with skies clear, the moonlight made visibility on both sides almost as clear as day. At 12:46 a.m., *Skeena*'s LCdr James Hibbard got word that SS *Muneric*, a merchant ship in the first column, had been torpedoed. Then Hibbard's sister escort, corvette *Kenogami*, reported a U-boat sighting on the surface and opened fire.[52] But Hibbard faced the reality that his was the only warship fast enough to keep pace with any of the attacking U-boats. He knew he had to keep his three corvettes tightly screening the convoy and, where possible, picking up survivors, not chasing U-boats.

Radio silence was suddenly broken as merchant ships reported sightings of many U-boats from several locations within the convoy. Hibbard spotted distress rockets on the opposite side of the convoy. KK Georg-Werner Fraatz, commanding *U652* on just his second patrol, had fired a spread of torpedoes into the convoy's starboard quarter. Increasing his speed to eighteen knots to get to the scene of the latest attack, LCdr Hibbard deftly threaded *Skeena* back through the centre of the convoy. Instead of firing off starshells, which would have blinded warship and merchant crews alike, he turned on navigation lights to avoid colliding with any merchant ships.

Then a succession of explosions erupted. At 2:50 a.m., merchant steamship *Winterswijk* blew up. Four minutes later it was SS *Tahchee*'s turn, and then SS *Baron Pentland*—within 200 yards of *Skeena*. Hibbard suddenly had *U652* in his sights.

"It [was my intention] to ram the submarine inside the convoy," he wrote. "On completion of the turn, closed the position where the U-boat had been sighted, illuminated with starshell and dropped depth charges."[53]

In spite of Hibbard's success in overtaking his adversary, *U652* had successfully crash-dived to elude *Skeena*'s attack. And though KK Fraatz had managed to torpedo *Tahchee*, carrying 6,500 tons of fuel oil in her holds, the tanker stayed afloat. LCdr Ted Briggs, commander of the corvette *Orillia*, realized the importance of saving the tanker, her load, and her merchant sailors, so his crew secured a line to the burning ship to tow her to the nearest port in Iceland. Of course, that reduced the number of warships escorting the convoy to three. LCdr Hibbard legitimately feared he might lose the majority of Convoy SC 42. He received word that some relief escorts had set out from the Western Approaches, but they were forty-eight hours away. Then Hibbard's crew made a new sighting—the most welcome of the week—unexpected escorts approaching from the southwest.

Lookouts onboard HMCS *Chambly* reported to Cdr James Prentice that they'd spotted an arc of white distress rockets from SC 42 on the horizon. Prentice signalled Lt Frederick Grubb and HMCS *Moose Jaw* to a position on *Chambly*'s starboard beam, and together, just the way Prentice had practised, the two corvettes approached the convoy from its dark side so they might not be spotted, away from the moonlight. His hunch proved right. Six miles in front of

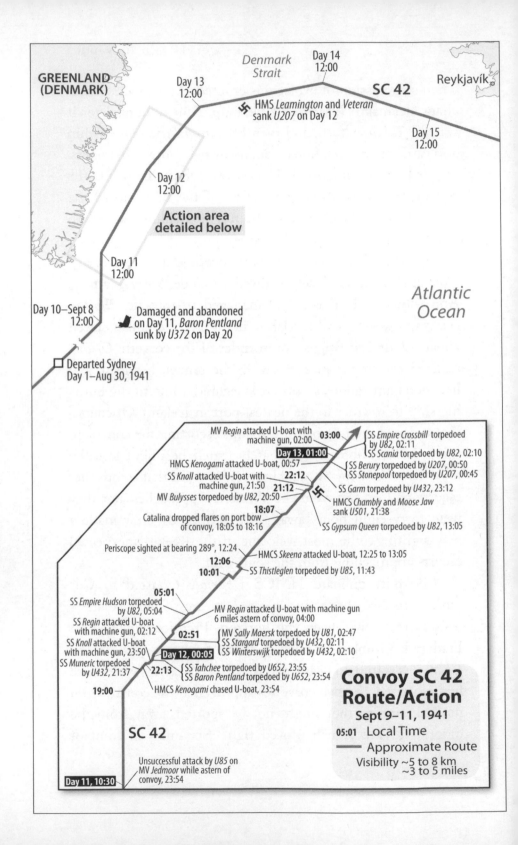

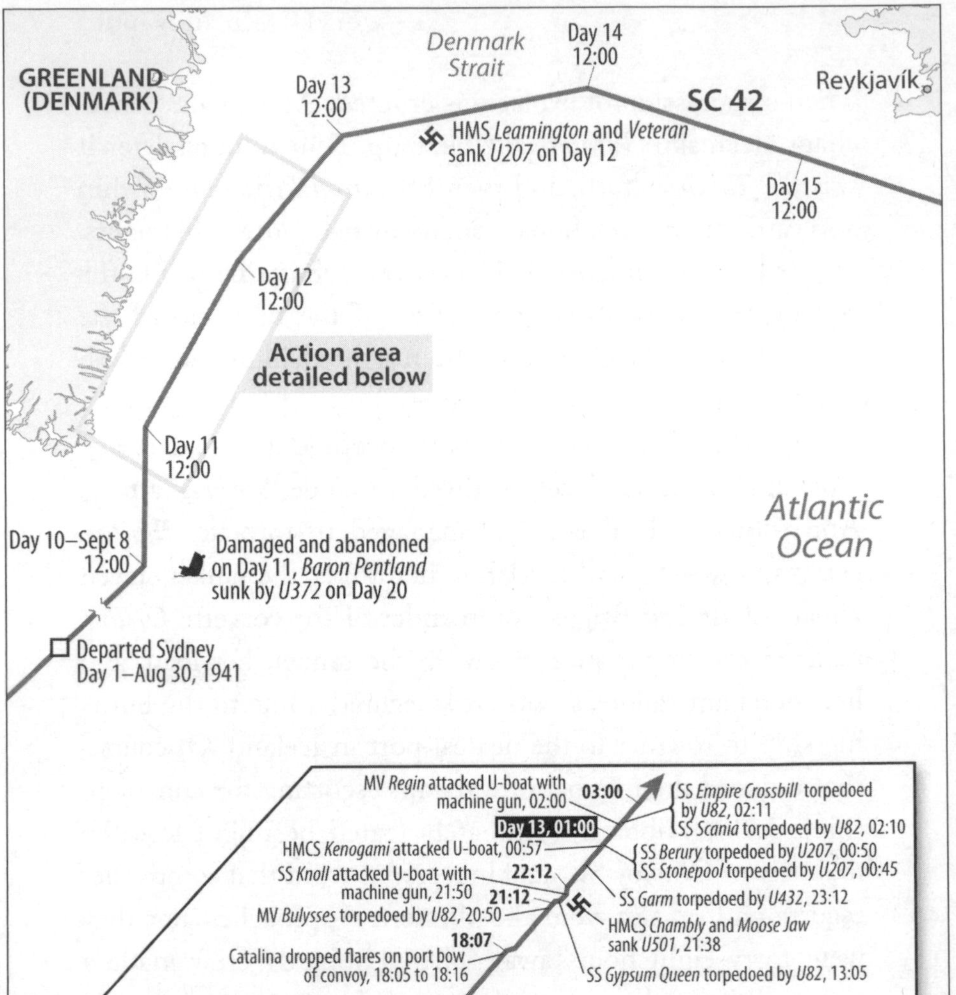

GREENLAND (DENMARK)
Denmark Strait
Day 14 12:00
Reykjavík
Day 13 12:00
SC 42
HMS *Leamington* and *Veteran* sank *U207* on Day 12
Day 15 12:00
Day 12 12:00
Action area detailed below
Day 11 12:00
Atlantic Ocean
Day 10–Sept 8 12:00
Damaged and abandoned on Day 11, *Baron Pentland* sunk by *U372* on Day 20
Departed Sydney Day 1–Aug 30, 1941
MV *Regin* attacked U-boat with machine gun, 02:00
03:00
SS *Empire Crossbill* torpedoed by *U82*, 02:11
SS *Scania* torpedoed by *U82*, 02:10
Day 13, 01:00
HMCS *Kenogami* attacked U-boat, 00:57
SS *Berury* torpedoed by *U207*, 00:50
SS *Stonepool* torpedoed by *U207*, 00:45
SS *Knoll* attacked U-boat with machine gun, 21:50
22:12
21:12
SS *Garm* torpedoed by *U432*, 23:12
MV *Bulysses* torpedoed by *U82*, 20:50
HMCS *Chambly* and *Moose Jaw* sank *U501*, 21:38
18:07
Catalina dropped flares on port bow of convoy, 18:05 to 18:16
SS *Gypsum Queen* torpedoed by *U82*, 13:05
Periscope sighted at bearing 289°, 12:24
HMCS *Skeena* attacked U-boat, 12:25 to 13:05
12:06
10:01
SS *Thistleglen* torpedoed by *U85*, 11:43
05:01
SS *Empire Hudson* torpedoed by *U82*, 05:04
MV *Regin* attacked U-boat with machine gun 6 miles astern of convoy, 04:00
SS *Regin* attacked U-boat with machine gun, 02:12
02:51
MV *Sally Maersk* torpedoed by *U81*, 02:47
SS *Stargard* torpedoed by *U432*, 02:11
SS *Winterswijk* torpedoed by *U432*, 02:10
SS *Knoll* attacked U-boat with machine gun, 23:50
Day 12, 00:05
SS *Muneric* torpedoed by *U432*, 21:37
22:13
SS *Tahchee* torpedoed by *U652*, 23:55
SS *Baron Pentland* torpedoed by *U652*, 23:54
19:00
HMCS *Kenogami* chased U-boat, 23:54
SC 42
Unsuccessful attack by *U85* on MV *Jedmoor* while astern of convoy, 23:54
Day 11, 10:30
Convoy SC 42 Route/Action
Sept 9–11, 1941
05:01 Local Time
Approximate Route
Visibility ~5 to 8 km ~3 to 5 miles

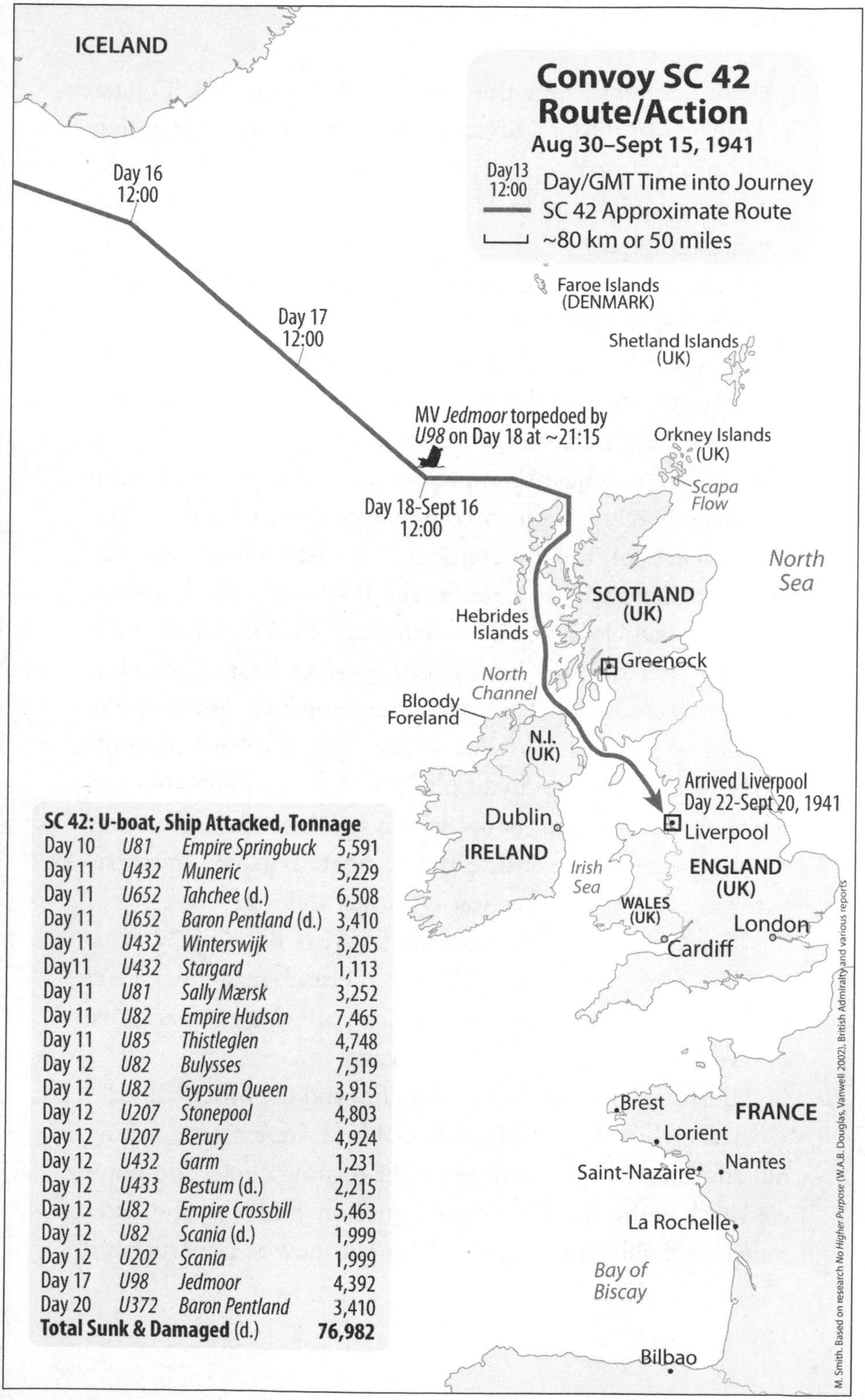

SC 42: U-boat, Ship Attacked, Tonnage

Day 10	*U81*	*Empire Springbuck*	5,591
Day 11	*U432*	*Muneric*	5,229
Day 11	*U652*	*Tahchee* (d.)	6,508
Day 11	*U652*	*Baron Pentland* (d.)	3,410
Day 11	*U432*	*Winterswijk*	3,205
Day11	*U432*	*Stargard*	1,113
Day 11	*U81*	*Sally Mærsk*	3,252
Day 11	*U82*	*Empire Hudson*	7,465
Day 11	*U85*	*Thistleglen*	4,748
Day 12	*U82*	*Bulysses*	7,519
Day 12	*U82*	*Gypsum Queen*	3,915
Day 12	*U207*	*Stonepool*	4,803
Day 12	*U207*	*Berury*	4,924
Day 12	*U432*	*Garm*	1,231
Day 12	*U433*	*Bestum* (d.)	2,215
Day 12	*U82*	*Empire Crossbill*	5,463
Day 12	*U82*	*Scania* (d.)	1,999
Day 12	*U202*	*Scania*	1,999
Day 17	*U98*	*Jedmoor*	4,392
Day 20	*U372*	*Baron Pentland*	3,410
Total Sunk & Damaged (d.)			**76,982**

Chambly, coming from the opposite direction, KK Förster jockeyed *U501* into an advantageous line of attack, running at full speed at periscope depth, just under the surface. It was just past midnight when *U501*'s engines and propeller noise became audible.

"Echo bearing 020 degrees," called out *Chambly*'s ASDIC operator. "Range 700 yards. Submarine contact."[54]

U501 and HMCS *Chambly* were closing rapidly, head-on on opposite courses. Prentice reduced *Chambly*'s speed. He knew the depth charges were set for over 100 feet, and it was too late to adjust them, so he called for an earlier drop of a five-charge pattern to compensate. But, because of the inexperience of the quarterdeck depth-charge crews, the firing was irregular; as a result, the first and second charges were dropped close together. Astern of *Chambly*, Lt Grubb abruptly altered *Moose Jaw*'s course to steer clear of the blast he knew was coming. The concussion struck *Chambly* aft like the kick of a wild horse. Worse for *U501*, the blast blew off the U-boat's stern port hydroplane outside the hull while also smashing her regulator tanks, which sent high-pressure water shooting everywhere inside the U-boat. Förster's inexperience gave him the impression *U501* was sinking.

"Surface! Surface!" he screamed. "We're flooding."

"We must go down to ninety metres," machinist Fritz Weinrich called out to his commander, offering an alternative to save the U-boat and possibly escape.

"Surface!" the captain called again, and the order "Blow!"[55]

Meanwhile, Lt Grubb altered *Moose Jaw*'s course, taking full advantage of his corvette's tight turning circle, and powered back in the direction of the explosion. Suddenly the water roiled and bubbled 400 yards off his port bow as *U501* surfaced and stopped dead. Grubb called for *Moose Jaw*'s four-inch gun to open fire and directed his corvette on a ramming course.

"I managed to go alongside the submarine . . . and called on her to surrender," Lt Grubb reported. "To my surprise, I saw a man make a magnificent leap from the submarine's deck into our waist [mid-part of the corvette], and the remainder of her crew move to do likewise. . . . The submarine altered across my bows and I rammed her."[56]

The U-boat officer who'd leapt onto *Moose Jaw*'s deck turned out to be KK Hugo Förster. But the drama wasn't over. Cdr Prentice, wanting to complete the capture, rushed *Chambly* astern of the U-boat, and at fifty yards, launched a skiff with an armed boarding party. First aboard *U501* was *Chambly* stoker William Brown, who ordered German crew, at gunpoint, to assist in preventing the U-boat from being scuttled.

"Herr Oberleutnant," machinist Weinrich called to engineer Schiemann, "the enemy are on board!"[57]

From *Moose Jaw* came backup troops. First Lt Edward Simmons mounted the conning tower to descend through the hatchway. His Mae West life jacket got caught on entry. It was too late. The U-boat crew, most of them having abandoned ship, had opened *U501*'s stern torpedo hatch to scuttle it, and water was rushing through the hull and now up through the hatchway. The U-boat lurched and began pulling everything and everyone down. Stoker Brown was nowhere to be found, and it was all Simmons could do to save himself.

"There was no sensation of being sucked under, just a hopeless feeling of not being able to last out," he said. "When I did reach the surface, I popped out like a champagne cork . . . I was alongside our lifeboat which had picked up our boys and some Germans."[58]

As quickly as the battle on the surface had begun, it ended. In minutes, *U501* was gone. KK Förster was a prisoner of war. Corvette crews aboard *Moose Jaw* and *Chambly* hauled aboard the remaining U-boat survivors. The Canadians managed to save thirty-five of *U501*'s officers and men from the sea, while William Brown and ten German U-boat sailors died when the submarine went down. The two corvettes' decks suddenly revealed an odd visual contradiction—U-boat and merchant navy sailors shivering and shipless, sharing the same space.

Over the next few days, Allied escorts and Coastal Command aircraft guided what was left of Convoy SC 42 to safer waters near their destination ports around the UK. By September 15, HMCS *Orillia* had towed the tanker *Tahchee* and her crew safely to Iceland; although LCdr Briggs took criticism for his decision to leave the convoy to salvage the tanker, ultimately he was awarded the Distinguished Service Cross for his actions.[59] The battle for Convoy SC 42 had taken its toll. Of the original sixty-seven ships, only forty-eight arrived in the UK safely. The Kriegsmarine wolf pack had sunk fifteen merchant ships and damaged several others. In the attack, more than 200 merchant sailors died in explosions and fires, or by drowning or exposure in Arctic waters. And more than 70,000 tons of cargo had gone down. The lost materials would have fed thousands of people, become countless war munitions, and built several ships.

The four-day ordeal at sea, meantime, had also nearly broken escort commander LCdr James Hibbard. The escorts of Convoy SC 42 had been outnumbered by Kriegsmarine U-boats, three and four to one. Despite the losses, however, the Canadians completed the operation, and *Skeena*'s captain received the highest praise from NEF Cmdre Leonard Murray.

"[Hibbard's] mental and physical stamina was sufficient to keep him alert and active from the first report of attack at 1004, 9th September, until . . . 0400, 12th September, a period of sixty-six hours [of] continuous battle," Murray reported.[60]

Lt Frederick Grubb admitted to feeling a certain discomfort that *Moose Jaw* was sailing with a crew numbering just forty-seven and his prisoners twenty-nine. Grubb wisely took the precaution of separating his POWs—locking Förster and his watch officers in the captain's cabin while putting the remaining German crewmen in aft cabins under guard. It didn't take long for *U501*'s crewmen to begin expressing their bitterness, blaming their captain for the loss of the U-boat and their imprisonment. On September 18, *Moose Jaw* tied up at Greenock in the Firth of Clyde. Armed guards escorted the German prisoners of war away; unlike the night of their capture, when KK Förster was the first to land on *Moose Jaw*'s decks, the Korvettenkapitän was last down the gangway and into custody.*

For Cdr James Prentice and his crew aboard *Chambly*, the encounter and engagement with *U501*, if nothing else, had proven his point: that Canadian corvette crews were much more than sheepdogs. What his orders had prescribed as a ten-day exercise, designed to introduce his corvette crews to the rigours of the North Atlantic, had overnight evolved into on-the-job training. Coincidence had played a role. So too had the inexperience of both his own crew and his adversary. But Prentice's patience and his direction to "find the enemy

* The consequences of KK Förster's controversial capture—as well as *U501*'s sudden surfacing and surrender—haunted him thereafter. As a POW in the UK, he was ostracized by fellow officers, and then returned to Germany in a prisoner exchange and faced court martial for cowardice in the face of the enemy. In February 1945, he committed suicide with a pistol smuggled into his cell.

and kill him" had yielded something the Royal Canadian Navy didn't have before that September night in 1941—its first corvette U-boat kill of the war. He was later awarded the Distinguished Service Order (DSO).[61]

Chapter Six

"BLOOD BROTHERS TO A CORK"

Despite Britain's "Dig for Victory" campaign to raise homegrown food, the Board of Trade's motto "Make Do and Mend," and the Ministry of Food's strict rationing programs, most Britons recognized their survival depended on merchant navy ships successfully running the gauntlet of U-boat attacks. Just about every consumable came from offshore. Thus, losses at sea altered British household habits for the duration of the Battle of the Atlantic. Every sunken tanker meant less heating oil and certainly empty pumps at petrol stations for civilian drivers across the UK. A reduced flow of iron ore, lumber, cotton, and chemicals translated to cutbacks at factories, fewer workdays, lost wages, and spartan budgets for homemakers. In just the first two years of the war, freighters lost at sea cut food imports in Britain to less than half their pre-war levels. And successful U-boat attacks in the North Atlantic choked off vital supplies of wheat from Canada, sugar from the Caribbean, maize from the United States, and meat from New Zealand.

When he served as First Lord of the Admiralty in 1939, Winston Churchill called rationing "folly." U-boat attacks on the Atlantic quickly changed his perspective. Initially the government rationed sugar, butter, ham, and bacon—eight ounces per person per week. Fresh imported fruit disappeared altogether. In July 1940, the British public sensed things had really gotten serious when tea became scarce. Rationing was no longer folly but a fact of life.[1]

John Birnie Dougall, one of the sailors working that vital ocean lifeline between North America and the UK, saw first-hand the value of his wartime service as well as the hardships that Britons faced trying to make do. While many Canadian merchant seamen completed their contracts when their freighters or tankers docked at a home port in Sydney, Halifax, or St. John's, Dougall always finished his trips in Britain. From 1939 through 1941, his tanker, *San Felix*, owned and operated by Eagle Oil and Shipping, finished each trans-atlantic circuit in Glasgow. That left the twenty-year-old Canadian waiting in the UK for his next trip, on the opposite side of the ocean from his hometown of Cornwall, Ontario. However, because his mother's sister Peg and his uncle James lived in Aberdeen, each time he finished a trip his Scottish family members welcomed him into their home.

"As usual, your son is being looked after by these good-natured aunts and uncles," Dougall wrote his mother in the spring of 1941. "[But] things are becoming harder to buy. Tinned foods are fast disappearing. . . . The fruit shops are now transformed into flower shops, and the tobacconists still have walking sticks [to sell]. With that spirit, they will likely pull through. But it is going to be a hard fight in more ways than one."[2]

By 1941, John Dougall had passed exams for his Certificate of Merit. He eagerly wrote to other shipping firms around the

UK in search of a promotion and a hike in pay—in his first and second years he'd received twenty shillings per month, in his third and fourth years forty shillings per month. When neither opportunity came, he did an additional transatlantic circuit aboard *San Felix*, transporting another load of bunker oil from Curaçao to Britain. Winter weather played havoc with his watch at the helm that trip, when he was tempted to "let the old ship prance about for a while, but a crooked wake shows lack of seamanship," he wrote.[3] That trip they practised action stations and gun drills, when Dougall had to stand a few feet from the gunner as he trained his sights, pressed the anti-aircraft gun trigger, and blasted an imaginary Focke-Wulf Condor bomber. Still, he loved the rhythm, the responsibility, and even the risk of it.

Another year at sea with Eagle Oil and Shipping brought more transatlantic crossings aboard *San Felix*. John had completed a further round of examinations for his Certificate of Merit with high marks. He desperately wanted an officer's position. Then his mother became ill and he managed to get leave to spend a short time with his family back in Canada. But his most recent trip had left a sour taste in his mouth. He'd grown tired of the tanker crewman's life. And worse, he'd recognized what seemed a disparity in the credit due his profession for ferrying a precious cargo that fuelled both the civilian and military wartime economies of Britain. The navy always seemed to steal the spotlight.

"The Forces take the credit," he wrote his mother, "while the mercantile marine, those men who carry the ammunition . . . get nothing."[4]

By the fall, Dougall had landed a position away from tankers, aboard a freighter working the North Atlantic run between North America and Britain. The steam merchant *Gretavale* regularly sailed from Glasgow for Andrew Crawford and Company, and the ship needed a third officer. Dougall applied, met with master of the ship Frank Passmore, and got the position.

In late 1941, while Dougall waited for his next trip, he stayed with his Scottish family and realized their situation had deteriorated. His aunt and uncle now made do with ration cards and whatever farm produce they could procure. But rationing took away "luxuries" such as flour, sugar, and even tea. Blackouts and air raids had grown more frequent, and the population in and around Aberdeen attended "fighting lectures," which organized defence of the city by neighbourhood, block, and even household.[5] In his letters home, Dougall offered his perspective on Allied progress in the war. But most often he applauded his aunts and uncles for their stoic resolve.

"It will be impossible to break the British spirit," he wrote his mother, "and though it may take many years, we shall prevail."[6]

In November 1941, John Dougall's good luck as a merchant seaman ran out. His new ship, *Gretavale*, steamed from Sydney, Nova Scotia, to join Convoy SC 52, consisting of thirty-three other merchant vessels and three escorting corvettes bound for Loch Ewe, Scotland. *Gretavale* was fully loaded with 6,700 tons of steel and seventeen trucks for the war effort. Aboard were five Royal Navy gunners and a crew of forty-two. Just before dawn on November 3, the ship passed Notre Dame Bay, on the coast of Newfoundland, where she entered the sights of *U202*, on only her third North Atlantic patrol; Kptlt Hans-Heinz Linder had few victories to show for his patrols, so he and his crew were hungry. *U202* fired a spread of three torpedoes that exploded into *Gretavale*'s cargo holds. With such a dense cargo of steel and air space above it in her holds, the sea rapidly flooded the holds and the ship sank in minutes, taking the five gunners and thirty-seven crew with her, including John Birnie Dougall, serving on just his first official crossing as Third Officer.

"If I should go down, don't you fret," he had written his mother, just in case, "for I shall be angry either above or below. After all, the sea is my life and likely always will be. And if I have to be splashing about in it, it is the way I would want to go, always living with the spirit of the sea—restless.

"Now that I have that off my chest . . . Cheerio till you hear from me again. Yours . . . J. Dougall."[7]

The irony of Convoy SC 52—which was probably never explained to John Dougall's grief-stricken mother, Rachel—was that the British Admiralty might have saved her son's ship. Even as the convoy departed Sydney, Allied intelligence strongly indicated that its course would lead it into a concentration of U-boats off Newfoundland. First, Admiralty redirected the merchant ships north. But because it feared another SC 42 debacle if the new convoy sailed through the Denmark Strait, Admiralty decision-makers recalled SC 52 back to Sydney. It was then, during the dispersion of the convoy through the Strait of Belle Isle, that four merchant ships were torpedoed, including *Gretavale*, while another two ran aground in fog. SC 52 was the only convoy of the war to fully retreat from the threat of a wolf pack attack.

✪ ✪ ✪

THE loss of *Gretavale* and the retreat of Convoy SC 52 to Sydney revealed all that was inadequate about Allied convoy defence in the western Atlantic. First, the agreement reached between Roosevelt and Churchill at Argentia in August 1941 meant that US Navy destroyers would henceforth escort fast convoys (the HX and ON series) between Newfoundland and the Mid-Ocean Meeting Point (MOMP) south of Iceland, where convoys were handed off to the Western Approaches escorts. Second, by process of elimination, that left the Royal Canadian Navy to escort the slow convoys (the SC and ONS series). And statistics reflected what Canadian crews knew first-hand—that ships in slow convoys were 30 percent more likely to be torpedoed. Finally, the Anglo-American agreement dictated that all operations in the northwest Atlantic would be controlled by a USN admiral at Argentia. Despite all these changes, Canada had no say. In effect, Canada, a belligerent state, now came under operational command of the United States, a neutral state.

Through the fall of 1941, however, conditions at sea and in Washington began to blur that American neutrality. On September 4, the USN announced that *U652* had fired two torpedoes at the destroyer USS *Greer* off the coast of Iceland. Nazi propagandists claimed the U-boat was attacked by depth charges in a German blockade zone. The truth was somewhere in between. During his "fireside chat" broadcast on September 11, President Roosevelt made clear his intention to help the Allies crush Hitler. The president delineated a US security zone in Atlantic waters west of Iceland, explaining the US position as "self defense surrounding outposts of American protection in the Atlantic."[8] Roosevelt denounced the attack on *Greer* as "piracy" and threatened the Axis powers. "From now on, if German or Italian vessels of war enter the waters, the protection of which is necessary for American defense, they do so at their own peril."

To make his point, the president assigned forty-eight destroyers to escort and protect convoys across the US security zone. The fireworks increased soon after. In mid-October, USS *Kearny* responded to distress calls from an eastbound slow convoy. U-boats had already sunk nine merchant ships over three days and nights. When *Kearny* joined the escort, she was torpedoed by *U568* but not sunk, just managing to stay afloat and reach Iceland. USN casualties rose dramatically two weeks later.

Kptlt Erich Topp, beginning his sixth war patrol in command of *U552*, joined a wolf pack shadowing fast convoy HX 156 east of the Grand Banks off Newfoundland. In response to a strong direction-finding bearing, the destroyer USS *Reuben James* moved to a screening position off the port beam of the convoy of forty-two ships, and subsequently took two of *U552*'s torpedoes in her port side. The resulting explosion in *Reuben James*'s forward magazine ripped the ship aft to her fourth funnel and sent her to the bottom within five minutes.[9] Of the ship's company of 160, only forty-five survived. There was no question about this attack. A Kriegsmarine U-boat had sunk a USN warship. But neither Roosevelt nor Hitler blinked. Days later, the US Congress voted to revise the Neutrality Act, but strong America First Committee forces continued to keep Congress from declaring war against Germany.

Meanwhile, Allied strategists called upon the Royal Canadian Navy to pick up the slack in the western Atlantic. The British and Americans asked the Canadians what size warship force they could provide. Ottawa's reply: thirteen destroyers (a third of which would always be out of action for refit and repairs) and twenty-five corvettes (with as many as half away for refit or repairs). The pressure shunted down the line. The system desperately needed the last twenty of the original sixty-four corvettes (under construction in Canadian shipyards) commissioned and ordered into immediate front-line operations.[10]

At the same time, the Newfoundland Escort Force needed more and better anti-submarine warfare equipment, which was never available. Capt Eric Stevens, a Royal Navy destroyer captain with the NEF in St. John's, considered the anti-submarine warfare equipment available to the NEF "a beggar's portion." "At present," he added, "most escorts are equipped with one weapon of approximate precision—the ram."[11]

The Admiralty appeared to complicate the process in the fall of 1941 by enlarging and doubling the frequency of slow convoys. The British also began routing convoys farther north to avoid U-boat contact. Those routes added distance to the transit and increased escort service time at sea, which meant additional strain on ships, fuel supplies, and crew performance. At the same time, as some British escorts were diverted to more southerly routes across the Atlantic, the USN and RCN escorts compensated and found themselves travelling farther east than Iceland. In October 1941, NEF corvettes were averaging twenty-eight out of every thirty-one days at sea.[12]

The first NEF assignment for HMCS *Pictou* typified the challenges Canada's sheepdog navy faced that fall. In the captain's cabin aboard the Flower-class corvette, commissioned just six months earlier, sat twenty-nine-year-old

Lt Anthony Griffin, anticipating the day. *Pictou* was his first command, her crew the ship's first complement. Positioned on the bridge, with the eyes of the ship's company on him, Lt Griffin felt apprehensive.

"This is the blind leading the blind," he thought, but then dismissed it as a salutary reminder of human limitation.[13]

Mindful that just weeks had passed since the debacle of SC 42, and attentive to the orders of NEF's senior escort commander, James Prentice, Griffin took *Pictou* to sea. Initially they screened the port side of Convoy SC 48. Griffin watched an old Greek tramp steamer next to *Pictou* lurch and creak through the water, seemingly bending amidships from the thousands of tons of cargo in her holds. Suddenly Western Approaches Command diverted *Pictou* to the sinking of the steam freighter *Vancouver Island*. But by the time the corvette reached the spot, there was no ship, no debris, nor any of the sixty-five crew, eight gunners, and thirty-two passengers to be found. By the time *Pictou* rejoined SC 48, six more ships had been torpedoed. Starshells burst, rockets arced, and merchantmen were sinking at every turn.

Amid the confusion around them, *Pictou*'s navigator, next to Lt Griffin, suddenly pointed from the bridge. "Do you see what I see?"

Off *Pictou*'s port bow they spotted broken water.

"Strong hydrophone effect," reported the ASDIC operator.

Then a full U-boat sighting ahead of them. Griffin called "Full ahead . . . Open fire" to the crew of the corvette's four-inch gun, which had no night-sighting equipment.

"Am chasing U-boat on surface," the commander had his radio operator transmit by Morse code as he warned those on the bridge a torpedo attack was likely. And instantly he saw a long, bubbling wake as a torpedo passed just fifteen feet off *Pictou*'s port side.

Pictou was closing on the U-boat as she cut starboard in a crash dive. "Stand by to ram," Griffin called. Then he ordered a full pattern of depth charges. He circled *Pictou* as tightly as he could and raced over the same water turbulence, releasing all remaining depth charges with throwers and off the corvette's stern. When the water settled from the explosions, a search revealed no debris or evidence of a kill. And because *Pictou* remained at sea, continuing her search for survivors of SC 48 sinkings, well beyond her patrol time, the corvette didn't return to St. John's until she was nearly out of fuel. In the meantime, WAC had transmitted an all-points signal asking, "Is anything known of whereabouts of *Pictou*?"

Anthony Griffin considered his first combat operation successful. His command was confirmed. His superiors recognized his actions with a Mentioned in Dispatches award. But he seemed haunted by the one that got away. "Without the U-boat being sunk, there were no awards possible for my crew," he wrote. "My failure actually to sink this U-boat was a great disappointment. Later in the war, I often reconstructed the circumstances in the context of greater experience, equipment, and training."

EQUIPMENT and training were things that Lorne Elley and his older brother Norm took seriously from the moment the war broke out. Just sixteen and nineteen, respectively, in 1939, the Elley boys took to the woods with some friends near their home in Beamsville, Ontario. They started a bonfire and heaved a box of ammunition onto the flames. This, they figured, would test their mettle should they ever be thrown into the front lines of an infantry battlefield. When bullets whizzed by their hiding places with an alarming racket and speed, both Lorne and Norm made up their minds to join the navy instead. By the time Norm had qualified as an ASDIC operator, the Bangor-class minesweeper HMCS *Red Deer* needed one, so the RCN posted him aboard. *Red Deer* served with the NEF in the defence of the harbours at Halifax, Sydney, and St. John's.

Just as with Lt Griffin aboard *Pictou*, AB Elley's commander was right out of the Naval Academy and suddenly on the bridge of a warship, forced to learn on the job. Often it was more obvious than the crew cared to admit. On a refit and resupply trip into the naval yard on the island of Bermuda, for example, Elley said the serpentine nature of the harbour's entrance tested his captain's piloting skills. On the first corner, *Red Deer* came in too quickly and bounced off a ship moored on the bend. The same thing happened on the second turn.

"On the third bend," Elley told his daughter, "*Red Deer* hit another ship and the force of the collision resulted in depth charges falling off the stern. They weren't set, so no harm done. [But] from then on, when the Bermuda harbour master saw HMCS *Red Deer* approaching, he sent out a pilot to guide them in."[14]

Unlike *Red Deer*'s novice commander, RCN telegraphist Gordon Baines readily admitted his shortcomings, and he spent as much time riding a classroom chair as he did the North Atlantic. Once he'd completed basic telegraphy instruction ashore in Halifax at HMCS *Stadacona* in 1940, and then advanced to signal school in 1941, he'd joined his first crew as a qualified telegraphist aboard HMCS *Amherst*. Attached to the NEF, the Canadian-built corvette escorted from St. John's out to the MOMP and back. Whenever *Amherst* went into drydock for refit or repair, Baines readily upgraded his skills, taking anti-submarine and radar training.

At sea, sufficient training wasn't the immediate problem; under fire, men who'd been task-oriented ashore—railwaymen, farmers, lumberjacks, labourers, and students—tended to learn quickly. The greater liabilities were outdated equipment and weapons. Most early corvettes went to war with obsolete instruments—no radar, no gyro compass, only primitive Type 123 ASDIC submarine detection devices. Corvettes were generally under-gunned, with a four-inch naval gun (some dating back to 1916), two machine guns, and depth charges as their principal anti-submarine weapons. Even communication between escorts and merchant ships was rudimentary. If escorts used key-operated wireless, their Morse code messages could be detected by U-boats. That left escorts contacting each other and their merchant convoys via signal lights, semaphore flags, and even megaphones.*

Like telegraphist Baines, Lt Louis Audette had crammed in as much training ashore as he could. After surviving the torpedoing of HMCS *Saguenay* in 1940, Audette had taken additional instruction in gunnery and navigation. In 1942 he became *Amherst*'s commanding officer.† But it wasn't enough just to build strong esprit de corps onboard his warship. Each

* By 1943, Allied navies had introduced a secret communications weapon in escorting warships. "Talk Between Ships" radios allowed radio operators to transmit/receive quick verbal messages in the heat of battle, on which U-boat wireless could not direction-find.

† The day Louis Audette arrived in St. John's to take command of HMCS *Amherst*, he learned the entire crew had mutinied against then commanding officer Lt Harry Denyer, who had not appeared on the bridge at all on the previous escort. Denyer was removed by force as Audette took command.

trip, he had to scrounge even basic instruments and expect the unexpected. During one nighttime escort, the gun crew aboard an American defensively equipped merchant ship (DEMS) mistook *Amherst* for a U-boat and opened fire. Lt Audette had to improvise.

"Instead of signalling to him [and breaking radio silence]," Audette said, "I made a wild lunge for the signal lamp, and ran the light up and down the side of the ship. Finally, the firing stopped, [but] for a few seconds the whole ship was illuminated."[15]

Identification was vital intelligence. It had to be instantaneous. Was a ship friend or foe? Was an ASDIC contact a real U-boat, a school of fish, a temperature layer in the sea, or a decoy? Was surface turbulence just the movement of sea mammals or a torpedo? During an inbound convoy in 1942, Lt Audette arrived on the bridge at 8 a.m. Within minutes, a lookout atop *Amherst*'s crow's nest called out a U-boat sighting. Nobody on the bridge could see it. Suppressing his acute acrophobia, the commanding officer climbed the mast himself to verify the call. He sat on the rung below the lookout, wrapped one arm around the mast, holding on for dear life, and peered through his binoculars. Sure enough, a U-boat was prowling on the surface dead ahead. Audette had no compass to give a course, so again he improvised.

"A bit to port," he called down to the bridge, conning his corvette toward the U-boat. Then he directed fire at the enemy boat, if only to force it to crash-dive, depriving the enemy of any direct visual contact with the convoy.

Of course, throughout the exchange, the corvette rolled back and forth on the sea's surface. Far up the mast, Audette felt every crest and trough with even greater severity.

"Oh sir, I'll get out and you get in," the lookout said, offering the crow's nest to his commanding officer.

Audette thanked his young lookout and admitted later, "If I'd ever gotten into that crow's nest, they'd have found my mouldering body there at the end of the war, because I'd never have had the guts to get out at that height."[16]

Another skill that AB Baines brought aboard HMCS *Amherst* was his photography hobby. While the navy discouraged taking personal pictures, Baines's position in the radio shack gave him a unique perspective. So, when he was off watch, he took photos of escort life. He shot images of torpedoed merchant ships, survivors being hauled aboard, depth charges exploding, ice floes at sea, and ice buildup on deck. But the sea and the sky, especially when they showed their temper, seemed to dominate Baines's photo collection. There were passing squalls, roiling seas, winds that tore away anything left unsecured, and waves he called "green ones," which cascaded over *Amherst*'s short fo'c'sle as if taking his ship under forever. No doubt such experiences gave rise to corvettes being referred to as "semi-submersibles."[17]

That fall and winter of 1941, as *Amherst* and her sister corvettes completed each of their gruelling escorts from St. John's to Iceland and back, they faced an opponent that was, at times, more wicked than any mortal enemy. While trying to fend off or destroy their U-boat adversaries, escort crews had to contend with North Atlantic gales. All sailors who'd witnessed their force—engulfing great ships, crumpling steel bulkheads, or carrying away men and gear with a single breaker—never took their fury lightly.

One such storm nearly swallowed up a Canadian destroyer and her escorts in December 1941. Sailing south from Iceland to pick up Convoy ON 44, outbound from the Western Approaches, HMCS *Restigouche* and her company soon faced a developing snowstorm that obscured their path and masked their convoy. With no radar, the corvettes were sailing blind. Using her superior speed, *Restigouche* surged ahead to where she expected the convoy to be, but found nothing. Eventually the escorts spread out in a line abreast, about a mile apart, and crawled into the nighttime storm.

By midnight on December 13, winds had accelerated to over a hundred miles per hour. The barometer dropped steadily. The escort group abandoned the search for the convoy and "hove to" for two days, each escort doing her best to ride out the hurricane. Aboard the corvettes they doubled the watches, one officer sheltering behind the ASDIC house momentarily, then relieving another crouched behind the canvas bridge dodger. Snow, sleet, and spray flew horizontally across their vantage point. One man's call to another was drowned out by winds that shrieked to the pain threshold.

The notorious liveliness of the escorting corvettes, while uncomfortable for crews below decks, proved to be their saving grace. Leslie McLean, an engine room artificer aboard the corvette HMCS *Port Arthur*, captured the essence of the corvette experience surviving gales on the open North Atlantic. "We were blood brothers to a cork, when it came to riding out a rough sea," he said.[18]

The destroyer experience was completely unlike the bone-rattling liveliness afforded by the corvettes' buoyancy. The long, narrow hull of *Restigouche* slashed through the rough seas all right, but she paid a price. What the watches could see of the path ahead appeared as mountains towering over their ship. Nobody dared guess their height and weight.

And for the moments spent in each climb, the rising wave blotted out the rest of the world. Then, going over the top, they faced the full force of the gale, every part of the descent exposing the ship to thunderous winds until the bow plunged into the hollow of the trough and somehow, miraculously, rose to begin the climb again. Anything small or breakable was swept away or torn to shreds.

Commanding officer Lt Desmond Piers remembered the eerie squeal of *Restigouche*'s siren wires. "On each side of the funnel there are siren wires, operated from the bridge," he wrote. "These shrouds caught both of the steam sirens and they both went off at the same time with the most devilish sound you've ever heard, with the howling of the wind and both of these sirens going madly out of tune, and shrieking."[19]

Late on the second day of the gale, *Restigouche* was in peril. The power of the winds had knocked the ship's mast down onto her fore-funnel, and the pounding of the sea had damaged rudder gear so badly that the crew resorted to alternating starboard and port propellers to navigate. Depth charges and lashings had long since gone, and with her main mast down, so too the wireless. Lt Piers continued to receive damage reports of the most unsettling kind.

"The next report was, 'Captain, we're sorry to tell you, but there's some ugly noises underneath the fo'c'sle mess deck. The ammunition cases are rattling around,'" Piers said. "And they took the lid off the ammunition [magazine] up forward and found it was flooded. The pounding of the seas had pushed the [hull] rivets in and there it was filling up with water [to a depth of seven feet]."[20]

The Admiralty recognized the futility of maintaining the convoy and dispersed it, relieving the escorts of further responsibility. *Restigouche* turned eastward to save herself, and four days she later crawled into Greenock, Scotland. The escorting corvettes finally found some of the convoy and punched on through the storm, but by then their main concern was just surviving the weather.

As horrid as the December elements seemed between Iceland and Scotland, there was a corner of the Battle of the Atlantic where convoys and U-boats both faced winter weather almost year-round. In mid-1941, the vagaries of the British Commonwealth's alliance with the Soviet Union suddenly had Allied military and merchant navy sailors exchanging tales of convoy work north of the seventieth parallel, into the Barents Sea. Serving on an Arctic convoy—also known as the Murmansk Run—presented an entirely new set of challenges for the war's combatants: from gales that registered beyond barometer extremes to green ones that towered over ships like Goliaths, to pack ice and ice floes that reached south like murderous tentacles into shipping lanes, to cold that tested the endurance of even the most hardened seafarers.

Since 1939, a pact between Joseph Stalin, the secretary general of the Soviet Union, and Adolf Hitler had decreed non-aggression by both nations. But in the early hours of June 22, 1941, Hitler's Operation Barbarossa, the invasion of Russia, left Stalin's forces in disarray. By day's end, the Luftwaffe had claimed destruction of 400 Russian aircraft in the air and another 800 on the ground. Within a week, the Germans had advanced fifty miles inside Russia and captured 2,500 tanks and 1,500 pieces of artillery.

Before Barbarossa was even twenty-four hours old,

and despite his strong opposition to communism, Winston Churchill pledged his full support to the Soviets. "The Russian danger is our danger," he announced on the BBC on June 22. "We shall give whatever help we can."[21]

Later that summer, even as the German armies were moving to within 100 miles of Moscow, Churchill asked his minister of aircraft production, Lord Beaverbrook, to travel with US emissary Averell Harriman to Moscow. Beaverbrook, a.k.a. Max Aitken, a former Canadian newspaper magnate, would personally deliver Britain's promise to support Stalin with "all we could spare and dare."[22] The challenge became delivering on that promise. The quickest, most efficient way to provide a lifeline to Russia proved to be the sea route, up and around Norway's North Cape (occupied by German forces) and through the Barents Sea to the Soviet ports of Murmansk and Archangel.

In theory, the route required a sea voyage of about 2,300 miles. In practice, each Arctic convoy potentially had to fight its way past occupied Norway—teeming with fully operational Luftwaffe bases and fjords full of Kriegsmarine U-boats and surface raiders—to reach the Soviet ports. Remarkably, of the forty-one convoys that left either Loch Ewe, Scotland, or Reykjavík, Iceland, for Russia, between 1941 and 1945, thirty completed the trip without loss to enemy action. Of the thirty-four homebound convoys, twenty-four made it without loss.[23]

Among the exceptions, Convoy PQ 17 departed Hvalfjord, Iceland, on June 27, 1942, with an assembly of thirty-seven merchant ships destined for Archangel in the White Sea. Its escort force consisted of trawlers, sweepers, corvettes, destroyers, subs, and anti-aircraft ships, about a dozen warships in all. Four days later, on July 1, as the convoy approached Bear Island in the Barents Sea, Luftwaffe bombers intercepted the convoy and attacked. Confusion reigned back at the Admiralty, while Bletchley Park could not confirm whether *Tirpitz*, sister battleship to *Bismarck*, had left her fjord to engage the convoy or not. Fearing the worst, Cdr Norman Denning at the Admiralty's Operational Intelligence Centre recalled RN destroyers and ordered the convoy to disperse.

When PQ 17's slow-moving merchant freighters and tankers scattered in thirty-five different directions, undoing any value that solidarity might provide, it doomed them all. Most were quickly overtaken and at the mercy of Luftwaffe and U-boat attackers. Of the thirty-seven ships that had sailed from Iceland, two returned to Reykjavík, eight were sunk by air attacks, and nine by U-boats. Seven more were torpedoed by U-boats after air bombings. Only eleven reached Archangel. One hundred and fifty-three merchant seamen died in the sinkings or from exposure in life rafts to Arctic conditions. The munitions lost included 430 tanks, 210 crated aircraft, 3,350 vehicles, and nearly 100,000 tons of cargo.[24]

The impact was immediate. The Germans had launched a summer offensive at the southern end of the Eastern Front; the Red Army was desperately short of resupply, and in two weeks it was pushed back in that sector. "This is the biggest success ever achieved against the enemy with one blow," claimed the German Naval War Staff diary.[25]

The human enemy was deadly enough, but around every Russian convoy lurked the worst natural elements the top of the world could deliver. Above the Arctic Circle, storms grew so powerful they drove merchant ships into each other. In the cold temperatures, welds could become brittle and fail, and hulls could crack and leak. Ice lurked everywhere, every day, and in every possible way. Arctic pack ice either crept southward into shipping lanes in the winter months and retreated north only briefly in summer. It never went away completely. And even if it melted, polar ice often calved icebergs or floes, making navigation unpredictable and treacherous. Attempting to evade a U-boat up an ice-lead—an apparent break in the ice—could take ships to a dead end. Just as easily, the ice could freeze up behind, stranding ships and damaging their machinery. If they could, most convoys stayed thirty to forty miles clear of pack ice.[26]

The ice that accumulated on ships from falling snow, hail, freezing rain, or sea spray posed an additional problem. Since the air temperatures rarely exceeded the freezing mark, whatever began in the air as precipitation generally froze on contact with decks, gun mounts, lifeboats, masts, and guy wires. The minute ice began to accumulate on a ship's surface, crews were dispatched with picks, ice clubs, and steam hoses to clear it away; their work was as vital to a ship's survival as gunners, depth-charge teams, ASDIC operators, or lookouts. Ice buildup on any part of a ship's superstructure could make it top-heavy and liable to lose stability. In March 1942, heavy sea ice formed on the superstructure of the Allied armed trawler escort HMS *Shera* in a Russia-bound convoy; the vessel was lost when she capsized from the burden of ice on her upperworks.

Oddly, RCNVR telegraphist Howard Hazzard learned to welcome the wild weather conditions. Forced from school after his father died in 1933, Howard had worked as a machinist's apprentice at Massey-Harris in Brantford, Ontario. When the war broke out, he'd joined the Royal Canadian Naval Volunteer Reserve and quickly earned his telegraphist certificate at HMCS *St. Hyacinthe*. On his way overseas, he'd served in the radio room of RMS *Queen Mary*; then, on operations, he joined the wireless staff aboard HMCS *Huron* in time for the escort of Convoy JW 55B to Russia. Immediately out of Loch Ewe, the Tribal-class destroyer ploughed into a typical gale.

"*Huron* had difficulty if we had to turn," Hazzard said. "The ship would go into a trough and nose into the water. Then, on the crest when the propellers came out of the water, the ship would shake all to hell. It went on for a day and a half."[27]

Hazzard considered Arctic waters the worst piece of sea in the world, with waves in a tempest easily rising to sixty feet. If there was a saving grace to these gruesome conditions, it was that U-boat torpedoes didn't function very well in rough seas. "We welcomed the stormy weather," he said. "It meant we were safer."

Not because they wanted to but because they were needed, the RCN's Tribal-class destroyers reinforced the first outward-bound convoy of the winter cycle, JW 54A, in November 1943. HMCS *Huron*, *Iroquois*, and *Haida* joined eight RN destroyers and four cruisers in the escort of eighteen merchant ships to Kola Inlet. And even though the Kriegsmarine's B-Dienst monitoring service detected the flotilla, the Arctic convoy arrived without mishap.

The following month, the three Tribals repeated the Murmansk Run, escorting JW 55B. But this time Adm Dönitz deployed the German battle cruiser *Scharnhorst* to intercept the convoy. Over 700 feet long, capable of speeds of thirty-one knots, and armed with (among others) nine eleven-inch naval guns, *Scharnhorst* could pounce virtually unmatched from her berth along the Norwegian coast. The day after Christmas 1943, the massive battle cruiser came within thirty miles of

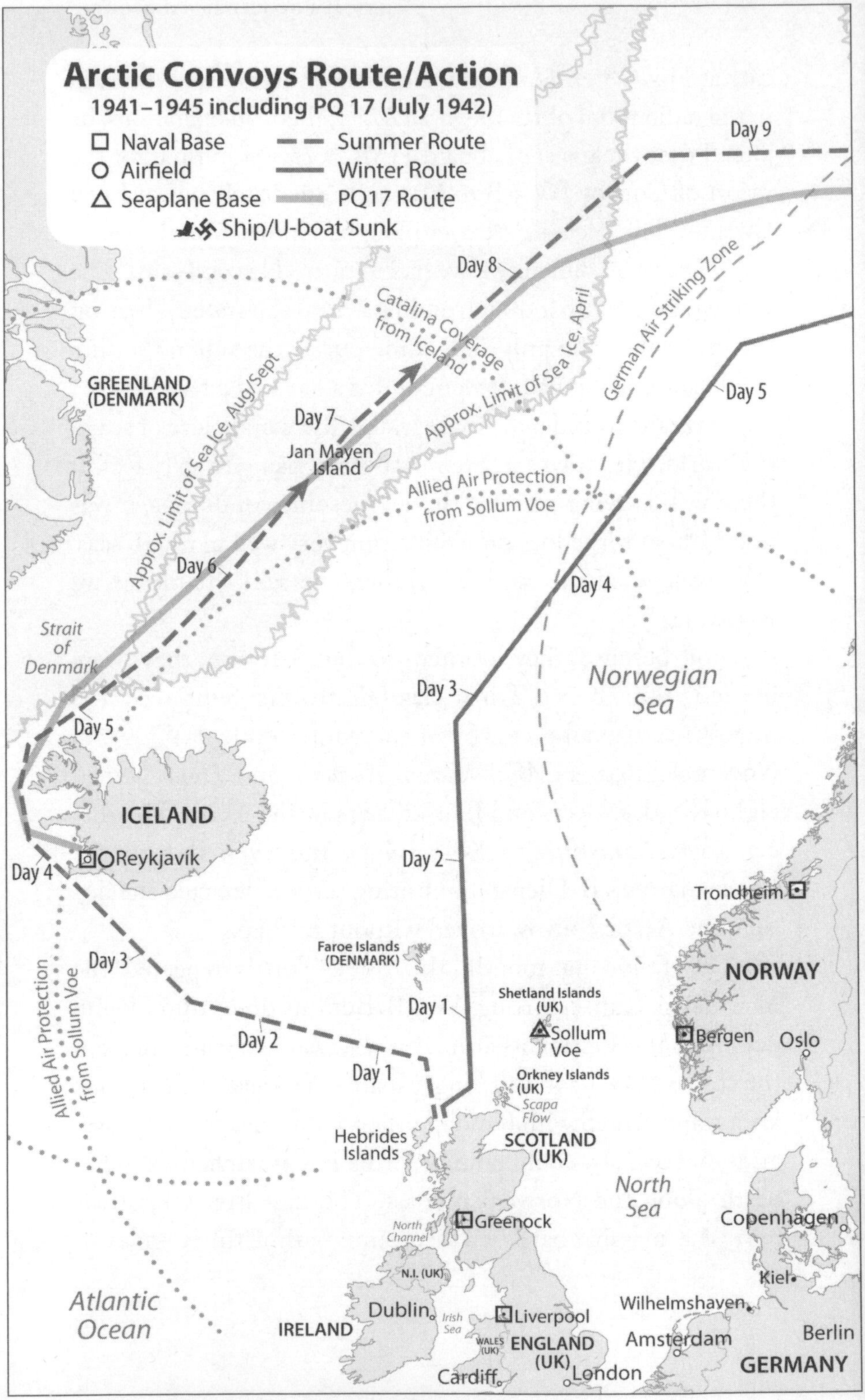

Arctic Convoys Route/Action
1941–1945 including PQ 17 (July 1942)
Naval Base
Airfield
Seaplane Base
Summer Route
Winter Route
PQ17 Route
Ship/U-boat Sunk
GREENLAND (DENMARK)
Approx. Limit of Sea Ice, Aug/Sept
Catalina Coverage from Iceland
Approx. Limit of Sea Ice, April
German Air Striking Zone
Allied Air Protection from Sollum Voe
Jan Mayen Island
Strait of Denmark
ICELAND
Reykjavík
Norwegian Sea
Faroe Islands (DENMARK)
Shetland Islands (UK)
Sollum Voe
Orkney Islands (UK)
Scapa Flow
Hebrides Islands
SCOTLAND (UK)
North Sea
NORWAY
Trondheim
Bergen
Oslo
Copenhagen
Kiel
Wilhelmshaven
Amsterdam
Berlin
GERMANY
Greenock
North Channel
N.I. (UK)
Dublin
Irish Sea
IRELAND
Liverpool
WALES (UK)
ENGLAND (UK)
Cardiff
London
Atlantic Ocean
Day 1
Day 2
Day 3
Day 4
Day 5
Day 6
Day 7
Day 8
Day 9

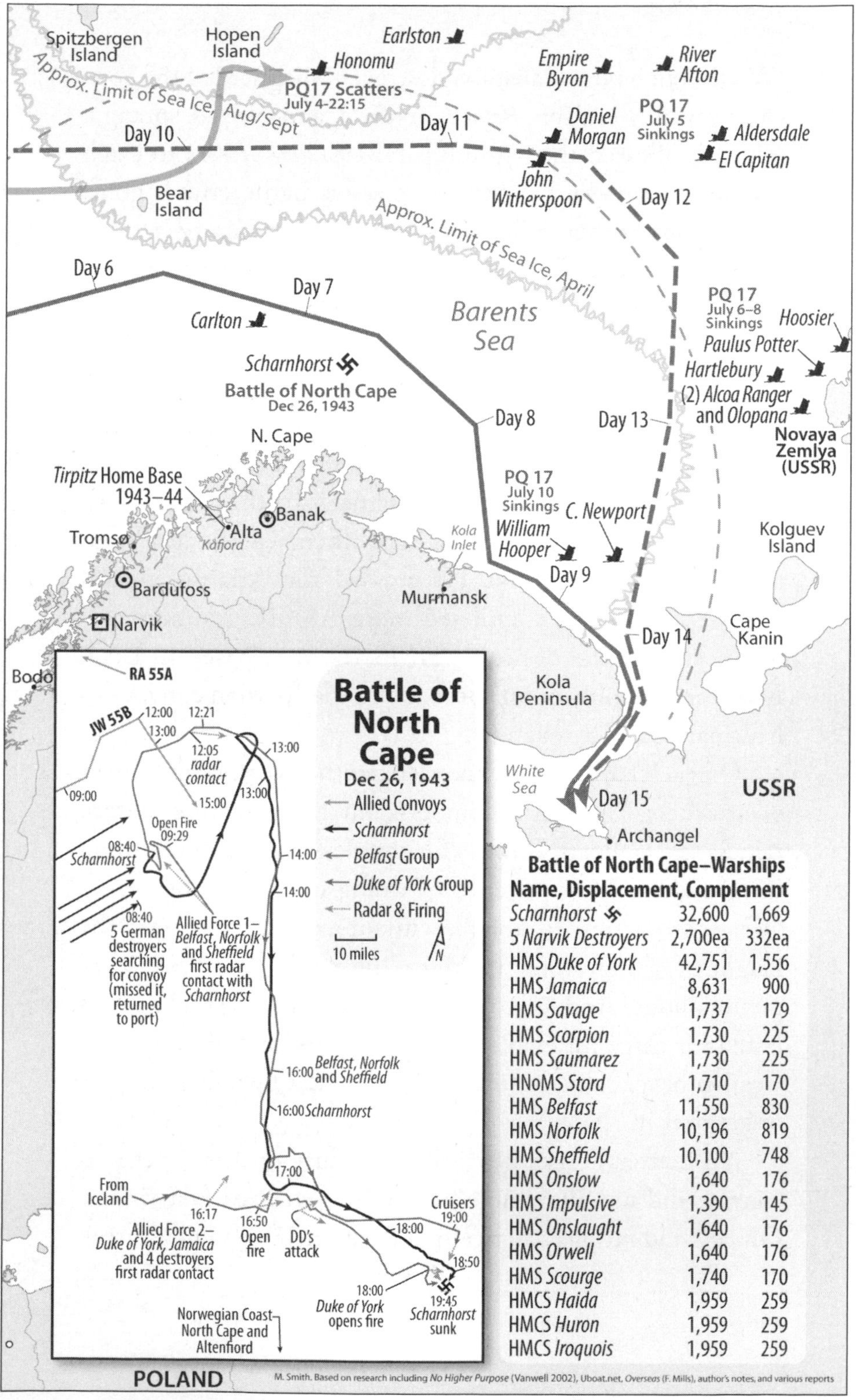

Battle of North Cape–Warships

Name	Displacement	Complement
Scharnhorst ✠	32,600	1,669
5 *Narvik Destroyers*	2,700ea	332ea
HMS *Duke of York*	42,751	1,556
HMS *Jamaica*	8,631	900
HMS *Savage*	1,737	179
HMS *Scorpion*	1,730	225
HMS *Saumarez*	1,730	225
HNoMS *Stord*	1,710	170
HMS *Belfast*	11,550	830
HMS *Norfolk*	10,196	819
HMS *Sheffield*	10,100	748
HMS *Onslow*	1,640	176
HMS *Impulsive*	1,390	145
HMS *Onslaught*	1,640	176
HMS *Orwell*	1,640	176
HMS *Scourge*	1,740	170
HMCS *Haida*	1,959	259
HMCS *Huron*	1,959	259
HMCS *Iroquois*	1,959	259

M. Smith. Based on research including *No Higher Purpose* (Vanwell 2002), Uboat.net, *Overseas* (F. Mills), author's notes, and various reports

JW 55B, but as the Canadian destroyers shepherded the convoy away, RN cruisers *Belfast*, *Sheffield*, and *Norfolk* sprang a trap that allowed the battleship HMS *Duke of York* to catch and sink *Scharnhorst*. With the massive battle cruiser gone, *Huron* joined other Allied destroyers pulling *Scharnhorst* survivors from the frigid Arctic waters. Of 1,968 crewmen aboard the German warship, only thirty-six were rescued.

Cliff Perry, a Canadian sub-lieutenant in the Royal Navy, also served on the Murmansk Run. He'd joined the Royal Canadian Navy in 1940, and at age twenty-two he received a promotion to probationary sub-lieutenant and extra training in gunnery, telegraphy, and signals. In the fall of 1943, the RN posted openings for ten officer candidates from the RCN. Cliff got one. He crossed the Atlantic aboard RMS *Queen Mary*, completed more ASDIC training, and was posted to the destroyer HMS *Westcott,* based in Loch Ewe, the assembly point for many of the Russian convoys to Murmansk and Archangel.

On each trip, Perry acknowledged the ever-present threat of attack by Luftwaffe bombers and Kriegsmarine surface raiders and U-boats. It made for sleepless nights. But nothing compared to the experience of riding out an Arctic storm. "Waves from crest to trough, without exaggeration, were the height of a four-storey building," he wrote. "The seas were mountainous. And, of course, I was violently seasick. . . . It lasted for three miserable days and nights, and although the weather never changed, nature decided that I would either die or get over it."[28]

No matter Perry's physical state, duty on these perilous convoys did not allow time in sick bay, even for first-timers. Officers and ratings had to either fulfill their watches or break the chain of escort surveillance the convoy demanded. Perry noted that *Westcott*, one of the RN's longest-serving destroyers, had been built in 1917, and he marvelled at how the older ship withstood such pounding from the elements. But after several days of being battered and scattered by the weather, the escorts had to round up the merchant ships into an orderly convoy again. And all those extra miles necessitated an emergency manoeuvre at sea.

"We must have used up much more fuel than expected, herding up strays," Perry wrote. "The captain decided he'd better top up the fuel tanks, and called in the oil tanker, part of the convoy. What followed was the most extraordinary feat of seamanship I could have imagined."

HMS *Westcott* steamed as close as she dared to the stern of the supply tanker. Meanwhile, a sailor wearing a lifeline crawled as far forward on the destroyer—close to one of the anchor cable hawsers—as he could go. Sailors aboard the tanker dropped a thin line with a small floating buoy over the stern. The man in the bow of *Westcott* used a grappling hook to scoop up the buoy and then pulled in the line, which was attached to a stronger line, and in turn to an even stronger line. The heaviest line kept the tanker and destroyer at a safe distance while helmsmen and engineers kept the two vessels moving in tandem at the same speed. A second line brought aboard the destroyer was attached to the tanker's fuel hose. So far, so good. But as the tanker crews pumped fuel through the hose, it was imperative that the hose not go taut or take any excess weight.

As the pumping progressed and the ships rose and fell with each swell, SLt Perry watched the entire refuelling procedure breathlessly from the bridge. "At one moment I was staring down the funnel of the tanker, and the next staring up at its propeller spinning out of the water," he wrote.

Over the lifespan of the Arctic convoys—between June 1941 and September 1945—the Allies shipped nearly four million tons of cargo via Reykjavík or Loch Ewe. And 93 percent of it arrived safely at the Soviet ports.[29] By the end of 1942, a crucial year for resupplying the Red Army, Allied navies had escorted twenty-one convoys to north Russia, delivering 310 merchant ships safely to Murmansk and Archangel. Among their valuable munitions—7,652 aircraft, 9,848 tanks, and 111,301 trucks, offloaded and delivered to Soviet forces. Records show that Anglo-American resupply, arriving when it did, assisted the Red Army in breaking the siege at Stalingrad early in 1943[30] and further fuelled Russian counteroffensives against the invading German armies throughout the remainder of the war.[31]

But those successful deliveries came at a high price. Over the four years of Russian convoys, 2,773 sailors died in the sinking of eighteen Allied warships and 104 merchant ships. On the German side, thirty-one U-boats were sunk in Arctic waters, and nearly 2,000 submariners killed.

In spite of the dishevelled state of convoy defence through the fall of 1941, Adm Dönitz's prospects for an advantage in the Battle of the Atlantic had suddenly dwindled dramatically. His "effective U-boat quotient" (tonnage sunk per U-boat per day at sea) had plummeted. Between April and December 1940, the U-Bootwaffe had sunk on average 727 tons per U-boat per day; during the period from July to November 1941, Dönitz's sea wolves had sunk on average only 124 tons per U-boat per day.

And then there were the U-boat losses. In December 1941 in the North Atlantic, the U-Bootwaffe sank just forty-four merchant ships, for a total of 50,682 tons, while losing ten U-boats there that same month (the highest monthly loss of the war thus far).[32] This despite the fact that Dönitz had more U-boats at his disposal—thirty-six in August and thirty-eight by November.[33] Consequently, by the end of 1941, Dönitz suspected that the British were breaking German codes and ciphers enough to warn convoys away from his patrols.

In fact, Allied naval crews had pulled off a series of successful Enigma pinches. During Operation Claymore in March, for example, Royal Navy crews ran a German trawler, *Krebs*, aground off the Lofoten Islands in Norway. Concealed in the captain's cabin were discs containing Kriegsmarine Enigma settings, which provided Bletchley's chief cryptographer, Alan Turing, with bigram tables (two-letter groupings of Enigma code). In May the German weather ship *München* was captured and yielded Enigma settings for the following month. Operation Primrose had also borne fruit in May. As Kptlt Fritz-Julius Lemp and *U110* (the crew that had sunk *Athenia* on the first day of the war) pursued Convoy OB 318, they were run down and boarded off the coast of Iceland. Lemp drowned in the assault, but RN destroyers captured more Enigma settings. In August, British and Canadian escorts captured an inexperienced crew and their *U570*, also off Iceland, and that pinch scored plain-language German code text.[34]

Most important to the Admiralty, and in particular the Operational Intelligence Centre in London, was Bletchley Park's breakthrough in August 1941. Cryptographers in Hut 8 had managed to break Kriegsmarine's Triton (in English, "Shark"), the three-rotor Enigma, and could now decrypt its codes within twenty-four hours on average. That meant Bletchley—now under the umbrella of "Ultra," the designation the British military used to cover all wartime intelligence—could inform the Submarine Tracking Room at Naval Intelligence where U-boat packs were patrolling and gathering. Capt Rodger Winn and his tracking staff could then redirect convoys away from U-boat concentrations.

Jürgen Rohwer, who served in the Kriegsmarine through 1942, assessed the opposing naval forces during this period of the Battle of the Atlantic. "The Admiralty, using Ultra decrypts, rerouted the convoys so cleverly around the German wolf packs," Rohwer wrote, "that about 300 [Allied] ships were saved* by avoiding battles."[35]

THE approach of winter could not have felt colder for Cmdre Leonard Murray and his RCN escort crews in December 1941. The pace of the slow convoy schedules from Sydney and Halifax to the Mid-Ocean Meeting Point had been gruelling, and the merchant ship losses disheartening. To boot, their RN superiors had not been kind in their assessment of the RCN contribution, calling the Canadians sloppy at signalling, cavalier in the use of lights, and overall lacking in discipline in convoy operations. The British still directed traffic on the eastern side of the North Atlantic, however, and promised they would redirect every available Royal Canadian Navy warship to buttress Murray's escort strength. By early December, almost 80 percent of Canada's wartime fleet was directly tied to the Newfoundland Escort Force.

* While consensus among naval historians points to convoy/U-boat battles of 1943 as the turning point in the Battle of the Atlantic, Rohwer claims these decrypts were more decisive.

At least the presence of US Navy destroyers at nearby Argentia gave Murray some solace in his darkest moments. Then December 7 happened. The Sunday morning attack on the US Pacific Fleet in Pearl Harbor by Japanese torpedo and dive-bomber aircraft changed everything yet again. The next day in Congress, President Roosevelt announced that "a state of war" with Japan existed from that moment. And almost as quickly, the USN presence in the western Atlantic dissolved. En masse, American warships moved through the Panama Canal to the Pacific. By February 1942, only two US coast-guard cutters remained available for escort duty at Argentia.[36]

Despite provocations on both sides in the northwestern Atlantic—USN ships depth-charging U-boats between Iceland and North America, and U-boats torpedoing the American destroyers *Kearny* and *Reuben James*—neither Hitler nor Roosevelt had officially declared war. The führer had no desire to provoke the Americans that far, particularly when the fortunes of his June 1941 invasion of the Soviet Union remained in question. However, Japan's surprise attack on Pearl Harbor gave Hitler cause to declare war on the US on December 11 and, in turn, to issue the all-ahead-full order to U-boat operations in American and Canadian coastal waters.

Almost immediately, U-boats were ordered to the western Atlantic in Operation Paukenschlag, or "Drumbeat," in search of targets all along the eastern seaboard. This U-boat equivalent of Blitzkrieg against Allied shipping from Newfoundland to the Caribbean yielded unexpected returns for Germany's U-boat flotillas—more than 400 Allied ships sunk during the campaign. Some calculated that Paukenschlag caused greater loss of raw resources and material for the US than all the devastation at Pearl Harbor.[37]

On December 17, Karl Dönitz summoned six U-boat commanders to his headquarters at Kernével, outside Lorient, France. He briefed them about their new target zones and methods of attack. Heinrich Bleichrodt and *U109*, as well as Ernst Kals aboard *U130*, would patrol in Type VII U-boats off Newfoundland. Simultaneously, Richard Zapp in command of *U66*, Ulrich Folkers with *U125*, Jürgen von Rosenstiel with his *U502* crew, and Reinhard Hardegen aboard *U123* would seek targets with their Type IXs between New York City and Cape Hatteras, North Carolina. Since these first attacks would occur close to American ports—where coastal waters were shallow—Dönitz advised his U-boat commanders to attack at night, seeking shelter in deeper water during the day. He suggested they use deck guns to sink some of their targets, avoid engagements with naval escorts, and strike principally merchant ships larger than 10,000 tons.[38]

Kptlt Hardegen approached his attack area early in January 1942. Since Hardegen had served on two different U-boats through three previous patrols before taking command of *U123*, Dönitz assigned him the prize of all the western Atlantic targets—New York Harbor. However, passing Sable Island off Nova Scotia en route to American waters, the twenty-nine-year-old commander spotted the 9,076-ton British steamer *Cyclops*. On January 11, just before 2 a.m., he fired a single torpedo that struck the merchantman just aft of the smokestack. The ship immediately began to settle. But *U123*'s radio operator then heard a distress call coming from *Cyclops*'s wireless shack.

Hardegen ordered his U-boat to the surface and for deck gunners to silence the merchant ship's radio centre. Hardegen fired a second torpedo, the *coup de grâce*, and five minutes later the steamer went down. Most of the merchant ship's 181 crew and passengers managed to get free of the sinking vessel in lifeboats and rafts, but when the minesweeper HMCS *Red Deer* reached the scene the following day, her crew found that ninety-seven survivors had died of exposure.[39] It was, after all, winter across the North Atlantic. By that time, *U123* had also sunk the tanker *Norness* off Rhode Island Sound and then had proceeded to her assigned target zone. Kptlt Hardegen had delivered the first drumbeats of Operation Paukenschlag.

The evening that *U123* surfaced for a first look at New York City, on January 15, Kptlt Hardegen could not believe his eyes. Rather than the featureless horizon of dark shapes and shadows he'd commonly seen at blacked-out European coastal cities, he witnessed from his conning tower a shoreline alive with lights and detail; even the lights of the harbour's navigation system were lit. "No blackouts. No dimming. Nothing," he remarked later. "It was unbelievably beautiful and great."[40]

But Hardegen didn't stop there. Strict operational secrecy meant that none of the U-boats sent to the western Atlantic could carry local mapping of their target areas. Clandestinely, however, Hardegen had managed to procure a souvenir pamphlet from the 1939 New York World's Fair. When the brochure was unfolded, the reverse side displayed a layout of New York subway lines, directions to the fair, and ferry routes criss-crossing a map of the city's harbour.[41] *U123* proceeded far enough into Ambrose Channel that crewmen in her conning tower could plainly see automobile headlights moving along the roadway through Coney Island amusement park.

"We were the first to be here," Hardegen said, "the first time in this war a German soldier looked upon the coast of the U.S.A."[42]

Even with the United States officially at war, American authorities did not mandate blackouts along the eastern seaboard. Consequently, U-boat commanders such as Hardegen took full advantage, targeting unprotected tankers and freighters vividly silhouetted at night by the glow of east-coast city lights. Completely unnoticed amid other vessels in New York Harbor, *U123* caught the British tanker *Coimbra* weighing anchor and torpedoed her on the spot. By January 18, Kptlt Hardegen had slipped into the shipping lanes off Cape Hatteras, North Carolina, and sunk another four merchantmen. Hardegen described it as a shooting gallery, and he increased his tonnage for the patrol to nine ships, or 53,173 tons sunk. On January 22, via radio, Kptlt Hardegen was awarded a Knight's Cross for his victories.

Operation Paukenschlag also delivered Adm Dönitz and his U-Bootwaffe crews the start of their "Second Happy Time."

Later in the year, following another successful patrol off the US coast, Hardegen learned he would receive the Knight's Cross with Oak Leaves, and that Hitler would make the presentation personally at a private dinner. The U-boat commander took the opportunity to voice what had long been his and his admiral's chief criticism of German High Command.

"It would be better to have more air forces and submarines, and fewer tanks," he told the führer.

"I know better," Hitler responded.

"[We] look too much to the land," Hardegen persisted.[43]

Hitler didn't much appreciate Hardegen's candour. And the U-boat commander felt he was unfairly chided for his criticism of decision-making at the top. But Hardegen had a point. The U-Bootwaffe had a fleet of 248 boats at the beginning of 1942; however, the führer had only commissioned twenty-one new U-boats in December. A breakdown of U-boat strength indicates that of the 248 U-boats afloat, only ninety were actually available to Dönitz in January 1942—seventy-one Type VIICs and nineteen Type IXs—and of those, fifty-four were in submarine pens for repair. Once other theatres of war were accounted for, only twenty-two combat-ready U-boats could be assigned to duty in the North Atlantic, just when Adm Dönitz needed them most.[44]

If resources for the U-Bootwaffe seemed limited and German High Command deaf to its front-line commanders' pleas, it was no better for Cdr James Prentice, the RCN's Senior Officer Corvettes. But neither was he afraid to tell Naval Service Headquarters in Ottawa about it. In November 1941 he'd produced a report provocatively assessing the net worth of his own escort force. As he had earlier in the year, Prentice called for improved equipment and training, without which the NEF would not meet its commitment to escort convoys safely to and from the MOMP. He claimed that RCN corvettes hadn't had the chance to become efficient. Why not? Prentice accused authorities in Ottawa and Halifax of hurrying to bring new ships into service. And whenever NEF ships were ordered to Halifax for refit, he said, authorities stripped the vessels-in-repair of their experienced crews in order to man the newly constructed ships.

"Ships' companies arrive at a certain average state of efficiency in spite of the complete lack of sea experience or training of the personnel, only because they are keen, energetic, and work as a team," Prentice reported. "[But] as soon as that team is broken up, the ship again becomes inefficient."[45]

The service record of AB William Bint reflected that kind of pinball career path. Born in 1923 and raised in Saskatoon, when the war broke out, Bill decided he'd prefer the navy over high-school matriculation, so he and three friends lied about their age and enlisted in the RCNVR. One thing he learned during his training was that even though most prairie boys had grown up landlocked in Manitoba, Saskatchewan, or Alberta, they had an innate capacity to deal with wide-open spaces, big skies, and unending horizons—conditions they would constantly face at sea.

"I trained with a salty group of Saskatchewan boys," Bint wrote. "Once we finished all our work-ups, we began regular duty off Nova Scotia. . . . I was very seasick, but I never missed a watch, and before we'd returned to Halifax, I was over my seasickness."[46]

During Bint's first weeks of active service, the navy discovered he had a good ear for small pitch differences; reading the Doppler effect of a returning ASDIC transmission, he could easily differentiate the echoes he was hearing. Consequently, each time a newly commissioned warship arrived in Halifax, Bint got bumped to that vessel. In early 1942 he'd just become used to the routine and conditions aboard corvette HMCS *Kenogami* when they transferred him to the brand-new minesweeper HMCS *Melville*. As Cdr Prentice had suggested in his critical report, with each new assignment ASDIC operator Bint had to acclimatize to a new ship, new CO, new shipmates, and new schedule.

"This [prevents] the development of even the most rudimentary form of cohesive action," Prentice concluded. "It is as though we were attempting to play against a professional hockey team with a collection of individuals who had not even learned to skate."[47]

On February 22, 1942, Bill Bint was with his new crew

in *Melville* on her first patrol, twenty-five miles southwest of Halifax, when the minesweeper's wireless operator received a distress call from a tanker that had fallen behind the rest of Convoy HX 175. At 11 p.m. the Scottish motor tanker *Kars* radioed that she'd been struck by a single torpedo, which had ignited massive fires onboard and in the water around the ship. *Kars* was loaded with 12,700 tons of aviation fuel and oil.

"It was the first ship I'd ever seen torpedoed," Bint wrote. "Suddenly, the U-boat surfaced off our portside, maybe half a mile away. I suspect she hadn't noticed us, likely because both [the minesweeper] and the tanker were diesel powered."[48]

Melville's commander immediately altered course for the U-boat at full speed—eighteen knots—and called for fire from the sweeper's four-inch gun. But just as quickly as the gunners trained on the U-boat, it crash-dived. Then, as happened so often in these sorts of engagements, the minesweeper's accelerating engines made it difficult for Bint's ASDIC to discern between sweeper and U-boat, and he couldn't pinpoint her descent. Nevertheless, *Melville* launched depth charges.

By the time the RCN minesweeper returned to the burning tanker, *Kars* was enveloped in fire. The sweeper crew couldn't even make out the ship amid the flames and black smoke. AB Bint volunteered for the rescue boat that *Melville* launched to search for survivors around the flaming wreck.

"As we pulled towards the burning tanker, which we couldn't see, it suddenly emerged from the smoke and flame still gushing burning gas and heading right for us," Bint wrote. "It was still underway, but turning in a circle.

"There were only two men moving in the water. We picked them up—one a Norwegian fireman, the other the ship's carpenter, not wearing a life jacket; he'd been able to swim under the burning gas," Bint continued. "We checked for more victims, but there were none. . . . The Norwegian died as we pulled him into the boat. The [carpenter] was out of his head and still swimming through the fire for several hours after we got him aboard."

The carpenter was the sole survivor of a crew of fifty men aboard *Kars*. Two days later, the tanker broke in two. The forward section sank; the aft portion was towed to Halifax and beached. The ship was a total loss.

"It had been quite an exciting day," Bint wrote finally, "for an eighteen-year-old."[49]

THE sinking of the tanker *Kars* in February 1942, as well as other merchant ships that fell victim to Dönitz's Operation Paukenschlag, was in part the result of a strategic decision by Adm Ernest J. King, the commander-in-chief (COMINCH) of the US Navy. Despite the advice of British and Canadian veterans of the North Atlantic convoy experience, King discarded the convoy system in favour of "offensive patrols." Such ventures to track down U-boats opened US mercantile shipping—in particular, the vital oil run from South America up the eastern seaboard and east to Britain—to U-boat harassment.

Adm Dönitz dispatched every U-boat available to join the open season on American shipping. In January the U-boat offensive on the US seaboard sank forty-eight ships, in February seventy-three ships (including some in the Caribbean), and in March ninety-five ships.[50] "[It was] the most successful period of the U-boat war against Allied supplies," Kriegsmarine veteran Jürgen Rohwer concluded.[51]

Such large merchant shipping losses very quickly appeared

on the radar of the Operational Intelligence Centre at the Admiralty in London. In particular, RAdm John Godfrey, director of Naval Intelligence, recognized that his department needed to address these setbacks in American waters. Somehow he had to convince the head of the US Navy to adopt the convoy concept and to open communications channels with Royal Navy intelligence to stop the bleeding.

But Adm King could not see his service playing second fiddle to the RN, much less adopting its tactics or accepting its intelligence as instructive. This even though, as early as 1940, the Americans had visited Godfrey's Tracking Room at the Operational Intelligence Centre and recognized its critical role in the Battle of the Atlantic. Following the Americans' visit, Godfrey had reciprocated in 1941, visiting Washington, D.C., and suggesting the establishment of a Joint Intelligence Committee.[52] His intelligence assistant, Ian Fleming, had even drafted plans to pool the intelligence of the US Navy, the Royal Canadian Navy, and the Royal Navy.

To get King to change his tactics, Godfrey knew he had to play a trump card. Another visit to the US was necessary. This time, the Royal Navy intelligence emissary had to have a commanding knowledge of the problems merchant convoys and their escorts faced, not to mention exceptional powers of advocacy. Godfrey's civilian assistant, Capt Rodger Winn, not only fit the bill with his experience in the Tracking Room, but he'd also studied at Harvard and would therefore be perfectly at ease on the Americans' turf. Capt Winn would have to persuade Adm King and his assistant, RAdm Ralph Edwards, that an Operational Intelligence Centre arrangement *within his own staff* would deliver King and the US Atlantic Fleet a valuable weapon against the U-boats.

First, Capt Winn spent three days persuading the officers at COMINCH headquarters that its strategic activity could profit by adding RN operational intelligence to the mix. Winn illustrated some of the methods he'd used in the Tracking Room—attempting to forecast the movements of U-boats and then, based on those forecasts, planning the disposition of escorts and the routing of convoys.[53] All of which seemed to make sense. The catch was convincing King and Edwards. Winn repeated his pitch to Edwards. But when the discussion reached an impasse, Winn decided to go for broke and resorted to plain speaking.

"The trouble is, Admiral," Winn said, "it's not only your bloody ships you are losing. A lot of them are ours!"

Caught off guard, Edwards relented. "Well, maybe you've got a point there."[54]

Winn was immediately given an audience with Adm King himself. And the group thus set about creating an Atlantic Section Operational Intelligence room at COMINCH headquarters. On his way back to the UK, Capt Winn travelled to Canada and met with Lt John McDiarmid, newly appointed head of the Foreign Intelligence Section at NSHQ in Ottawa. McDiarmid had studied classics at the University of Toronto and had been teaching Greek and Sanskrit at Johns Hopkins University in Baltimore when the war broke out. He admitted that he had little in his background that led him to the navy; in fact, he said he'd never seen the ocean. But once he'd joined the RCN, he was streamed to NSHQ, where he began correlating data and preparing daily situation reports on U-boat activity.[55]

"I set about educating myself in the nature and behaviour of U-boats," he wrote, "keeping constant watch on the evidence from both sides and reading everything that was known or thought about submarines past and present."[56]

Lt McDiarmid appeared to fit perfectly into Winn's integrated intelligence model. In one quick trip to North America, then, Winn had hastened the collaboration of intelligence gathering and opened the door to greater co-operation among the Allied navies. At further meetings in Washington, senior Canadian, British, and American officers agreed to better integrate escort duties among all three navies. All convoys—slow and fast—would now take more southerly routes (closer to the Great Circle Route), which would require fewer escorts than the Iceland route, and Royal Navy warships would be reintroduced to the Atlantic run.

To assist the RCN in its defence west of Cape Race, Newfoundland, the Allies initiated the Western Local Escort Force (WLEF). It would reorganize into six groups (equal in strength to the mid-ocean escorts). The RN would reassign thirteen of the former US lend-lease destroyers to join the RCN's five lend-lease destroyers in the WLEF. The RCN would send thirty corvettes from Halifax as well.

It took time, however, to adjust to new coverage areas and to adapt to new teammates on escort duty. The first week of February, as Convoy ON 60 made its way west, U-boats torpedoed and sank *Alysse*, a Free French corvette, as well as a merchant ship. To fill the gap, the captains of corvettes HMCS *Sherbrooke* and HMCS *Barrie* risked running out of fuel but chose to maintain screening of the convoy through to Halifax. Just short of the safety of the Halifax WLEF zone, an Operation Paukenschlag U-boat sank a straggling merchantman. By the time the two Canadian corvettes managed to pick up survivors and shepherd the rest of the convoy to Halifax, they had been at sea for sixteen days straight.

Initially, losses in the WLEF protection areas dropped in the first months of 1942, mostly because Dönitz's U-boat flotilla had set its sights on the rich hunting grounds off New York and the Carolinas. In February, U-boats sank only nine ships in Canadian waters, and in March the total fell to eight. That same month, the WLEF began escorting convoys between Halifax and Boston. Then, in April, it picked up those convoys coming from Britain and guided them to American ports as well. This unique route—Sydney or Halifax to St. John's escorting SC or HX convoys eastbound, then picking up ON or ONS convoys headed westbound for Boston or New York, and finally back to Halifax or Sydney—became known among its veteran RCN corvette crews as the Triangle Run.

As menacing as the U-boat threat became off the eastern seaboard, however, it was often the uncertainty of escort duty on that run that posed the greatest challenge to RCN crews. Could they hope to meet and shepherd their convoys safely? Would they come under attack by day or night? What if they had to rescue the crew of a sunken merchantman? And how long would a particular escort sortie last? Days? Weeks?

"I calculated everything in terms of five-pound cans of corned beef, powdered eggs, and powdered milk," said Leonard Philbrook, who served as victualler aboard HMCS *Sorel* on the Triangle Run. "So many cans of this, jars of that, and we could stay out for seven days, or ten at most."[57]

Victuallers were worth their weight in gold. They came from the navy's supply service. As victualler under a logistics officer, Philbrook's task was to supply *Sorel*'s company of seventy-five men, and especially the cook and his helper (who was often Philbrook himself), with provisions. That generally meant procuring food for the galley, but a true victualler might also keep tabs on all provisions aboard, from fuel oil to fresh water to toilet paper.[58] Whenever *Sorel* landed back in Halifax or St. John's, Philbrook's job was to dash to the quartermaster's, get his next order in, and arrange for all hands on deck to load provisions aboard when the transport arrived at *Sorel*'s gangway. Turnarounds sometimes happened within hours.

From the outset, Philbrook was a marked man. His enlistment papers indicated that his father had run a butcher shop on Roncesvalles Avenue in Toronto's west end. When the navy lined everybody up at HMCS *Stadacona* for assignment in 1941, Philbrook could have anticipated his fate.

"Philbrook? You a butcher?" the posting officer said.

"Yes, sir," he answered.

"HMCS *St. Hyacinth*, Montreal."

The instructors the navy hired to train their cooks came from fishing boats, lumber and mining camps, restaurants, and railway companies.[59] After two or three weeks of instruction, they put Philbrook on a train back to Halifax, and just as quickly aboard *Sorel*. As much experience as his father's butcher shop and the courses at *St. Hyacinth* had provided, he acquired most of his skills on the job. On minesweepers and corvettes the galley was no more than six feet by six feet, with a sink, an oil stove, some cupboards, and a small refrigerator. The staples—corned beef, peas, corn, and fruit desserts—were all canned. Eggs and milk were powdered. If Philbrook could procure some fresh beef, the cook roasted it and stored it for soup or stew. Cold weather conditions at sea meant he could easily find spots onboard for cool storage, given the limited refrigerator space. And heat from the funnel kept frost off the vegetables stored nearby.

A standard breakfast was "red lead and bacon"—hot tomatoes and bacon swimming in fat. Spam or Klik could substitute for the bacon. Another regular was "square eggs," made from egg powder spread in a large pan and baked with water or milk. There were "collision mats" (a reference to any material used to plug holes in a ship)—thick, tough-to-chew pancakes. And for a change, the cook would mush porridge with white sugar and powdered milk.[60] The beverage most sailors enjoyed was "kai," a drink made of melted cooking chocolate, condensed milk, and boiling water. But no matter how innovative the cooks and victualler became with their concoctions, conditions at sea generally dictated the way a sailor's meal was presented.

"*Sorel* was a wet ship," said Philbrook, referring to the corvette's proclivity for taking sea water aboard. Food was delivered in covered pails, each mess of six or eight seamen sending a man to bring their meal. "Men picked up their food in the galley. But they ate in the mess deck. If you ran one to the other in the rain or the waves came over, very often dinner was gone before you got to the mess deck."

Of course, if action stations were called, everything in the galley or the mess was left as is, and would likely be little more than muck on the deck by the time the cooks and sailors stood down.

If his job had a perk at all, Philbrook learned that as a petty officer and victualler he played a key role when "Up Spirits" was announced. Aboard *Sorel* (and most RCN ships), the rum ration was issued daily to each sailor by 11 a.m. The senior officer in charge had keys to the locker holding the ten-gallon keg of rum. After a while he didn't bother with the keys and left the distribution in Philbrook's charge. As the crew lined up to receive the tots of rum, an officer called out, "Everything all right, Petty Officer?"

"Yes, sir."

"You sure?" he'd ask again.

"Yes, sir," Philbrook assured him. But he also admitted that he made a lot of friends in the transaction.

ON one of those rare days that winter of 1942, when escorting corvette HMCS *Amherst* was not at sea but tied up in St. John's, commanding officer Louis Audette received an old friend. John Connolly, then the executive assistant to Angus L. Macdonald, minister of national defence for naval services, arrived with a second visitor, Eric Brand. Despite his career as an RN officer and, at the start of the war, his appointment as RCN's director of Naval Intelligence and Plans at NSHQ in Ottawa, Eric Brand had never seen a corvette in the flesh. Audette gave Connolly and Brand a personal tour. Then, over a post-tour drink in *Amherst*'s wardroom, Brand commented on what he'd seen.

"I can't imagine how you get the bloody thing from A to B, or how you fight [with] it," he said.[61]

Chapter Seven

SWIM MEET IN THE GULF

U-BOAT COMMANDERS ON WARTIME PATROLS IN the North Atlantic endured their share of close calls. By the winter of 1942, Kptlt Karl Thurmann was no exception. Raised along the River Ruhr in western Germany, he had joined the Reichsmarine in 1928 and served as a sea cadet aboard the light cruisers *Emden* and *Köln* in the peacetime navy. In the spring of 1940 he began his wartime U-boat training and in December joined *U553*, a Type VIIC U-boat. A year later, he was commander of *U553* on his inaugural patrol from Bergen, Norway, into the Atlantic gap between the Faroe and Shetland islands. But right away Thurmann's U-boat encountered serious engine troubles and just managed to limp back to the sub pens at St. Nazaire.

Four patrols later, in October 1941, Thurmann discovered the ill-fated Convoy SC 48 at its Mid-Ocean Meeting Point, and he began shadowing the fifty-two eastbound merchant ships until the rest of the wolf pack arrived. Early on the evening of October 15, the four-stack lend-lease Canadian destroyer HMCS *Columbia* sighted *U553* off the port beam of the convoy; as the U-boat submerged in a crash dive, *Columbia* launched depth charges at the target. Thurmann recorded the next minutes in his war diary. "I quickly go to great depth," he wrote.[1]

Inside a U-boat, those minutes seemed an eternity. The depth gauge raced past its key markers—fifty, seventy-five, a hundred metres. Sounds of the destroyer's ASDIC and its propellers, growing louder as the enemy warship passed overhead, seemed to amplify the anxiety inside the U-boat. The commander, in heavy sea boots and raincoat, positioned himself in the control room with his back against the base of the sky periscope. He was focused on the sounds coming through the sonic hydrophones in the sub's radio shack. Everyone braced for the pounding that was coming. Then it arrived. "Three depth charges in a very tight pattern land [directly above]," Thurmann continued. "Everything that can be knocked out is."

The rumble outside the hull and the concussion waves arrived nearly together—the blasts were that close. Bits of flaked paint on the boat's ceiling fluttered down. The whole vessel shook and swayed. The lights failed, and the unsettling seconds of uncertainty in total darkness passed until the reserve light system kicked in. Submariners had no choice but to hold on and endure.

For two more days and nights, Thurmann and *U553* remained in the fray, shadowing, surfacing, attacking merchant vessels—they sank three of the nine merchant ships torpedoed in that convoy—and crash-dived again to nearly 300 feet to escape another pursuing Allied warship. This time it was USS *Kearny* that had dropped the pattern of depth charges. And again, *U553* managed to escape major damage.

"Dying is hard work aboard a [U-boat]," wrote Lothar-Günther Buchheim, Kriegsmarine lieutenant and propaganda writer. "There's no shooting people dead. No sparks of life just simply snuffed out. The devil likes to keep you dangling."[2]

Kptlt Thurmann's seventh patrol began on the heels of the U-Bootwaffe's successful Operation Paukenschlag, in search of targets along the North American coastline. The entire Kreigsmarine fleet had experienced a euphoric boost because of the U-boats' productive patrols off the US and Canadian eastern seaboard in January and February 1942. In March the Allied shipping loss rose to more than half a million tons,[3] and Thurmann's commander, Karl Dönitz, was promoted to full admiral. When Thurmann departed the U-boat base at St. Nazaire on April 19, 1942, destined for shipping lanes off the Canadian coast, his commander's words of encouragement rang in Thurmann's head.

"Every ship . . . sunk counts not only as a ship sunk, but at the same time damages the enemy's shipbuilding and armament at its inception," Dönitz reminded his U-boat commanders. "Tonnage must be taken where it can be destroyed most reasonably."[4]

Dönitz did caution, however, that U-boat operations in North American waters had to remain wary of the Allied response, including an acceleration of shipbuilding in North American ports to compensate for losses; the eventual implementation of convoy tactics to protect merchant vessels where that response had been absent in US waters; and, perhaps most critical, increased air surveillance from a growing number of Allied air bases where shipping traffic was busiest and most vulnerable.

Mindful of his commander's mandate to sink merchant ships wherever it seemed most reasonable, Kptlt Thurmann made an unprecedented decision in the first week of May 1942.

He and his crew had not added to their tonnage accumulation since January. Adding insult to injury, *U553* continued to suffer from equipment problems during her transatlantic crossing. With no immediate targets in his sights when he reached Canadian coastal waters on the night of May 8/9, Thurmann considered a novel course change. He directed *U553* into a body of water he anticipated might be quieter but productive—through the Cabot Strait and into potentially new hunting grounds—the Gulf of the St. Lawrence River.

MURRAY Westgate had always looked for a chance to go to sea. Growing up in landlocked Regina, Saskatchewan, during the 1930s, he decided to join the Royal Canadian Naval Volunteer Reserve. But Murray also had a flair for transposing what he saw—landscapes, buildings, machines, and faces—onto a sketch pad. He hoped either his interest in the navy or a course he'd taken in commercial art would lead him away from his home on the Canadian Prairies. When the war broke out in 1939, the RCNVR learned that Murray was also skilled in wireless telegraphy. When there was suddenly a navy draft to train leading telegraphists, Murray was quickly posted to Halifax. But he never gave up his sketching, including mischievous caricatures of his instructor. When he got caught one day on the course, he had to do some punishment time.

"But I actually like your work," his wireless instructor admitted.

"Really?" Westgate said.

"I think we should set up a drawing office. Would you like to be in charge?" his teacher asked.

"Whatever you want, sir."[5]

By 1941, the RCN had packed AB Westgate off to the signals training school at HMCS *St. Hyacinthe*, near Montreal, where he was tasked with setting up the school's official drawing office. He taught other recruits how to create detailed maps, charts, drawings of flags, and circuit diagrams for transmitters and receivers. But diagram drawing was not getting AB Westgate to sea. He applied for a commission, moved to HMCS *Kings* back in Halifax, and began basic training as a probationary sub-lieutenant. By 1942 he'd graduated and been posted closer to the sea, just not on it. The navy put him in command of the main coding office near HMCS *Fort Ramsay*, a land base still under construction in Gaspé, Quebec.

"I was sent out to man the Port Wave* signal station," Westgate said. "I was the officer in charge, with about three or four signalmen and a cook."

Westgate figured the navy couldn't have sent him to a more remote outpost. But there, twenty miles from Gaspé at the village of Saint-Georges-de-Malbaie, and atop a 300-foot cliff, he became the first communications line of defence on the south shore of the Gulf of St. Lawrence. At the signal station, now SLt Westgate and the cook built a bridge and hooked up a generator in order to flash light signals to passing ships.

"We challenged all ships that came into our vicinity," he said, deducing that if a vessel didn't respond the navy should be suspicious. It wasn't out of the realm of possibility that German surface raiders or U-boats would come his way.

As early as March 1942, Mackenzie King had addressed the U-boat threat in Canadian waters during a speech in

* Port Waves were small naval radio stations positioned along the coast to communicate with vessels not far from shore. Gaspé's frequency was 125 kilocycles with a call sign of "CFL."

the House of Commons. In his warning, the prime minister waxed eloquent about the history of the gulf and about its geographical signficance. Then he noted that the RCN had informed him that U-boats "may well be found operating within the gulf and even the St. Lawrence River. . . . [But] if enemy submarines do operate in the St. Lawrence, an additional burden will be thrown on the Canadian navy."[6]

King had stated the obvious. In the Gulf of St. Lawrence, the RCN faced a formidable task. Not only did the gulf stretch at its widest nearly 250 miles (from the north shore of New Brunswick to the Strait of Belle Isle, at the northern tip of Newfoundland), but the main current of the river offered a 300-mile-long waterway and easy passage for ships of friend or foe as far west as Quebec City. The gulf had strategic importance in both peace and war; about one-fifth of Canada's wealth came through the Gulf of St. Lawrence.[7] The river and gulf had provided a highway from the Great Lakes, Quebec, and New Brunswick shipyards for all of the Canadian-built warships on their way to active service in the North Atlantic. And yet, when it came to considering early warning of enemy warships and protection of that gateway to eastern Canada, the federal government and RCN headquarters in Ottawa had allotted only the Bangor-class minesweeper HMCS *Medicine Hat* and a couple of motor launches to keep the entire gulf safe.

"Not since Lewis Carroll's *Hunting of the Snark*," mused one RCN sailor, "has an elusive prey been pursued by such a motley band of hunters—corvettes, armed yachts, minesweepers, and Fairmiles."[8]

With its options limited early in the war, the RCN considered a lightweight, quick-accelerating motor launch, the

Fairmile, to supplement corvettes and minesweepers in anti-submarine patrols, particularly in the Gulf of St. Lawrence. The Canadian government initially ordered twenty-four for the RCN in May 1940.* Across Ontario there were dozens of yacht builders capable of constructing them; among them, Greavette Boats, in central Ontario, was contracted to build nine. Coincidentally, Greavette had recently engaged a German Navy veteran and yacht designer who'd emigrated to Canada between the wars.

Hans Sachau had grown up north of Hamburg, Germany. In 1907, at the age of sixteen, he was apprenticed to the shipbuilding yard at Kiel. During the Great War he served in the Germany Navy aboard warships laying mines in the North Sea. Between the wars, back in Kiel, he designed and built pleasure craft, including a sailing yacht for Prince Heinrich, brother of the exiled Kaiser Wilhelm. In 1928, on the eve of the Depression, Hans immigrated to Canada. He first found work building boats in Toronto but quickly chose to buy property on Lake Ontario, west of Toronto, and launched his own boatbuilding business on the shores of Humber Bay. He had yards, sheds, and a 600-foot marine railway that allowed him to launch his watercraft directly into Lake Ontario. That's when Tom Greavette entered the picture.

"Tom Greavette had won a contract to build Fairmiles, but he had no water access to Lake Ontario," said Elsa-Ann Pickard, Sachau's daughter. And despite the Mackenzie King government's policy of routinely interning German-born immigrants it considered "enemy aliens," Greavette managed to get her father the work he loved and needed. The government

* Canada's boat builders produced eighty-eight Fairmile B-type motor launches—fourteen on the west coast, fifteen in Nova Scotia, and fifty-nine in Ontario.

contracted Greavette to deliver the Fairmiles, and Greavette hired Hans Sachau to build and launch them from his boat-building site on Lake Ontario. "It was a perfect match."[9]

Sachau fashioned his Fairmile hulls with a double layer of mahogany wood and a keel made of oak. Each launch was 112 feet long and 17 feet wide and weighed 80 tons. Twin V-12 American Hall-Scott "Defender" gas engines could deliver a maximum continuous speed of 16.5 knots, and in an emergency up to 20 knots. A Fairmile had a range of 1,455 miles and was armed with three twenty-millimetre Oerlikon guns, two .303 Lewis machine guns, rifles, a Sten gun, revolvers, and as many as twenty depth charges.[10] Its crew consisted of fifteen men.

In combat, the Fairmile was no match for a surfaced U-boat; so the motor launch's job was to detect subs, pin them down with ASDIC, and keep them submerged while larger warships arrived to inflict greater damage.[11] In the fall of 1941, the first three Fairmiles (*Q054*, *Q055*, and *Q056*) were commissioned and launched from Sachau's Humber Bay shipyard.[12]

"Each launch brought dignitaries out to the ceremony," Pickard continued. "And each time the wife of a dignitary would smash a bottle of Champagne over the bow [of the Fairmile]. Either I or my sisters Greta or Elizabeth got to present her with a bouquet of flowers."

Greavette's first Fairmiles sailed into a sea of uncertainty that spring of 1942. The government of Mackenzie King was facing a unique dilemma in its relationship with Quebec, and in particular with voters in Gaspé. In April, under pressure from both francophone voters in Quebec and anglophone voters in the rest of Canada, King's Liberal government had conducted a national plebiscite asking to be released from the anti-conscription promises it had made after the First World

War. At the time, Bill 80 authorized conscription for overseas service only if it were deemed necessary. Wary that Quebec sentiment was building against him, but fearing the U-boat threat in the Gulf of St. Lawrence even more, the prime minister had raised the issue in the House of Commons. At the same time, he reassured citizens around the gulf that the Canadian government and the military were prepared, even if they weren't.

While not as busy as the shipping lanes of the Triangle Run, ocean-going traffic in and out of the St. Lawrence River was substantial. In the 1941 season, as an example, no fewer than 750 ocean-going vessels had arrived at and departed from the Port of Montreal.[13] Defence plans for the volume of traffic between Sydney and Quebec demanded escorts for (SQ and QS) convoys in each direction every three days. In 1942 Cdr Horatio Nelson Lay, director of the Operations Division, warned that increasing the number of escorts in the gulf would reduce the navy's supply of escorts for duty in the Atlantic; so instead, RCN staff chose to rely more heavily on minesweepers, yachts, and Fairmiles to protect the SQ and QS convoys.[14]

Around Gaspé Harbour, the concern about the proximity of the war was palpable. Perhaps apocryphally, there had been rumours during the 1930s that Adolf Hitler had expressed interest in purchasing Anticosti Island, just off the Gaspé Peninsula. In any case, Quebec authorities did not wish to be caught flat-footed. Capt Colin Donald, the RCN officer in charge of the defence of Gaspé since 1940, busily marshalled men, transport, and munitions. As the navy built the new jetty, barracks, radio towers, and administrative buildings of HMCS *Fort Ramsay*, Capt Donald directed construction of concrete bunkers and installation of 4.7-inch naval guns (mothballed since the Great War) overlooking Gaspé Harbour, and anti-submarine nets at its entrance.

However, there hadn't been the time, allocation of funds, or equipment available to install effective radio direction-finders around the St. Lawrence basin. Commercial telephone lines provided the only reliable long-distance communication in the region. Nor had a St. Lawrence Escort Force of warships, promised two years earlier, been deployed to the gulf. In early May 1942, the only vessels protecting the waters in the Gaspé approaches were the minesweeper HMCS *Medicine Hat* and the Greavette Fairmiles.

On May 1, 1942, RCN officers and staff raised the White Ensign to officially open HMCS *Fort Ramsay*. Coincidentally, the Canadian government had invited the press to tell Canadians how the government was protecting them. Sent to cover the proceedings were two eager reporters—René Lévesque to write for francophone readers, and seasoned Canadian Press (CP) correspondent Jack Brayley, who would file through CP to major English-speaking newspapers across the country.[15] Also on hand for the opening ceremonies, and the unofficial photographer of the event, was RCNVR sub-lieutenant Ian Tate. Tate had recently graduated from the University of Toronto and, like Murray Westgate, had campaigned for the navy to post him to the front lines at sea. Instead they shipped him off to *Fort Ramsay* as the outpost's cipher officer.[16] All of the players in the opening act of the Battle of the St. Lawrence were on their marks.

Perched on the exposed side of the peninsula and up the coastline from Gaspé Harbour, the Cap-des-Rosiers lighthouse had provided boats and ships in the Gulf of St. Lawrence a guiding beacon since 1858. But during the day on May 10, 1942, lightkeeper Joseph Ferguson had paused for a chat with a neighbour on the cape long enough to learn that fishermen had reported unexplained torn nets. Soon after, Ferguson spotted the wake of what appeared to be a half-submerged vessel. He didn't waste any time getting to a telephone to report what he'd seen to navy authorities at HMCS *Fort Ramsay*.[17] His sighting was relayed to the signal station at Saint-Georges-de-Malbaie.

"Suddenly we got report of a U-boat," SLt Murray Westgate said. "It was in the Gulf!"

As the chief navy signal officer in the region, Westgate had wireless connection to air force bases in New Brunswick, Nova Scotia, and Newfoundland. His message was relayed, as were the civilian sightings, to a US Army Air Forces base at Gander, Newfoundland. That afternoon, a B-17 Flying Fortress dispatched from the Gander station made visual contact with *U553* and dropped depth-charges.[18] The charges exploded wide of the mark. The next day, two Canso flying boats from RCAF No. 5 (BR) Squadron at Dartmouth, Nova Scotia, swept the gulf but made no contact. The presence of air surveillance, however, kept *U553* submerged and slowed Kptlt Karl Thurmann's progress farther up the Gaspé coast.

Back on the surface after dark on May 11, *U553* found shipping lanes and unescorted merchant targets eastbound from Montreal. First he shadowed the 5,364-ton freighter SS *Nicoya*. Then, just south of Anticosti Island, he fired one torpedo, which brought the steamer to a stop, and then a second *coup de grâce* shot to sink it. The explosions and sinking killed five crewmen and one gunner. Eighty-two survived. Two hours later, *U553* sighted the unescorted SS *Leto*, north of Cape-de-la-Madeleine, and torpedoed her too; forty-one aboard managed to get to lifeboats and rafts as she went down.

The first evidence of the merchant ship sinkings came during the day on May 12, from residents on the Gaspé shoreline closest to the attacks. At L'Anse-à-Valleau, twenty miles up the coast from the Cap-des-Rosiers lighthouse, thirty-nine survivors had come ashore from *Nicoya* in lifeboats. With no roads to the shoreline, local fishermen rushed their horse-drawn wagons overland to the scene to bring out the injured. Meantime, RCN photographer Ian Tate found his way there to capture the rescue in still photos, and Jack Brayley talked to survivors and rescuers, wrote his copy, and phoned his story in to the Canadian Press office in Montreal. Two news stories appeared the next day on the front pages of newspapers across the country.

Brayley's account was datelined "A St. Lawrence River Port, May 13 (Wednesday) (CP)." "With the number of survivors from the first vessel torpedoed in the St. Lawrence River reported to be 87 or 88," the story began, "the Mayor of a fishing centre near here said early today that, 'there may have been some losses.' . . . Censorship would not permit the use of his name.

"An informant said over the telephone that residents for two miles around one fishing village were awakened 'by a terrible explosion that rocked our houses as though there was an earthquake. [We] saw lights appear offshore and we knew that something had happened to a ship.'

"'Early on Tuesday,' he said, 'two lifeboats drifted ashore bearing the forty-two crewmen from the torpedoed freighter. The boats were not equipped with oars and were carried ashore by wind and tide.'"[19]

A second story, carried on the front pages of newspapers

such as the *Globe and Mail* and the *Ottawa Evening Journal*, contained the federal government's official press-release response to the attack. But Angus L. Macdonald, the minister of defence for naval services, explicitly omitted mention of the merchant ship, the location of the sinking, or even where survivors had come ashore. The story merely said, "the first enemy submarine attack upon shipping in the St. Lawrence River took place on May 11. . . . Forty-one survivors have been landed."

The minister finished his statement by proclaiming that "any future sinkings in this area will not be made public. . . . [But] the Canadian public should be . . . assured that every step is being taken to grapple with the situation."[20]

Jack Brayley didn't need to read the minister's pronouncement about prohibiting publication of further sinkings. Ottawa and the navy censors already had. In Brayley's original copy filed to Canadian Press, he described two sinkings, not one. But before the censors could close the door on his reporting, on May 13 the *Ottawa Evening Journal* printed what Brayley had learned from interviews with villagers:

"Nearly half of more than four score survivors of a vessel torpedoed Monday in the St. Lawrence River were reported to the Canadian Press to have come from a vessel other than the one sunk by the first enemy submarine ever to invade the river waters.

"Residents along the river were said to have heard gunfire either indicating that the submarine had fired shells at the ship or that the ship was fighting back. . . . A tight censorship of news from a nearby fishing village where some of the survivors are resting, prevented confirmation of reports some lives have been lost."[21]

Undaunted by the government's attempts to keep a lid on the sinkings and to prevent general panic,* Brayley had a backup plan that would at least alert Forbes Rhude, the Canadian Press bureau chief in Montreal, about what was happening in the waters off Gaspé. He'd composed a series of code words that censors would likely overlook but which Rhude would recognize. Brayley would simply refer to a laundry list of additional clothing he needed while on the case in Gaspé: "Socks" were U-boats. "Shirts" were torpedoes. "Shorts" were freighters.

Meanwhile, as Gaspé Quebecers digested what was unfolding off their shores and as Ottawa scrambled to invent the long-promised St. Lawrence Escort Force, *U553* slipped quietly back through the Cabot Strait to the open Atlantic. Kptlt Thurmann transmitted a quick summary of what he'd seen to Kriegsmarine headquarters. "No shipping traffic, very alert air surveillance, warship patrols by patrol boats"[22] was his review from the gulf.

In June, while still on his seventh patrol in the western Atlantic—his longest, at sixty-seven days—Thurmann sank the British motor freighter *Mattawin* to push his total tonnage sunk to over 50,000; in August the Kriegsmarine awarded him the Knight's Cross. He didn't return to the Gulf of St. Lawrence, but by the end of 1942 he had sunk over 77,000 tons of merchant shipping. On her tenth patrol, in January 1943, however, *U553* disappeared mysteriously. Thurmann's final message, like others he'd issued from this U-boat, dealt with an apparent mechanical problem. "Periscope not clear" was all it said. *U553* was never seen or heard from again.

* Prime Minister King revealed news of the sinkings to his caucus the next day, admitting candidly that the attacks in the Gaspé validated his concern about the U-boat threat to Quebecers and further justified his call to marshal military resources in Canada.

Within weeks of *U553*'s exit from the gulf, fellow U-Bootwaffe commander Kptlt Ernst Vogelsang steered *U132* through Cabot Strait into the gulf, just as Thurmann had done in May. Vogelsang had first served aboard a German destroyer in the Spanish Civil War. After U-boat training in 1940, he took command of *U132*, a Type VIIC U-boat, in 1941. On just his third patrol, Kptlt Vogelsang worked his way northwest to Cap Chat, where the St. Lawrence estuary begins to narrow, a spot more than 100 miles beyond where *U553* had sunk the first two merchant ships. Vogelsang piloted his U-boat back and forth across the shipping channel until, on July 6, Convoy QS 15, in transit between Quebec City and Sydney, entered his sights. He attacked on the surface and torpedoed two freighters—SS *Anastassios Pateras* and SS *Hainaut*—in different columns of the convoy. The principal escort, minesweeper HMCS *Drummondville*, was steaming well ahead of the convoy, and since the stricken merchantmen hadn't had time to fire distress rockets, the sweeper's crew initially knew nothing of the attack. The remaining merchant ships began to scatter.

"The convoy disperses in all directions," Vogelsang recorded, "the larger portion turns inbound [back to port of origin]."[23]

Fairmile *Q060*, also escorting, began dropping depth charges, but in the confusion the U-boat remained on the surface and fired a torpedo into the British freighter SS *Dinaric*. The ship was suddenly blowing steam and listing to starboard. That explosion attracted *Drummondville*. The minesweeper commander, Lt James Fraser, recounted his counterattack. "The SS *Dinaric* was passed, with a torpedo hole in her starboard side and the crew in a lifeboat," he wrote. "Rounding the stern of *Dinaric* the submarine was sighted directly ahead in the light of the starshell, laying on the surface stopped—distance about 900 to 1,000 yards."[24]

Fraser completed his turn and headed straight for *U132*, calling on CPO George Jamieson and his anti-submarine crew to drop three depth charges (set for fifty feet and released at three-second intervals) over the phosphorescence in the water where the U-boat had dived. The blasts brought up debris and the U-boat surfaced. But Fraser couldn't make out the conning tower. He realized that he was staring at the underside of *U132* as she lay on her side. Fraser ordered *Drummondville* up to ramming speed, but Vogelsang had managed to regain control of his U-boat and commenced another crash dive.

The U-boat captain didn't realize it at the time, but gulf and river currents were mixing beneath the surface, and their different water densities would ultimately save him. At that particular location in the estuary, a relatively warm layer of freshwater from the river flowed over the colder, and therefore denser and heavier, saltwater present in the gulf. Tides tended to mix the two. Vogelsang discovered that this layering effect offered *U132* adequate protection when close to surface escorts, by both reflecting ASDIC signals and masking his own sounds. The gulf's natural properties were giving the invading U-boats the upper hand.*

The water layering effect hampered anti-submarine gear aboard the corvettes too. Sub-detector operator Martin Franchetto learned this early in his time aboard corvettes in

* Air action July 6 involved a flight of Kittyhawk fighters from RCAF 130 Squadron at Mont-Joli, Quebec. S/L Jacques Chevrier (Canadian veteran of the Battle of Britain) scrambled to chase *U132*; patrolling to his fuel limit, Chevrier ditched in the St. Lawrence River a mile offshore Cap Chat. His body was never recovered.

the gulf. After his basic training at HMCS *York* in Toronto, and advanced training at HMCS *Naden* in Esquimalt, BC, he went on active service aboard a minesweeper. The Bangor-class sweepers used gyro compasses and state-of-the-art retractable-dome sonar during their anti-submarine patrols in the Pacific. However, when the navy reassigned him to HMCS *Moncton*, a corvette in the St. Lawrence Escort Force, he discovered it only had magnetic compasses and Type 123A ASDIC.[25] As a result, when his corvette entered waters where the fresh and saltwater mixed, ASDIC efficiency was compromised.

"Salt water is very dense, so it carries the underwater sound beam very well," he wrote. "[But] our sonar was useless in the fresh water of the St. Lawrence River."[26]

And when U-boat commanders began to realize this inadequacy in their escort adversaries, they took full advantage.

In the case of Kptlt Vogelsang and *U132*, the U-boat likely had a buoyancy problem after *Drummondville*'s first attack. The U-boat descended rapidly; then Vogelsang blew his buoyancy tanks to resurface and used his greater speed on the surface to outrun the sweeper. Lt Fraser and *Drummondville* attempted to make ASDIC contact. But again, in the upper, freshwater layers of the gulf, sonic sensing devices produced confusing results. *U132* made it to the shelter of the south shore of the St. Lawrence, where she remained submerged for eighteen hours, until July 6/7. Vogelsang and *U132* then received orders from BdU to move northeast to the Strait of Belle Isle and patrol in search of convoys. Behind them they left a political tempest.

Within hours, CP reporter Jack Brayley knew that three merchant ships had been sunk. He also knew that government censors would dissect or block anything he wrote. With that in mind, he sent editor Forbes Rhude his latest laundry list: "Three shirts, three shorts and three pairs of socks"—meaning U-boats had fired at least three torpedoes at three freighters.

"What the hell is this?" responded a news editor—not Rhude—on the desk in Montreal. "The isolation has finally gotten to Brayley."[27]

Before long, the RCMP in Gaspé had arrived to put an end to Brayley's laundry lists and his reporting. But neither law enforcement officials nor federal censors could silence the uproar in the House of Commons. On July 10, Joseph Roy, an independent Member of Parliament from Gaspé, used parliamentary immunity in the House to deliver the bombshell story to the nation.

"According to information received from my constituency," Roy announced, "three ships forming part of a fourteen-ship convoy were torpedoed . . . opposite Cap Chat in the St. Lawrence River." He went on to demand a secret session in Ottawa to discuss "the seriousness of the situation."[28]

Angus L. Macdonald attacked Roy for revealing information that he contended could be used by the enemy. "If [Roy] thinks . . . the whole Canadian navy is going to line up along his shores and defend those shores only . . . he's making a tremendous mistake," Macdonald fumed. "I'm not ready to change the disposition of one ship for him or all the questions he may ask from now until doomsday."

At this point in the summer of 1942, the RCN's St. Lawrence Escort Force looked pretty meagre. The force stationed at HMCS *Fort Ramsay* in Gaspé and responsible for the SQ and QS convoys in the gulf consisted of five minesweepers, an armed yacht, and three Fairmiles. The RCN force based at Sydney consisted of two sweepers, two armed yachts, and six Fairmiles. And the latter was responsible for escorting passenger and railway ferries across the Cabot Strait, and merchant ships running between the west coast of Newfoundland and ports in eastern Canada. However, all RCN warships had an able ally in the RCAF Eastern Air Command.

Thanks to Canada's early commitment to the training of aircrew—pilots, observers, wireless radio operators, and gunners—the British Commonwealth Air Training Plan (BCATP) had already established eight Air Force stations, all on the southern perimeter of the gulf. Each school included fully serviced airfields, hangars, barracks, administration facilities, and aircrew to back up operations of Canada's EAC, the wing of RCAF operations over eastern Canada, Newfoundland, and the Gulf of St. Lawrence. Yarmouth had also become the base of operations for RCAF No. 113 (BR) Squadron, with its Lockheed Hudson bombers and its experienced commanding officer, S/L Norville "Molly" Small.

Originally from Ontario, Small had served in the RCAF between the wars, and in commercial aviation flying bush planes in the late 1930s. When the war broke out, he rejoined the Air Force, and because of his experience, EAC posted him to bombing and gunnery squadrons to both instruct and fly operational sorties. It was on April 28, 1942, while serving in RCAF No. 10 (BR) Squadron at Dartmouth that Small's keenness to fight and to teach intersected.

On a Catalina training flight he located a U-boat and closed in for an attack. As yet untrained for anti-submarine tactics with Catalinas, Small and crew unleashed two 250-pound bombs; one got stuck in the plane's bomb rack and the other was a dud. Small had learned by trial and error that bombs with contact fuses were useless against U-boats; however, depth charges dropped from a low level and triggered by water pressure (hydrostatic detonation) had a better chance of inflicting more severe damage.[29]

"The captain of the aircraft," Small reported drily about his own attack, "feels that though the possibility of a clean kill is not very strong, he is certain that he made their back teeth rattle."[30] He added that he'd be better prepared the next time.

In addition to changing weaponry, Small borrowed a couple of tricks from other experienced aircrews with RAF Coastal Command. Until that time, Air Force U-boat hunters had not mastered the element of surprise. Too often U-boats on the surface spotted enemy aircraft—dark fuselages against a bright sky—and managed to submerge long before the Allied bomber got within range to attack. RAF veterans recommended painting the Hudson bomber bellies white, to blend into the sky. They also noted that attacking from higher altitudes, where U-boat lookouts might not be scanning, would give attackers a slight edge. Eastern Air Command recommended abandoning attacks from 100 feet in favour of attacks from 5,000 feet.

That summer, S/L Small was posted to No. 113 (BR) Squadron, back flying Hudson bombers. And on July 31, 1942, he was piloting a white-bellied Hudson when he caught *U754* unawares off the Nova Scotia coast.

"[Spotted] a submarine fully surfaced approximately three miles ahead and one mile to port of aircraft track," Small reported. "The approach to the target was made at a slight angle to the submarine's track and from astern."[31]

Date	U-boat	Ship Attacked	Tonnage
May 12/42	*U553*	*Nicoya*	5,364
May 12	*U553*	*Leto*	4,712
July 6	*U132*	*Dinaric*	2,555
July 6	*U132*	*Hainaut*	4,312
July 6	*U132*	*Anastassios Pateras*	3,382
July 20	*U132*	*Frederika Lensen*	4,367
Aug 27	*U517*	*Chatham*	5,649
Aug 28	*U517*	*Arlyn*	3,304
Aug 28	*U165*	*Laramie**	7,252
Sept 3	*U517*	*Donald Stewart*	1,781
Sept 6	*U165*	*Aeas*	4,729
Sept 7	*U165*	HMCS *Raccoon*	358
Sept 7	*U517*	*Mount Pindus*	5,729
Sept 7	*U517*	*Mount Taygetus*	3,286
Sept 7	*U517*	*Oakton*	1,727
Sept 11/42	*U517*	HMCS *Charlottetown*	900
Sept 15	*U517*	*Saturnus*	2,741
Sept 15	*U517*	*Inger Elizabeth*	2,166
Sept 16	*U165*	*Joannis*	3,667
Sept 16	*U165*	*Essex Lance*	6,625 (d.)
Oct 9	*U69*	*Carolus*	2,375
Oct 11	*U106*	*Waterton*	2,140
Oct 14	*U69*	*Caribou*	2,222
Oct 14	*U1223*	HMCS *Magog*	1,370
Nov 2	*U1223*	*Fort Thompson*	7,134 (d.)
Nov 25	*U1228*	HMCS *Shawinigan*	900
Dec 24	*U806*	HMCS *Clayoquot*	672
Apr 16/45	*U190*	HMCS *Esquimalt*	590
Total Sunk & Damaged (d.)			**92,009**

* Location not known

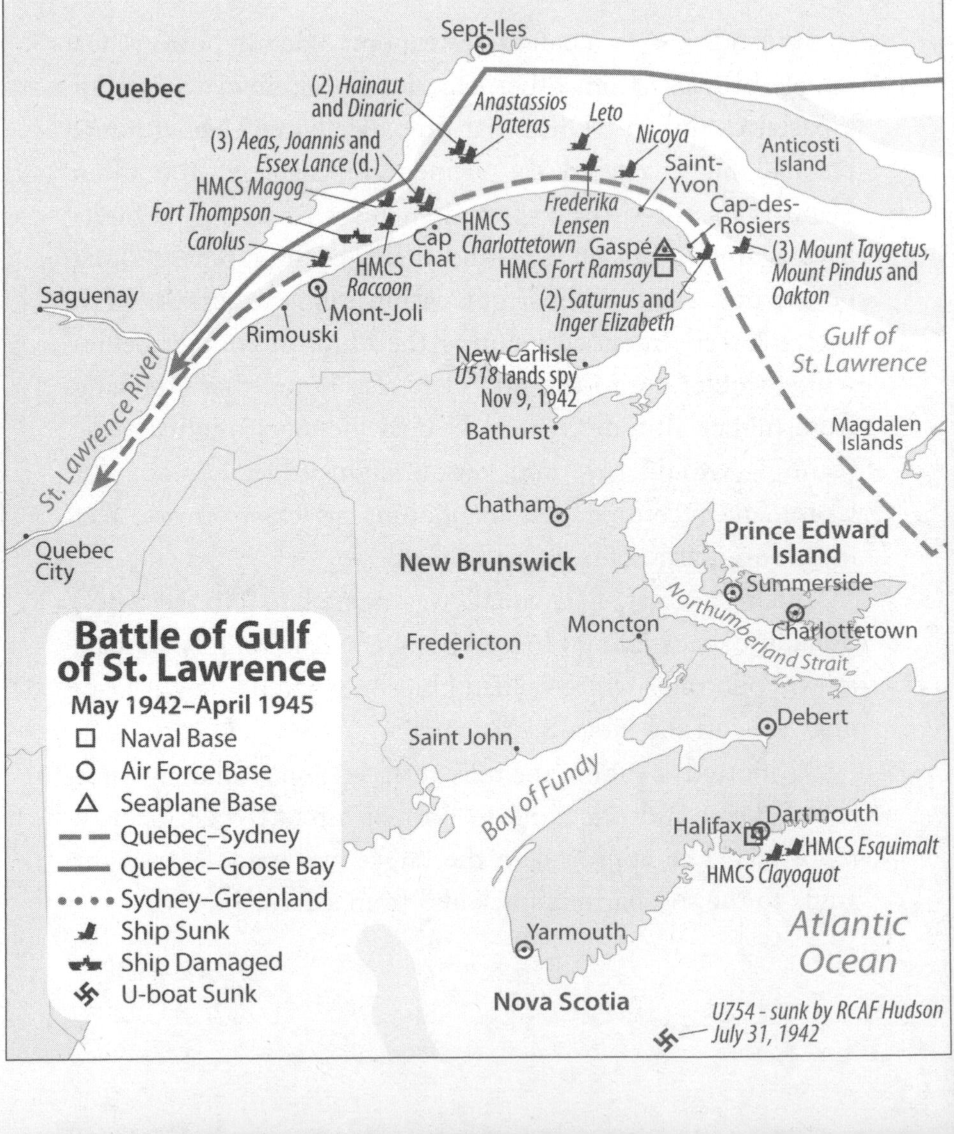

Conception Bay–Bell Island

Date	U-boat	Ship Attacked	Tonnage
Sept 5/42	*U513*	*Saganaga*	5,545
Sept 5	*U513*	*Lord Strathcona*	7,335
Nov 2	*U518*	*Rose Castle*	7,803
Nov 2	*U518*	*PLM 27*	5,633

Atlantic Ocean off Cape Race, Nfld

Date	U-boat	Ship Attacked	Tonnage
May 7/44	*U548*	HMCS *Valleyfield*	1,445

Small's severe dive and rapid attack finally caught the lookout's attention, and the Hudson aircrew could plainly see the U-boat's submariners dashing for the conning tower hatch. The U-boat loomed with her battleship-grey colouring, the entire deck visible. Small levelled off at fifty feet above the surface, straddled the submarine, and released a cluster of four depth charges. Set for shallow ignition, the charges exploded just as *U754* began her crash dive. She briefly resurfaced, and Small's gunners strafed the conning tower. The U-boat submerged again.

"Fifty-five minutes [later]," the anti-submarine report noted, "a heavy explosion was seen to take place at a point five miles from the point where the depth charges exploded."

U754 was gone. S/L Small and his crew were the first anti-submarine aircraft crew in RCAF Eastern Air Command to destroy a U-boat.[32]

TRIAL and error became the teachers of Royal Canadian Navy crews thrown into this new battlefield too. With U-boat attacks mounting in the gulf, RCN strategists began redirecting more potent escorts, including corvette HMCS *Trail*, from the Triangle Run to convoys moving through the Strait of Belle Isle, at the northern tip of Newfoundland. The ship's ASDIC operators had learned from other escorts about the way gulf water-layering interfered with onboard listening devices, but experience told them the U-boats would always be lurking at that bottleneck.

On August 27, 1942, an American convoy worked its way from Sydney, Cape Breton Island, north across the gulf toward the Strait of Belle Isle, en route to Greenland. The convoy had split into two groups, with the US Army troopship *Chatham* coursing ahead in a faster group (Convoy SG 6) with US Coast Guard Cutter (USCGC) *Mojave*. The 5,649-ton *Chatham* carried a crew of 134 as well as 428 Canadian and American labourers bound for air bases at Thule, Greenland. Close behind the first convoy, HMCS *Trail* escorted two slower merchantmen in Convoy LN 6, sailing from Quebec City to Goose Bay, Labrador. RCAF aircrews were providing air cover for the slower convoy, but not for SG 6.

Ahead of the troopship lay the first of a dozen U-boats Adm Karl Dönitz had dispatched that fall to hunt along the Atlantic coast of Newfoundland and into the Gulf of St. Lawrence via the Strait of Belle Isle. Preparing to work in tandem, Kptlt Paul Hartwig—commanding *U517*—and Kptlt Eberhard Hoffmann—commanding *U165*—were both young officers on their first patrols, in search of their first victories. Just before nine in the morning, *U517* surfaced and fired two torpedoes into *Chatham*, the second striking the engine room and causing the ship's boilers to explode. In spite of the destruction amidships, the vessel remained afloat for half an hour, allowing most to get to lifeboats and rafts. *Chatham* was the first American troopship sunk by enemy action.[33]

Alerted to the sinking, *Trail*, under the command of Lt George Hall, raced ahead to assist but suddenly faced an unexpected dilemma. Ahead of her—along the exact line of telltale ASDIC soundings of an escaping submerged U-boat—the water was littered with troops and crewmen from the sunken troopship, all thrashing in the water to survive. Hall knew that to plough into the shipwrecked men would kill innocents. Worse, while pursuing a U-boat, which was his duty and priority, he would ultimately have to drop depth charges, whose massive explosions would certainly kill more *Chatham* survivors. The cantankerous gulf waters made the decision for the corvette crew.

"ASDIC conditions were bad," Lt Hall reported. "Non-sub contacts [were] obtained all around the ship. . . . Effectiveness of an [anti-submarine] screen [was] greatly affected."[34]

Trail's crew began a rescue operation instead. But U-boat commanders Hartwig and Hoffmann had just begun their sinking spree. That same day, *U165* and *U517* torpedoed three more US ships. Even within the confined area of the Gulf of St. Lawrence, the U-boats found plenty of room to continue their hunt. On the evening of September 6, Kptlt Hoffmann and *U165* penetrated Convoy QS 33 in the Strait of Belle Isle and sank the Greek freighter *Aeas*, and then fired a single torpedo into the armed yacht at the rear of the convoy. HMCS *Raccoon*'s boiler exploded with the impact, and though the remaining escorts searched in the morning, they found no remnants or survivors from *Raccoon*.

Meanwhile, a third member of the U-boat flotilla, KK Rolf Rüggeberg and *U513*, got BdU clearance to hunt the waters off Newfoundland's east coast. At thirty-five, Rüggeberg had served in the German Navy between the wars, and in 1939 as a senior naval attaché in Spain and Portugal. In 1941 he had transferred to U-boats, and when Adm Dönitz sent him to the North Atlantic in August 1942, both *U513* and Rüggeberg were on their maiden patrol. While Hartwig and Hoffmann had taken the Strait of Belle Isle assignment, BdU cleared Rüggeberg to take his Type IXC U-boat south along the east coast of Newfoundland.[35]

Undetected, on September 4 he followed an armed merchant ship, SS *Evelyn B*, into Conception Bay, to the west end of Bell Island. There he spotted several fully loaded iron-ore carriers anchored at the Wabana mine's loading docks. KK Rüggeberg put *U513* on the bottom of the channel in about eighty feet of water, preparing to make Wabana a wartime target.

In the morning, he scanned the scene at periscope depth. At the extreme left of his view, still at the Wabana loading pier, was the 5,633-ton ore carrier SS *PLM* 47. Dead ahead, all lying at anchor, sat the 5,454-ton SS *Saganaga*, 7,335-ton SS *Lord Strathcona*, and, slightly to starboard, SS *Evelyn B*, the ship *U513* had followed to the spot in the darkness overnight.[36] Rüggeberg fired two torpedoes from his forward tubes. It was just after 11:30 a.m. local time.

"No detonation. Neither of the fish could be heard on the hydrophones. They failed to run," his report said. "Kept going. Prepared to attack with stern tubes. Fired two single shots. Scored a hit at front [of *Saganaga*]."[37]

Half a mile away, the explosion threw Ross Creaser out of his bunk aboard SS *Lord Strathcona*. He'd finished his watch at eight o'clock, had breakfast, and turned in. Chief Officer Creaser dashed on deck just as the third mate sounded the alarm.

"I saw the second explosion," Creaser said. "It was pretty heavy because it shook [our fully] loaded ship. I went back to my room, put on my hat and life jacket."[38]

Creaser and his shipmates took to *Strathcona*'s lifeboats—one off the starboard side and Creaser's from the port side. They weren't abandoning ship but launching their boats to assist their brother merchant sailors in *Saganaga*. Laden with ore, she was sinking fast.

Meantime, Rüggeberg called for *U513* to surface to assess

the damage inflicted. But as the U-boat rose through the shallow water, her conning tower collided with the hull of the other ore carrier. Rüggeberg quickly repositioned the U-boat, lined up the carrier he'd just struck, and fired another two torpedoes. Less than a minute later, the weapons struck SS *Lord Strathcona*.

"We were nearly to the [*Saganaga*] wreckage," Creaser continued, "when we heard two sounds under the water and then our ship blew up. It was 11:45 and a minute and a half later she was completely underwater."[39]

Creaser and *Strathcona*'s rescuers managed to save fourteen of the forty-four aboard *Saganaga*, while all forty-four aboard his own ship managed to get to lifeboats and rafts to save themselves. But by that time, a full-scale naval engagement was raging on the surface around them. Gunners aboard *Evelyn B* as well as shore batteries on Bell Island had spotted *U513*'s wake in the daylight, but Rüggeberg escaped through the Tickle, the strait between the island and the mainland. A Hudson bomber arrived within an hour, followed by a Digby; then four Fairmiles and a corvette completed a sweep. None found any trace of the attacker.

THE pace of the battle in the Gulf of St. Lawrence—an extension of the larger North Atlantic siege that summer of 1942—never let up. In August alone, Adm Dönitz's U-boats had sunk 508,426 tons of shipping across the North Atlantic, their third-best month of the year thus far.[40] During just fourteen days in the gulf, Kptlt Hartwig and his crew aboard *U517* had sunk five freighters and a US troopship, nearly 22,000 tons of shipping. And all three U-boats in this joint patrol of the gulf—*U513*, *U517*, and *U165*—were the larger, longer-range Type IXC U-boats, each carrying at least twenty torpedoes. As long as they remained undetected and had fuel and food supplies sufficient to last them, there was much more they could accomplish. Anticipating even better hunting prospects, Dönitz sent another handful of U-boats to probe the waters of the gulf. Meanwhile, on September 11, Hartwig and *U517* encountered their seventh target.

Travelling in tandem with Bangor-class minesweeper HMCS *Clayoquot*, LCdr John W. Bonner and his corvette crew aboard HMCS *Charlottetown* had just completed their eleventh Sydney-to-Quebec convoy escort since July. The two warships hadn't bothered to refuel at Rimouski, Quebec, so they were steaming at an efficient speed of eleven knots but were not zigzagging. It was about eight o'clock in the morning and *Charlottetown*'s crewmen were changing watches when *U517*'s first torpedo struck the corvette's starboard quarter; a few seconds later a second hit farther forward.

The corvette immediately listed to starboard, water pouring in at the waterline; she would only remain afloat for four minutes. In that time, her RCN sailors scrambled to save themselves. Most below decks in the engine room hadn't a chance to escape, while those on deck had just enough time to make it to a railing and jump overboard. But even as the first survivors swam frantically to get clear of the now rolling and sinking corvette, a worse fate awaited them in the frigid water. Since *Charlottetown* had gone to action stations, all her depth charges had been activated and set for shallow depth. As the ship sank, those charges began exploding, killing crew in the water or heaving them skyward. *Charlottetown*'s own charges killed more of her crew than *U517*'s two torpedoes had.

Meanwhile, the corvette's sister sweeper *Clayoquot* had raced from a mile away to where *Charlottetown* had gone down. Lt Henry Lade, the CO aboard *Clayoquot*, faced an oft-repeated decision: whether to attempt to destroy the submerging U-boat with depth charges and, in doing so, injure or kill the Canadian crewmen struggling in the very same waters. Lade quickly called off the attack and began retrieving survivors in water that was just above freezing. Of sixty-eight crew aboard *Charlottetown*, ten, including LCdr Bonner, died in the sinking.

DURING the fall of 1942, as the see-saw battle in the St. Lawrence reached its climax, the Canadian government made a crucial decision that changed defensive strategies for both navy and air force operations in the gulf. The Mackenzie King Cabinet approved a navy recommendation to send seventeen of its corvettes to support Operation Torch, the invasion of North Africa planned for November. Within hours of the Cabinet decision, NSHQ in Ottawa signalled the Admiralty that the St. Lawrence was closed to all overseas shipping.

At the same time, Allied convoy planners had decided to assemble transatlantic convoys in New York rather than in Sydney and Halifax. With convoys growing larger and sailing more frequently from American ports, their continuous passage to the UK seemed more economical; however, they would then require the Western Local Escort Force to extend its patrols substantially in order to escort convoys to the mid-ocean handoff points. All this left fewer RCN warships patrolling East Coast shipping. To compensate, EAC moved a detachment of Hudson bombers from Yarmouth, Nova Scotia, to Mont-Joli, Quebec; with all BCATP schools across the region alerted, the RCAF felt it could fill that gap against U-boat incursion in the gulf from the air.

His torpedo attack on HMCS *Charlottetown* on September 11 had emboldened Kptlt Paul Hartwig. Four days later, *U517* added a Norwegian coal-carrier and a Dutch freighter to her tonnage sunk total. But try as he might, from then until his patrol ended in mid-October, Hartwig enjoyed no further victories in the gulf. He blamed "constantly strengthened" air patrols.[41] His nemesis was F/O M.J. Bélanger, a Hudson bomber pilot flying from the training and operational station at Chatham, New Brunswick. Just before midnight on September 24, Bélanger executed a perfect moonlight attack. Off the north shore of the St. Lawrence, his Hudson caught *U517* on the surface and dropped depth charges astern of the U-boat. Hartwig escaped. But then, four days later, twenty miles off Gaspé, Bélanger surprised Hartwig on the surface again.

"The charges were seen to explode all around the hull slightly ahead of the conning tower," Bélanger reported. "The U-boat's bow came up out of the water and all forward action stopped. It then appeared to settle straight down."[42]

Despite the violent impact, all Bélanger detected after the attack was oil or air bubbles. *U517* had escaped again. However, the strain was getting to the U-boat commander. As he made his way back to Lorient in October 1942, Hartwig noted his frustration.* "Planes would unexpectedly swoop down . . .

* Kptlt Hartwig had sunk nine ships on his first patrol—all in the Gulf of St. Lawrence; four days into his second patrol in November 1942, *U517* was sunk by Fairey Albacores from the aircraft carrier HMS *Victorious*, and Hartwig was captured.

buzz . . . drop out of a cloud, or skim low over the water out of the sun and drop bombs," Hartwig later said. "One hell of a ruckus."[43]

Harassment by EAC sub-hunters from stations at Mont-Joli and Gander prevented sinkings in the gulf for three weeks—from September 16 to October 9—until a new U-boat arriving on the scene sank *Carolus*, in the Goose Bay–bound Convoy LN 9 along the south shore of the St. Lawrence, just 200 miles from Quebec City. The newcomer in the gulf was *U69*, under the command of Kptlt Ulrich Gräf. The Type VIIC U-boat had seen a lot of action—eight patrols since 1940—but this was only Gräf's second trip as her commander. *U69* did, however, have the latest in anti-radar technology. Called Metox, after its French inventor Metox Grandin, this new German radar search receiver had an antenna attached to a wooden cross (dubbed the Biscay Cross) that stuck into a fitting on the U-boat's conning tower. The Metox receiver detected long-wave radar emissions, including those emitted by radar sets aboard RCAF Eastern Air Command aircraft. So, after *U69* attacked and sank *Carolus*, attracting EAC Hudson bombers to the area, the searching aircraft set off *U69*'s Metox alarms in plenty of time for the U-boat to dive to safety.

Forced to submerge longer than he liked, however, Gräf chose next to reposition his U-boat away from the mouth of the St. Lawrence, southward to the relative safety of Cabot Strait. There he could surface, recharge his batteries, take advantage of easy access to the open ocean if he needed it, and keep a lookout for potential targets. At 3:21 a.m. on October 14, 1942, under a moonless, clear sky, on seas with two-foot swells, Kptlt Gräf spotted one.

"Bearing 300. One shadow in sight, behind it a second small one," read *U69*'s log. "Freighter-passenger vessel belching heavy smoke, approx. 6,500 GRT [tonnage]. Starboard aft, a two-stacked destroyer [*sic*] escorting. Visibility good, weak aurora borealis."[44]

Gräf's assessments did not correctly identify either vessel. In fact, the second shadow was not a destroyer but the Bangor-class minesweeper HMCS *Grandmère*, escorting the lead vessel. The freighter-passenger was more accurately a ferry, weighing closer to 2,000 tons, and bearing not freight but seventy-three civilians, including eleven children, 118 military personnel, and forty-six crew members serving aboard Newfoundland Railway's SS *Caribou.*

The steamer was making one of its thrice-weekly trips between North Sydney on Cape Breton Island and Port-aux-Basques, at the southwestern tip of Newfoundland. Despite the clear skies and calm seas, it was pitch dark, and neither the ferry *Caribou* nor the warship *Grandmère* (positioned according to RN protocol about 2,500 yards off the starboard quarter of the ferry) spotted *U69* travelling on the surface. The sweeper also had no radar; her ASDIC hydrophone, not suited for surface pickup of the U-boat, delivered only the sound of *Caribou*'s steam engines and propeller. *Caribou* and *Grandmère* had cleared the anti-submarine defence boom at the entrance to North Sydney Harbour at 8:30 the previous evening. At 3:21 a.m. they were just twenty-three miles from their Newfoundland destination.

U69, still on the surface and still undetected, had managed to race ahead on the starboard side of her target, and had turned back to line up a torpedo shot at a right angle to the ferry. Gräf headed straight to the target and fired from less than half a mile away. Forty-three seconds later, the torpedo ploughed into *Caribou* amidships, directly into the engine room, causing the ferry's boilers to explode. The blast not only punctured the ferry's hull for sea water to rush in, it also shattered everything above—lifeboats, fittings, and the first-class berths amidships.

Among the 191 passengers travelling to Port-aux-Basques, two nursing sisters, Margaret Brooke and Agnes Wilkie, were returning from two weeks of leave, on their way back to the naval hospital in St. John's. During the early evening hours of their trip, the two sub-lieutenants had taken the time to look for life jackets and practise putting them on.

"When the torpedo struck, I was thrown across the room right on top of Agnes [Wilkie]," Sister Brooke wrote later. "She jumped up and grabbed the flashlight to find our life belts."[45] The two nursing sisters quickly probed their way to the boat deck and found "one terrified mob." With all lights blacked out or dead without power from the engine room, the darkness sent passengers into panic. Too many clambered into lifeboats and refused to give up their spots, preventing the boats from being turned out and launched.

On *Grandmère*'s open bridge, the watch saw the flash of the torpedo detonation off the sweeper's port bow. Her commander, Lt James Cuthbert, dashed to the bridge amid a call to action stations. Within moments *U69* was spotted—350 yards away—veering sharply to starboard. Cuthbert called for full speed from the engine room and for depth charges to be readied. It was *Grandmère*'s job to attack. If he could intercept the U-boat before she dove, Cuthbert intended to ram her, or at least to lay down a pattern of depth charges over her likely course underwater.

Gräf saw the escort racing his way. He cleared the conning tower and ordered a crash dive. In addition, as he took *U69* down, Gräf called for the release of a couple of *Pillenwerfer* bubble targets* to cloak his escape.

Over the U-boat's wake, Cuthbert's depth-charge crew dropped a six-charge pattern. But once again with the layering effect of gulf waters, *Grandmère* could not maintain ASDIC contact with the sub.

Gräf turned his U-boat toward the sinking ferry, thinking that the surface warship would not drop charges where passengers were floating in lifeboats and jackets.

For two hours Cuthbert searched, listened, and waited for evidence of the U-boat so he could attack again; he knew, however, that every moment his sweeper spent in pursuit might well be the last for *Caribou*'s survivors, thrown into the frigid October waters of the gulf. Finally he ended the hunt with no evidence of damage or destruction, and addressed his other obligation as escort. "05.20–6.30. Searched for survivors," *Grandmère*'s log read.[46]

In the water just minutes after they reached the boat deck, nursing sisters Brooke and Wilkie found themselves fighting the weight of the waterlogged Burberry coats they'd put on to keep out the cold. "We were sucked under with [the sinking ferry]," continued Brooke's account. "We clung together somehow all the time we were under and when we finally reached the surface, we managed to grab a piece of wreckage."[47]

Eventually an overturned lifeboat floated near them and

* By 1942, Kriegsmarine scientists had developed the *Pillenwerfer* ("pill thrower")—a metal canister, four inches in diameter, with calcium hydride inside. When mixed with sea water, those contents generated hydrogen, which bubbled out of the canister and presented a false sonar target. The decoy could last about twenty-five minutes at a depth of 100 feet, while the U-boat slipped away.

others in the water. Survivors pulled on ropes attached to the boat to lift themselves onto the hull. But quickly the cold conditions brought on hypothermia. Sister Wilkie lost consciousness; with one hand gripping a rope on the boat and the other holding Sister Wilkie's hand, Sister Brooke kept trying to revive her comrade. "I did manage to hold her until daybreak, but then a wave pulled her right away from me. It was so terrible to see her go."[48]

HMCS *Grandmère* eventually found SLt Brooke* and several others clinging to that lifeboat. But with the sunrise, the sweeper wasn't the only vessel attempting a rescue. From the moment *Grandmère* issued her mayday wireless call, an amphibious Canso spotter, four navy ships, and a crash boat had all responded. Cpl Charles Richardson and his shipmates aboard RCAF B109, a high-speed ocean-going rescue craft, raced the eighty miles from North Sydney during the predawn hours to join the search.† [49]

Among the others rescued were fifteen-month-old Leonard Shiers and his mother, Gladys. Carrying him, she was climbing steps to the ferry's bridge when waters washed them overboard; Leonard was the only one of eleven children on board to survive. *Grandmère* managed to retrieve 103 survivors. In all, 137 men, women, and children died in the ferry sinking, including fifty-seven in military uniform, and thirty-one of the ferry's forty-six-man crew.[50] By 9 a.m.

* SLt Wilkie was the only nurse in all three services killed by enemy action in the Second World War. For her heroism, SLt Brooke was made a military Member of the Order of the British Empire.

† RCAF crash boats were seventy feet long, purpose-built for their role by the Canadian Power Boat Company in Montreal. As the name suggests, they raced to crash sites to assist in rescue. All six craft adopted First Nations names; B109 was dubbed *Abnaki* (although *Abenaki*, of the Algonquian-speaking peoples, is the correct spelling).

HMCS *Grandmère* had received orders to make for Sydney, where a hospital could handle the bruises and hypothermia of *Caribou*'s survivors. Despite the first-aid efforts of *Grandmère*'s crew, two of the injured died en route.

Aboard the minesweeper-turned-hospital-ship, there began equally desperate post-trauma activity. One of the survivors, William Lundrigan, a lumber company owner from Corner Brook, said officers aboard *Grandmère* spoke on the warship's public address system and demanded that "no one was to give out any information when they arrived in Sydney."[51] Nevertheless, once ashore, Lundrigan paid a boy ten dollars to have a message sent to his wife: "Arrived in Sydney. All well."

The news spread. The British United Press (BUP) office in Montreal wired a part-time Sydney reporter, asking him to get the story; they tried to bury the request in code by asking about a "swim meet" in the area.[52] By coincidence, Ottawa censor Warren Baldwin had recently arrived in Halifax to assist district censor H. Bruce Jefferson in dealing with attempts by Canadian Press and others to publish stories about the summertime sinkings in the Gulf of St. Lawrence. Baldwin and Jefferson caught BUP's request and blocked its transmission. Meanwhile, reporters at the *Halifax Herald* demanded permission to interview victims' relatives. They'd already composed telegrams to the families of known casualties, but the censors blocked them as well. Undeterred, the *Herald* found Gladys Shiers, mother of infant survivor Leonard, wrote up her story of mother-and-child survival, and submitted it to the censors. Jefferson edited out Shiers's account of the counterattack by *Grandmère* against the U-boat, but the story of baby Shiers's survival was published.

At CP in Halifax, reporter Bob Daldorph had gathered interviews and details of the ordeal by telephone and telegraph and reported on what he'd found. Two days later, on October 16, his story was published with the heading "BULLETIN," and next to it the approval "Passed by Censor" scribbled in pencil. The lead included the phrase "greatest announced Marine disaster of this war, in the coastal waters fringing on Canada."

The story continued: "Struck as she neared the end of her overnight run from North Sydney, N.S., to Port-aux-Basques, Newfoundland, the ferry sank within a few minutes. Servicemen and civilians, men, women, and children from Canada, Newfoundland, and the United States perished."

The censors blacked out when and where the ferry was torpedoed and the names of Capt Ben Taverner and his two sons, lost in the sinking. They also ran black pencil through Daldorph's description of the response by RCN warships and the RCAF crash boat and aircraft. "After the sub had slipped under the surface, she was attacked heavily by ships of the Canadian Navy that raced up to the scene," the redacted copy read. "With the area lit by flares, the survivors watched from their lifeboats and the water as the war craft tossed a bombardment of depth charges after the sub. . . . There was no word from the Navy on the results of the attack."[53]

Meanwhile, newspaper op-ed columns had begun to print criticism, including Toronto's *Globe and Mail*, which asked: "Why was the *Caribou* not protected when it was known U-boats are slinking off the eastern shores?" It stated further that "Canada must have more ships of war."[54]

On October 17 the navy minister, Angus L. Macdonald, rose in the House of Commons. With more details and questions being published and broadcast each hour, he had no choice but to address the growing outrage. "The sinking of the SS *Caribou* brings the war to Canada with tragic emphasis," he said. "If anything were needed to prove the hideousness of Nazi warfare, surely this is it. Canada can never forget the SS *Caribou*."[55]

As Macdonald spoke, another tempest over the release of sensitive information was brewing in Quebec media. *L'Action catholique*, the major newspaper in Quebec City, had published stories about U-boat attacks across the Gulf of St. Lawrence over the summer. Reports written by the paper's Edouard Laurent characterized the RCN's response as a failure to protect citizens of the province. *L'Action catholique* editor Eugène L'Heureux claimed the stories were not designed as malicious criticism but "to stimulate . . . the men responsible for the defence of our shores and the river."[56] While the Mackenzie King government briefed the premier of Quebec, Adélard Godbout, about events in the Battle of the St. Lawrence, the federal air minister, Charles G. "Chubby" Power, forwarded data about the various sinkings—ship names, locations of attacks—to the premier, hoping he would share details with *L'Action catholique* to soften its criticism of the government and the navy.

For his part, Lt James Cuthbert, the commander of *Grandmère*, continued to be haunted by that night. "I felt the full complement of the things you feel at a time like that. Things you had to live with," Cuthbert said later. "You are torn. Demoralized. Terribly alone . . . I should have gone on looking for the submarine, but I couldn't. Not with women and children out there somewhere."[57]

✪ ✪ ✪

THE Battle of the St. Lawrence had a few more scenes to play out that fall of 1942. While waiting for the new moon period of October to help disguise their nighttime movements, three more of the U-Bootwaffe's Type IX U-boats bided their time near or in the gulf. Recently arrived *U183* probed the Cabot Strait on October 18 and lay low, awaiting further instructions. Already idling south of Newfoundland was *U522*; she would later become engaged in a battle with Convoy SC 107. Meanwhile, *U518*, with Kptlt Friedrich-Wilhelm Wissmann commanding, probed the east coast of Newfoundland on her way to the Cabot Strait. Just as *U513* had in the spring, *U518* crept into Conception Bay to the Wabana mines loading docks on Bell Island. There in the darkness and light rain, on November 2, he spotted three ore carriers at anchor. He fired six torpedoes, sinking the ore-carrier *Rose Castle* and the Free French carrier *PLM 27*, but missing *Fylingdale*; the sixth torpedo exploded against a loading pier. In a matter of minutes, forty merchant sailors died in the explosions and sinking wreckage of the two carriers.

Just as quickly, *U518* submerged, escaped aerial attack with minor damage, and dashed for deeper water off Newfoundland. BdU orders then directed Wissmann through the Cabot Strait back toward Gaspé, and to a position offshore New Carlisle, Quebec. There, on the morning of November 9, *U518* landed a spy on the beach.

Werner Alfred Waldemar von Janowski had lived in Canada before the war. In 1932 he'd even married a woman in Ontario. But late in the Great Depression he'd deserted his wife and returned to Germany. Ashore in Quebec that November morning, Janowski buried his naval uniform. Then, carrying a couple of suitcases (one containing a radio transmitter), he entered the village. He used the assumed name William Branton, lately arrived from Toronto. Not surprisingly for a small community, his presence raised eyebrows. When he arrived at a local hotel, the owner noticed his clothing smelled of diesel oil.[58] Hotelier Earl Annett also secretly checked Branton's room and discovered matches from Belgium, out of place since Canada had not had trade with that country for more than three years. The last straw came as Janowski arrived at the hotel's front desk to pay for his room.

"He was using old big one-dollar Canadian bills," said Murray Westgate, the RCN telegraphist at HMCS *Fort Ramsay*, fifty miles up the coast. "The hotel manager got suspicious and reported him to the [Quebec Provincial] police on board a train to Montreal."

Confronted by a QPP constable who sat beside him on the train, Janowski yielded his identification papers, one of which was flawed; he was arrested. He informed both the Quebec authorities and later Inspector C.W. Harvison, the commissioner of the RCMP, that he was a German naval officer and wanted to defect. Harvison then proposed that Janowski turn on his native Germany and become a double agent for the Allies—or else. Janowski assumed that he'd be hanged and consented to Harvison's proposal.[59] Over the next year, those handling Janowski watched as he manufactured false information about military activity in and around Montreal for his contacts in Hamburg.

"Just another aspect of enemy activity in the Gulf," Westgate said, "but at the time nobody knew about it."

The Battle of the St. Lawrence might best be described as ending in a draw. On one hand, the U-Bootwaffe had sunk seventeen merchant freighters, three American ships in the service of the US Navy, and the two RCN warships *Raccoon* and *Charlottetown*. The layered nature of the gulf's salt and fresh water interplay virtually undermined any escort detection via ASDIC.

On the other hand, Allied warships sank no U-boats. But throughout the summer and fall of 1942, both RCN escort patterns and RCAF air surveillance had increased dramatically; between May and October Eastern Air Command had dedicated 1,590 operational sorties over the gulf.[60] Such ramped-up air cover forced Adm Dönitz to reconsider further large-scale incursions into the gulf. Indeed, his U-Bootwaffe sank no shipping in the gulf for another year.

From the first appearance of U-boats in the gulf in May 1942 to the push to make the sinking of SS *Caribou* public, reporters and news agencies exposed the Canadian government's underestimation of the threat and the RCN's inability to meet the escort demands of every ship's passage in the gulf. However, as quickly as U-boats seemed to threaten catastrophe inside Canadian territorial waters, the enemy's emphasis shifted again. Worldwide, November had been a record month for U-boat victories—807,754 tons of shipping sunk, and nearly two-thirds of that in the North Atlantic.[61]

For Dönitz, the time for his wolf packs to strike a lethal blow against North Atlantic shipping lanes was at hand. "The time has come to regard these results in a true light," he entered in his diary, "and to give propaganda suitable guidance."[62]

Brushes with death, and worse, did, however, continue to plague his U-boats. Ulrich Gräf and the crew of *U69* returned to the U-boat pens on the French coast in time for Christmas 1942. Their second patrol—some eighty-three days long—had only increased their tonnage sunk total by two ships, *Carolus* and *Caribou*, and by 5,000 tons. Early in 1943, Kptlt Gräf and the same crew departed Lorient on their third patrol together. On February 17, HMS *Viscount*, a British destroyer escorting Convoy SC 104, got a bead on the attacking U-boat and sank it. None of *U69*'s submariners survived.

Chapter Eight

"A YEAR ASTERN"

On February 1, 1942, the bombes in Hut 8 at Bletchley Park—the same ones that had so consistently delivered the whereabouts and movements of U-boat packs in the North Atlantic—suddenly came up empty, their drums whirring on and on without solving the Enigma codes in the usual way. Unbeknownst to the codebreakers at Bletchley, that was the day the Germans issued a new model Naval Enigma machine to their Atlantic U-boats, an Enigma that featured four rotors, not three, as in the older device. As a consequence, the Germans' Triton cipher prevented the bombes at Bletchley from deciphering weather transmissions and U-boat movements in the North Atlantic.[1]

The Kriegsmarine continued to employ three-rotor ciphers for U-boat activity in the Arctic, the Baltic, and bodies of water around western Europe. This meant that the Submarine Tracking Room at Naval Intelligence could still make reasonable estimates about the numbers of U-boats in those regions.[2] Otherwise, though, Allied convoy planners, merchant ship commodores, escort commanders, and defensive stations all along North Atlantic shipping routes remained largely in the dark about looming U-boat attacks. Not until Bletchley managed to crack the four-rotor Naval Enigma—ten months later—would the flow of accurate U-boat intelligence return to the Allied side. To add to the Germans' advantage, in early 1942, B-Dienst, the Kriegsmarine's radio monitoring and cryptographic service, broke the Admiralty's cipher for signals about the movement of convoys and stragglers; the Germans could now read roughly 10 percent of their enemy's convoy intelligence.[3]

Coincidentally, in the same month that Triton and B-Dienst trumped Bletchley, the Allies were experimenting with a new anti-submarine weapon. On Valentine's Day 1942, Convoy ON 67 left Liverpool, England, westbound with an escort of four USN destroyers and the RCN corvette HMCS *Algoma*. The convoy was following the Great Circle Route, the shortest distance between the UK and North America. Among its thirty-nine cargo vessels, the convoy included an unassuming 1,500-ton steamer. For all the world, SS *Toward* looked like a small merchantman travelling in the convoy. Aboard was an oversized sick bay, a surgeon and full medical staff, special rescue equipment, and space for several hundred survivors.[4] *Toward* looked like a rescue ship. Indeed, during the crossing, her crew became extremely busy, rescuing survivors from eight sunken freight vessels.

However, SS *Toward* carried one additional apparatus on board—a high-frequency radio direction-finding device. Huff-Duff could give bearings at sea (the way shore stations did on land) triggered by U-boat radio signals. An experienced operator could easily distinguish between a distant transmission and one sent to or from a U-boat nearby. With that information passed along, one of the USN destroyer escorts could run down the bearing of the transmission, confront the U-boat, and force it to crash-dive and consequently lose contact with the convoy. While not always used effectively, Huff-Duff at least provided convoys with an active tracing weapon.

Three months later, on May 6, another outbound assembly of forty-two merchant ships left Liverpool heading for Halifax. The next day, Convoy ONS 92 rendezvoused with its Mid-Ocean Escort Force (MOEF), led by American warships USS *Gleaves* and USCGC *Spencer* and accompanied by four Canadian corvettes: HMCS *Algoma*, *Arvida*, *Bittersweet*, and *Shediac*. None of the warships had yet been equipped with Huff-Duff, but HMS *Bury*, the rescue ship assigned to the convoy, carried the tracing device on board.

Adm Dönitz had dispatched a wolf pack to the area with orders to assemble, search, and attack on May 14. But *U569* made an early contact with the convoy on May 11, the same day that *Bury*'s Huff-Duff operators picked up U-boat transmissions; *U124* and *U94* had joined *U569*. Admiralty warned the senior officer escort aboard *Gleaves* that three U-boats were nearby and five more were closing. It appeared that the available alert mechanisms were working on both sides.

Given the Huff-Duff data, *Bury*'s captain anticipated that *Gleaves* would commence a chase to drive the U-boats away from the convoy and simultaneously order the convoy to move away from the perceived threat. Neither happened. Instead, the American senior officer concluded that *Gleaves*, the only destroyer in the escort, should not break away from the convoy. Apparently he didn't trust what *Bury*'s Huff-Duff was reporting. The devices were new. Not all USN warships carried them, and in truth, in order to make an accurate fix, locators had to come from at least two different Huff-Duff sets triangulating on the enemy transmitter. *Bury* had a bearing but not a fix on the U-boats.[5]

Gleaves's commander therefore opted for normal US Navy escort response, placing his destroyer and cutter at the vanguard to clear the way for the convoy following. Not long into that strategy, the destroyer spotted *U569*, and both USN ships left the convoy in pursuit, which continued through the night into May 12. That left the four Canadian corvettes screening Convoy ONS 92. KK Johann Mohr and *U124* attacked first, torpedoing the ore-carrier *Empire Dell* and then the cargo vessel *Llanover*, forcing *Bury* and one of the corvettes into rescue operations. The screen around the convoy had now been reduced by three warships, and the next day that brought on one new attack, by Kptlt Otto Ites and *U94*, and a second by *U124*. By the time the USN ships returned to the convoy, U-boats had sunk five ships. The attacks continued into the next day, in rough seas, when the wolf pack sank two more merchantmen. The convoy had lost seven ships. The escorts had not damaged or sunk any U-boats in response.

On May 14, with the convoy out of reach, Adm Dönitz called off the pack. He applauded the results of his new mid-Atlantic initiative, concluding that convoys at these longitudes were easy prey—not heavily armed, not screened in sufficient numbers, and not aggressively escorted. Remarkably, the American senior officer escort considered the outcome the best possible under the circumstances, and in his report he included praise for the Canadian corvettes attempting to screen while conducting rescue work.

That's not the way Western Approaches Command saw it, or the convoy commodore, or the captain of HMS *Bury*. All three called Convoy ONS 92 a failure. The Canadian corvettes took it on the chin from WAC too. *Arvida* took criticism for picking up survivors instead of launching a counterattack, and *Bittersweet* crews were chastised for avoiding a collision with what they thought was another escort but turned out to be one of the attacking U-boats on the surface. The RN view of the capability of RCN escort ships and crews remained as dim as it had been in 1941. And, by year's end, it would grow dimmer.

The frequency of convoys kept climbing—by mid-1942, eighteen convoys a month[6]—and so did the loss statistics. U-boats accumulated the highest North Atlantic tonnage sunk of the war so far: 429,891 tons in February, including seventy-three ships, up to a high for the year in June with 623,545 tons, including 124 ships. These dramatic figures stacked up favourably for the U-Bootwaffe when compared to a total of just twenty-one U-boats lost to the Allies in the first six months of 1942.[7]

MOST veterans on the North Atlantic run agreed: "Happy is the convoy with no history."[8] Convoys that met action, endured sinkings, and suffered crew deaths attracted criticism and post-mortem reprimand. Those convoys that delivered successfully thanks to skilful evasion, convoy discipline, steadfast seamanship, and a dash of good luck were rarely noted as victories, just missions accomplished.

For example, Acting Lieutenant Commander (A/LCdr) Leslie Foxall and HMCS *Chilliwack* served among the handful of escorts that helped to deliver Convoy HX 195 safely to the Western Approaches on July 1, 1942. It was the first escort assignment with the MOEF for Foxall and his corvette crew, but their thirteenth escort assignment in eleven months on the North Atlantic. Of those thirteen trips—from August 1941 through April 1942—only one (SC 67) had seen a merchant ship torpedoed in transit. In a dozen trips escorting between Newfoundland and Iceland, *Chilliwack* and her sister escorts (from the RN or RCN) had delivered 488 merchant ships to their hand-off locations at sea without incident.[9]

All of this occurred while the RCN's escort inventory was stretched to its limit. The Navy received eleven more corvettes in 1942: *Regina* and *New Westminster* in January; *Timmins* in February; *Vancouver* in March; and *La Malbaie* and *Moncton* in April. *Woodstock*, *Ville de Québec*, *Port Arthur*, and *Brantford* arrived in May, and *Kitchener* in June. *Moncton* was the last of the 950-ton corvettes with a short fo'c'sle. Those that followed were 1,015 tons with extended fo'c'sles; by extending the fo'c'sle aft, the design eliminated the well-deck, creating more liveable space for crew and dry access to the galley. Canadian shipyards had built eighty corvettes—thirteen in 1940, fifty-six in 1941, and eleven in 1942.[10] Even with the additions, however, the RCN could only supply the MOEF's eleven groups with about fifty corvettes at the beginning of the year.

Meanwhile, the RCN's escorting destroyers had slipped from eleven to eight MOEF warships. Its Town-class destroyers—*Niagara*, *Columbia*, and *St. Clair*—didn't have the durability to continue operating on the long Newfy-to-Derry (Newfoundland-to-Londonderry) runs, particularly since the Admiralty had directed those convoys farther south, increasing the distance of each trip. That left the MOEF operations to Canada's six pre-war River-class destroyers—*St. Laurent*, *Saguenay*, *Skeena*, *Restigouche*, *Ottawa*, and *Assiniboine*—backed up by the two longer-range Town-class lend-lease destroyers *St. Francis* and *St. Croix*. This reduced strength posed a real problem, particularly when RCN escorts had become responsible for the defence of one-third of the main ocean shipping routes.[11]

Halfway through 1942, the RCN calculated it needed 200 escorts to protect convoys in the mid-ocean, the Western Local, and the Gulf of St. Lawrence, plus the oil convoys sailing from the Caribbean. On paper, it had 188 warships available, but in actual service just thirty-four minesweepers, seventy corvettes, and thirteen destroyers—nearly 100 ships fewer than what was needed. In plain terms, the merchant navy commodores departing Londonderry or Liverpool for North America, and those leading convoys from Sydney or Halifax for the UK, learned in 1942 that the Mid-Ocean Escort Force had shrunk.

This meant that a commodore's convoy of thirty or forty or fifty merchant ships would now have to cross the Black Pit—the most dangerous stretch of mid-Atlantic water, with the greatest threat of U-boat attack and no air cover—protected by just two destroyers and four corvettes. Each MOEF would bring together a variety of escorts in a "B" (British) group, an "A" (American) group, or a "C" (Canadian) group. Not surprisingly, the escort skill level varied from ship to ship, group to group, and nationality to nationality.

In addition, with escorts and crews in such demand on so many operations, the time allotted for both ship maintenance and crew training suffered. To compensate, new Cdr (Destroyers) Rollo Mainguy—a respected officer with both RCN and RN credentials and transatlantic service as commander in RCN destroyers *Assiniboine* and *Ottawa*—drafted a plan. He suggested to RAdm Murray that Chummy Prentice and his corvette *Chambly* be reassigned to operational training, a practice that Prentice had inaugurated the year before in the Newfoundland Escort Force. In April and May, Cdr Prentice put a handful of escorts through exercises in towing, manoeuvring, gunnery, depth charges, and anti-aircraft training. During both months escorts made U-boat sightings, which ratcheted up the intensity of the exercises. But just like the dearth of warships in Canada's escort fleet, there were too few hours the navy could allow its crews to be away from their principal role of shepherding convoys.

Canadian crews also faced a nagging equipment gap.[12] Sub-hunting escorts had often experienced the operational problem of losing ASDIC contact with a U-boat amid the noise of a depth-charge attack. Navy technical wizards manufactured a gadget they called "Hedgehog." It was a forward-firing mortar-type weapon that propelled depth charges from spigotted heads skyward in an arc to enter the water about 100 feet ahead of the warship, rather than from the ship's side or stern. Each of the Hedgehog's sixty-five-pound depth charges contained thirty pounds of Torpex.[13] Firing them from a distance allowed the warship to attack a U-boat with haste, without having to wait to pass over where the sub had submerged before dropping charges.* Naturally the RN was the first to acquire Hedgehogs; it would be another year before RCN warships got them.

Similarly, British warships and crews had come to understand the benefits of centimetre-band Type 271 radar, since Cdr Donald Macintyre and HMS *Walker* had used it to attack *U99* and capture Otto Kretschmer in March 1941. Type 271

* During the Second World War, RN warships made more than 5,000 depth-charge attacks, which yielded eighty-four U-boat kills; by comparison, about 250 Hedgehog attacks yielded forty-seven kills.

radar could detect U-boats, but U-boats could not detect 271. As a consequence, Type 271 radar sets were common in RN escorts thereafter. To assist RCN destroyers (which didn't have 271) as they tried to detect surface U-boats at night in waters around the UK, the British had installed the naval equivalent of the RAF's Aerial Vessel and Ship (AVS) radar equipment, known as Type 286 radar, into those Canadian ships.

Initially, Canadian corvettes operating in North American or mid-Atlantic waters had no access to Type 286. So they made do with Surface Warning 1st Canadian (SW1C) sets developed by the National Research Council of Canada.[14] In operation, SW1C sets provided only weak echoes from small, distant objects such as U-boats on the surface of the ocean. As well, RCN corvettes had difficulty mounting antennas high enough on masts to improve SW1C range, the impulses being "line of sight." In effect, unless the escort was operating on relatively calm seas, a moderate swell could mask a U-boat hull on the surface. Making do was not making a difference.

"Our ships were a year astern," noted one RCN commander.[15]

JUST as front-line Royal Canadian Navy crews struggled to make do with insufficient operational training, lack of anti-submarine warfare gear, and 100 fewer ships than they actually needed, the U-Bootwaffe had gained the advantage in all of those categories. While the Kriegsmarine U-boat strength in January 1942 had been sixty-five, by July it had ballooned to ninety-nine. Where in 1941 German maintenance and repair crews could keep only about half the U-boat fleet operational, by mid-1942 they constantly kept more than two-thirds of their fleet on station at occupied bases in France. As well, the greater availability of U-tankers—the so-called *milch*-cows for resupply at sea—gave U-boats the potential for greater range and even longer patrols into the Atlantic, in some cases up to eighty-one days.[16]

HMCS *Spikenard* became a casualty of inexperience and lack of proper equipment. After serving a short stint with the NEF, the corvette began escorting merchantmen from Newfoundland to mid-ocean. On February 10, *Spikenard* was screening ahead of Convoy SC 67 after dark. With no radar at his disposal, LCdr Bert Shadforth was zigzagging ahead of a starboard column, when *U136* aimed and fired two torpedoes. One struck the Norwegian freighter *Heina*; the second hit directly below *Spikenard*'s bridge. The corvette disintegrated in minutes. But no other vessel recognized that the second explosion had sunk *Spikenard*. Fifty-seven of sixty-five aboard, including LCdr Shadforth, were lost. Later, at an inquiry, the corvette's last moments became clear. The ship had not been at action stations when the torpedo struck, which meant most crewmen were below decks in their messes. And in the water on Carley floats, *Spikenard* survivors had no flares or lights to draw the attention of the other ships.[17]

It took five months for *Spikenard*'s sister escorts and their crews to deliver a noticeable response to the German attack. But in the summer of 1942, the RCN's under-equipped, less trained, and allegedly less experienced destroyers and corvettes finally struck back. Notably, that response had little to do with leading-edge equipment or traditional seamanship, and more to do with calm calculation and improvising in the heat of battle—something the Canadians were learning the hard way.

On July 24, the Town-class destroyer HMCS *St. Croix* led Convoy ON 113 westbound from the UK, screening thirty-three merchant ships. The convoy and Canadian (C-2) escorts were two-thirds of the way across the Atlantic. *St. Croix* had no Huff-Duff detector equipment, but she did have an alert masthead lookout. AB Jim Pullen spotted the profiles of two U-boats five and twelve miles ahead of the convoy.[18] They were part of a patrol of nine U-boats. The escorting RN destroyer HMS *Burnham* chased but lost contact with the U-boat to the starboard, while LCdr Andrew Dobson and *St. Croix* veered off to port to chase the other. His target turned out to be *U90*.

Kptlt Hans-Jürgen Oldörp was just three weeks into his first patrol command, and *U90* had previously only served in training exercises. Oldörp tried outrunning *St. Croix* on the surface. LCdr Dobson withheld fire to keep him there and to improve the odds of eventual ASDIC detection if *U90* submerged. After an hour of surface pursuit, the Canadian destroyer had closed to within 6,000 yards when *U90* made a crash dive.

Dobson turned to his anti-submarine team—Lt Leslie Earl and PO M.E. Biggs—to maintain contact and direct the Canadian destroyer's weapons. *St. Croix*'s SW1C radar delivered "no pip whatever"; however, when the destroyer reached *U90*'s diving location, her Type 141 ASDIC picked up an echo. Dobson and his team deduced that the U-boat had commenced a deep dive. *St. Croix*'s depth-charge crew responded by adjusting to a deep detonation during the run-in and released a pattern of six charges. Dobson ordered a quick circle back and discovered that the target showed no movement. His depth-charge crew unleashed a second set of charges for detonation between 150 and 350 feet underwater.[19] In minutes, debris and air bubbles surfaced.*

Dobson made a third and a fourth run-in and dropped more charges. "This time the results were definite," *St. Croix*'s war diary stated. "Gathering slowly from the depths beneath was a nasty, oily litter of timber, clothing, pocket books, cigarettes, food packages and bits of human flesh."[20]

Despite the clear evidence that *St. Croix* had scored the RCN's second U-boat kill in the North Atlantic, LCdr Dobson knew staff at WAC and the British Admiralty would need more than just his report of surface debris. So *St. Croix* crew went over the side to collect human remains and placed them in jars for delivery to an assessment committee.

The battle to drive off U-boats and protect Convoy ON 113, however, wasn't over. The remaining U-boats continued intermittent attacks for two more days and nights, sinking five merchant ships in total. Once again, while not recognized or credited for their skill in these situations, Canadian escort crews improvised when *U552* torpedoed the 8,000-ton tanker *British Merit* and the 5,000-ton freighter *Broompark*, both near the rear of the convoy. In the darkness on July 25, Lt John Littler, in command of HMCS *Brandon*, raced to the torpedoed merchant ships to offer assistance. "The ocean seemed to be covered with little lights attached to life-jackets, indicating men in the water," he noted.[21]

Before the war, Littler had served in the British merchant service; he'd become a master mariner in 1936. Better than most, he understood that injury due to hypothermia escalated every minute the surviving sailor remained in the water. He also struggled with strict Admiralty orders *not to stop*.

* When under attack, more experienced U-boat commandeers had their crews deliberately release debris through torpedo tubes to give the impression of a kill.

"So, we went in, my crew lining the sides [of the ship] with ropes and rope nets . . . without stopping," he explained. "It wasn't long before merchant seamen were coming over the side into *Brandon* like tunny fish and being rushed off into the bowels of the ship to be warmed up or treated."[22] Their innovative rescue technique saved forty-five men from *Broompark*.

JUST seven days later, another predominantly Canadian escort group, westbound with Convoy ON 115 from Londonderry to North America, illustrated yet more Canadian on-the-spot improvisation. Leading this C-3 escort group (nicknamed the "Barber Pole Brigade"* for the red-and-white-striped bands painted on their funnels) were destroyers HMCS *Saguenay* and *Skeena*, while corvettes HMCS *Wetaskiwin*, *Galt*, *Louisburg*, and *Sackville* screened the convoy. Once again, the Barber Pole Brigade was operating without the benefit of air cover or Huff-Duff. However, they had one notable asset—they'd all benefited from Chummy Prentice's team-training patrols at sea earlier in the year.

Overnight on July 30/31, three U-boats began to shadow the fast-moving convoy of forty-one merchant ships. The commodore ship's Huff-Duff had intercepted medium-frequency radio transmissions from U-boats astern of the convoy. Aboard *Saguenay*, A/Cdr Dickson Wallace sent *Skeena* seven

* Canadian warships also acquired nicknames—*Restigouche* "Rustyguts," *St. Laurent* "Sally Rand" (after the 1930s fan dancer), and *Assiniboine* "Bones." When *Wetaskiwin* (after the Alberta town) was nicknamed "Wet Ass Queen," AB Burnie Forbes, an amateur painter onboard, created a logo of a shapely queen of hearts sitting in a puddle. "With every repaint job," Forbes said, "I couldn't resist lifting her skirt a little and making her bust one size larger." (Quoted in Mac Johnston, *Corvettes Canada: Convoy Veterans of World War II Tell Their True Stories* [Whitby, ON: McGraw-Hill Ryerson, 1994], 178.)

miles out on the starboard beam of the convoy; even if her Type 286 radar couldn't detect the shadowing U-boats, she could keep them submerged. At first light, *Skeena* lookouts spotted *U511* and *U588*, and A/Cdr Kenneth Dyer gave chase, commencing one of the RCN's more memorable episodes of sub-chasing teamwork.

Both U-boats crash-dived, and Dyer dropped depth charges at the farthest points of a diamond-shaped area he calculated the enemy boats could reach. Wallace knew that *Skeena*'s Dyer and *Wetaskiwin*'s LCdr Guy Windeyer had worked in tandem in Chummy Prentice's training runs the previous May, when they'd practised pursuing a tame submarine at Conception Bay. They'd refined a tactic in which one ship maintained contact with the U-boat while directing the other ship's charges over the target. Their joint attack on *U588* began with the destroyer's signal to the corvette, using a witty biblical reference style that became popular in the RCN during the Battle of the Atlantic.

Skeena to *Wetaskiwin*: "ACTS 16, VERSE 9"—a reference to the scripture lines "A vision appeared to Paul in the night. There stood a man of Macedonia, and prayed him, saying, Come over into Macedonia, and help us."[23]

Wetaskiwin was full-ahead making her way toward *Skeena* and signalled, "REVELATIONS 13, VERSE 1," which affirmed, "And I stood upon the sand of the sea, and saw a beast rise up out of the sea."

When *Wetaskiwin* reached the Canadian destroyer's position, it was the second submerged U-boat, *U588*, that became the target. LCdr Windeyer gained and lost contact with the submarine several times before making a strong contact and laying down depth charges. *Wetaskiwin* then stood off, matching the U-boat's low speed and keeping contact while guiding *Skeena* to each attack.

Wetaskiwin: "I will try to help you by directing."

Skeena then dropped a pattern of depth charges with settings changed from a depth of 350 feet to one of 550 feet.

Wetaskiwin: "Excellent."

Skeena: "Did you hear that underwater explosion?"

Wetaskiwin: "Plenty of wreckage over this way."

Skeena: "I am lowering a whaler to pick up the guts."[24]

The Canadian escorts had conducted the pursuit for five hours and dropped more than 100 depth charges to achieve the kill. The sinking of *U588* brought to eleven the number of U-boats sunk in July 1942.[25] But it came with an unfortunate admission. After a week's steaming from Liverpool and the pursuit of *U588*, *Skeena* and *Wetaskiwin* had nearly exhausted their fuel supplies; with no refuelling options at sea, they had to steam 400 miles directly to St. John's to replenish. However, there remained another half-dozen U-boats fuelled, loaded, and eager to press their attack well east of Newfoundland. The long transatlantic trek of Convoy ON 115 had spilled over into a new month.

That's when Lt Alan Easton and HMCS *Sackville*, who'd joined the convoy on July 25, entered the fray. Despite the heroic actions of fellow C-3 escorts, Lt Easton found himself weighing every escorting warship's persistent dilemma: defending the convoy versus chasing the enemy. At noon on August 2, following a Sunday service at sea, Lt Easton climbed to the crow's nest to take advantage of the morning's good visibility. He spotted a surfaced U-boat and ordered pursuit, but by the time *Sackville* reached the spot where the U-boat had dived, the corvette couldn't regain contact. That night two merchantmen were torpedoed, and as rescue ships moved into position, *Sackville* detected *U43* just 400 yards away, fired a starshell to illuminate, and attempted a ram. Easton's ship passed above the crash-diving U-boat without making contact, but his depth-charge crew delivered two patterns over the spot.[26] This scenario of spotting, chasing, and then attacking continued in thick fog through the night without a definitive result.

Eventually the onset of Grand Banks fog and daylight brought the action to an end. Convoy ON 115 had lost three merchant ships to the U-boats, while C-3 had sunk *U588* and damaged at least two other members of the wolf pack. Kudos and criticism followed the report on the convoy. *Saguenay*'s Wallace was pleased with the portion of the escort he'd led. So was *Skeena*'s Dyer. But final judgment on C-3's success or failure came from a review of the convoy's minutes by the Admiralty, and the Western Approaches Commander, Clarence Dinsmore Howard-Johnston, didn't mince words.

"This is an example of reckless expenditure of fuel and disregard of the object which must always include timely arrival," he complained. "The success achieved against the enemy in destroying a U-boat should not be allowed to cover up this basic failure."[27]

It appeared that the Barber Pole Brigade was damned if it did and damned if it didn't. In its attempt to satisfy the Admiralty's priorities for North Atlantic escort duty, the Canadians continued to make do with substandard detecting equipment, or none at all. If the escorts themselves were not scheduled to receive seaborne Huff-Duff sets, experienced convoy officers argued, then rescue ships with Huff-Duff needed to accompany all convoys to fill that void.

Further, most understood that C-3's less than adequate radar capability needed addressing. Indeed, the radar officer aboard *Sackville* went further. "*Sackville*'s two U-boats would have been a gift," he surmised, "if [*Sackville*] had been fitted with RDF [radio direction-finder] Type 271."[28]

Technical deficiencies were not limited to members of the Canadian escort groups. While the crews aboard aging RCN Town-class destroyers and first-generation Flower-class corvettes had to jury-rig Type 286 devices on mastheads as improvised radar, U-boat crews were also coping with shortcomings in their equipment. In the third week of July 1942, as *U210* embarked on her first operational patrol to the mid-Atlantic, the crew had already found one of her echo-sounders faulty; on July 20, during a practice dive near Kristiansand, off the Norwegian coast, the U-boat struck a rock and damaged a port torpedo tube. Later, meeting another U-boat on the surface, *U210*'s Kptlt Rudolf Lemcke tried to communicate with the other captain by signal lamp; the light wouldn't function, so Lemcke resorted to using semaphore with signal flags. Then, a wireless radio failed inside the U-boat, leaving them without a link to BdU in Lorient.[29]

Neither was sailors' discomfort limited to the RCN's cramped escorts. While crews aboard the first generation of short-fo'c'sle corvettes regularly got drenched while carrying meals between the galley and the crew's mess deck forward, German submariners ran the gauntlet from the galley amidships through circular bulkheads to the after compartment "like circus lions through a hoop." However, unlike the Allied crews, who could only procure fresh provisions at either end of a convoy escort operation, the *milch*-cow submarines could replenish the patrol U-boats in the middle of the Atlantic with nets full of sausage, sides of bacon, and crates of fresh fruit, which hung from instruments and overhead pipes "like the hanging gardens of Babylon."[30]

Typical was the meal laid out for the crew of *U210* on the evening of August 6, 1942. The submariners had lined up at the galley for portions of sausage, chicken, fresh bread, and other foods "we couldn't even think of getting at home before the war."[31] That night Kptlt Lemcke and *U210* were shadowing some eastbound merchant ships of Convoy SC 94, but the area was cloaked in fog, so Lemcke left the bridge to go below for his meal. Twenty minutes later, OS Karl Mueller interrupted the feast, saying he had heard shouts and firing above them. The general alarm was sounded.

Six days into the escort of SC 94 from Sydney to Liverpool, HMCS *Assiniboine* had suddenly made contact with a U-boat six miles off the slow convoy's port bow. Following their Type 286 radar detection, the destroyer's lookouts had spotted *U210* on the surface, coming out of the fog just fifty yards away and about to cross *Assiniboine*'s bow.[32] LCdr John Stubbs called for action stations and full speed, hoping to ram the U-boat.

By this time Lemcke had dashed back to the conning tower, where he began snapping out orders. He fully intended to fight it out on the surface. As both U-boat and destroyer opened fire at point-blank range, Lemcke directed *U210* into a path where the destroyer's guns would inflict less damage, and the chance of being rammed was less likely.

"I was forced to go full astern on the inside engine to prevent him getting inside our turning circle," LCdr Stubbs noted.[33] This manipulation, employing the destroyer's twin engines, tightened her turn but couldn't match the tighter turn capability of the U-boat.

U210's flak gunner was already pumping 20mm cannon fire into *Assiniboine*'s bridge, forecastle, and forward gun positions. Since the two vessels were charging forward nearly beside each other at better than sixteen knots, *Assiniboine*'s gunners couldn't initially lower the barrels of their 4.7-inch guns enough to land hits on the U-boat. But their quad .5-inch machine guns managed to sweep the U-boat's deck, preventing the submariners from manning their 88mm deck gun.

"During most of the action we were so close that I could make out the Commanding Officer on the conning tower bending down to pass wheel orders," Stubbs reported.

The two vessels jostled for a position of advantage for over thirty minutes, *Assiniboine* attempting to ram, and *U210* trying to stay beneath the destroyer's line of gunfire. Finally some of the destroyer's shells smashed into the U-boat's forward torpedo tubes, forward torpedo hatch, and propellers.

But *U210*'s 88mm deck gun had already scored a hit on the destroyer's forward 4.7-inch "A" gun shield, where OS Kenneth Watson and Fred Addy were feeding ammunition; Watson died in the exchange of gunfire.[34] As well, the U-boat's 20mm flak gunfire had ignited petrol drums stored outside *Assiniboine*'s wheelhouse. Lt Ralph Hennessy deployed a damage-control party that fought to keep the blaze from spreading. Meantime, CPO Max Bernays had ordered the helmsman and telegraphist out of the wheelhouse to safety, even as the fire cut off the wheelhouse. Bernays then took the helm himself and passed course-change orders to the engine room via the ship's telegraph.[35]

Kptlt Lemcke chose to keep *U210* on the surface, perhaps believing he could lose the destroyer in the mist. But *Assiniboine*'s 4.7-inch "Y" gun scored a direct hit on the conning tower—the shell passing directly through it—killing Lemcke and three others. Moments later, *U210*'s engineer officer, Heinz Sorber, called for a crash dive.

"In the few seconds during which he was on a steady course to dive," Stubbs reported, "we rammed him just abaft the conning tower. I turned as quickly as possible . . . After a little manoeuvring, we rammed him again. . . . Also, one 4.7-inch shell scored a direct hit on his bows. He sank by the head in about two minutes."

With the battle finished, submariner enemies became shipwrecked sailors, and *Assiniboine*'s crew began hauling *U210*'s survivors aboard. All but six of the U-boat's crew of forty-three were rescued, but one wasn't particularly grateful. Fished from the swirling waters around the sunken U-boat, the German officer spat in the face of one of *Assiniboine*'s rescuers. A junior Canadian officer, Bill LaNauze, stepped forward and levelled the German with a punch to the jaw, knocking him over the rail and back into the sea. "Leave him for someone else to pick up," LaNauze said.[36]

Indeed, Royal Navy corvette HMS *Dianthus* rescued him a second time. Most of *U210*'s survivors ended up aboard *Assiniboine*; the non-commissioned officers (NCOs) were locked in an unused boiler room, while two German officers were locked inside the doctor's burned-out cabin, outside of which stood an armed guard with orders to shoot if either attempted to escape.[37] Interrogated later, *U210*'s crew appeared to have low morale and repeated Nazi propaganda that their enemies would carry out "sterilization of all Germans in the event of an Allied victory."[38]

"The ship's company behaved excellently," Stubbs concluded in his report, "although this was their first taste of any sort of action." Lt Ralph Hennessy received a Distinguished Service Cross and CPO Max Bernays the Conspicuous Gallantry Medal; four other *Assiniboine* crewmen received Distinguished Service Medals (DSMs), and Lt Stubbs was awarded the Distinguished Service Order for "gallantry, devotion to duty, and distinguished service under fire."[39]

THAT same summer, in the battle of one-upmanship, Allied strategists gave their Coastal Command anti-submarine aircraft a new tool to tip the balance on the North Atlantic yet again. The innovation of the Leigh Light quickly gave Wellington and Catalina aircrew eyes at night. RAF Squadron Leader Humphrey de Verd Leigh, a former First World War pilot, had long considered the idea of Coastal Command aircraft equipped with lights rather than fast-expiring flares. In March 1941 one of S/L Leigh's Wellington crews experimented with a twenty-four-inch searchlight in a mock attack first against a corvette, then a submarine. The exercise proved successful. It allowed the air-to-surface radar aboard the aircraft to home on the enemy vessel in the dark, then illuminate the U-boat with the switched-on Leigh Light, and finally deliver a surprise attack before the sub's crew could react and dive.[40] The concept was expedited, and by summer's end Coastal Command had equipped six Wellingtons and six Catalinas with Leigh Lights.

The following spring, after further trials, RAF No. 172 Squadron began operating over the Bay of Biscay, where U-boats entered and exited the occupied ports in France. The Leigh-Light Wellingtons sighted and illuminated seven U-boats during 230 hours over the bay, while ordinary night-flying Whitleys using flares accumulated 260 hours without making a single sighting. The first successful strike, in June 1942, caught an Italian submarine on the surface, and the Wellington's depth-charge attack inflicted heavy damage.[41]

The Leigh Light triggered an instant response from U-Bootwaffe command headquarters. On June 24, with darkness no longer a protection for U-boats travelling on the surface at night, Adm Dönitz ordered all U-boats passing through the bay to travel submerged both day and night, surfacing as briefly as possible only to recharge batteries and refresh air. The new Allied weapon would make life for German U-boat crews more uncomfortable, if not more dangerous. It also indirectly forced U-boats to spend more transit time submerged, increased their travel time to and from operations, and decreased time spent looking for and attacking convoys.

JUST weeks after HMCS *Assiniboine*'s tangle with *U210*, an equally vicious surface battle between two seasoned warriors played out in the Atlantic waters of the Caribbean. Just twenty-four when he assumed command of *U94*, and in only four war patrols, Kptlt Otto Ites had already sunk fifteen ships, a total of 76,882 tons.[42] Considered by his crew to be just one of the men, he was openly addressed as "Onkel Otto." In April 1942, Adolf Hitler had awarded him the Knight's Cross of the Iron Cross. On the other side, the Canadian corvette HMCS *Oakville* had completed a winter's service piling up the hours and experience at sea with the Western Local Escort Force, protecting merchantmen on the Triangle Run between American ports and Sydney and Halifax. In May, LCdr Clarence King became *Oakville*'s new CO. King had been awarded a Distinguished Service Cross in the Great War, sinking one U-boat and earning two probables. In August 1942 he and *Oakville* were diverted to a new front line, escorting tankers through the Caribbean.

"His [kill] score in this war was zero," wrote *Oakville*'s SLt Hal Lawrence, "and he didn't like it."[43]

Late that same month, Kptlt Ites and his Type VIIC *U94* teamed up with *U511* searching for convoys near the Windward Passage, south of Haiti. Meanwhile, HMCS *Oakville* had joined warships escorting Convoy TAW 15, outbound from Trinidad via Aruba to Key West. For added security, the convoy of twenty-nine merchant ships received airborne protection from a US Navy Catalina flying boat. When Ites spotted the flying boat on August 27, he knew a convoy was near; he'd located it by 6 p.m. and remained astern of it until after dark. Then, in the moonlight, *U94* penetrated the escort screen between Canadian corvettes *Oakville* and *Snowberry* and the sparks began to fly.

First, the Catalina pilot spotted the surfaced U-boat amid the shimmer of moonlight on the water, swooped in, and dropped four 650-pound depth charges. The attack and explosion took *U94*'s crew by surprise, and the concussion catapulted the stern of the U-boat clear out of the water and damaged her diving planes. Nevertheless, Ites managed to put the submarine into a crash dive.[44]

The lookout on watch on *Oakville*'s bridge woke LCdr King, who quickly ordered full speed and sent gun crews and depth-charge parties to their action stations.[45] Meanwhile, SLt Lawrence, an English-born Canadian, arrived at his position, with the ASDIC operator on earphones attempting to pinpoint the U-boat's underwater course. *Oakville* dropped a pattern of two depth charges from throwers and rolled three more over the stern rails. The combination of the Catalina's and the corvette's depth charges had debilitated *U94* to the point where Ites was having great difficulty controlling the U-boat. First the bow appeared; then the U-boat's conning tower pierced the surface, and *U94* was fully exposed ahead of *Oakville*.

King's first attempt to ram was a glancing blow that scraped along the full length of the U-boat. Then *Oakville*'s commander turned to put distance between the corvette and the U-boat so his gunners could bring fire down on *U94*. Machine gun bullets raked the U-boat and kept her crew from manning her more lethal 88mm deck gun; *Oakville*'s four-inch gun got off a shot that smashed the 88 and blew it off the U-boat's deck.[46] With the two vessels so close together, the intensity of the exchange of fire motivated *Oakville*'s now idle depth charge crew; they grabbed empty Coke bottles (stored abaft of the funnel), pelted *U94*'s conning tower, and shouted "Yah! Yah!" each time they scored a hit.[47] LCdr King lined up *Oakville* to ram again. This time the corvette glanced off *U94*'s starboard side, but her crew also released a shallow charge off the stern.[48] It exploded directly beneath the U-boat.[49]

Not only did the blast cut *U94*'s speed, the concussion also caused *Oakville*'s lights to flicker. Still, King brought the corvette in for a third strike, squarely abaft *U94*'s conning tower. The U-boat was done. But King wasn't finished; he'd gone to the trouble of training his crew for what came next.

"Away, boarding party," he shouted. "Come on, Lawrence! Get cracking!"[50] And he put *Oakville* alongside the U-boat to allow the assault team easy access to the deck. SLt Lawrence joined stoker PO Arthur Powell—formerly a hard-rock miner from Timmins, Ontario—and others outfitted with .45

revolvers, grenades, gas masks, torches, Mae West lifebelts, and a length of chain, preparing to leap to the U-boat's deck. They'd all been sleeping when action stations was called, so most were shirtless, shoeless, and in their shorts. Lawrence and Powell launched themselves down onto the U-boat deck to confront any Germans emerging from the conning tower hatch. But the impact of hitting the deck snapped the elastic in Lawrence's shorts, so aside from his gun belt and lifebelt, he was virtually naked as he and Powell rushed the U-boat bridge.

At the conning tower, the two Canadians draped their chain into the hatch, making it impossible for the Germans to dive the U-boat without drowning themselves. At the open hatch, Lawrence called out in broken German for the U-boat crew to surrender, but when that didn't flush anybody out, he put his weapon down, shone the flashlight on his face, and spoke as reassuringly as he could. "Come on up. It's all right," he said. "See—no gun."[51]

Before long, with his pistol and flashlight at his feet, the sub-lieutenant was surrounded by a mob of surrendering Germans. Among them was Kptlt Ites, still wearing his Knight's Cross and limping with wounds to his leg. Powell ordered the prisoners aft while Lawrence climbed down in search of anything that looked like codes or intelligence, but he eventually found himself in water up to his chest. Lawrence retraced his steps and scurried back on deck. Then Powell motioned with his thumb and all their prisoners leapt overboard. The two Canadians followed. Lawrence wrote later that he felt genuine disappointment that he and his shipmates couldn't tow the captured U-boat into Guantanamo Bay, "a prize of war."[52] *U94* sank minutes later. Of forty-five crew aboard, twenty survived, including Kptlt Ites. It had been three-quarters of an hour since *Oakville*'s lookout originally spotted the U-boat, and LCdr King had his first U-boat kill of this war. It would not be his last.

While word of *Oakville*'s audacious victory spread among the escorting warships of Convoy TAW 15, RCN and government censors kept the story secret back home in Canada for three months.[53] Eventually, on November 10, 1942, Navy Minister Angus L. Macdonald issued a press release about *Oakville*'s "relentless surface engagement,"[54] but with reference to little else. A month later, Macdonald announced awards to the crew, including a DSM for PO Arthur Powell, a DSC for (promoted) Lt Hal Lawrence, and a DSO for now A/Cdr Clarence King. Then, publicly recognized as national heroes, Lawrence and Powell were sent on a propaganda tour, including a stop in Oakville, Ontario, the corvette's namesake town. The navy even created a poster titled "Men of Valor: They fight for you," depicting the two Canadians, pistols in hand, rushing *U94*'s conning tower.

ROYAL Canadian Navy efforts in the summer of 1942 had delivered significant victories to the Allied cause. In just five weeks, RCN escorts had destroyed five U-boats on the Atlantic. *St. Croix* had sunk *U90* on July 24. A week later, *Skeena* and *Wetaskiwin* had teamed up to destroy *U558*. *Assiniboine* had rammed and sunk *U210* on August 6. *Oakville* accomplished the same against *U94* on August 27/28. And (while it was not confirmed until 1987) corvette HMCS *Morden* had sunk *U756* while escorting Convoy SC 97 early on September 1. In total, over the same weeks, all the Allied navies had sunk twenty-one U-boats.[55]

However, all the good press and propaganda of the summertime success against repeated U-boat attacks could not overshadow the realities of the ongoing fight in the mid-Atlantic. Lack of proper detecting equipment, insufficient escort strength, shortcomings in team training, and the virtual silence from the Bletchley Park codebreakers all plagued operations on the North Atlantic—which were largely the responsibility of RCN escort groups. And if the summer had offered hope, the fall ultimately became Canada's darkest time at sea.

Right in the country's backyard, U-boats—mostly attacking alone—had penetrated the Gulf of the St. Lawrence and sunk two Canadian warships, seventeen merchant freighters, three USN ships, and the passenger ferry *Caribou*. The U-Bootwaffe had suffered no losses there. Out in the Atlantic, on the night of September 13, just as Escort Group C-4 neared Newfoundland, where the WLEF escorts would relieve MOEF escorts, a U-boat pack closed in on HMCS *Ottawa*. For the previous four days the Canadian destroyer, with destroyer HMCS *St. Croix* and four corvettes, had struggled to protect Convoy ON 127's westward passage against a wolf pack of thirteen U-boats; the submarines had sunk seven of its thirty-four merchant ships. Then, on that final night before handing off to WLEF, *Ottawa* was leading the convoy without benefit of radar when *U91* scored a torpedo strike into the destroyer's port bow.

Following first impact, Lt Thomas Pullen, executive officer aboard *Ottawa*, grabbed a flashlight, knife, morphine, pistol, and lifebelt and bolted to the bridge.

"The scene greeting me . . . was memorable," he wrote. "Forward of 'B' gun [position] there was nothing but water. The bow, including 'A' gun and all had vanished. . . . Fortunately, the torpedo just missed the forward 4.7-inch magazine or half the ship or more, not just the bow, would have 'gone west.'"[56]

Less than thirty seconds later, a second torpedo from *U91* hit *Ottawa* on her starboard side beneath the forward funnel.

"From the grinding, tearing sounds all about, the ship was breaking up," Pullen continued. "There was nothing to be done but clear out in what few seconds remained."[57]

The second explosion broke the destroyer in two, and both parts shortly stood on end and went straight down. Of the ship's 175-man crew, only sixty-nine survived the sinking and the four hours on rafts before being rescued.

"Had we been fitted with radar Type 271 as we should have been," Pullen wrote finally, "the lurking enemy would most likely have been detected."[58]

If improper or inadequate weaponry didn't impede Canadian escorts, then diminished escort strength did. On October 30, SC 107, a slow convoy of thirty-nine freighters en route to the UK passed the easternmost tip of Newfoundland. Six days out of New York, the convoy was picked up by Escort Group C-4. The Allied escort consisted of the British corvette HMS *Celandine* and three Canadian corvettes, HMCS *Amherst*, *Arvida*, and *Sherbrooke*. As well, C-4 should have had two destroyers at the vanguard. It didn't because destroyer HMCS *St. Croix* was forced to stay behind for repairs. That left HMCS *Restigouche*, with Lt Desmond Piers commanding, as the lone destroyer spearheading the escort. That evening, on her way to the Gulf of St. Lawrence, *U522* spotted the convoy and was ordered to shadow. A wolf pack began to coalesce.

To its credit, because of land-based Huff-Duff intelligence, EAC sent aircrews more than 300 miles east of Newfoundland to pursue U-boats in SC 107's path. Even forcing them to dive would allow the convoy to outrun them. It paid off. That very day, a pair of Hudson bombers from RCAF No. 145 (BR) Squadron at Torbay, Newfoundland, flew as far out to sea as they dared. They sighted and sank *U658*. Meanwhile, a Digby bomber from No. 10 (BR) Squadron located and sank *U520*.* Catalinas from No. 116 Squadron forced several other U-boats to dive. But by November 1, SC 107 was entering the Black Pit, where its air cover would disappear. And that's where the rest of the U-boat patrol was waiting.

The convoy's defensive system was aided by a Huff-Duff set that Lt Piers had scrounged and installed aboard *Restigouche* just months earlier, and there was a similar set aboard the rescue steamship *Stockport*.[59] That gave Piers the means to establish the bearing and distance of U-boat transmissions. However, aboard his screening corvettes the radar sets had failed; both *Arvida*'s SW1C set and *Celandine*'s Type 271 set were unserviceable. *Restigouche* was leading the convoy virtually blind. And while he didn't know it, Piers faced thirteen U-boats stretched across his path like a dragnet. Among his adversaries were experienced captains Siegfried von Forstner in *U402* and Herbert Schneider in *U522*. Von Forstner attacked on the starboard side of the convoy. Using the moonlight, which silhouetted his targets, Schneider penetrated the port columns. By night's end, eight merchant ships were gone.

Fog and rain shrouded the convoy over the next twenty-four hours, but German intelligence had intercepted and decoded the convoy's routing signal, and the U-boats' Metox

* RCAF F/O E.L. Robinson located and sank *U658*; he was awarded the DFC for his actions. RCAF F/O D.R. Raymes sank *U520*.

radar detectors kept the pack within striking distance while the defenders' radar sets were functioning. Lt Piers tried to take advantage of the low visibility to direct the convoy through evasive turns,[60] but when the convoy emerged from the fog bank, the wolf pack regained contact. The cat-and-mouse game of U-boats surfacing to reconnoitre and escorts forcing them down with charges and gunfire continued through the day.

Into the night of November 3/4, the carnage continued. *U132* took advantage of a gap, slipped between two columns of the convoy, and unleashed three torpedoes, striking the freighters *Hobbema* and *Hatimura*, each loaded with 7,000 tons of explosives and ammunition. The resulting explosions knocked *Arvida*'s stern out of the water, concussed *Algoma*'s engine, and—in what was later described as the largest pre-nuclear explosion of the war—sent *U132* to the bottom as well.[61] By November 5 air support had resumed on the UK side of the Black Pit, and reinforcement escorts arrived. Five days later, SC 107 limped into Liverpool.

Piers reflected on being so young and assigned the role of escort commander for that convoy. He was so junior in the MOEF that his pay was less than the doctor's on board *Restigouche*. Still, he'd improvised with limited resources, guided his relatively inexperienced escorts round-the-clock during critical moments, and fought his way across a thousand miles of Atlantic. In seven days his convoy had lost fifteen of forty-two ships. "With three years as a lieutenant," he said. "I'd suddenly been in command of a convoy crossing the Atlantic."[62]

The flag officer, Newfoundland, Cmdre Howard E. Reid, described SC 107 as "one of the most disastrous convoys we have ever had."[63] Just days later, the new C-in-C of Western

Approaches, Adm Max Horton, went further, demanding that a convoy's defence be entrusted to more experienced commanders, *not* young lieutenants.[64]

Winston Churchill felt he needed to act. He wrote to Prime Minister Mackenzie King. "A careful analysis of our transatlantic convoys has clearly shown that in those cases where heavy losses have occurred, lack of training of the escorts, both individually and as a team, has largely been responsible," Churchill wrote King on December 17, 1942. (He didn't know it was King's birthday.)

"I appreciate the grand contribution of the Royal Canadian Navy to the Battle of the Atlantic," Churchill concluded, "but the expansion of the RCN has created a training problem which must take time to resolve."[65]

To be clear, Churchill told King he was pulling the Canadians from the mid-Atlantic completely. But almost before he'd suggested, as an alternative, that RCN crews be reassigned to the easier UK-to-Gibraltar route, Convoy ONS 154 happened. LCdr Guy Windeyer, with more peacetime service than active combat in his career, led the outbound "Christmas convoy" in destroyer HMCS *St. Laurent*. Through five days of gruelling escort (December 26–31), ONS 154 lost fourteen of forty-six merchant ships and 486 lives; in response, the Canadian escorts had sunk one enemy U-boat, *U356*.[66] The loss of so many merchantmen in one crossing left Churchill's confidence in the Canadians in tatters.

In the final two months of 1942, 80 percent of shipping losses in transatlantic convoys had occurred when Canadian warships were escorting.[67] It was no coincidence that during the same period, the U-Bootwaffe had ninety-five U-boats in the North Atlantic (twice as many as in January of that year).

In other words, Canadian escorts had faced better than half the entire U-boat force operating at sea in 1942.

HAL Lawrence and his shipmates in *Oakville* spent Christmas 1942 at sea, en route from Curaçao to Haiti, back where they'd sunk *U94* in August. The newly promoted and decorated Lt Lawrence had experienced quite a year facing the enemy on the Atlantic and then an adoring public back home in Canada. But he also knew the loss statistics from 1942. The war was going the wrong way. Allied convoys had lost 1,664 ships in twelve months, 1,160 of them sunk by U-boats.

"[But] the loss of over a thousand ships means little to the individual," Lawrence wrote. "Instead, [one] remembers the sight of a lifeboat full of merchant sailors rowing frantically from the side of a burning tanker, and the sound of their screams as the flames engulf them."[68]

If such carnage hadn't given members of the merchant navy pause about their choice to serve at sea, an event in the fall of 1942 made the prospect of survival in the Atlantic sea lanes even more bleak.

On the evening of September 12, KK Werner Hartenstein and the crew of *U156*—on their fourth patrol—spotted RMS *Laconia*, a British troopship sailing unescorted in the Atlantic from Cape Town to Sierra Leone. On board were 366 passengers, 200 tons of cargo, and 1,809 Italian prisoners of war. KK Hartenstien fired two torpedoes into the 19,695-ton ship, which immediately listed and began to sink. The U-boat commander hoped to capture the troopship's senior officers, but as he approached the sinking liner he realized there were nearly 2,000 people struggling to survive in the water, many of them women and children, as well as Germany's Axis allies—the Italian POWs. *U156* radioed U-boat Command for instructions.

Adm Dönitz recognized the complication of potentially abandoning his Italian allies; he ordered a nearby wolf pack (*U507*, *U506*, and *U459*) to race to the scene to help gather survivors and then rendezvous with Vichy French surface vessels to complete a rescue.

"If any ship will assist, I will not attack," Hartenstein transmitted on an international radio wavelength, "providing I am not attacked by ship or air forces."[69]

Three days later, a USAAF Liberator, patrolling east from its 343d Bomb Squadron on Ascension Island, came across *U156* on the surface. The U-boat crew had draped a Red Cross flag across her bridge as she towed a cluster of life rafts and carried scores of other survivors on her open deck. The Liberator circled and then left, but a second bomber arrived soon after and, despite clearly appreciating the situation, commenced to attack. Its bombing run killed many survivors on the life rafts and forced *U156* to crash-dive. KK Hartenstein later surfaced and radioed his experience to BdU. By September 20 the Vichy ships had collected 1,083 *Laconia* survivors (including 415 Italian POWs).

Meanwhile, in Berlin, German High Command debated a response to the Liberator attack on *U156*. Hitler had wanted an excuse to slaughter survivors of torpedoed ships in order to terrorize or deter merchant navy crews.[70] On the other hand, Dönitz knew he couldn't be seen ordering his crews to shoot survivors of merchant sinkings. It would play into enemy propagandists' hands. Nonetheless, by September 17 he had issued new orders to his U-boat commanders:

"Efforts to save survivors of sunken ships must stop," his directive began. "Rescue contradicts the most basic demands of the war—the destruction of hostile ships and their crews." His orders further stated the capture of captains and engineers would continue only if it gained valuable intelligence. Finally he said, "Stay firm. Remember that the enemy has no regard for women and children when bombing German cities."[71]

The document became known as the "Laconia Order." Taken a step further, did such an order give Kriegsmarine crews licence to murder shipwrecked survivors? For Adolf Hitler, it did. On September 28, when he and Dönitz met in the Reich Chancellery in Berlin, the führer was unequivocal: "It is very much to our disadvantage if a large percentage of the crews of sunken ships is able to go to sea again in new ships," Hitler stated.[72]

Dönitz didn't argue.

Chapter Nine

"TOUGH-LOOKING BUNCH OF BASTARDS"

CHRISTMAS 1942 AT THE RICKERS HOUSEHOLD IN Port Dalhousie, Ontario, brought little joy. While Cyril and his wife, Lillian, prepared a Yuletide meal for themselves and three of their children, there remained an empty chair at the table for their eldest son, Ken. Days before the holidays, the family had received a telegram with the dreaded "We regret to inform you . . ." introduction. The cable informed them that the British merchant ship MV *Empire Sailor*, on which Ken had served for two years, had suffered a mechanical breakdown during her westbound transatlantic crossing to Canada. Somewhere off the Newfoundland coast, she was forced to pull out of her position in the protection of Convoy ON 145. And 200 miles short of her destination—Sydney, Nova Scotia—the ship had been struck by a torpedo and sunk. Finally, the notification explained, while Ken, just twenty-four, had survived the sinking, he'd later died aboard a rescue ship and was buried at sea.

Cyril Rickers was a veteran of the Royal Navy in the Great War and was no stranger to loss. He chose to channel his grief over his son's death into an open letter of patriotic encouragement at his place of employment, the McKinnon Industries car manufacturing plant in Port Dalhousie. First, he admitted how Christmas had been difficult, gazing at his son's vacant chair. He explained that the family had honoured his son's service in the merchant navy with the donation of a baptismal font to their local church in Ken's memory. But his message also expressed worry.

"It may be you, next time," it warned. "A breakdown somewhere in the machinery of his ship caused it to fall prey to a Nazi torpedo. Perhaps a bolt came loose, a nut came off, a pin fractured. . . . We can do something right here at McKinnon's by making our assembly lines, benches and machines battle lines."[1]

Rickers encouraged his co-workers to put extra punch into every aspect of their jobs, and to make sure that nothing but the best craftmanship left their plant. He entreated his colleagues to consider the troops driving the tanks and trucks they built, and to keep top of mind that soldiers' lives depended on the quality of their work.

"Let's [remember] that lost time and accidents . . . are vicious torpedoes striking the Ship of Industry," he continued. "Let's get down to business, so that when our heroes return, we can say, 'We served you to the utmost.'"

It was sometime after Cyril Rickers wrote his open letter that the actual details of *Empire Sailor*'s destruction and the fate of her crew emerged. Stationed within the convoy for most of the crossing, *Empire Sailor* unexpectedly had to move to the outer column (presumably to deal with mechanical problems). Just past 4 a.m. on November 21, *U518* closed on the convoy and Kptlt Friedrich-Wilhelm Wissmann called for three torpedo shots, one of which struck *Empire Sailor* on her port side. The explosion in her No. 4 hold proved more lethal than most of the crew aboard could have anticipated.

"Only three senior officers aboard *Empire Sailor* were aware of the dangerous cargo the ship carried below decks," explained Don Rickers, Ken's nephew. "Specially sealed and fitted with ventilating pipes [were] 270 tons of phosgene gas in cylinders, sixty tons of mustard gas in drums, and 100 tons of commercial cyanide."[2]

The torpedo explosion blew the hatches of No. 4 hold. Within moments, the debris that crashed back onto *Empire Sailor*'s open deck included six phosgene gas cylinders. They shattered immediately and released their poisonous contents into the air, which then enveloped the crewmen attempting to save themselves as the merchant ship went down.

"Unfathomably, only the ship's senior officers had been issued gas masks," Don Rickers continued. "The sixty crew had none, and were totally unaware of what toxins were stored below decks."

It didn't matter that the master of the freighter immediately gave the order to abandon ship, or that sixty of the sixty-three crew on board managed to escape in four lifeboats within eight minutes of impact. The damage to the unmasked crewmen was done. Those aboard the escort minesweeper HMCS *Minas* and corvette HMCS *Trail*, who came to *Empire Sailor*'s assistance, reported soon after that several of the survivors began to cough and struggle and fall into delirium. Someone disclosed the freighter's secret cargo—poison gas, presumably for an Allied retaliatory attack should the Nazis resort to chemical warfare.

"Into the eyes of the remaining survivors came the look of dawning realization," wrote *Trail* crewman James Lamb.

"They were all doomed. Within hours, the last one lay cold and still. *Minas*, who had rescued a joyous party of live survivors, steamed on with a cargo of corpses."[3]

Fourteen merchant sailors saved by *Minas* died before the sweeper reached Halifax. Another died en route to hospital. Four of seventeen survivors whom *Trail* rescued died on board the corvette and another in a Halifax hospital. A report to the Admiralty criticized the lack of precautions aboard *Empire Sailor*. It stated emphatically that ordinary service respirators would have protected the crew. Naval officers who'd witnessed the excruciating deaths of Rickers and the others called for a full enquiry. None was held. They warned that "the effect of this occurrence on the morale of Merchant Seamen . . . can readily be imagined."[4]

RAdm Leonard Murray didn't have to imagine the state of mind of sailors on both sides of his home harbour in Halifax—his escort crews and the merchant sailors on freighters and tankers. The evidence was all around him. Throughout 1942 the Commanding Officer Atlantic Coast grappled with the realities that members of his Mid-Ocean Escort Force (formerly the Newfoundland Escort Force) had endured. MOEF crews regularly served in thirty-five-day cycles—twenty-nine days at sea without fresh provisions.

When the masters of the merchant navy vessels gathered for the requisite briefing conference at Admiralty House in Halifax before departing on their transatlantic convoys, Murray made a point of attending. In particular during that gruelling winter of 1942–43 when merchantmen losses escalated, the experience wore on him.

"I could see that they knew very well and that they knew in spite of my brave words, that up to twenty-five per cent of them probably would not arrive in the UK in their own ships, and that probably half of that number would not arrive in the UK at all," Murray said. "But there was never a waver in their resolve."[5] So, there couldn't be in Murray's either.

In the Cabinet War Rooms, Winston Churchill sensed the same grave impact. The prime minister worried that merchant navy sailors who were enduring such catastrophic losses at sea and seeing little or no security in their occupation would abandon the service all together. As he often did, Churchill confided in his friend and ally Franklin Roosevelt: "the spectacle of all these splendid ships being built, sent to sea crammed with priceless food and munitions, and being sunk—three or four a day—torments me day and night."[6]

And if waning confidence among merchant mariners and losing shiploads of valuable supplies didn't keep Churchill awake at night, Britain's dwindling oil reserves did. In mid-December, Albert Alexander, First Lord of the Admiralty, advised the prime minister that the disparity between oil usage and imports was 250,000 tons per month, and if dipping into British emergency oil reserves didn't stop, Alexander said, the country's last-ditch supply would shrink to as little as twelve weeks' worth by February.[7]

For these reasons and others, Churchill followed through on the note he'd sent to the Canadian prime minister on December 17, 1942. In no uncertain terms, he told Mackenzie King that he wanted the Canadian escorts redeployed to the eastern Atlantic, where they could receive training and facilities support. Not coincidentally, Western Approaches Command had recently passed from Adm Percy Noble to the former commander of the RN's submarine force, Max Horton, who made *professionalism* the watchword in anti-submarine warfare.[8] That the Admiralty's own Monthly Anti-Submarine Report in January 1943 accurately noted, "the Canadians have had to bear the brunt of the U-Boat attack in the North Atlantic for the last six months [or] about half of the German U-boats at sea," didn't change the numbers. "Eighty per cent of all ships torpedoed in Trans-Atlantic convoys in the last two months were hit while being escorted by Canadian groups," the report concluded.[9] Ultimately, that's all that mattered.

For the moment, then, the Canadians left the North Atlantic battleground for reassignment to the Mediterranean.

PAUL Morse, stoker aboard the recently commissioned HMCS *Ville de Québec*, had an inkling about the new deployment. His corvette (among the first with an extended fo'c'sle[10]) had initially served in the Western Local Escort Force on the Triangle Run. But the crew had barely learned the ropes of escort duty between Boston and Halifax when, overnight, the ship's stores received six-month supplies of light bulbs, gloves, and paint; the canteen stocked up on cigarettes, soap, razor blades, chocolate bars, and toothpaste.

"When we left Halifax for overseas, there was an extra issue of heavy winter wear," he said. "The buzz was that we were being trained for the Murmansk Run."[11]

In fact, the Admiralty had given orders for all four "C" groups, the seventeen active Canadian corvettes, to cross the Atlantic and rendezvous with RN transports and warships spearheading Operation Torch, the Allied invasion of North Africa. On November 8, 1942, in what was the greatest amphibious landing of the war to date, the Allies landed

35,000 US troops near Casablanca, 39,000 US troops at Oran,* and a combined force of 23,000 British and 10,000 American troops against German-occupied Algiers. In the process, the Canadian corvettes adapted to their new escort duties in distinctly different conditions than they'd known in the North Atlantic's Black Pit. First, the battlefield was smaller. Second, the enemy—usually single U-boats, not packs—was always close. Third, the escorts endured shorter hauls on the Mediterranean than on the Atlantic, and much better air cover. And finally, the calmer seas and more moderate weather conditions improved the accuracy of the corvettes' new Type 271 radar and ASDIC detecting.[12]

Charged with the responsibility of escorting the landing craft, the Canadian flotilla rose to the challenge. On January 13, 1943, while steaming ninety miles from Algiers and zigzagging ahead of the fifteen-ship Convoy TE 13, *Ville de Québec*'s ASDIC crew picked up a U-boat submerged to periscope depth just 900 yards away.[13] Her shallow pattern of ten depth charges forced *U224* to the surface, where the corvette rammed and sank the U-boat in minutes. The sinking brought an immediate response from the nearby merchant crews, who were "cheering and shouting as if we had won the war."[14] HMCS *Port Arthur* launched a similar attack the same week, while escorting the twenty-nine-ship Convoy MKS 6 east of Algiers, and sank the Italian sub *Tritone*. Days later, HMCS *Regina* sank the Italian sub *Avorio*.

Just weeks after Torch, the Canadian corvette crews were

* The attack on Oran Harbour also witnessed Canadian Capt Frederick Peters (in the RN) breaching the harbour boom using the former USCGC *Walney*; though captured briefly and killed in a later plane crash, he was one of two Canadian navy personnel awarded the Victoria Cross in the Second World War. The other was aviator SLt Hampton Gray in the Pacific War in 1945.

the talk of Algiers. Admiral of the Fleet Sir Dudley Pound arrived and led an inspection of the Canadians. Joining him were Adm Sir Andrew Cunningham, C-in-C of the Mediterranean; Field Marshal Sir John Dill, chief of the Imperial General Staff; and VAdm Lord Louis Mountbatten, chief of Combined Operations. Mountbatten even tossed a backhanded compliment to the Canadians. "They're a bloody tough-looking bunch of bastards," he said.[15]

Despite their anti-submarine acuity in the Mediterranean, all the Canadian groups went on hiatus that winter of 1943. First the C-1 crews spent down time in the UK while their ships underwent rapid refits. In addition to Type 271 radar upgrades and Oerlikon guns, the Canadian destroyers and corvettes received long-overdue repairs and alterations. Armament crews installed Hedgehog anti-submarine mortar weapons, and instrument techs added Huff-Duff devices. Meantime, everybody—captains, officers, and ratings—became students again. At Londonderry's training facilities, British instructors put them through depth-charge exercises, night-lookout practice, and anti-aircraft drills and tutored them on their new ASDIC and radar equipment.[16]

Then, in mid-February, almost as if returning to boot camp, the Canadians headed to the land-based training facility at HMS *Western Isles* and the tutelage of legendary Cmdre Gilbert Owen Stephenson. Though his headquarters—an Edwardian-era steam yacht at the Tobermory anchorage in Scotland—gave little impression of authority, the commodore had a service record dating back half a century, to 1892, when he began training in the Royal Navy College at age fourteen. An officer aboard destroyers, on staff at torpedo school, attached to the Admiralty's naval intelligence, and decorated in the Great War, he became vice-admiral in 1934. Often seen with heavy whiskers, Stephenson earned the moniker "Monkey Brand" after a household cleaning product.

When the Second World War began, he became Commodore of Convoy and served during the Dunkirk evacuation. In 1940 he was tasked with setting up the RN Anti-Submarine Training School on the Isle of Mull; it was there he earned his second nickname, "the Terror of Tobermory." If he thought an officer was not up to his job, Stephenson would remove him, whether their lordships in London approved or not.[17] In four and a half years, however, Stephenson had put more than 900 ships' crews—including the Canadians that winter—through over 1,100 training courses.

"What have you heard about this base?" Stephenson asked an arriving commanding officer.

"I've heard you're tortured until you're efficient," the CO replied. "Then, if you've any strength left, you're allowed to go."[18]

When a Canadian corvette arrived for the two-week course, the crusty commodore often stepped aboard to meet the new crop of trainees. He removed his braided cap, threw it on deck, and in a foghorn bellow called out, "This is a small unexploded bomb. What're you going to do about it?"

On this occasion, a bosun's mate coolly stepped forward and kicked the cap overboard. The ship's company waited for the rebuke. Instead, Stephenson offered praise for the man's reflexes, but then pointed to his floating cap on the water and shouted, "Man overboard! What're you going to do about it?"[19]

For the next fourteen days, the "Terror" unleashed an equally fearsome staff on the newly initiated Canadian crews. The instructors had concocted a wide array of battle predicaments and anti-submarine manoeuvres, pushing the escort sailors' ability to respond faster, better, and as efficiently in darkness as daylight. And just when a crew thought they had things under control, the Tobermory staff knocked out the ship's power, unleashed smoke and mock explosions, or artificially killed off the captain and senior officers to test the company's flexibility to improvise and survive.[20] Following ten days of theory, training took to sea for four days of exercises chasing a tame submarine.

"Take for granted that everyone knows nothing about his job and start from rock bottom," Stephenson preached, while also choosing not "to teach any but the simplest tactics."[21]

Canadian corvette crews had demonstrated the value of the "simplest tactics" during and immediately after Operation Torch. With access to better listening and sensing devices and more powerful armament, and a growing sense of teamwork, *Ville de Québec*, *Port Arthur*, and *Regina* had taken full advantage of their opportunities versus enemy submarines in the Mediterranean early that winter of 1943. The Canadian groups also suffered setbacks—the loss of HMCS *Louisburg* to an Italian torpedo bomber on February 6, and on February 22 the sinking of HMCS *Weyburn* when a mine west of Gibraltar detonated. But there were steps forward too. On March 13, while screening Convoy MKS 9, HMCS *Prescott* chased a contact and twice attacked a Type IXC U-boat, but she could not confirm a sinking.

REPORTS from the Mediterranean and other key battlefields gave Prime Minister Churchill some hope that winter. He diarized that "the aggressors in Europe and Asia" had been driven to the defensive. In February 1943 the German surrender at Stalingrad marked a turn of fortunes for the Soviets. The Americans had secured victories in the Coral Sea and at Midway Island. And most of the German and Italian forces in Africa had been killed, pushed back to Italy, or captured. Indeed, on January 14, 1943, Churchill took great delight in meeting President Roosevelt at Casablanca, Morocco, on what he described as "conquered or liberated territory."[22] However, the two leaders kept returning to the outstanding Achilles heel of the Allied campaign—the apparently unstoppable assault by U-boats on merchant shipping lanes in the Atlantic.

The tonnage losses haunted the prime minister. In both 1940 and 1941, the Kriegsmarine had sunk four million tons of merchant shipping. Losses doubled to nearly eight million tons in 1942. When the two Allied leaders met in Casablanca, they acknowledged the bleakest statistic of all: U-boats were sinking ships faster than the Allies could build new ones. And until they turned the tables—until Allied navies destroyed more U-boats than the Nazis could build—victory was not assured.

"[Without] mastery of the lifelines across the Atlantic," Churchill wrote, "no amphibious operations . . . to liberate Europe would [be] possible. . . . The Battle of the Atlantic [is] the dominating factor . . . [and] everything happening elsewhere—on land, at sea, or in the air—depend[s] ultimately on its outcome."[23]

The American industrial juggernaut was beginning to turn the tide, however. By 1940, US merchant ship production had reached 200 vessels per year; by 1941, over 300 ships annually. That year, the US government dubbed the merchant ships its "Liberty Fleet." The first cargo ships had each taken 230 days to build, but by 1943 American assembly-line shipyards were completing three Liberty ships every day. Over the course of the war, the US Maritime Commission employed 650,000 Americans and built a total of 2,710 Liberty ships.[24]

With a tenth the population, Canada kept pace. At the beginning of the war, the country boasted but a handful of shipyards (in the Maritimes, up the St. Lawrence River, and along the BC coast) capable of warship production; in all they employed fewer than 4,000 workers. Over the six war years, however, 126,000 Canadians were working in ninety shipyards, contributing to the construction of 4,047 naval vessels and 410 cargo ships.[25] The arrival of the government's Wartime Merchant Shipping Ltd. in 1941 pushed shipyard employment numbers to an annual wartime high of 75,847 workers in 1943, largely centred in Quebec and British Columbia.[26] And among those stepping up to meet the so-called manpower crisis in the yards were thousands of skilled women. In Britain women comprised 2 percent of the workforce in shipyards. In the US it was much higher; as many as 150,000 women wage earners worked in American shipyards. In Canada, about 4,000 women came to the yards.[27]

Among them, Ethel Harvey had trained at a trades school in Victoria. Then she broke the gender barrier by becoming the first certified female welder in British Columbia.[28] And in 1942, when the shipbuilding yards on the Pacific coast suddenly needed welders by the score to fulfill the merchant shipbuilding contracts with the Canadian government, she had applied and was hired. The *Vancouver Sun* reported that male welders threatened to walk off the job in protest.

"I'm not doing any man out of a job," Harvey told the newspaper. "So far as I know, I'm being paid the same scale as the men."[29]

The *Sun* further reported that C.D. Howe, the minister of munitions and supply, was alarmed that a work stoppage would violate union contracts and deal a damaging blow to the war effort. Harvey said she had not been asked to join the union, but would if that solved the problem. The local representative of the Canadian Congress of Labour said the union (Boilermakers and Iron Shipbuilders) was without prejudice and welcomed Harvey into its ranks.

"I'm just proving that women can do this type of work satisfactorily," she said.

In a somewhat more welcoming move, the Canadian government created the Women's Royal Canadian Naval Service on July 31, 1942. While the navy did not allow any of the 7,100 women who joined* between 1942 and 1945 in combat or "arms-bearing" duty, the Order-in-Council did ensure that women navy officers "received the King's Commission, held the same ranks as men, and were entitled to salutes and all marks of respect from non-commissioned and commissioned men and women of the three armed forces."[30] Canada was the first nation in the British Commonwealth to admit women into the naval service as integral members, not as an auxiliary force.[31]

Canadian women volunteers could not enlist in ship-related trades, but initially they could train as stenographers, postal clerks, cooks, stewards, coders, teletype operators, and motor transport drivers; additionally, they could serve as librarians, tailors, dieticians, supply clerks, plotters, sick-berth attendants, photographers, dental assistants, messengers, mess

* During the Second World War, 50,000 Canadian women served in uniform—21,600 in the Canadian Women's Army Corps; 17,400 in the Women's Division of the RCAF; 4,480 nursing sisters; and 7,100 in the Wrens.

women, switchboard operators, regulators (police), classifiers, sailmakers, censors, signallers, and Hollerith (punch-card) operators.[32] In most respects, women serving in the navy had the same responsibilities, were subject to the same chain of command, took the same oath of allegiance, followed the same grievance procedures, strived for the same objectives, and were expected to endure all the same inconveniences as men.

Well, almost all. PO Buckley-Beevers prided herself as a loyal and obedient servicewoman in the Royal Canadian Navy—as loyal and obedient as any other woman or man. But in 1943, when she arrived at HMCS *Stadacona* as PO in charge of the Wrens' barracks at the Halifax naval base, she faced unexpected antagonism.

"The Navy is no place for girls," an RN petty officer said out loud in her presence one day.[33]

Buckley-Beevers made sure his comments did not go unchallenged. Not that the then twenty-year-old volunteer from Vancouver went out of her way to hurt fellow non-commissioned officers. It was just that if the King's Regulations considered such judgment inappropriate, then her navy should know about it and respond accordingly. The navy was everything to Rodine Doris Mary Buckley-Beevers, "Ronnie" to her friends. Her father had been a Conway boy and had served in the Royal Navy in the Great War. So, the moment the government announced formation of the Women's Royal Canadian Naval Service, she volunteered. They trained her at HMCS *Conestoga* in Galt, Ontario, and then posted her to Halifax, in the engineering department of RCN's Mechanical Training Establishment at HMCS *Stadacona*. She relished any extra responsibility they gave her, riding herd on all the junior Wrens at *Stadacona*, "tucking them in" at the barracks at night, and even conducting Wren marching drills on the base parade square.

"I even drilled the men," she said, "putting [male] sailors through their paces—close-order drill—marching and all the rest of it. I really enjoyed that."

PO Buckley-Beevers did everything by the book, right down to the last detail. If some of her more adventurous Wren subordinates chose to show off their glamorous silk stockings on duty, Ronnie quickly hauled them out of the line to revert to navy-issue lisle stockings. Nor did she shirk tougher responsibilities, such as processing the names of navy crewmen lost at sea, or informing the wife or girlfriend when a male relative in the navy was in hospital for treatment of venereal disease.

Ronnie worked and lived in Halifax long enough to recognize that tensions existed there simply because of the war. Haligonians—approximately 70,000 permanent residents—went about their daily lives facing wartime shortages, rationing, blackouts, curfews, and general overcrowding in everything from restaurants to department stores to streetcars. Meanwhile, RN, RCN, and merchant navy personnel—as many as 55,000 people, mostly passing through—had status in the services, some amenities, and a regular paycheque. There was real disparity between the civilians and the services. Consequently, when some city merchants saw off-duty navy personnel coming into their shops, cafés, theatres, and bars, they often jacked up prices. Some even posted signs expressing their discontent: "No Sailors or Dogs Allowed!"[34]

Whatever his reason, the Royal Navy PO working alongside Buckley-Beevers let show his frustrations about women serving in *his* navy. And because she wasn't about to let him get away with such prejudice, Ronnie grieved; soon afterward, he was posted away from *Stadacona* permanently.

"I saw to that," Ronnie said.

As crusty as she could appear, PO Buckley-Beevers had a soft side too. One night she gladly escorted fifty Wren comrades to a Canadian Army dance across the harbour in Dartmouth. She knew her trainees deserved the chance to let their hair down. And it's a good thing she went to that dance. That was the night she met an army chauffeur named Willis Egan. He told a friend at the dance, "That's the girl I'm going to marry."[35] And he did, the following year.

But by far Ronnie's greatest stress relievers were her periodic walks from *Stadacona* up to the Citadel, where she could see Bedford Basin in the distance. "It was the most beautiful sight of all," she said, "just gazing at a convoy coming together in the basin."

JUST two weeks after Allied leaders met in Casablanca and lamented that the war could not be won without mastery of the Atlantic shipping lanes, their military adversary Adm Karl Dönitz saw his star rising. With Gen Erwin Rommel's Afrika Korps retreating at El Alamein, the German 6th Army surrounded at Stalingrad, and Allied escorts thwarting the Kriegsmarine's surface battleships on Arctic convoys, Adolf Hitler's only bearer of good news was Dönitz. The Admiral told the führer—at Berghof, his mountain retreat—that U-boat successes in November 1942 had climbed to a new high and "will probably amount to 900,000 tons" sunk,[36] and that the Reich's propaganda machine should trumpet such a feat.

Hitler did him one better. He accepted the resignation of Grossadmiral Erich Raeder, commander-in-chief of the Kriegsmarine, and anointed Dönitz as his successor. Further, he agreed to direct all naval resources to construction, maintenance, and refitting of U-boats. No doubt in the same breath, Hitler would have reminded Dönitz that in September 1939 the admiral had predicted "if 300 boats were available . . . that the U-boat arm can achieve decisive success."[37] In fact, at the beginning of 1943, Hitler's new Grossadmiral had 382 U-boats to press into the Battle of the Atlantic.[38]

Dönitz, then age fifty-one, sensed that the pendulum was swinging his way in the Atlantic struggle, at least for the moment; nevertheless, he realized the battle was a race against time. He still believed that surprise gave U-boats the tactical advantage in the Black Pit, and that his wolf pack numbers could still overwhelm surface escorts and deliver victory. Along with his new title, Dönitz acquired new headquarters—combining his office as BdU with his post as C-in-C of the Kriegsmarine—at the Hotel am Steinplatz in Berlin. His two sons now proudly joined him in the U-boat arm—Peter as an officer aboard *U954*, and Klaus also an officer with the 5th U-boat flotilla at Kiel. His first directive didn't mince words: "It is a question of winning the war," he said. "The sea war is the U-boat war [and] all has to be subordinated to this main goal."[39]

But Dönitz's adversaries had not stood still during this critical winter of the war. On December 13, 1942, the experts at the Government Code & Cypher School in England had cracked Triton, the Kriegsmarine's encrypting system (the one the Allies referred to as Shark). For most of the year, Alan Turing and his fellow cryptographers at Bletchley

Park had worked to solve the four-wheeled Naval Enigma machine that the Atlantic U-boats used to communicate with headquarters, and vice versa. By accident, the Germans had reverted to using three-wheel settings for short signals, which in turn were decipherable on the three-wheel bombes in Hut 8 at Bletchley.[40] And since directing Rüdeltaktik required highly centralized control and frequent radio communication with individual U-boats, when Bletchley broke the code for even small messages, the Submarine Tracking Room at Naval Intelligence in London was able to determine a pack's position and objective.* The key was the quick turnaround. Any delay—a day or a week—prevented the timely diversion of a convoy around wolf packs lying in wait.

For both sides in the Battle of the Atlantic, the greatest misery at sea in early 1943 was nature's work, not man's. North Atlantic storms were the worst in thirty years. For the Allies, the ice and wind left a third of escorts unserviceable, sank eight merchant ships in a month, and caused a rescue ship to capsize with a top-heavy coating of ice.[41] Dönitz sent thirty-seven U-boats into the Black Pit south of Greenland at the end of January, but the same rough seas plagued his wolf packs and their patrols came up empty.

In February he ordered twenty-one U-boats, with adequate fuel reserves to move farther west, closer to Newfoundland. On February 4, two RCAF Canso aircraft from Gander spotted U-boats in this pack on the surface. Despite air turbulence, rough seas, snow flurries, and limited visibility, they dropped

* On January 8, 1943, a U-boat pack west of the Azores found a nine-tanker convoy routed from Trinidad to Anglo-American forces in North Africa, and sank all but two tankers (55,000 tons of ships, 100,000 tons of oil). The next day, Ultra codebreakers mastered a set of Enigma settings and rerouted similar transatlantic oil convoys around the wolf packs.

depth charges, driving the U-boats underwater. This amphibious air attack and several others in the middle of the winter introduced a new combatant to the North Atlantic battlefield.

One of Eastern Air Command's oldest units—No. 5 (BR) Squadron—had begun stepping up its anti-submarine operations. The RCAF had recently supplied No. 5 crews with eleven modified Catalina/Canso A flying boats; the redesigned Canso A featured a tricycle undercarriage so it could take off and land on airfields as well as water. Designed as a long-range patrol bomber, the Montreal-built amphibious Canso included a parasol wing, twin engines, and two waist blisters where observers had a clear view of the sea, and where (if needed) gunners could man the seaplane's Browning machine guns. For its anti-submarine work, the Canso could carry up to 4,000 pounds of depth charges or bombs for up to twenty-three hours of flying time (at a cruising speed of 110 miles per hour) while providing convoy air cover and chasing U-boats well out to sea. That meant a Canso could conduct a sweep as far as 700 miles from its base—in this case Gander—and then straight back. The range fell to 550 miles if the Canso stayed with a convoy for four hours, or 450 miles if it escorted for about six hours.[42]

As a result, EAC continued to face a daunting challenge—how to extend the Canso's time aloft and therefore pose a greater deterrent to the U-boat packs. Determined to meet that challenge, S/L Norville "Molly" Small—perhaps EAC's most experienced Catalina/Canso pilot—made a series of test flights. Working with No. 5 (BR) Squadron, he and his crew had stripped their Canso down to bare-minimum weight—removing food canisters, spare parts, mooring gear, anything that wasn't essential—in order to carry more fuel to extend the aircraft's range over water. On January 6, 1943, Small's seven-man crew boarded their modified Canso, which was loaded with additional fuel, ammunition, and depth charges to within a few pounds of its maximum 34,000-pound takeoff weight. Just before 7 a.m., Small got the Canso airborne over Gander Lake, but the aircraft suddenly encountered severe air turbulence. The winds forced Small down to treetop level, where the plane crashed and burned. Two of the crew survived the impact, but five were killed, including S/L Small.

Despite the loss of a decorated and beloved squadron leader, No. 5 (BR) Squadron benefited from Small's initiative. By reducing the Canso's weight by some 1,200 pounds during his test flights,[43] he and his crew had proven they could increase the amphibious bomber's range by hundreds of miles and its time aloft by several hours. In lieu of the faster very-long-range (VLR) B-24 Liberator bombers,* Canso crews from Gander were about to turn Small's test flights into a valuable sub-chasing weapon. In the process, their operations would take an important bite out of the advantage enjoyed by Hitler's U-boats in the Black Pit.

ON her fourth patrol, *U604* departed the pens at Brest, France, on February 8, 1943, but after patrolling for ten days Kptlt Horst Höltring and his Type VIIC had nothing to show for it except a crew nearly exhausted from battling the elements.[44] Höltring had a reputation for being ambitious, demanding, and daring. He carried a pistol on his person at all times. He'd risen quickly in the ranks of the Reichsmarine in the 1930s, received

* Despite repeated requests for VLR Liberators—with a cruising speed of 215 mph, endurance of twenty hours, and a depth-charge load of 5,000 pounds—USAAF refused to send the RCAF any VLR aircraft.

a U-boat command in 1940, and turned his early patrols at the helm of *U604* into immediate successes. In 203 days at sea, he and his crew had sunk seven merchant ships (40,000 tons) and he'd been recognized with two Iron Cross awards.

On the eleventh day of their fourth patrol, Höltring's lookouts spotted a convoy of merchant ships westbound from Liverpool. Just as *U604* had, the merchant ships of Convoy ON 166 were emerging from eight days of battling a northwesterly gale; of sixty-three original ships, thirteen had returned to the UK, one had put into Iceland, and nine others had lost touch with the convoy and were straggling.[45] Their A-3 escort group included USCGC *Spencer* and *Campbell*, British corvette HMS *Dianthus*, and four Canadian corvettes: HMCS *Chilliwack*, *Dauphin*, *Trillium*, and *Rosthern*.

Before long, *U604* (shadowing the convoy) had drawn eighteen other U-boats from three different attack packs into the fray. To Höltring's immense displeasure, *U604* was ordered not to fire any torpedoes but simply to act as "contact keeper."[46] At nightfall, straggling merchant ships began to disappear, and the escorts dashed from one sinking merchantman to the next, trying to harass or drive off the U-boats. Positioned at *Rosthern*'s stern depth-charge rail, Leading Stoker John Dennis watched some of the confusion unfold as the American cutter *Spencer* suddenly emerged from the darkness, heading straight for his corvette.

"At about 500 yards from us and closing in at full speed preparing to ram, *Spencer* turned on her searchlight, fully illuminating *Rosthern*," Dennis said.

Frozen by what looked like an inevitable collision, Dennis's attention was only broken by the fluorescent wake of two torpedoes whizzing past *Rosthern*'s stern.

"This was almost a double play by the U-boats," he said. "*Spencer* realized her error and both escorts took evasive action, with *Spencer* passing at full speed within yards of our stern."[47]

During two days and two nights of carnage in the Black Pit, U-boat wolf packs had sunk four Norwegian freighters, four British cargo ships, four US Liberty ships, and a Panamanian tanker. All the while, *U604* had been patrolling to the port side of the westbound convoy, maintaining contact and waiting her turn. Late on the night of February 23, Kptlt Höltring took advantage of a situation unfolding away from the convoy. The British rescue ship SS *Stockport* had pulled alongside the torpedoed freighter *Empire Trader*, attempting to rescue her crew. Höltring fired a single torpedo into *Stockport* and the rescue ship went down, taking all of her crew and 106 merchant mariners rescued that same night to their deaths.

Early on the morning of February 24, however, predator became prey.

"We were at 3,000 feet altitude when I saw the U-boat, six miles ahead and slightly to port," reported F/L Fred Colborne, pilot of Canso 9738.[48] He wouldn't know until sometime later that his target was Kptlt Horst Höltring in *U604*.

Colborne and his all-Canadian crew had taken off from RCAF No. 5 (BR) Squadron's Gander airfield at about 5 a.m. and headed southeast, straight into the Wednesday morning sunrise. At the ops briefing just before they left, they'd learned that about twenty U-boats had been harassing Convoy ON 166 for several days, that seven ships had been sunk during the night, and that they were to rendezvous with the remainder of the convoy as it came within their range, approximately 600 miles from Gander—about half again as far as their Cansos had flown up until S/L Small's stripped-down test flights. Colborne and his navigator, F/O Bill Irving, had therefore calculated that Canso 9738 could deliver perhaps two and a half hours of air cover over the convoy before a shortage of fuel forced them home.

Several hours into their outbound flight, a message from Gander updated them. Another merchant ship had been torpedoed and six U-boats had been sighted east of the convoy. Irving altered his course to the sighting position. That's when Colborne spotted *U604*.

"No chance to sneak up on him," Colborne continued, so "I slapped open the throttles and started to dive to gain speed." Earlier in the month, he and his crew had depth-charged a U-boat shadowing another convoy. And while the result was inconclusive, Colborne had made several alterations to his Canso that he hoped would improve the results next time—white camouflaging of the aircraft, a fixed camera forward and yellow smoke floats to mark the attack position.

As Colborne nosed the Canso down into the dive, first engineer F/Sgt G.H. Thomson, seated right behind the cockpit, adjusted the carburetor mixture (less air, more gas) for the aircraft's twin Wright Cyclone radial engines and flashed the adjustment to Colborne so he knew the engines were primed for emergency performance.

"Submarine! Submarine!" F/Sgt R. Duncan shouted into the aircraft intercom. Sitting in the right-hand seat in the cockpit, the second pilot then started taking photographs through the windscreen.

Wireless Air Gunner WO Jimmy Elden knew protocol demanded that he send the first sighting report back to Gander. He glanced at the ampere reading on his control panel to ensure the electrical system wasn't overloaded (which would prevent Colborne from releasing the Canso's depth charges). Then he signalled the U-boat abbreviation, the longitude and latitude, and his aircraft call sign. Elden admitted later that Colborne's dive created such a strong gravity force on his body that it was difficult to tap out his transmission as quickly as he wanted to.

Elden also noted the thoughts that had crossed his mind. "I was wondering what the sub was like? Was it shooting at us? . . . What is my wife doing right now? Is she all right?" he wrote later. "Seconds seemed like years as I was sitting there."

Halfway back along the fuselage, Leading Aircraftman (LAC) Johnny Watson arrived at the starboard blister, opened it, and swung his machine gun out in readiness, thinking he was "dying to get a crack at one of Hitler's little pets."

Meantime, across from where Watson sat, an unexpected drama was unfolding. Irving had rushed from his position behind the cockpit to take photographs of the attack from the port-side blister. Right behind the co-pilot on the starboard side of the Canso, manning the air-to-surface vessel radar, was wireless air gunner F/Sgt L.H. Blain. The moment co-pilot Duncan shouted "submarine," Blain knew his second responsibility was to man the port-side machine gun. But gunner Blain also understood that Irving's getting pictures—proof of the attack—was more important than his manning the gun. The two men arrived at the port-side blister nearly simultaneously. Blain opened the blister and Irving leaned out to aim the camera. Exactly at that moment, Colborne pushed the Canso's nose into an even steeper dive, which nearly catapulted Irving out of the airplane. With catlike reflexes, Blain grabbed Irving by the legs. Irving, an ordained minister, blurted out, "Thank God!"

Blain shouted to Irving that as gunner he had to get his machine guns ready. "To hell with the guns!" Irving called back, mindful that his attempt to photograph the attack on a U-boat eighteen days before had yielded no images. "We want pictures!"

So, with Blain hanging on to Irving, the navigator kept pointing the camera, clicking shots, and winding the film ahead. "Take another. Take another," Blain called out.

In the final seconds before releasing his depth charges, F/L Colborne saw *U604* begin her crash dive. At an altitude of just 800 feet, he cut the throttles and nosed down yet again. Then, at nearly 200 miles an hour, he flew the Canso over the length of *U604* as he released four depth charges from the aircraft. Colborne reported seeing the U-boat's deck gun, conning tower, and all of her stern still above the surface as the charges fell. One landed on the U-boat deck, the rest in a pattern around the diving sub. Colborne then banked to the left, and everybody on the port side of the aircraft could see the depth charges explode.

"A big cloud of spray was blown about fifty feet into the air," Blain reported from the port-side blister. He was still hanging on to Irving's legs as the latter madly snapped more photographs. "And before [the spray] had time to fall back into the ocean, there was another very sharp explosion which must have come from the U-boat. . . . The column of water was blown much higher than before . . . like a huge funnel."

Co-pilot Duncan continued to photograph from his cockpit vantage point. "I took [a] picture of the air bubbles that were coming to the surface. They lasted from ten to twelve minutes and looked like a great cauldron of boiling water. . . . a good indication that the sub has been split open and the air inside is escaping." He was sure that Canso 9738 had sunk the U-boat.

The sight sparked euphoric whooping, and in the cramped space of their Canso the crew back of the cockpit moved back and forth congratulating each other on their apparent victory. Colborne stayed focused on the oil slick and debris field and circled there for almost an hour. Irving prepared an amplifying report, cleared it with Colborne, and had Elden send it to Gander—their exact position and the success of the attack—in plain language. For Irving, the message held special meaning.

"I have two brothers in the navy," he wrote later, "and realize that every U-boat we down, gives them one more chance to live through the hell . . . in an endeavour to get vital food and supplies to the battle fronts of war-torn Europe."

Back at No. 5 (BR) Squadron station in Gander, the crew of Canso 9738 was debriefed by an intelligence officer, their individual reports written up and signed off, and their photos developed. S/L F.J. Ewart, the CO at No. 5, declared the U-boat "definitely destroyed."[49] On March 2, Air Cmdre F.V. Heakes wrote that the "attack and coverage undoubtedly saved the convoy that day." By July 7, 1943, the US Navy had recorded Canso 9738's target as "probably damaged."[50]

That assessment turned out to be the most accurate. Kptlt Höltring, in his report back to Kriegsmarine headquarters, summed up the damage to *U604* this way: "Both compressors torn off. Shafts displaced in axial direction. Diesel clutches are pounding hard. Main clutches cannot be fully disengaged. Main ballast tank V has 50-centimetre long crack. Tank vents air very rapidly. Moved off at 50 degrees to make repairs."[51] The sub arrived back in Brest on March 9, 1943.

✪ ✪ ✪

GRAND Adm Dönitz called the attack on Convoy ON 166 a victory, attributing its success to U-boat commanders who "were for the most part experienced older men."[52] He claimed that his three U-boat packs had sunk twenty-three ships, or 132,171 tons of shipping. In fact, Allied losses amounted to fourteen merchant ships and 78,700 tons lost. During the six-day running battle in the Black Pit, three U-boats were sunk—*U529*, *U606*, and *U623*—while *U604* was heavily damaged. This time, Royal Navy staff at Western Approaches Command had little to complain about in terms of Canadian performance, particularly since ON 166 had experienced a week-long gale, no destroyer support, attacks from nineteen U-boats, and tactical demands that had spread thin the Canadian corvette escorts.

"Their aggressive actions prevented at least five additional attacks on the convoy," reported USN Cmdre Paul Heineman, in charge of the convoy. "They were a tower of strength."[53]

On February 26, twenty-eight of the original forty-nine merchantmen from Convoy ON 166 limped into East Coast harbours. Evidence of the previous week's carnage could be seen on deck aboard HMCS *Trillium*—scores of merchant navy survivors at the rails. Leading Seaman Harry Mann described the rescues he and his corvette shipmates had managed during the battle. "We burnt the paint off the side of our ship trying to get close to a torpedoed tanker," he said. "The water was burning with high-test gas all around her."

With so many burned or wounded sailors aboard the Canadian corvette, USCGC *Spencer* had transferred a doctor to *Trillium* at sea to attend them. Despite these efforts, however, two of those who'd survived the sinkings died aboard

Trillium, and the Canadian crew wrapped and lashed down their bodies at the stern. Elsewhere, with barely room in the ship's extended fo'c'sle for the crew, *Trillium*'s complement offered every bit of space aboard so that survivors could rest, share galley food provisions, and receive treatment from the visiting medical officer.

"We picked up 167 survivors and a cat from the sunken ships," Mann said.[54]

While not a death blow for either side, Convoy ON 166 proved one of the largest, bloodiest actions in the Battle of the Atlantic, involving U-boats, convoy escorts, and Allied bombers. More than 120 German submariners and over 260 Allied merchant navy sailors died in the clash. And yet neither side blinked. Allied logistical needs demanded that escorts make rapid turnarounds to protect an increasing number of convoys laden with goods for the UK civilian population, and for the resupply of military operations in North Africa and (later in 1943) the invasion of Sicily.

Escort group A-3, including its three Canadian corvettes—*Dauphin*, *Rosthern*, and *Trillium*—had less than a week in port to rest, repair, and replenish before they were ordered to sea again, this time to protect the fifty-nine merchantmen of Convoy SC 121. More tempestuous seas slowed these eastbound ships, eliminated their air cover, and scattered the cohesion of the convoy. The first week of March, Bletchley Park's attempts to decode Triton came up empty, and that, combined with B-Dienst decryption of RN ciphers, allowed two wolf packs of twenty-seven U-boats to intercept the convoy south of Greenland. The packs sank thirteen merchant ships, and 270 sailors died. There were no U-boat losses.[55]

In January 1943, in the North Atlantic alone, U-boats had sunk 172,691 tons of shipping, and in February, 288,625. But in March they nearly doubled the total to 476,349 tons.[56] Those numbers represented the loss of 155 merchant ships. Of note, particularly since the Admiralty had levelled so much criticism at Canadian escorts, were the efforts of escort groups B-4 and B-5, shepherding three convoys—SC 122, HX 229, and HX 229A—through the mid-North Atlantic from March 16 to 20. In nearly textbook Rüdeltaktik conditions (ninety-six hours in the Black Pit, rough but navigable seas, and a nearly full moon at night), forty-five U-boats had swarmed the three convoys. They'd sunk twenty-one ships with the loss of only one U-boat. These were totals reminiscent of the Kriegsmarine's Happy Times of mid-1940 and early 1942. The Admiralty's Monthly Anti-Submarine Report revealed that U-boats had destroyed 120 ships (82 in the North Atlantic) in March, the highest monthly total of tonnage sunk in convoys since the war began.

And this time the Admiralty Sea Lords couldn't blame their usual scapegoats, the Canadian escort groups.

FAR from the mess decks of Canada's corvette navy, but as politically stormy as the Atlantic's winter gales, a power struggle was brewing over who commanded what and where as a crisis loomed in the Battle of the Atlantic. Following the pronouncements of the Casablanca Conference in January 1943, the highest officials of the three Allied navies assembled at the Navy Department in Washington from March 1 to 12. The Atlantic Convoy Conference meeting rooms got crowded—if not physically, then certainly in terms of creden-

The human adversary on the North Atlantic was deadly enough, but the natural elements of winter—howling gales, blinding snow, and pack ice—posed an equal threat. Ice buildup on a ship's superstructure had the potential to capsize it. When ice accumulated on HMCS *Outremont*'s surface, often on the Murmansk run, RCN artificer Frank Mills (1) recalled all hands worked in shifts with ice clubs, axes, and steam hoses clearing it away (2). As tricky as any ice-removal measures were, Cliff Perry (3), a Canadian officer in the RN, recalled "the most extraordinary feat of seamanship," refuelling (4) his warship at sea: "One moment I was staring down the funnel of the tanker and the next staring up at its propeller spinning out of the water."

1

2

3

4

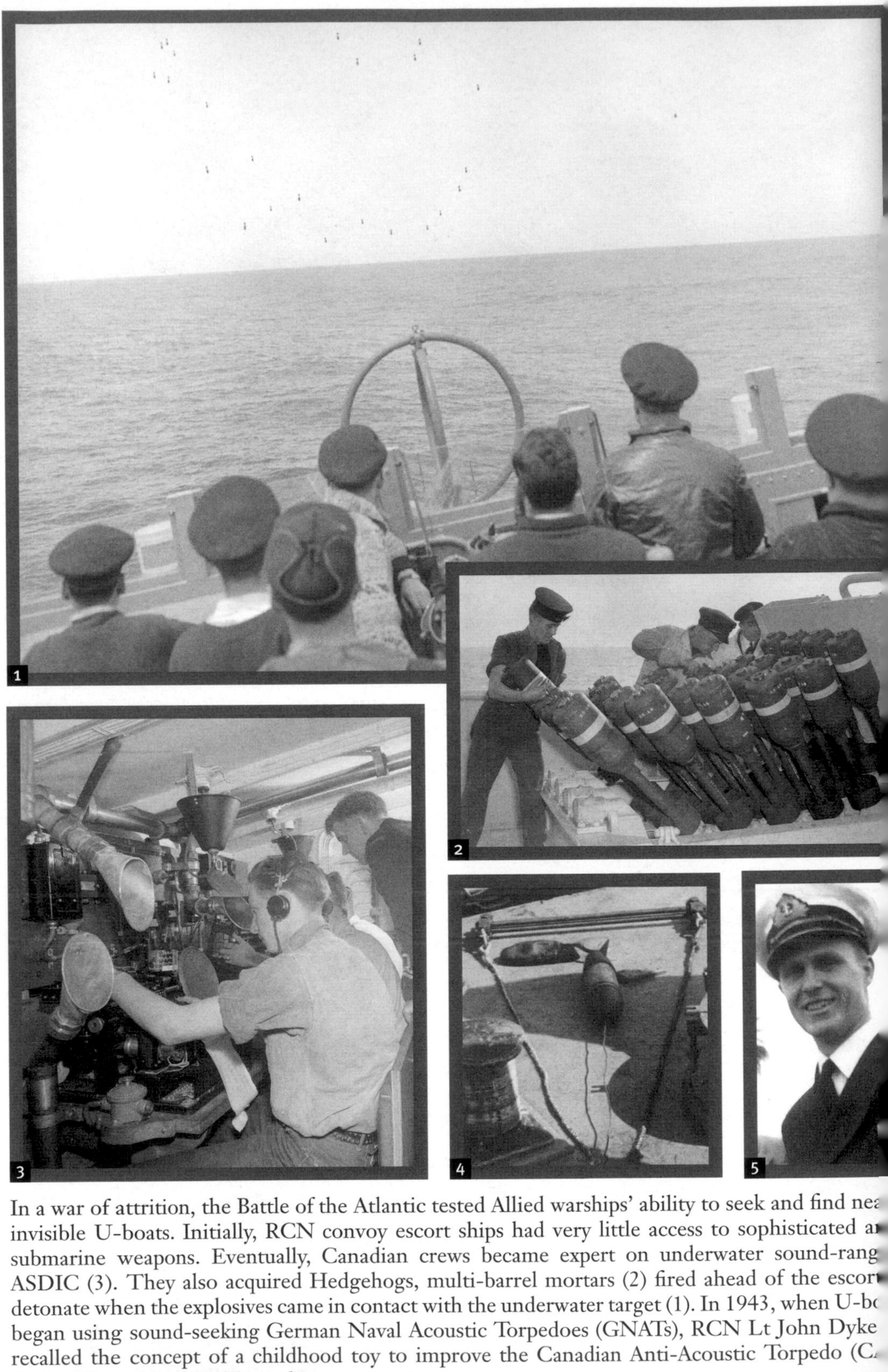

In a war of attrition, the Battle of the Atlantic tested Allied warships' ability to seek and find nea invisible U-boats. Initially, RCN convoy escort ships had very little access to sophisticated a submarine weapons. Eventually, Canadian crews became expert on underwater sound-rang ASDIC (3). They also acquired Hedgehogs, multi-barrel mortars (2) fired ahead of the escor detonate when the explosives came in contact with the underwater target (1). In 1943, when U-bo began using sound-seeking German Naval Acoustic Torpedoes (GNATs), RCN Lt John Dyke recalled the concept of a childhood toy to improve the Canadian Anti-Acoustic Torpedo (C device (4) against GNAT attacks.

1

2

Despite often carrying explosives (1), during the war Allied merchant ships completed 25,343 transatlantic trips delivering 165 million tons of cargo to Britain. On November 21, 1941, however, the merchant ship carrying Ken Rickers (2) was attacked and sunk; its secret contents proved more dangerous than the U-boat attack. George and Harold Doig (3) both served in the RCN, and endured the trauma of mutual loss. Shipwrecked sailors often survived on the flimsiest of rafts, such as this Carley float (4) full of HMCS *Clayoquot* survivors in December 1944. In September 1943, a GNAT struck and sank Canadian destroyer *St. Croix*; miraculously, William Fisher (5) survived that sinking and, soon after, the sinking of his rescue ship. Similarly, Walter Schmietenknop (6) was the sole survivor from *U767* when it was attacked and sunk two weeks after D-Day.

3

4

TORONTO DAILY STAR

TORONTO, FRIDAY, OCTOBER 1, 1943

THE WEATHER

DESTROYER ST. CROIX TORPEDOED
146 OF 147 CANADIANS MISSING

Nazi Munitions Ship Blown Up At Naples

FINANCIAL EDITION
CLOSING MARKETS

Gomel Capture Nears As Russians Close In

10-DAY SEA FIGHT ON ARCTIC RIM REVEALED IN SINKING OF WARSHIP 14 TORONTO CASUALTIES REPORTED

ALBERTA SAILOR ONLY KNOWN SURVIVOR WHEN ST. CROIX TORPEDOED

300 FLEE BY SEA AS DENMARK JEWS GESTAPO SOUGHT

DESTROYER WAS ON RESCUE MISSION WHEN U-BOAT DEALT DEATHBLOW

JOINT MILITARY TALKS PLANNED

5

6

1

2

3

4

5

Hollywood could not have scripted two more dramatic Atlantic battles than those involving U-boats and Canadian escort ships in the summer of 1942. When HMCS *Assiniboine* forced *U210* to surface on August 6, destroyer commander John Stubbs (3) outmanouvered the U-boat on the surface (1) before ultimately ramming it, as depicted in the *Halifax Mail* newspaper (2). Adm Leonard Murray personally congratulated *Assiniboine*'s crew (4). Then, on August 28, HMCS *Oakville* commander Clarence King (5) chased *U94* to the surface, eventually enabling corvette officers Hal Lawrence and Arthur Powell (6) to board and capture the sub before it sank. Government posters depicted the moment in a propaganda "Men of Valor" poster (7).

6

MEN of VALOR
They fight for you
Two-man boarding party from the
Canadian corvette 'Oakville' subdues
crew of German sub in Caribbean

7

1

2

3

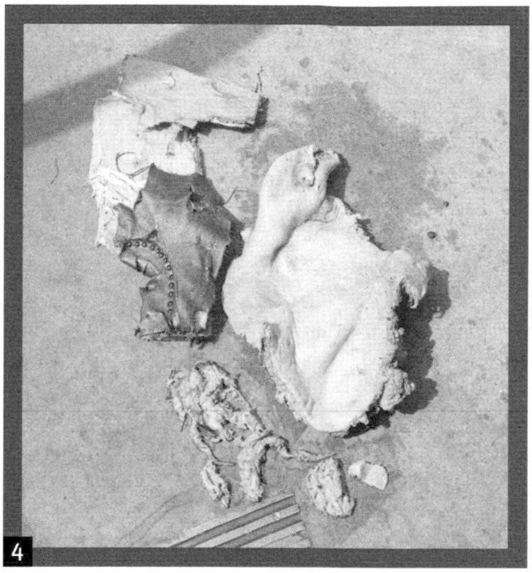

4

5

Describing the minutes following his U-boat's attack on a convoy, and the deep dive to escape the escorts' response with depth charges (1) and strafing (2), one submariner commented, "Dying is hard work aboard a U-boat." By 1943, when Allied hunter-killer escort groups gained the upper hand, the life expectancy of a German submariner was only 100 days. On March 6, 1944, after a thirty-two-hour chase, crewmen from HMCS *Chilliwack* boarded (3) and captured *U744*. Following their sinking of Italian U-boat *Avorio*, HMCS *Regina* crew posed around the corvette's gun shield logo (5). When no submariners survived an apparent U-boat sinking, the British Admiralty only verified the victory if Allied crews collected human remains (4) from surface debris as evidence.

1

2

3

4

5

6

When the RCN posted Ian Tate (1, far right) to frigate HMCS *Valleyfield*, he took great pride in his anti-submarine crew, calling them "my white-haired boys"; only he and two of his seven-man crew survived when they were torpedoed by *U548* in May 1944. To evade Allied air surveillance, U-boats developed a Schnorchel device allowing subs to take in air while travelling just under the surface (2). Consequently, the mid–North Atlantic, a.k.a. the Black Pit, remained dominated by wolf packs for much of the war. RCAF pilot Don Rollins (5, far right) and his crew anticipated a leave over Christmas in 1943; however, a last-minute bombing op over the Bay of Biscay on December 24 nearly ended in disaster. In June 1944, David Hornell (4 second from right) and his all-Canadian Canso aircrew were shot down by *U1225* off the Faroe Islands, but depth-charged the sub in the battle (3); Hornell managed to keep five of his eight crew alive in a dinghy until rescue, receiving the VC posthumously. Ultimately, the VLR Liberator aircraft (6) delivered very-long-range coverage to the convoys, and helped end the slaughter of ships in the Black Pit.

1

2

3

4

Just days before the war ended, HMCS *Esquimalt* (1) conducted operations outside Halifax Harbour; there on April 16, 1945, *U190* (3), with Werner Hirschmann (4) serving as her engineer, fired a single torpedo into the minesweeper. In the minutes he had, *Esquimalt*'s Terry Manuel, 2, wearing life jacket, scrambled with forty-three others to escape the sinking sweeper (twenty-eight died when the ship sank), but exposure to the cold on life rafts killed half of those before rescue. On May 4, 1945, Adm Dönitz ordered U-boats to surrender to Allied ports. *U190* surrendered at Bay Bulls, Newfoundland. Meanwhile, RCN sailor Martin Franchetto (6) was assigned gunnery duty to help oversee the surrender of *U889* at Shelburne, NS. Never able to fire on a U-boat during the war, his anger watching Canadian film crews and reporters (5) fuss over the surrendering Germans tempted his trigger finger.

5

6

1

2

3

4

5

6

7

Aboard HMCS *Montreal*, Roy Harbin (1) experienced many calls to action stations as a torpedoman, but in December 1944, was ordered to guard captured German sailors (2), though he'd never handled a pistol in his life. The RCN's Rodine Egan (5) served ashore in Halifax, responsible for hundreds of Wrens at HMCS *Stadacona* barracks. When VE-Day sparked riots in downtown Halifax, she thwarted rioters at the Zellers store (4) on Barrington Street. Bob Rae (6) served in the Canadian merchant navy from 1942-45, but had to wait until 1992 before the federal government recognized merchant sailors as veterans; only then did he wear his medals proudly (7). As a sick bay attendant aboard HMCS *Forest Hill*, Ken Davy (3) dealt with everything from seasickness to VD; at the end of the war, however, there was nothing he could do to save his ship from being cut up for scrap in Hamilton Harbour.

tials. Representing the Americans were Adm Ernest J. King (COMINCH of the US Navy) and RAdm R.M. Brainard (commander of Task Force 24). The British delegation was led by Adm Percy Noble of WAC. And the Canadian contingent comprised RAdm Victor Brodeur, Cdr Horatio Nelson Lay (director of operations), and Cdr Harry DeWolf (director of plans). Opening statements from the US Navy spoke of "unification of effort," and from the Royal Navy about "common policy."[57]

Brodeur, who'd served in the RCN since 1910, was openly suspicious of both the Royal and US Navies. He admired both services for their legacies but was a fierce nationalist when it came to Canadian protection of the northwest Atlantic. At the outset, he proposed emphatically that control of convoys and anti-submarine warfare off the Canadian and Newfoundland coasts "be exercised solely by British and Canadian authorities," and that "the present COAC [Commanding Officer Atlantic Coast] become C-in-C NW Atlantic [directing] all surface and Air Forces deployed in [anti-submarine] warfare in NW Atlantic."[58]

Since the days of the Atlantic Charter in 1941, Britain and the United States had made most decisions about the Battle of the Atlantic bilaterally. They had divided up the battlefield into zones governed by either the US or Royal Navies, while assigning to the RCN its fair share of escort duties and anti-submarine warfare. Still, throughout the post–Atlantic Charter period, Canada had no voice. The RCN had always gone without Type 271 radar, Huff-Duff, and the latest armament while the other two services had been first and second in line. Experienced RCN officers had trained its volunteer ranks between escort patrols, during refits, and on their leave time.

Every patrol escort had been catch-as-catch-can and had then routinely caught hell if things went wrong. Meantime, when Canadian waters, such as the Gulf of St. Lawrence, came under threat, the RCN was left to its own devices. But when operations such as Torch demanded additional warships and crews halfway around the globe, Canada had selflessly contributed more than its share to the Allied cause.

"This has been done quite often . . . as a result of requests from the Admiralty and COMINCH," Capt Lay had calmly pointed out. "At the present time [Canada has] forty-eight per cent of the escorts in North Atlantic Trade Convoys, and two Commands on the Atlantic with staffs capable of dealing with all escort matters."[59]

A combination of Brodeur's pro-Canada declarations and Lay's low-key provision of the facts contributed to the decision at the conference to finally make Canada a full partner in the Battle of the Atlantic. After twelve days of deliberation, the delegates had changed the convoy timetables, reframed the division of responsibility, recognized the need for more powerful long-range air cover, and reorganized the chain of command.

By the end of May 1943, the Admiralty had instituted an alternating cycle of seven to eight days for fast convoys and eleven days for slow ones, limiting the size of each to eighty merchant ships (instead of sixty) to make up for less frequent sailings. To protect the convoys, the Admiralty created nine close escort groups, five of them Canadian. As a result, the RCN assumed responsibility for two-thirds of close escort between Newfoundland and the UK.[60] As well, the Americans promised to introduce light aircraft carriers in support of the Atlantic escorts and within a short time deliver forty-eight VLR Liberator bombers to Newfoundland bases to help bridge the Black Pit.[61]

Meanwhile, the North Atlantic battlefield was being reconfigured. All ocean convoys and U-boat battles north of latitude 40 degrees now came under British and Canadian control, while east-west, the shipping lanes were divided at 47 degrees longitude. The C-in-C Western Approaches assumed responsibility for the eastern half, and the new C-in-C Northwest Atlantic took control of all anti-submarine surface and air forces to the west. That new C-in-C in the west would be RCN RAdm Leonard Murray, the only Canadian to command an Allied theatre during the Second World War.

As of April 30, 1943, then, the RCN would take back responsibility for trade convoys in the northwest Atlantic. The C-group warships would officially return to active service in the waters from just off New York City to the ocean approaches of Newfoundland and Labrador, and in partnership with the RN they would ensure the protection of merchant shipping across the entire breadth of the North Atlantic.

Just prior to the Atlantic Convoy Conference, the Canadian government had made its case for the navy's re-entry into the Battle of the Atlantic: "[The] Canadian Navy can serve no higher purpose," it declared. "We have come to look upon [this task] as a national responsibility for Canada and one which geographically and strategically we are well placed to undertake."[62]

Chapter Ten

HUNTER-KILLERS

Dave Broadfoot got his initial taste of war work building Park cargo ships at North Van Repairs, in Vancouver. At the beginning of the war, there were only four large shipbuilding berths on the west coast. But by 1943, at peak wartime production, Canadian west-coast shipyards were averaging a new 10,000-ton ship every week, while across Canada shipbuilders averaged three 10,000-ton vessels per week.[1] The Park Steamship Company (a Crown corporation) oversaw construction of merchant ships in Canada for the British Merchant Navy. During the war, the firm built 160 cargo ships and twenty tankers. Broadfoot earned thirty-five dollars a week as a labourer in the North Van Repairs yard.[2] But as attractive as a shipbuilder's wage seemed, at sixteen, Broadfoot wanted to go to sea.

"Can I enlist?" he asked at HMCS *Discovery*'s Vancouver recruiting office.

"Sure," the recruiting officer said, "but there's 25,000 guys ahead of you."[3]

Too impatient to wait, Broadfoot joined the merchant navy, and for six months he worked aboard small freighters servicing ports on Vancouver Island, where he got over his seasickness. Next, as a fireman in the engine room aboard SS *Brentwood Bay Park*, one of the ships he'd helped to build, he quickly set his primary goal of working his way out of the engine room and getting off tankers. He didn't appreciate that tankers always docked in fuelling yards, usually quite distant from the port city's population and night life. Tankers also tended to be the least safe place in a convoy at sea.

"You got into thick fog and you are maybe one of sixty ships in a convoy," he said. "You'd walk out onto the bow, and suddenly you'd see this other ship right up tight to you. . . . [Tankers] are so volatile, when they did collide it was usually a tragedy."[4]

On one trip up from South America to join a North Atlantic convoy to the UK, his tanker received a signal from the commodore's ship that a U-boat pack was assembling around them. The tankers had to disperse immediately. The captain ordered full speed to get away from the threat; Broadfoot said the engines were running so fast that "deck plates were bouncing off the engine-room beams, we'd opened it up so much." Later, on an outbound trip from the UK to North America, north of the Azores Broadfoot's tanker broke down with a damaged propeller. The convoy was already a slow convoy, but his tanker had to drop out and make her way at an even slower speed, "across the whole Atlantic at seven knots," until he saw the most welcome sight ever. "I'll never forget the joy of seeing one of those [merchant] aircraft carriers coming over the horizon," he said.

This was no mirage. Originally laid down at a Pennsylvania shipyard in December 1939 and launched a year later as a mercantile ship, *Rio Parana* had been requisitioned by the

USN for conversion to a merchant aircraft carrier (MAC). Shipbuilders in Brooklyn added trusses to support a wooden flight deck covering nearly three-quarters of the ship's length, with a hangar and a lift aft of the flight deck.[5] Christened HMS *Biter* in the spring of 1942, the carrier provided air support in Operation Torch, and for scores of merchant ships passing through the mid-Atlantic gap where none had sailed before. Among *Biter*'s beneficiaries early in 1943 were the members of Dave Broadfoot's crew coaxing their crippled tanker westbound—at seven knots—alone across the Atlantic.

"When we saw the carrier," Broadfoot said, "we knew we were going to make it back to Canada."[6]

PART of the strategy that ensured stoker Dave Broadfoot's ship made it safely to Canada included the introduction of the merchant aircraft carrier *Biter*. The rest had finally dawned on those who'd debated the state of military escorts at the Atlantic Convoy Conference in March 1943. Heavy merchant ship losses in the first three months of the year made it clear that even the Allies' best close escorts, be they British, American, or Canadian, could not deflect groups of thirty and forty U-boats at a time. The only response was to rapidly deploy reinforced escort groups to locations where Allied intelligence knew U-boat patrols were assembling.

The idea of "support groups" was not new. RCN Cdr Chummy Prentice had proven their worth when he led HMCS *Chambly* and *Moose Jaw* to the aid of Convoy SC 42 in 1942. This time, Western Approaches Cdr Max Horton chose to build not one but five anti-submarine support groups with more warships in each, more experienced crews, the best detecting equipment available, and as much firepower as he could spare. These would become "hunter-killers" whose prime purpose was to destroy U-boats.

The Canadian escort groups—with some additional training at HMS *Western Isles* and recent experience in the Mediterranean—simply needed more dependable warships to compensate for the RCN's lack of destroyers. So the Admiralty assigned new British frigates—HMS *Itchen* (C-1), *Lagan* (C-2), and *Jed* (C-3)—as well as refitted Town-class destroyers—HMS *Broadway* (C-2), *Burnham* (C-3), and *Churchill* (C-4). All would be commanded by experienced British group commanders, which RCN headquarters in Ottawa welcomed.

In addition, the Admiralty would lend two fleet destroyers—HMCS *Ottawa II* and HMCS *Kootenay*—commanded by RCN Cdr Hugh Pullen and RCN A/Cdr Kenneth Dyer, respectively, and later River-class destroyers—HMCS *Saskatchewan* and HMCS *Gatineau*—commanded by RN Cdr Ralph Medley and RN Cdr Philip Burnett, respectively. To round out the support groups' strength, the Admiralty added merchant aircraft carriers—HMS *Biter* and HMS *Archer,* plus USS *Bogue*—to provide convoys with immediate access to air cover in the mid-Atlantic.

Meanwhile, by the spring of 1943, escorting warships in all three Allied navies in the Battle of the Atlantic—the RN, RCN, and USN—enjoyed the benefits of a new secret weapon. Antennas atop their masts—a quarter-wave vertical with four horizontal rods to form a ground plane—were connected to a short-range, high-frequency transmitter/receiver radio aboard the ship. Its operator, often self-trained, understood that this radio had a limited power output of fifty watts, capable of sending and receiving verbal messages in a line-of-sight range, about ten miles. Known as "Talk Between Ships" (TBS), these sets offered escorts a means of communicating short verbal messages in the heat of battle in and around a convoy. U-boat wireless operators might accidentally intercept and listen to TBS messages, but they could not direction-find (locate the sources) on TBS signals. Each set weighed about 250 pounds and occupied eight cubic feet (the size of a chest of drawers). But, for its rapid communications capability, Allied strategists considered TBS worth its weight in gold.

Allied strategists added one final weapon to the new Atlantic convoy arsenal—land-based heavy bombers capable of flying a very long range out to the convoys to provide cover. In late March they doubled the strength of RAF No. 120 Squadron, flying from RAF Nutts Corner, Northern Ireland, bringing their total number of VLR Liberators to thirty-eight.[7] And on the other side of the ocean, over several months they delivered fifteen VLR Liberators to Canadian crews flying from RCAF No. 10 (BR) Squadron at Gander.[8] The Newfoundland-based bomber reconnaissance aircraft would quickly accumulate a record number of anti-submarine sorties—twenty-two—successfully sinking three U-boats.[9]

In early March, U-boats had intercepted every single convoy that ventured into the North Atlantic. Wolf packs had attacked more than half of them. And when the smoke cleared, after the first three weeks in March, nearly a quarter of all shipping that had attempted an Atlantic crossing had never arrived.[10] But in April the tables began to turn. The introduction of beefed-up escort support groups, the addition of MACs in the air gap, the availability of VLR bombers, better weather conditions, and, finally, solving the U-boat cipher Triton all sparked an Allied offensive in the North Atlantic and reduced shipping losses.

Ultra intelligence gave convoy planners safer routes around Dönitz's wolf packs. So WAC assigned most of the Canadian warships returning to the North Atlantic to close escort of those diverted convoys, away from the perceived danger zones. And that freed the British and American support groups—the "hunter-killers"—to go on the offensive. Without the constant responsibility of delivering the convoys safely to their destinations, those specialists could chase U-boat contacts until they eliminated them.[11]

For Nan Adair, this period at Bletchley Park proved to be one of the busiest. She had worked with the brain trust in Hut 8 for months, watching as they assembled intelligence and built apparatuses to decode Kriegsmarine communications. She spent her shifts listening to or reading German naval transmissions and feeding any stereotyped greetings or standardized content she discovered to the team of codebreakers. U-boats shadowing merchant ships sent weather reports back through U-Bootwaffe headquarters to help direct packs into the path of a convoy. When the telegraphist aboard a U-boat sent a weather report, he encoded it into a condensed seven-letter message. That message was enciphered using the naval Enigma machine and then transmitted to intercept stations in Lorient, France, or Germany. There the message was deciphered by the onshore Enigma and the weather report reconstructed. Thanks to the Operation Primrose pinch in May 1941, Bletchley Park codebreakers had succeeded in decoding the meteorological station's code. That meant that Bletchley staff in Hut 8 had gained access to cribs (plain-text letter combinations) that reduced the number of possible letter combinations in the coded messages.[12]

"All we did was handle the German U-boat traffic," Adair said. "The intercepts, where the cryptographers got their cribs, meant [monitoring] one form of traffic. They were all weather messages."[13]

Nan had never studied German at school, but she had a knack for recognizing words phonetically or visually, even if she couldn't translate them. Hut 8 codebreakers taught her what German words and numbers to look and listen for in naval weather messages. The transmissions were short, often repetitive, and her job was to spot recurring words or phrases, because their appearance usually indicated something of importance followed.

"One phrase I learned was *Vorhersage Reichsegen*," she said. She didn't know what it meant, but "whenever it came up on my machine, I made note of it. Once [codebreakers] broke one pattern and took note of the operator's call sign, they could understand what was said."

Work shifts were long and intense, and Hut 8 was generally cold. Someone managed to find an electric hot plate, however, and often during the night shifts she and Joan Clarke boiled water in a kettle. Most of the time they prepared a concoction of Marmite (concentrated yeast extract left over from brewing beer), but occasionally, when Nan received a gift package from former neighbours in Canada, there was a warm treat for all.

"Friends of the family would send this chocolate mix that was already sweetened. All you had to do was add hot water to it and you had a lovely hot chocolate," Nan said. "It was like gold. . . . And yours truly was very popular."

If Nan's imported delicacy didn't take the edge off those chilly nights, she said, the discussions and debates shared around the hot chocolate table certainly did. Whenever there was a slack period, the younger members of the cryptography team would often draw out the veterans—Shaun Wylie, Rolf Noskwith, Hugh Alexander, Gordon Welchman, and Alan Turing—just to listen to their discourse on politics, religion, and the war. Then, after an edifying and lively conversation, the group would return to work, but not before Turing had wiped his mug clean, strung a chain through its handle, and locked it onto a radiator on the wall.

"Here was the brains of Ultra," Nan said, "locking his mug to a radiator to keep someone from stealing it."

THE showdown between Karl Dönitz's wolf packs and the Admiralty's hunter-killers began with the launch of the fifth Outward North Atlantic slow convoy, ONS 5. In the final week of April 1943, fifty-two ships assembled in the North Channel off Londonderry—forty-three merchant ships and eventually sixteen escorts (destroyers, frigates, corvettes, and trawlers). Royal Navy Cdr Peter Gretton led the B-7 escort group shepherding the slow convoy at 7.5 knots, bound for Halifax. Western Approaches Command routed the convoy south of Iceland and past the southern tip of Greenland, where RN forecasters predicted that gale-force winds, pack ice, and icebergs would make passage uncomfortable. But so would it be, they hoped, for the U-boats.

B-Dienst intercepts of RN data prompted the grand admiral to deploy three wolf packs—nearly sixty U-boats in all—across a 500-mile arc south of Greenland and east of

Newfoundland. Kriegsmarine strategists sent the packs deep enough into the Black Pit, they anticipated, to be immune to Allied air attacks. Apparently not deep enough. Several days out, the escorts' Huff-Duff sets picked up U-boat transmissions. That brought a Flying Fortress from RAF No. 206 Squadron Coastal Command in the Hebrides, and the B-17 attacked *U170* with two sticks of depth charges and sank her.

Meanwhile, BdU in Berlin and WAC in Liverpool were engaging in a crucial cat-and-mouse game, each side waiting for its decryption specialists to pick up the other's transmissions and break their codes. Using B-Dienst to listen to RN ciphers, Dönitz spread his dragnet of U-boats farther afield in anticipation of convoy sightings. At the same time, WAC used every Enigma message that the Bletchley Park decoders could decipher to keep Allied convoys—not just ONS 5—out of danger. That same week, there were 350 Allied ships in motion on the Atlantic.* Initially, the Allies had managed to keep four westbound convoys and five eastbound ones from being detected.

But suddenly—at noon on April 26—Berlin changed the Naval Enigma settings, and Bletchley's flow of information stopped. At the same time, the expected Atlantic gale descended on ONS 5. Aboard the rescue trawler HMS *Northern Spray*, Arthur Howell, a former banker turned navy coder, tried to stay dry and put down his thoughts in a diary.

"Weather bad now. Green seas and decks under water all the time. Life almost intolerable on a small ship. Difficult to write," he wrote on April 27. "Many interceptions on the Huff-Duff. It appears the enemy is waiting."[14]

---

* Bad weather had scattered eastbound Convoy HX 234, leaving British motor merchant *Amerika* straggling; after midnight on April 22, *U306* torpedoed and sank her; eighty-six of 140 died, including thirty-seven RCAF aircrew en route to Allied air bases in the UK.

The storm persisted for days. It slowed the convoy to 3.5 knots and scattered all ten columns of ships across miles of open Atlantic. Howell noted that even the crow's nest was repeatedly deluged as his ship crashed through troughs. At times they also had to dodge icebergs and pack ice. Keeping merchant ships from straggling forced the escorts to do endless circuits, which expended precious fuel. The destroyers couldn't refuel at sea, which forced some to withdraw for Halifax or Reykjavík. As to Howell's other observation, even in the storm, U-boats in overwhelming numbers found the convoy. By May 4, 1943, forty-one subs had amassed for the attack on ONS 5. They became the largest wolf pack assembled against a single convoy of the war. That day they sank two merchant ships, and the next day ten more.

Among the ten attacked and sunk on May 5, the British merchant steamer *Bristol City* carried a cargo of china clay on her way to New York for military cargo on the return trip. Every morning during the westbound crossing, just before the four-to-eight watch began in the engine room, one stoker was designated to brew a pot of tea on the mess deck and take it below to the rest of the watch. That morning, it was Bernard McCluskey's turn. Originally from Charlottetown, Prince Edward Island, McCluskey had gone to sea at thirteen, lying about his age. He'd served on buoy boats around the Maritimes, on a Norwegian merchant ship carrying ammunition to the UK as the war began, and later aboard *Rideau Park*, one of the Park company's 10,000-ton freighters. But at 4 a.m. on May 5, his job was getting tea for his fellow stokers aboard *Bristol City*.

"I didn't feel like goin' for the tea," he said. "Course, they'd grab lumps of coal and fire 'em at you, if you didn't. I'd just put my foot over the mess room door back aft, and she took [a torpedo] right in the engine room. All the engine room was gone. Being on the four-to-eight watch, I'd be gone."[15]

Instead, McCluskey managed to retrieve his life jacket and climb over the stern of the ship as she sank; he was rescued by the corvette HMS *Loosestrife*. *Bristol City* sank in less than twenty minutes with a loss of fifteen crew, mostly from the lower decks where McCluskey normally worked. "I was supposed to be gone."

Picking up the pieces of their besieged convoy, Arthur Howell and the rescue trawler *Northern Spray* faced the prospect of searching for the survivors of sunken merchant ships in mountainous seas.

"We sighted lights in the water. They were survivors aboard a waterlogged life raft," he wrote during the night of May 5. "The raft was brought alongside, time after time, but the men seemed unable to help themselves."

Northern Spray's crew rushed to every raft, pulling aboard the men clinging to them. But even as they did, others disappeared beneath the waves and were lost. Of forty men serving aboard SS *North Britain*, just ten were saved. Next they raced to the scene of three more sunken freighters astern of the convoy. Instead of lights in the water, there were voices calling to their rescue boat, "Tender! Tender!" The sea around the bobbing lifeboats was awash with black fuel oil from the wrecked ships, and the men in the boats were coated with it. The rescuers managed to get a line to one lifeboat. Then, with the swell of the storm waters still running, they tried to pass the lifeboat astern—hoping to keep it from getting under the counter, the overhang of the stern of the rescue trawler.

"Alas, the stern rose up and fell back, crushing the boat and killing the men outright, so we had to cut them adrift," Howell continued. "It was desperate work trying to drag others aboard as they were covered in oil and kept slipping back into the boats."

Northern Spray, a mere 160 feet long, was now crammed with 143 survivors of Convoy ONS 5. Arthur Howell wrote in his diary that his bunk was occupied by three merchant sailors, and the captain had three sleeping in his toilet compartment. The trawler's cook had prepared 200 suppers all by himself. And in the morning, every one of the survivors aboard joined a detail that cleaned the ship from stem to stern "without using any [fresh] water, since it had been rationed." The trawler and all her occupants docked safely in St. John's three days later.

Grossadmiral Dönitz's U-Bootwaffe had chalked up substantial tonnage figures during this convoy. In a week of fighting in the North Atlantic, his forty-two U-boats had sunk thirteen merchantmen, totalling 60,000 tons of lost ships and cargo. However, Allied escorts had also demonstrated skill in repelling the attacks. On May 5, HMS *Sunflower* sank *U638*, and HMS *Vidette* sank *U531*. The support group ships fared even better on May 6, when HMS *Loosestrife* sank *U192*, HMS *Oribi* and *Snowflake* combined to sink *U125*, and HMS *Pelican* sank *U438*. Including *U701*, early in the engagement, that totalled six U-boats sunk.

The warships had been backed up by land-based air support. Taking a page from the late S/L "Molly" Small's test flights in January 1943, S/L B.H. Moffit flew his Canso more than 750 miles from the RCAF No. 5 (BR) Squadron base at Torbay, Newfoundland, in search of the convoy. Moffit's air-to-surface vessel radar made initial contact, leading him to a lone U-boat, *U630*, on the surface thirty miles behind ONS 5. He pushed the Canso's nose down, opened the throttles, and achieved total surprise.

"Coming in straight on, we let our depth charges go," Moffit reported. "As the aircraft passed over the sub I could see two of the Jerries still on the conning tower platform."[16]

U630 had just begun to crash-dive as the Canso's depth charges landed—two to port and another just off the conning tower. The impact was so powerful that the explosion threw the U-boat back up to the surface. Then she sank in a mass of air bubbles, debris, and a growing oil slick. All aboard *U630*, on just their first patrol, were lost.

"As for myself," Moffit concluded, "all I can say is that after two and a half years of peering for subs, it really makes the pulse quicken when you finally click." The Air Force would later award Moffit a Distinguished Flying Cross for thirty-two months of service in anti-submarine patrols.

While not directly involved in the battle for ONS 5, members of the new Canadian escort group C-2 were operating in close support of Convoy HX 237, which was heading in the opposite direction during that same first week of May. Five escort ships shepherded forty-two merchant ships eastbound from Newfoundland to Liverpool. The commodore of the convoy, Roy Gill, reported that his surface support group "proved a valuable asset in spotting submarines and is just what the doctor ordered."[17] Early on the morning of May 13, corvette HMCS *Drumheller* received orders to pick up survivors of a merchant ship that had been sunk some distance from the convoy. In the process, a Sunderland aircraft circling in the vicinity signalled *Drumheller* by lamp that it was stalking a U-boat. Officer of the watch Lt Ken Culley altered *Drumheller*'s course to investigate. The captain, Lt Les Denny, and Culley conferred. (Culley had been serving aboard HMCS *Oakville* when she captured *U94* in the Caribbean in 1942.)

Aboard *U753*, the captain, Alfred von Mannstein, had his gunners on deck. They let loose anti-aircraft fire on the circling Sunderland, but they did not notice the approaching corvette until *Drumheller*'s crew began firing her four-inch gun.

"We opened fire at a relatively short range," Culley said. "As soon as we started shooting, he dived."[18]

Moments later, *Drumheller* raced over *U753*'s dive path and dropped a shallow pattern of ten depth charges. The corvette's ASDIC operator maintained contact and the Canadians dropped another pattern of charges. The engagement had also attracted a Swordfish fighter-bomber launched from auxiliary aircraft carrier HMS *Biter*, as well as the frigate escort HMS *Lagan*; her crew launched Hedgehog explosives. Eventually the Allied crews heard an explosion deep beneath them, and soon after *Drumheller*'s crew spotted the telltale debris and oil slick that indicated *U753* was no more. The corvette collected the evidence and returned to close support of Convoy HX 237. Of the original forty-two ships, all but three arrived safely in the UK.

"One [should] send a wire to Hitler," Cmdre Gill wrote in his convoy narrative, "telling him if any of his submarines are in the way, they will be sunk."[19]

The fortunes of Allied support groups securing UK lifelines had changed dramatically. More impressive, given the disjointed nature of Allied response to the U-boat threat over the previous winter, was the close co-operation among RCAF aircraft, the British hunter-killer groups, a USN carrier, and the RCN close support ships. Success had come as a result of months of building experience at sea, trust in the development of new tactics and leadership, and rapid deployment of new weapons and devices. It also could not have happened without the resolve of merchant mariners who, despite the odds of survival, never flinched. The battle for Convoy ONS 5 had provided a defining moment—thirteen merchant ships sunk versus six U-boats (and another eight damaged or driven from the fight).

And German losses escalated. In the first three weeks of May, thirty-one of Grossadmiral Dönitz's flotilla of 120 U-boats operating in the Atlantic had been destroyed. His staff knew the long-term picture looked even grimmer. In the first forty months of the war, the U-Bootwaffe had lost 148 U-boats and 6,356 submariners; in stark contrast, between January and June of 1943 alone, 112 U-boats and 5,534 crewmen had been lost.[20] Adding to the sting, a hunter-killer group supporting Convoy SC 130 off Greenland had pursued and sunk *U954* on May 19. All submariners were lost, including Peter Dönitz, the grand admiral's son. For the Kriegsmarine—its forces and its families—this had become "Black May."

"In May [1943] in the Atlantic, the sinking of about 10,000 tons had to be paid for, by the loss of a boat," Karl Dönitz noted in the U-boat war diaries. "Not long ago [such] a loss came with the sinking of 100,000 tons. Thus, losses in May have reached an intolerable level."[21]

Accordingly, on May 24 Dönitz ordered the U-boats to withdraw from the North Atlantic. It had taken the better part of three years, but Allied air, naval, merchant, and intelligence forces had finally broken the mystique of the grand admiral's Rüdeltaktik.

"Wolf-pack operations against the convoys in the North Atlantic, the main theatre of operations," Dönitz wrote later, "were no longer possible."[22]

POSITIVE news for the Allies came from a number of fronts that spring. German armies had sustained defeats on the Eastern Front and in North Africa, totalling the loss of nearly half a million men—twenty divisions at Stalingrad and six divisions in Tunisia, roughly one-eighth of the German order of battle.[23] On the heels of those Allied victories, the successful arrival of substantial convoys to Britain in the summer of 1943 signalled progress on the Western Front. Operation Bolero, the long-range plan to amass forces in the UK, was back on track. It would see the construction of hundreds of bases, airfields, warehouses, barracks, hospitals, and fuel depots to support three million US military personnel who would eventually be transported to the British Isles. Once the buildup was complete, according to Bolero, the Allies could launch a cross-channel invasion and deliver the long anticipated "second front" against Hitler's Fortress Europe.

In the Atlantic siege, the Kriegsmarine saw its tonnage numbers fall steadily throughout 1943. In the first five months—between January and May—the sea wolves destroyed 1,336,650 tons of Allied merchant shipping. But in the latter seven months—from June to December—total tonnage sunk fell to 322,951 tons.[24] During those same twelve months, the U-Bootwaffe suffered the largest losses of the war thus far—237 U-boats sunk or destroyed. Remarkably, during the same year, the nineteen shipbuilding yards in eleven different German cities had built a total of 286 U-boats, the greatest annual production of the war.[25] At the 1943 loss rate, however, Kriegsmarine strategists knew they could not sustain offensive pressure in the North Atlantic. Despite the setback, Dönitz challenged his U-Bootwaffe crews to greater tenacity.

"In his efforts to rob U-boats of their most valuable characteristic, invisibility, the enemy is some lengths ahead of us," he told his flotilla crews. "I expect you to continue your determined struggle with the enemy. . . . Research and development departments [in] the Navy are working to improve your weapons and apparatus."[26]

Grossadmiral Dönitz needed something new to prove that his U-Bootwaffe was not a spent force. He looked to a series of innovations from German scientists to help his U-boats regain the upper hand, even if they couldn't operate in wolf packs. In the short term, Dönitz ordered Kriegsmarine armourers to install more lethal anti-aircraft weapons on the open decks of U-boats. Further, he ordered his flotillas traversing the Bay of Biscay (immediately west of the U-boat bases on the French coast) to travel submerged at night, but back on the surface in groups by day. In addition, his Standing Order 483 required that U-boats under attack in the bay remain surfaced to shoot it out with the aircraft.[27] Dönitz expected such tactics would deter Allied aircrews from attacking. In fact, the new orders would have deadly consequences for many of his U-boat crews.

To spot the enemy searching for his U-boats, Dönitz wanted his crews equipped with the latest radar detectors. This included the improved Hagenuk Wanze search receivers, which were able to detect radar emissions from escorts. They would replace the older Metox radar detector. Eventually the Germans also experimented with a radar decoy device, Thetis, and the anti-radar decoy Aphrodite.[28] As important, Dönitz needed his U-boats to regain a torpedo advantage. He called for the delivery of so-called search-and-destroy torpedoes. The Flächenabsuchender torpedo, or FaT target-seeking torpedo, would follow a back-and-forth ladder course until it hit a target.[29] Meanwhile, the T5 Zaunkönig torpedo could be fired toward an enemy ship from any position; it used acoustic technology, a hydrophone that homed on the cavitation (bubbling effect) of propellers in the ten-to-eighteen-knot range, the operating speed of most Allied escort ships.[30] Most of the Type VIIC U-boats carried fourteen torpedoes including four FaTs and four T5s, which the U-Bootwaffe nicknamed "destroyer crackers."[31]

Finally, however, Dönitz craved the arrival of the ultimate U-boat, a submarine with long underwater endurance as well as high-speed capability when submerged. These combined characteristics would allow the U-boat to track convoys and attack without exposing itself on the surface. The "Walther" boat (designed by engineer Hellmuth Walther) would use self-oxygenating hydrogen peroxide fuel in diesel engines theoretically capable of delivering a surface speed of twenty-six knots and an underwater speed of thirty knots.[32]

While he awaited the ultimate boat, Dönitz pushed for a hybrid, the Type XXI, using Walther's design but with massive battery capacity to deliver seventeen knots of speed submerged. Dönitz was told that prototypes would be prefabricated in sections and welded together (similar to US shipyard construction) at any number of factories far from the coast, thus out of range of enemy bombers.[33] In the meantime, German scientists had given Dönitz's U-Bootwaffe one more valuable tool. The Schnorchel, a retractable pipe that supplied air to the diesel engines while at periscope depth, would give each U-boat the ability to cruise and recharge batteries while submerged.

"We'll get [the British] in the end," Dönitz told his staff. "But first we must have the new boat!"[34]

The Admiralty took full advantage of the U-Bootwaffe's temporary retreat from the North Atlantic shipping lanes. In May it redirected convoys that had previously navigated the far North Atlantic route south to the Great Circle Route. It was a provocation. If U-boat commanders were bold enough to chase convoys along this shorter route between the UK and North America, the largely British special support escorts, reinforced by air cover from MACs or Liberators from land bases, would make them pay.

Officials at the Atlantic Convoy Conference in March had decided that the B groups—the Mid-Ocean Escort Force—would comprise ten of the fourteen escort groups. In fact, the Admiralty had already diverted some RN ships to a new offensive against U-boats sailing through the Bay of Biscay, and others to support renewed shipping in the Mediterranean. By April and May 1943, the RCN had assumed responsibility for five of the dozen MOEF escort groups—more than 40 percent. Accordingly, the Canadian escorts—working in both transatlantic directions—safely delivered thirteen of thirty-five North Atlantic convoys. They also freed hunter-killer groups to go about their business.

The Bay of Biscay offensive seemed the obvious next step in eliminating the U-boat threat in the Atlantic. It would involve the targeted destruction of U-boats as they departed or returned to their pen sanctuaries at Brest, Lorient, St. Nazaire, and La Rochelle on the west coast of occupied France. The offensive would be a combined effort—RN, RCN, USN, and Allied air forces—from late spring through the summer of 1943. The commander-in-chief of RAF Coastal Command, Air Marshal John Slessor, saw the Atlantic U-boat menace as a tree trunk, with "the roots being in the Biscay ports and the branches spreading far and wide to the North Atlantic convoys." It was there, in that "little patch of water about 300 miles by 120 miles in the Bay, through which five out of six U-boats operating in the Atlantic had to pass," that a combined operation would fell the tree once and for all.[35]

Coastal Command's Operation Enclose, an effort to blanket the bay like a "spider web" with anti-submarine patrols, began in March.[36] Over the next two months, Coastal Command's Sunderland, Liberator, and Wellington aircraft accumulated more than 80,000 hours in the air and sank ten U-boats.[37] As the offensive continued into the fall, RCAF pilot Don Rollins joined the fray. Sporting a new single braid on his sleeve, the Canadian pilot officer from Estevan, Saskatchewan, arrived at the RAF station in Chivenor in southwest England in early September.

Chivenor was home to Coastal Command's storied No. 407 Demon Squadron, the RCAF unit in which Rollins had hoped to serve. The Canadian squadron had earned its nickname for its exploits against enemy shipping off the Dutch coast in 1941. At twenty-three, Rollins had trained more than a year in the BCATP in Canada, then received operational training in the United Kingdom. He'd flown sorties from Gibraltar into the Mediterranean but was finally posted to No. 407 Squadron to fly anti-submarine operations in the Bay of Biscay. By the fall of 1943, aircrews were flying Wellingtons, equipped with Leigh Lights and AVS Mark III search radar for tracking down U-boats and German surface warships at night.[38] It was combat activity for which Rollins seemed more than adequately equipped. Upon completion of his ops training, his CO offered an endorsement on his certificate: "Night vision . . . above average."[39]

Crewed up with new airmen, PO Rollins commenced weeks of special training aboard the upgraded Wellingtons, preparing for Operation Enclose. During 1943-44, Demon Squadron aircrews sank three U-boats. Throughout this time, Rollins and his Wellington bomber, Q for Quebec, completed numerous sorties—flying twelve-hour sweeps to Biscay and back—through gales, fog, low ceilings, or near-zero visibility.

Suddenly it was Christmas Eve 1943. It appeared there'd be a pause in combat operations. The officer's mess got a makeover with a real Christmas tree, holiday cards covering the walls, and carols playing on the radio. The base cooks planned a turkey supper with all the trimmings for the next day. Rollins took the day to read the newspapers and write letters home.

But that afternoon, three of 407's Wellington crews, including Rollins's six-man crew, were called to a briefing. Intelligence had revealed that the Kriegsmarine had taken advantage of the lull to assemble a convoy of transports and destroyers to resupply the U-boat pens on the west coast of France. No. 407 Squadron would dispatch a nighttime raid against the convoy.[40]

Five hours of night flying put Q for Quebec 500 miles south of England, over the Bay of Biscay and shadowing the convoy. "We picked [the convoy] up and did a circuit at about eight miles," Rollins wrote.[41] Though his Wellington was equipped with a powerful Leigh Light, experience told him not to turn it on; the bright light would reveal the precise location of the attacking bomber and surely attract flak gunners aboard the German warships. "Closed it to 1.5 miles upwind," he continued in his report, "and dropped a flare" to illuminate only the target for a visual attack.

"Did a tight 360-degree turn to starboard and went roaring in losing height. The flak was beginning to come close, so I did a bit of weaving and let go our load of 3 X 500-pound bombs, and then climbed up to 3,000 feet, weaving all the way."

Rollins was about to bank the aircraft to check on the results of his bombing run when, out of the blackness ahead, he spotted a shadow darker than the gloom of the night. It was another aircraft—an Allied Liberator, he learned later—heading in the opposite direction. During the seconds it took for Rollins to realize his Wellington was about to collide head-on with the Liberator, "I immediately slammed the stick forward [forcing Q for Quebec into a steep dive] and he seemed to go over my head by inches."

Then came the grinding, wrenching sound of tearing metal at the rear of his aircraft. The Wellington shuddered in protest. The rudder pedals below Rollins's feet snapped to the full-left position and the bomber lurched sharply in a death plunge toward the ocean. He later learned that the Liberator had struck the Wellington's tail and sheared off eight feet of rudder.

Rollins called to his second pilot, Sgt H.S. Butcher, to help him pull back hard on the controls. At least the control column appeared to be working. The bomber finally responded and levelled out of its dive. Rollins nursed the aircraft back to 3,000 feet to give him a margin of security above Biscay.

He now faced several uninviting options: ditch in the ocean and likely be captured; ditch and, if the convoy ignored the downed aircraft, likely die of exposure; or, finally, attempt a nearly impossible five-hour flight back to base, struggling with a crippled aircraft all the way. Rollins chose to try for home.

It was dawn when Rollins and Butcher nursed the wobbling Wellington into an approach to Chivenor airfield. While the aircraft's lateral control was difficult and imprecise, and nobody could predict how the bomber might respond to a configuration of flaps and gear down, Rollins sensed a landing was possible. He offered his crew the option of bailing out, if they preferred. Nobody did. They trusted their skipper to get them down safely.

Q for Quebec's wireless operator flashed a signal to base that they'd attempt a landing while damaged. Crash trucks quickly assembled at the end of the runway. Then, with no rudder control and the control column canted at an awkward angle, but with confidence in his hours of training and ops experience, Rollins brought his bomber down in one piece.

It was 8:30 in the morning by the time Rollins and his crew gathered around Q for Quebec's half-sheared-away tail section. When Rollins eventually met the pilot of the Liberator, he was told that the collision had torn away fourteen feet of the Liberator's port wing, but its pilot had likewise brought his aircraft safely home. The two shook hands and realized that, were it not for Rollins's sharp night vision and reflexes, neither the pilots nor any of the fifteen men in the two bombers would have lived to enjoy Christmas Day. In his journal, Don Rollins offered a final thought: "On X-mas Eve we did a shipping strike and how close we came to getting it, only me and the laundry man knows!"

Meanwhile, in probing operations through the summer and fall of 1943, Allied warships and aircraft destroyed sixteen U-boats, including most of the *milch*-cow submarines in the Bay of Biscay. When Allied air and sea forces sank four U-boats on the first two days of August, the grand admiral made an about-face on the flotilla's procedure through Biscay. He cancelled all group transits, re-mandated submerged passage of the bay in daylight, and ordered all returning U-boats to hug the Spanish coast en route to the Biscay ports; by routing his U-Bootwaffe closer to the coast, he ensured that the Luftwaffe's Ju 88s and Do 217s could provide the U-boats with air cover.[42]

In response to the Biscay offensive, German bombers introduced yet another innovative piece of weaponry against the Allied hunter-killer ships. Luftwaffe pilots had experimented with radio-controlled solid-fuel-propelled glider bombs that travelled at 400 miles per hour and contained a thousand pounds of explosive. On August 27, 1943, they successfully launched two Hs 293A glider bombs that sank the sloop HMS *Egret* and severely damaged the Tribal-class destroyer HMCS *Athabaskan*.[43] Only masterful seamanship enabled the Canadian warship to make it back to her home port of Plymouth, England. Even so, the Kriegsmarine was losing the war of attrition. While Dönitz had seventy-one operational U-boats available to him in July, by the end of August, that number had shrunk to forty.

The Bay of Biscay had lived up to its wartime moniker as *Tal des Todes*, or "Death Valley."[44]

✪ ✪ ✪

RODGER Winn paid close attention to events in the Bay of Biscay that summer. In some ways, his role assessing the next moves by Karl Dönitz and the U-Bootwaffe had come full circle. In 1939, when he'd stepped into the Submarine Tracking Room in the Old Admiralty Building for the first time, his job was estimating U-boat strength and tactics. He'd rarely been wrong. In four years of intense analysis of U-boats, their commanders, and their grand admiral, Winn found himself like the barrister he'd once been in court—not guessing the next move of his opponent, but weighing evidence. In July 1943 he'd written a report on what Dönitz might do next.

Winn surmised that Dönitz understood that the Allied ability to survive and then mount a military offensive against the Reich depended completely on delivering to Britain a continuous supply of food, armies of men, and weapons from the North America. Dönitz must therefore have withdrawn from the North Atlantic only with the hope of living to fight another day.[45] Finally, Winn gauged the grand admiral's likely return to that mid-ocean battlefield.

"If all hope is lost, there will be a sudden, drastic, and for [Dönitz], a fatal contest staged in the North Atlantic," Winn wrote. And though it wasn't his place, he recommended that "the time is ripe for confident, optimistic and bold enterprise, even if heavy losses on the North Atlantic convoy route were to be suffered."[46]

Winn had accurately outlined the scenario for the final acts in the Battle of the Atlantic. In August the Enigma decrypts from Bletchley Park showed a sudden increase in Kriegsmarine activity. U-boats were outbound from northwestern Europe. The first Operational Intelligence Centre estimates suggested sixteen, but by September 13 Winn had pinned down numbers, objectives, and timing. Dönitz's U-boats were indeed heading west—not in great numbers, but with renewed stealth and lethal force.

Royal Canadian Naval Volunteer Reserve sailor Bill Fisher was among the first to witness the return of the U-boats to the North Atlantic that fall of 1943. At the time, the former oil-well driller from Black Diamond, Alberta, served as a stoker aboard a Canadian destroyer with the MOEF. HMCS *St. Croix* had begun life as the four-stacker USS *McCook* in 1919. She was one of the famous fifty lend-lease destroyers to arrive in Canada in September 1940. During her early RCN years in the Battle of the Atlantic, *St. Croix* had served in the Newfoundland Escort Force and the Newfy-to-Derry run and had two U-boat kills to her credit (*U90* and *U87*). In August 1943 the destroyer had emerged from her latest refit, including the installation of Type 271 radar, Huff-Duff, and Hedgehog anti-submarine mortar launchers.

When stoker Bill Fisher served aboard *St. Croix*, LCdr Andrew Dobson was the commanding officer, and the aging warship had just begun her fourth year of RCN service. It was mid-September 1943 when Fisher wrote that *St. Croix* had slipped quietly from her wartime moorings at Plymouth. Something big was up. "The boys sitting around were discussing where we were going," Fisher wrote. "Some said the Med[iterranean], others the Bay of Biscay."[47]

By September 19, Fisher and his shipmates realized they weren't sailing southeast but northwest. They subsequently learned that two outbound convoys—ONS 18, with twenty-seven ships bound for Halifax, and ON 202, with forty-two ships headed for New York—were merging in mid-ocean. Western Approaches Command had assigned two escort groups—C-2 and B-2—to protect them. But British intelligence had new data that U-boats had spotted the two convoys and a wolf pack was likely. WAC decided to strengthen the escort screen by sending Support Group 9, including *St. Croix*, to its assistance. By the time the two convoys and their escort groups had assembled the next day, there were sixty-nine merchant ships escorted by nineteen warships. They would soon face an attacking force of twenty-two U-boats spread across a 350-mile-long patrol line in the mid-Atlantic gap.

About to begin his watch, stoker Fisher had just eaten his evening meal and gone out on *St. Croix*'s main deck for some air. He heard the engines of a Liberator bomber overhead and depth charges exploding well behind the convoy.

"The stokers flashed the two boilers. Black smoke was soon rising out of three and four funnels," Fisher wrote, indicating that the bridge had called for more speed to propel *St. Croix* to the scene of the attack. Fisher went below to the engine room to assist. "We revved up to twenty-four knots. . . . I came back up on deck sweating and very hot. We saw the plane flying low and circling."[48]

The Liberator had forced another U-boat on the surface to crash-dive. *U305*'s commander was Kptlt Rudolf Bahr. Just twenty-seven and a veteran of the wolf pack attacks on Convoys SC 122 and HX 229 back in the spring, Kptlt Bahr had returned from that May engagement flying two victory pennants. He and his crew had sunk two merchantmen on their inaugural patrol. But in the midst of this, his third patrol, Bahr had struggled for hours to catch the convoy.[49] Then suddenly, with *U305* at periscope depth, a Town-class destroyer appeared in his sights. Under normal circumstances, Bahr would have used a couple of torpedoes in a fan shot. Instead, he chose the "destroyer cracker"—the T5 torpedo that would home on the sound generated by Allied escort ships' propellers and explode on contact with the warship's stern.

It was just after 9:30 p.m., September 20.

"Tubes flooded and ready," the torpedo crew reported.

"Tube Two. Loose!" the commander ordered; then he called for an immediate deep dive.[50]

The T5 had a maximum effective range of 5.7 kilometres. Bahr had fired it from less than 1,500 metres and at a depth of four metres. So, to prevent becoming the acoustic torpedo's unintended victim, Bahr ordered *U305* to descend quickly and for his crew to listen.[51] Two and a half minutes later . . .

"There was a violent explosion," *St. Croix* stoker Fisher said. "The ship listed and stopped. . . . The captain was on the bridge looking aft and was very worried."[52]

The torpedo had locked on to *St. Croix*'s propeller noise and struck the destroyer's rear port quarter. The explosion, penetrating one of the ship's mess decks and the depth-charge magazine, spared the engine room but triggered the explosion of a depth charge aft, inflicting further damage to her stern. Some of the injured had already appeared on deck. The ship's doctor, W.L. Mackenzie King (nephew of the Canadian prime minister), had begun bandaging the wounded. The first lieutenant ordered the ship's whaler, Carley floats, and motor boat readied for evacuation, and Fisher helped load the wounded. Nearly an hour had passed with the lifeboats clear of the ship when Kptlt Bahr resurfaced *U305* and fired a second torpedo at the disabled destroyer. It hit abaft the bridge.

"A terrific explosion," Fisher reported. "The stern of the ship disappeared quickly. From amidship forward stayed up from three to five minutes. Then she turned her bow into the air and went down."

The speedy launch of the boats and rafts had saved eighty-one members of the ship's company. But it took more than thirteen hours before another of the convoy escorts, HMS *Itchen*, found *St. Croix*'s motor boat and assorted life rafts all tied together and began to bring survivors aboard.

"When I tried to move I was so stiff I almost fell overboard," Fisher continued. "They put a rope around me and pulled me up. I was never so happy in all my life as I was when I reached the deck of the *Itchen*."

Itchen's crew gave *St. Croix* survivors all they had—blankets, dry clothing, coffee, food, rum ration, and bunks to sleep in. But the RN frigate remained on duty, continuing her escort duties ahead of the combined Convoys ONS 18 and ON 202 for the next two days. At 8:45 p.m. on September 22, an action stations alarm sounded aboard *Itchen*. Just after dark, Bill Fisher and some fellow survivors climbed to the frigate's upper deck as the bridge called for a searchlight. When its beam lit up the water ahead, *U666* was caught in the light.

"I looked past the bridge and could see the sub about 300 yards ahead," Fisher wrote. He was holding on to a railing near *Itchen*'s funnel as the frigate's gun crew opened fire on the U-boat. "Then there was an explosion. We had been torpedoed. I was blown about thirty feet and landed against a gun deck."

Itchen began to list just the way *St. Croix* had, so Fisher grabbed a railing and jumped over the side. Within seconds of hitting the water, he heard and felt another explosion behind him. The torpedo from *U666* had struck *Itchen* close enough to her ammunition magazine that it detonated and tore the ship apart. Fisher said the frigate was gone in forty seconds; he swam as hard as he could to escape the vortex of *Itchen* going down.

"It has been forty-nine hours between torpedoing of the two ships," he wrote later. "I [was] in the water three hours when I was picked up for the second time."

The Polish freighter SS *Wisla* found Fisher and two other sailors bobbing around in the wreckage that night, and Capt Kazimierz Lipski courageously stopped to haul the men aboard. They proved to be the only three—of nearly 400 men—to survive the sinking of *Itchen*. And Fisher turned out to be the only man left alive from *St. Croix*'s crew, one survivor out of 147 officers and men. HMCS *St. Croix* and HMS *Itchen* were among the first victims of the T5 acoustic torpedo, known to the Allies as the German Naval Acoustic Torpedo (GNAT).* Its sole purpose was to destroy navy escorts.

"It was hard to take after serving fourteen months on the *St. Croix*," Fisher wrote finally. "The boys had all been old hands and old friends."

But if the Kriegsmarine considered its acoustic torpedoes a step ahead of the enemy, it was about to learn otherwise. On September 22, the combined Convoys ONS 18 and ON 202 emerged from a day of crawling through fog on the Grand Banks. What remained of the convoy was stretched across some thirty miles of the Atlantic. While the escorts tightened up the convoy columns, aircraft from the RCAF's Eastern Air Command arrived. They'd come 800 miles from Newfoundland with something new in their anti-submarine arsenal.

* The first Allied warship sunk by a T5 was HMS *Lagan*, a frigate originally escorting Convoy ON 202 but torpedoed earlier the same day, September 20.

A pair of Liberators from No. 10 (BR) Squadron immediately forced *U270* and *U377* into crash dives—the former with depth charges, the latter with a new weapon called the Mark 24. Twenty seconds after *U377* submerged, F/L J.R. Martin launched this 600-pound homing torpedo, which was attracted to the sound of a U-boat's cavitating propeller (not unlike the GNATs that U-boats had unleashed on *St. Croix* and *Itchen*);[53] while Martin did not sink *U377*, he forced her from the remainder of the battle. Now both sides had acoustic weaponry.

Quoting from inflated reports, Grossadmiral Dönitz claimed his packs had sunk twelve escort vessels and seven merchant ships, versus only two U-boats lost. The true tally proved less of a victory for either side. In the nearly two weeks of continuous engagement across a thousand miles of the mid-Atlantic, the combined Convoys ONS 18 and ON 202 had sustained the loss of six (of sixty-nine) merchant ships, while the MOEF Support Group had lost three (of nineteen) warships. On the Kriegsmarine side, Dönitz's U-Bootwaffe had lost three (of twenty-two) U-boats—*U341*, *U338*, and *U229*—and the services of several others damaged by Allied escorts and VLR aircraft.

"We regard this as a very satisfactory success," Dönitz stated.[54]

The Royal Navy's senior officer commanding the escorts called the acoustic torpedo "a menace," but he applauded the escort captains' offensive spirit by saying, "We should dictate our tactics to them."[55]

Allied strategists analyzed the evidence of the warships sunk by the GNATs. They quickly turned to an invention devised by Canadian scientists. As early as 1940, Royal

Canadian Navy minesweepers had employed a "pipe noise-maker" (PNM) to detonate enemy acoustic mines at safe distances from harbours and sea lanes. By coincidence, on September 20, the very day the GNAT had sunk HMCS *St. Croix*, John Johnstone, the RCN's director of operational research, reported on a potential countermeasure—the device used five-foot-long 1⅜-inch metal pipes towed 250 yards behind the warship; as the unit passed through the water at a speed between 8.5 and 17.5 knots, its vibration generated the same noise as an escort propeller.[56] The invention was dubbed the Canadian Anti-Acoustic Torpedo (CAT). By September 24, fifty sets were on their way to St. John's and were distributed to Canadian escorts. The Royal Navy modified its PNM and called it the "Foxer," but within weeks the RCN had manufactured 400 CATs for installation aboard all its warships.

Not long afterward, Martin McGregor, a telegraphist aboard the Canadian frigate HMCS *Grou*, witnessed CAT gear save his ship. At the time, *Grou* and a sister Canadian frigate, HMCS *Waskesiu*, were being attacked by U-boats while escorting a convoy to Murmansk. *Waskesiu* was steaming ahead of *Grou* and towing an activated CAT. McGregor happened to be standing at his action station on *Grou*'s bridge, looking forward.

"I saw the trail of an acoustic torpedo cross our bow and strike *Waskesiu*'s CAT," McGregor said. "There was quite an explosion, but no damage done."[57]

As was so often the case, Canadians tasked with solving day-to-day threats to the convoys and their escorts traversing the Atlantic went unnoticed—even if the solutions saved Allied lives and His Majesty's ships. With so much attention being focused on the derring-do of the killer-hunter groups, Canada's sizable share of MOEF duties rarely garnered any response, least of all among the senior Allies—the United States and Britain.

None felt that oversight more than the Mackenzie King government, which desperately craved accolades for its efforts. At least once during this tumultuous year of the Battle of the Atlantic, Prime Minister King campaigned for Canadian recognition. In August 1943, British, American, and Canadian leaders had gathered for the Quebec Conference. During the predominantly Anglo-American talks, Prime Minister King invited Winston Churchill to meet Angus L. Macdonald, the minister of defence for naval services, and other members of the Canadian War Cabinet at the Château Frontenac, in Quebec City.

King took advantage of his moments alone with Churchill. First he pushed the British leader for an apology for omitting Canadians from the official Allied communiqué announcing the successful Operation Husky landings in Sicily on July 10, 1943. And while he was at it, King wanted some overdue praise for Canada's protection of the Atlantic convoys, particularly since the reintroduction of RCN escorts to the transatlantic shipping lanes in the spring of the year.

"The Canadian Navy does about forty per cent of the work in the North Atlantic," King emphasized to Churchill.

"I didn't know it was forty per cent," Churchill responded.[58] And, always quick to take full advantage of such information, the British prime minister proceeded to thank Canada and Canadians at every opportunity thereafter.

✪ ✪ ✪

As 1944 began, German forces along the perimeter of occupied Europe began preparing for an Allied assault. German High Command upgraded the Atlantic U-boat bases to "Fortress" status and began to fortify them with additional land batteries and tighter security. Often the defence of the concrete pens and work sheds fell to the U-boat crews themselves. Early in January 1944, Walter Schmietenknop's sole enemy on duty was lack of sleep. Just nineteen and an electrical engineer aboard *U767*, Walter and his shipmates were still recovering from their New Year's revelry. The former blacksmith's apprentice from Kleefeld, Germany, had completed training and was awaiting his first combat patrol when his captain received new orders. *U767* had to rush to Hamburg for immediate alterations. There the entire crew, including Schmietenknop, began round-the-clock guard duty outside the work shed. Often the only intruders Schmietenknop faced were civilians seeking shelter in the reinforced concrete U-boat pens from nighttime Allied bombing raids. Inside the pen, U-Bootwaffe technicians set to work on *U767*'s superstructure.

"We were told that we were to be outfitted with a *Schnorchel*," he wrote. "[It] was so new, nobody knew how it worked."[59]

He soon learned from the technicians that the device would help his Type VIIC U-boat maintain a level of invisibility. Its mast-like structure would allow *U767* to conserve the power of her electric batteries by drawing in air for combustion in the diesel engines through one tube in the Schnorchel and emitting exhaust through a second tube, all while the U-boat remained underwater. *U767* could then run her diesel engines and charge her electric batteries without having to surface.

"The *Schnorchel* helped us not be detected by radar," Schmietenknop explained. "In the ocean, there is a lot of debris. . . . On a radar screen the *Schnorchel* would look like another piece of debris. If an [enemy] airplane saw the cap on its radar, it would [appear] too small to be worth investigating or bombing."[60]

The rhythm of attack and counterattack propelled the war in the North Atlantic into its fifth year. Victories came too infrequently and provided little satisfaction. Neither Axis nor Allied naval powers seemed capable of delivering a knockout. With every setback one side found new strategies, new responses to the other's game. When WAC found a safer path for a transatlantic convoy, the Kriegsmarine foiled it by casting a wider patrol net with larger and more potent wolf packs. When B-Dienst intercepted transmissions of the Admiralty's ciphers, Bletchley Park decoders cracked the Kriegsmarine's Triton with their bombes. And while U-boats found periodic gaps in what had been the Black Pit to operate unmolested, Allied navies now regularly deployed MACs and VLR bombers to take those gaps away. When sound became the weapon and the Kriegsmarine launched its propeller-seeking GNAT torpedoes, Commonwealth navy scientists countered with Foxers and CATs as decoys. If anti-submarine warships came too close to occupied Europe, the Luftwaffe pounced, occasionally using its new glider bombs. When Allied bombers used Leigh Lights to turn night into day to find U-boats on the surface, the U-Bootwaffe countered with Schnorchels to make their boats invisible again. And when the Admiralty deployed specialized dedicated support escorts—the hunter-killer groups—to chase submarines to the death, Grossadmiral Dönitz pulled his beleaguered crews out of the North

Atlantic in hopes his scientists would soon deliver his ultimate Walther boat, or at least his faster, longer-range hybrid Type XXI U-boat.

The battle of wits and wizardry persisted. The frustrations of its leaders did too.

"They know all our secrets," Dönitz had complained in 1943, "and we know none of theirs."[61]

His enemy knew many of his secrets. But not all.

Later in the fall of 1943, after the fireworks of Convoys ONS 18 and ON 202 in September, Dönitz sent a handful of U-boats on lone-wolf assignments to the western Atlantic.* On October 22, Kptlt Peter Schrewe and the crew of *U537*—on one of those secret missions—reached their objective, just above the sixtieth parallel at the northern tip of Labrador.

In the shelter and seclusion of Martin Bay, Kptlt Schrewe nosed his U-boat to the shore, where seven crewmen offloaded ten grey oil-drum-sized canisters. They hauled them to the top of a nearby hill and—complete with nickel-cadmium batteries and a ten-metre antenna—assembled what would become an automatic weather observatory. The station—code-named Kurt after its minder, Kurt Sommermeyer—would be powerful enough to transmit encoded weather readings around the clock to German naval headquarters in Europe. And Allied defenders had no idea it was there. To help disguise their mission, Schrewe's crew hand-painted fake identification on the canisters. *Canadian Meteor Service*, the words read.[62]

Then, for good measure, the submariners littered the site with American cigarette packs and departed. The data that

* Unlike the wolf-pack attacks used effectively in 1942–1943, Dönitz's lone-wolf, or "static," attacks used in the late stages of the war, saw an individual U-boat wait for a target of opportunity, ambush it, and then evade detection by manoeuvring into deep water for a prolonged period.

Kurt yielded proved nearly as valuable as the B-Dienst deciphering of Royal Navy transmissions. It marked the first time that the U-Bootwaffe would know remotely what weather conditions lay over its North Atlantic objectives, well before U-boat crews arrived to carry out attacks on Allied shipping.* It also turned out to be the only armed landing of German forces on the North American continent during the Second World War.[63]

* In *The Weather Machine*, author Andrew Blum explains that Kurt's transmissions lasted about a month before mysteriously being jammed. Not until Siemens employee/historian Franz Selinger searched for and found it in 1981 was the existence of Weather Station Kurt confirmed.

Chapter Eleven

HUNTED TO EXHAUSTION

Of all the weapons the Kriegsmarine, its U-boat commanders, and its commander-in-chief marshalled for the Battle of the Atlantic, perhaps the darkest one emerged when Hitler told Joseph Goebbels, his minister of propaganda, to inspire a greater war effort *at all cost*. Empowered to issue directives to civilians and high-ranking figures of the Reich, Goebbels staged a rally at the Berlin Sports Palace in front of 14,000 hand-picked party members. The speech was filmed and broadcast.

"Are you and the German people determined, if the Leader orders it," Goebbels asked, "to give your utmost for victory?"

A roar of approval and applause filled the palace in response.

"I ask you: Do you want total war?"

More cheers.

"Do you want it, if necessary, more total and more radical than we can even imagine it today?"[1]

On the surface, the "Total War" speech riled the party faithful against its usual array of enemies—the Jews, the Soviets, the British, the Americans—blaming them for inflicting terror, mass starvation, and anarchy on the German people. Goebbels's directive threatened death to shirkers in Germany who were not committed to total war as well. For the U-Bootwaffe, waging the war against the Allied convoys at sea, the implications of the edict, in addition to the existing Laconia Order, resonated and motivated.

In the Laconia Order of 1942, Grossadmiral Dönitz had decreed that U-boat commanders not consider rescuing sailors from ships they'd sunk, since "the annihilation of enemy ships and crews" was fundamental to the demands of war.[2] That meant U-boat crews should interrogate senior officers of sunken ships but then eliminate survivors to prevent them ever returning to the war in new ships. The object was to terrorize enemy crews. The tactic inspired Heinz-Wilhelm Eck.

Eck had received his first solo wartime command as kapitänleutnant of *U852*, a Type IXD2 U-boat, midway through 1943. Eck had served five years in minesweepers and a year training in the U-Bootwaffe before taking charge of *U852*. During months of instruction from senior U-boat commanders, Kptlt Eck had taken his mentors' recommendations to heart. Understand that Type IXD2 U-boats are larger, heavier, and more easily spotted by air reconnaissance than earlier U-boat models, they told him. More important, they warned that wreckage from ships he torpedoed could leave his U-boat more readily open to detection by enemy aircraft.[3] In other words, Eck inferred, don't leave telltale evidence after an attack.

Fully loaded, armed, and operating under yet another decree from the grand admiral—that all U-boats as of January 7, 1944, were ordered to patrol singly—Kptlt Eck and *U852* left Kiel in late January. On March 13, six weeks into their Atlantic patrol, Eck sighted the Greek steam merchant *Peleus*. He shadowed the freighter until dark and then fired two magnetic torpedoes into her. The 8,000-ton ship sank quickly, but on the surface Eck and his crew saw torchlight and heard calls from survivors amid the wreckage. Eck directed *U852* among the rafts, interrogated two crewmen, returned them to their rafts, and then turned on the mostly Greek survivors with machine guns and grenades. For five hours, members of *U852*'s crew—including the watch officer, the engineer, and even the doctor—joined the slaughter of the defenceless *Peleus* crew.[4]

Eighteen months later, during his war crimes trial in Hamburg, Germany, Eck was questioned by the prosecution.

"The decision [you made] was a decision to destroy among other things, survivors, was it not?"

"It was clear that [by] destroying the rafts and wreckage," Eck answered, "survivors also would die."[5] The U-boat commander expressed no remorse.*

Crewmen of the Flower-class corvette HMCS *Hepatica* had an antithetical view about the plight of shipwrecked sailors that same winter. The demands of Operation Bolero—transporting troops, munitions, and supplies to the UK for an anticipated invasion of the Continent that spring—meant larger and larger convoys through the winter. And though the number of merchant ships sunk by U-boats fell dramatically in the first three months of 1944—only three sunk of 3,360 ships making the crossing—convoys still faced the threat of lone-wolf attacks.

Meanwhile, the close escorts' orders remained the same. If the enemy torpedoed, sank, or otherwise disabled a merchant

* In October 1945, the British Military War Crimes court at Hamburg found Kptlt Heinz-Wilhelm Eck and four crewmen guilty of war crimes; Eck was executed by firing squad.

ship en route, the escort's first obligation was to remain with the convoy. It didn't matter how many shipwrecked survivors the escort vessels might have to leave behind. Rescue ships, now regularly sailing with the convoys, would attend to those forced to abandon their ships. Nevertheless, escorting an eastbound convoy in February 1944, Lt John Ferguson, commander of *Hepatica*, received word that two oil tankers had collided in rough seas and were ablaze.[6] He weighed the need to save lives and precious fuel bound for Britain, and ordered his crew to action stations.

George Doig, the youngest of three Winnipeg brothers in the armed forces, was serving aboard *Hepatica* that winter. All rudimentary jobs fell to AB Doig and his ratings shipmates—everything from gun loading and depth-charge operations to survivor rescue and ice-clearing detail. Every activity onboard a corvette on the mid-Atlantic in winter meant greater discomfort and higher risk.

"Ice on board was the challenge," Doig later told his family. "Everything, as well as men, became frozen."[7]

But when *Hepatica* arrived at the scene of the tanker collision, conditions grew even more threatening.

"*Hepatica* fought snow squalls and twenty-foot seas," crewmen later told reporters. "Although [the tanker's] bridge and superstructure were ablaze . . . Lt Ferguson laid *Hepatica* alongside."[8]

The corvette crew managed to rescue twenty-three injured crewmen while some of the tanker crew continued to fight the fire. Both merchant and escort sailors felt the need to save the twelve military aircraft stowed on the tanker, as well as the 7,000 tons of fuel oil in her hold.

"After two hours [the sailors] brought the fire under control," reports said, "signaling that they had decided against abandoning ship."[9]

Not only had *Hepatica*'s crew manoeuvred in treacherous conditions to save lives, but the corvette sailors had also ensured that vital fuel and munitions reached their UK destinations intact. Shortly after George Doig put ashore in Londonderry on that trip, he learned that his oldest brother, RCAF F/O John Doig, had been shot down and killed in a bombing raid over Nuremburg, Germany.[10] Eventually, when *Hepatica*'s crew got leave back in Canada, George caught up with his other brother, Harold, also serving in the RCN.

Harold noted how the stress had changed his younger sibling. "I saw my kid brother in Halifax after he'd finished a convoy," Harold Doig said. "And he was grey. He was twenty-two, and his hair had turned grey around his temples from what he'd seen."[11]

FRESH from their successful duties across the roof of the world—escorting Arctic convoys to Murmansk and Archangel in the Soviet Union through the winter of 1943–44—three of the Royal Canadian Navy's four Tribal-class destroyers were redeployed at Plymouth, England, to join the 10th Destroyer Flotilla. Assisted by Royal Navy cruisers, the Tribals—HMCS *Athabaskan*, *Haida*, and *Huron*—now organized into a powerful small-ship fighting force to carry out two types of offensive actions in preparation for Operation Neptune—the amphibious invasion of Normandy.

The first, Operation Tunnel, pitted the Canadian destroyers against German Biscay and Channel convoys, which were often escorted by Narvik-class and Elbing-built destroyers.

As well, in Operation Hostile, the Fighting Tenth served as a covering force. While fast RN minelayers dashed in to sow enemy waters with explosives, the Allied destroyers lay seaward of them, ready to deal with any German warships that might come out to interfere.

By the latter part of April 1944, *Haida* had conducted nineteen Tunnel and Hostile operations, *Huron* had carried out eleven, and *Athabaskan* nine. Between missions, the Tribal crews completed special exercises in night fighting, navigation, radar detection, and radar-controlled gunnery that would shortly be delivered with deadly effect. On April 25/26, in a Tunnel operation, all three Tribals tangled with three Elbing destroyers, sinking one and damaging another. Two nights later, *Haida* and *Athabaskan* joined a Hostile operation supporting minelaying boats near the tip of the Brittany peninsula. With their cover work done and heading for Plymouth, the two Canadian Tribals suddenly made contact and closed on two German destroyers. LCdr John Stubbs, recently transferred from *Assiniboine* to command *Athabaskan*, called for a starshell to illuminate the Elbings, and the Tribal gunners concentrated fire on their targets. The Elbings returned fire.

Bill Bint, previously an ASDIC operator on the minesweeper HMCS *Melville* and then posted to *Athabaskan*, recalled the intensity of the destroyer battle in the Channel. "We were banging away at them and they at us," he wrote. "Things seemed to be going OK, when they fired torpedoes back at us; [the torpedoes] were designed with a zigzag course at a pursuing enemy. They worked. Suddenly we had our stern blown off and were dead in the water."[12]

"I'm hit and losing power," Stubbs signalled *Haida*.[13] He then ordered the lifeboats turned out.

Bint worked furiously with his shipmates to receive a towline from *Haida*. Others hauled a massive pump toward the fires that now consumed *Athabaskan* amidships and aft. Then *Athabaskan*'s 4.7-inch magazine exploded, and Bint was blown off the flag deck to the fo'c'sle, landing on his back. "My clothes were on fire and I heard Capt Stubbs calling 'Abandon ship.'"[14]

Momentarily, LCdr Harry DeWolf held *Haida* in a defensive position across *Athabaskan*'s bow and released smoke to protect crew abandoning the stricken destroyer. But "the grim priorities of sea warfare had to be maintained,"[15] and DeWolf set off in pursuit of the Elbings, driving one of them ashore, where *Haida* gunners pounded its remains. When she returned to assist *Athabaskan* and her crew, however, her sister Tribal had already sunk.

"Haida came back and dropped nets over the side for survivors," said Bint, who by this time was hanging on to debris in the water. "I tried swimming, but was too groggy. It was a fair distance away."[16]

DeWolf called to his *Haida* crew that they would stay for fifteen minutes. His ship now lay just fifteen miles from the occupied coast (within striking distance of enemy aircraft) and was drifting toward a German minefield. He called for Allied air cover, but none was available.[17] Meanwhile, his crew had hauled aboard thirty-eight *Athabaskan* survivors. DeWolf extended the rescue another five minutes.

"Get away, *Haida*!" LCdr Stubbs called out to DeWolf from among his crew in the water. "Get clear!"[18] *Haida*'s crew rescued another seven survivors and departed the scene. Eighty-six men still scattered across the debris field became prisoners of war, including Bill Bint. Liberated in the spring of 1945, he arrived home to Saskatoon that summer in time to celebrate his twenty-second birthday. The action killed 128 crewmen from HMCS *Athabaskan*, including LCdr Stubbs, who was buried at the Plouescat Communal Cemetery in Finistère, France. Meanwhile, in the period leading up to the Allied invasion of Normandy six weeks later, HMCS *Haida* sank more enemy surface tonnage than any other Canadian warship, earning her moniker "the fightingest ship in the Royal Canadian Navy."

For the first half of the war, when upgrading, the Royal Canadian Navy had chosen to acquire rather than to build more modern warships. But while the appetite was there, the means were not. However, in 1942, the government of Mackenzie King had approved the British frigate design and allocated funds to build sixty-four of them in eastern Canada in 1943 and 1944.[19] Frigates were the most sophisticated naval vessels constructed in Canada during the war (until the larger, more powerful Tribal-class destroyers were launched from Canadian shipyards in 1943–45).

Compared to the cramped and utilitarian design of the RCN's minesweepers and corvettes, the frigates built in Canada for the navy seemed palatial. Just over 300 feet in length (corvettes were just over 200 feet), the Canadian frigates were driven by twin engines that delivered twenty knots of speed (four knots faster than corvettes) and offered a range of 7,200 miles (twice that of corvettes).[20] The few extra knots of speed were particularly valuable; no longer would escorts tarrying behind to hunt a U-boat take days to catch up with their convoy and resume screening.

From the moment the frigate construction program was announced, serving aboard one became a wartime obsession for SLt Ian Tate. He had fought his first days of the war from behind a desk at HMCS *Fort Ramsay*, the RCN's first land base in the Gulf of St. Lawrence. Just two weeks after Tate was posted there, *U553* had slipped into the Gulf and torpedoed SS *Nicoya*, the first freighter sunk in the Battle of the Gulf of St. Lawrence. But even as that theatre of war intensified that summer, all Tate wanted was to serve at sea.

He got his first taste of the Battle of the Atlantic in late 1942, aboard HMCS *Mulgrave*, on escort duty for convoys on the Triangle Run. Finally, in December 1943, at age twenty-two, Tate figured his ship had quite literally come in when the RCN transferred him to newly minted HMCS *Valleyfield*, as anti-submarine officer. The frigate was just joining Escort Group C-1.

"Not only were frigates sleek of line," Tate wrote, "but they were equipped with the finest anti-submarine devices then available."[21]

New in her U-boat detection technology, *Valleyfield* was fitted with the 147B "Sword" protruding below the hull. The device determined the depth of underwater targets with a horizontal fan of transmissions; this, combined with the older ASDIC vertical transmissions, gave anti-submarine personnel pinpoint accuracy for detecting U-boats. Also added to her ASW gear was an Admiralty Research Laboratory plotting table. A dot of light moved with the ship's course and speed and shone through a glass top onto a large sheet of paper, thus making it possible to trace the ship's movements and plot ASDIC and radar contacts during the hunt. This presented a total picture of *Valleyfield*'s course and attack points.[22]

The frigates also packed a punch that Tate relished. Each had four power-mounted twin Oerlikon guns, as well as twin four-inch guns, for double the capacity of artillery shells, including more starshells for illuminating surfaced targets at night. Every frigate carried no fewer than 150 depth charges, and all now featured the forward-firing mortar device Hedgehog. It fired twenty-four projectiles launched with a prolonged ripple fire in a wide elliptical pattern forward of the frigate. Hedgehog projectiles caused no disturbance in the sea unless they achieved a hit; that allowed either the frigate's ASDIC equipment or that of a sister ship to maintain contact with a target throughout the attack.

"Frigates were outstanding anti-submarine vessels," SLt Tate concluded. "They contributed mightily to the victory over the U-boats."[23]

Indeed, upon their arrival, Canada's frigates began logging the final chapter in the North Atlantic siege by lone-wolf U-boats. In just over seven hours on February 24, 1944, HMCS *Waskesiu* had hunted *U257* to exhaustion, driving the U-boat to the surface and then sinking it. The following week, members of Escort Group C-2—including destroyers HMCS *Chaudière* and *Gatineau*, with frigate HMCS *St. Catharines* and corvettes HMCS *Chilliwack* and *Fennel*—pursued *U744* in an epic chase. It took this hunter-killer force 1,500 signals, 291 depth charges, and more than thirty-two hours to bring the U-boat to surrender on the surface. On March 10, members of C-1—destroyer HMCS *St. Laurent* working with corvette HMCS *Owen Sound* and frigate *Swansea*—joined Escort Group 9 to destroy *U845*. In fact, that spring, *Swansea*'s commanding officer, Clarence King, extended his already impressive resumé. Formerly the commander of HMCS *Oakville*, which had rammed and sunk *U94* in the Caribbean in 1942, Cdr King and *Swansea* participated in the sinking of two more U-boats (*U448* and *U311*) in April 1944.

After dominating the North Atlantic for the better part of three years, in just nine months U-boats were abruptly put on the defensive. Despite their wolf-pack victories and Happy Times, life expectancy aboard a U-boat in 1944 had dropped to a hundred days. As well, in those first months of 1944, the RCN progressively took on the lion's share of mid-ocean escort duty. This coincided with the declining RN and USN involvement as Allied forces prepared their navies for the D-Day invasion of Normandy. Consequently, with more "C" groups on the mid-ocean run, Canadian frigates were proving their worth; either singly or accompanied by other escorts, they participated in the destruction of twelve U-boats.[24]

With their greater length and breadth, frigates also provided their crews with greater comfort than their sister Flower-class corvettes or even the older Town-class destroyers. It was an attribute not lost on Canadian sailors when they had a choice. That spring, three Canadian engineer officers completed a Royal Navy training course in England. Almost immediately, Stan Howe, John Storey, and John Dyke got word they were to travel to Londonderry for passage aboard RCN warships back to Canada.

"When Stan and I arrived . . . the convoy was steaming up to leave," Lt Dyke said. "There were two berths [available] in *Valleyfield*, and two berths in [corvette] *Frontenac*."[25]

Following navy tradition, the three officers tossed a coin to decide who went where. As the coin hit the ground, Dyke stomped his foot on top of it. He suggested, since he and Howe had chummed together on the course, that they agree to take the less spacious passage in *Frontenac* and allow Storey the trip home in greater comfort aboard the frigate on his own. The two chums nodded in agreement. Storey would take one of the berths in *Valleyfield*.

"John Storey never made it," Dyke said. "But for the corvette, neither would we."

Through most of April 1944, the Operational Intelligence Centre in Ottawa reported no U-boat activity in the Canadian theatre.[26] Then, on April 23, Enigma decrypts identified the presence of a U-boat transmitting weather conditions off the Avalon Peninsula. A week later, Kptlt Eberhard Zimmermann and *U548* surfaced and attacked HMS *Hargood* unsuccessfully, and then engaged with a Liberator bomber at the end of her escort sortie. The U-boat dived deep to escape, but her presence somehow was not communicated to warships approaching Newfoundland.

On May 6, HMCS *Valleyfield* and four corvettes of C-1—HMCS *Halifax*, *Giffard*, *Edmundston*, and *Frontenac*—had completed their westbound mid-ocean escort of Convoy ONM 243 (headed to New York City) and handed off to the Western Local Escort Force from Halifax. Then the C-1 group turned north for St. John's.

Though seas were calm and skies moonlit, it was a perfect setting for disaster. Travelling abreast about 2,000 yards apart, the five ships faced a line of ice floes and growlers. Radar consequently picked up echoes everywhere. Still, by 10:30 p.m. the group had safely passed the ice obstacles. It looked like clear sailing the rest of the way. Crews, weary from the week's escort and only fifty miles south of Cape Race, abandoned the safer zigzagging navigation and coursed straight for their home port at a modest thirteen knots. And none of the escorts had deployed their CATs, the anti-acoustic torpedo devices; their annoying clatter tended to mask the warships' ASDIC sensing, so it seemed safe and expedient not to stream the CATs behind the ships.[27]

In *Valleyfield*'s anti-submarine office, SLt Ian Tate had nearly finished his watch. He noticed how calm the sea swell looked and how bright the night. "With the convoy well on its way, I was thinking, 'A U-boat captain would be a damn fool to take on five anti-submarine ships!'" Tate said. "I mean, what are the chances? After all, it's a big ocean."[28]

At 11 p.m., Kptlt Zimmermann had *U548* moving southwesterly on the surface. The moonlight silhouetted ships some distance away but he was closing quickly. He was approaching the Canadian escorts between *Frontenac* and *Valleyfield* and dived for a submerged attack on the latter.[29] Zimmermann chose his acoustic weapon, the Zaunkönig, or GNAT, launching it from about 1,600 yards. He anticipated about three minutes to detonation.

On *Valleyfield*'s bridge, Tate listened to an ASDIC loudspeaker crackling out normal pings at his station. Just after 11:30, however, the transmission changed abruptly to distinct ticking sounds.

"Investigate 250 to 290!" Tate called to his ASDIC operator.[30]

It was the electric motor of the inbound acoustic torpedo off *Valleyfield*'s port bow. Five seconds later, it hit. It smashed into the frigate amidships, penetrating the boiler room with a massive explosion. On the bridge, navigator Jack Warren was thrown to the deck. Tate rang the engine room.

"Get the hell out, boys!" he shouted, just as the captain arrived at the bridge.[31]

"Is anyone trapped?" LCdr Dermot English asked, but the noise of the ship splitting into two drowned out any response. "Slip the Carley floats," he called out, then gave an "Abandon ship" order.

The frigate's bow section, now separated from the rest of the stricken frigate, had already rolled to starboard; within a couple of minutes, it was gone. The crew had managed to release three Carley floats. On the after section, three ratings—David E. Brown, David H. Brown, and M.H. Woods—rushed to *Valleyfield*'s depth charges, rendering their primers safe to keep them from exploding as the ship went down.[32] But the after section sank nearly as quickly as the bow. In four minutes, all that remained was wreckage, some flotation devices, and fuel oil coating the survivors. The water temperature was thirty-two degrees Fahrenheit.

"There she goes," Warren called out as he swam and looked back. "God bless her."

Nearby, Tate and the captain had managed to swim clear of the aft section as well. In the dark they'd found a Carley float, where other survivors were beating their hands and feet against the float, trying to keep extremities from freezing.

Cdr English had only managed to get a single strap of a life jacket secured on himself. He told those who could to tie any floats together. Then he got those around him to sing. "For she's a jolly good fellow . . . ," they heard him calling out.

Then the night went quiet. "Mr. Tate, are you still there?" English called out weakly.

"Yes, Tate here, sir," he replied.

"If I don't come through this, will you please write my wife?"

"Aye, sir," he answered, but Tate felt himself passing out from the cold.[33] He remembered a wave washing over them. He didn't hear or see English again.

Some of those aboard *Valleyfield*'s sister ships—*Frontenac* and *Giffard*—had heard a thump-like sound in the distance and signalled the frigate, "Is there anything wrong?" With no reply, *Giffard* turned for *Valleyfield*'s last known position and was soon among the frigate's survivors, some calling out with what strength they had left.

"I yelled so loud they must have heard me all over the ocean," said Irving Kaplan, *Valleyfield*'s yeoman of signals.[34] He'd gone to his hammock fully clothed, so he had some insulation while in the water.

LCdr Charles Petersen, in command on *Giffard*, was obliged under the circumstances to hunt for the U-boat. That took twenty minutes, after which the corvette returned to bring aboard *Valleyfield* survivors. Most had been in the water nearly ninety minutes. *Giffard* managed to find forty-three of the frigate's 163 crew. Five, including LCdr English, died on the way to St. John's. Meanwhile, *Valleyfield*'s sister escorts continued to search for *U548* for another four days, in vain.* For Lt John Dyke, aboard *Frontenac*, this proved doubly disheartening, particularly since he and his shipmate Lt Stan Howe had flipped a coin for berths in the C-1 escorts that ultimately sent their shipmate Lt John Storey to his death.

* *U548* finished her patrol having sunk one ship, HMCS *Valleyfield*. After leave in June 1944, Kptlt Zimmermann could not return to his U-boat at Lorient since the Normandy invasion overtook the port. Zimmermann was detained by the Allies. *U548* was sunk in April 1945, just a few hundred miles from *Valleyfield*'s sinking.

A board of inquiry on May 10, 1944, assigned blame for the lost frigate to mistakes that had compounded the disaster: failing to zigzag once the five escorts had passed the ice floes; delays in recognizing *Valleyfield*'s predicament; further time lost to launch the U-boat search versus rescuing the survivors; and perhaps the most egregious error—failing to deploy the CATs to decoy the German acoustic torpedo.

Lt Dyke had no role at the inquiry into *Valleyfield*'s sinking, but following his attendance at John Storey's funeral in St. John's, he got the opportunity to address the inquiry's criticism regarding the failure to deploy CATs. Back in Halifax after a month's leave, Dyke awaited his next wartime posting. Coincidentally, the officer in charge was a university chum, Doug Darling.

"We need somebody to work on the CAT gear," Darling told Dyke. "They can't get it working. Would you like to help?"

"I don't really like the sea," Dyke admitted. "I'd like to take up the task."[35]

The Canadian Anti-Acoustic Torpedo device had already proven itself immensely valuable, attracting the sound-seeking German GNAT torpedo during battles with the U-boats. Among its flaws, however, was that, once tethered and tossed from the stern of a warship, the CAT couldn't be turned on or off at will. Additionally, while the CAT lured the GNAT, its vibrating bars drowned out the escort's underwater ASDIC system. The racket also tended to attract other U-boats, which undermined the objective of helping convoys evade U-boats. After reviewing all the CAT specs and reports and then applying his civilian and military training as an engineer, Lt Dyke reached a solution that ultimately was as easy as child's play.

"At the age of ten, I had a bicycle," Dyke wrote. "My

dad brought home large elastic bands, which when stretched across the handlebars of my bike, [made] a noise when the air activated the bands as we peddled along."[36]

Dyke got an additional thrill from stopping and starting the noise, simply by slipping his hand between the pair of vibrating elastic bands. Why not, he thought in May 1944, employ the same concept to lock and unlock the CAT's vibrating bars? He eventually slipped a bight into the towline that created an impulse in the line to the CAT. The impulse compressed a spring. The motion turned a cam. And this allowed the water flowing over the two bars of the CAT and through the gap between them to make them vibrate or not.

"It worked," he wrote, "but [the rigging] was too big and cumbersome."

Still, he and his experiment team knew the concept could solve the problem. They took the prototype to sea trials in Bedford Basin, beyond Halifax Harbour. They recorded the sound of the CAT being deployed. One night, the recording revealed that the bight had turned the trip to shut off the CAT, which silenced the noise.

"Then, I remembered the elastic bands across my handlebars," Dyke wrote, recalling his boyhood days in Saint-Lambert, Quebec.

Dyke and his team redesigned the CAT so that instead of rotating the noisemaker's heavy bars to stop the vibration, the trip would rotate a tongue into the space between the bars—like his fingers between the elastic bands—to stop them from vibrating, or alternatively remove the tongue to allow the bars to vibrate again. That redesign reduced the CAT to a seventy-pound device, so that one sailor could easily launch it at the stern of the escort.

"Sea trials were conducted in the Bay of Fundy," Dyke wrote. "The new design was successfully tested and hailed by the Royal Navy as the best device for towing the CAT of any design!"

Lt John Morley Dyke's CAT Mk III was subsequently issued to all Allied navies. Nobody ever calculated the hundreds of lives his childhood-inspired device saved. No doubt Dyke wished it could have saved his friend John Storey's and those of all the men lost when *Valleyfield* went down.

DESPITE the sinking of HMCS *Valleyfield*, the anti-submarine escort groups were prevailing. They now controlled Allied shipping lanes. In the first half of 1944, merchant shipping losses on the Atlantic had averaged eleven ships and 41,906 tons per month.[37] During the same six months, the Kriegsmarine had lost 128 U-boats; by the end of the year that number would nearly double to 242.[38] And with convoys fortified by larger, more experienced close escorts, with killer-hunter specialists (no longer responsible for screening convoys but bent on hunting U-boats to exhaustion and a kill), and with the Black Pit shrinking to nothing, any U-boat choosing to attack (and thus revealing her position) faced less prospect of survival.

Equally alarming for Karl Dönitz, the perimeters of the Kriegsmarine's safe waters along the northwest European coast were receding, becoming more dangerous for the occupiers.* To compensate, the grand admiral withdrew his U-boats into a semicircle front line with Brest, France, at the south end and the Faroe Islands at the north.[39] For most of

* Dönitz also learned in May 1944 that son Klaus had died aboard a Schnellboot sunk by Allied warships off Cherbourg. Son Peter died when *U954* was sunk in May 1943.

the previous five years, U-boats had carried the war to the doorsteps of their enemies. Now they were being harassed on their own.

At the end of April, one of U-Bootwaffe's experienced commanders piloted *U415* home into the safety of the Brest shipyards. Oblt zS Herbert Werner had completed an aborted patrol in search of convoys at the Western Approaches to the English Channel. He'd survived attacks from both RAF bombers and RN hunter-killer groups. But after thirty-seven hours and more than 300 charges dropped over and around his U-boat, Werner had received orders to return to base immediately.[40] He did so readily. As they arrived home, Werner and *U415* picked up additional Armed Forces radio communiqués. Berlin, Hamburg, and Hanover had received heavy Allied air bombardments. The Soviets had launched a broad offensive in the south of Russia. In Italy, the German Army had fallen back to the Adolf Hitler Line. And during their few days at sea, three other U-boats had been sunk. With *U415* safely secured, Werner reported to his CO's office. He learned the reason he'd been recalled was that German High Command anticipated an Allied invasion of the Continent.

No surprise to Werner, given the state of things on land and sea. But perhaps more worrying was the meeting that followed. Oblt zS Werner joined a conference table at 1st Flotilla headquarters, where fifteen young but experienced U-boat commanders had assembled. Hans-Rudolf Rösing, senior U-boat commander for all the occupied French ports, presided at the urgent session.

"Gentlemen, as you know, the Allied invasion is expected momentarily," Rösing began. "You must be in the position to sail at any hour."[41] He reviewed the inventory of defences available to U-boat Command—twenty-two boats on alert in Norway, and twenty-one in the Biscay ports. He offered his best guess that the invasion fleet would take the shortest route across the Channel, within fifty miles of England.

"This is where you gentlemen step in," he said finally. "Headquarters' directive is short and precise: Attack and sink invasion fleet with the final objective of destroying enemy ships by ramming."

The conference room went silent with shock.

"Sir, does that mean we have to ram our boat into an enemy vessel, if we are able to return to port for more torpedoes?" Werner asked.

"As the order stands, it means ramming," Rösing said. "Total assault is ordered, even though it means deliberate self-destruction."

Werner recorded that each U-boat commander left the meeting struggling to reconcile his own grim thoughts. He himself worried, despite repeated calls for its installation, that *U415* had not been upgraded with a Schnorchel to give his U-boat a fighting chance for invisibility in the coming battle. If the deficiency remained unchanged, he deduced, that would leave a grand total of seven Schnorchel-equipped U-boats from Biscay with any chance of heading off an invasion in the Channel. Even if Rösing had made a Schnorchel available for Werner's *U415*, there wouldn't have been time to install it. Overnight on June 5 and into the early hours of June 6, the Allies' Operation Neptune (the naval portion of Overlord) launched and crossed the English Channel. The largest wartime amphibious assault against Hitler's Fortress Europe—almost 7,000 ships (including 1,213 warships, 4,126 landing craft, 736 support ships, and 864 merchant ships)[42]—at dawn delivered 156,000 troops to the five D-Day beaches, codenamed Utah, Omaha, Gold, Juno, and Sword.

Oblt zS Werner was wakened at 3:47 a.m. to learn the Allies were landing in the Bay of the Seine. He jumped into battle fatigues, collected a few belongings (including a toothbrush and tube of toothpaste), put on his lambskin jacket and boots, and dashed to the pen containing *U415*. However, not until 2:20 p.m. did Werner receive a sealed envelope with orders "to proceed on surface at top speed to English coast [to] attack and destroy Allied shipping." Werner considered the orders even more outrageous than Dönitz's directive to destroy enemy ships by ramming. It would require *U415* and seven other U-boats without Schnorchels to stay surfaced and race unprotected to the south English coast, with Allied aircraft and warships ready to pounce.

"Clearly, we would not survive long enough to commit suicide by ramming cargo ships in the English ports," Werner wrote.[43]

Even his doomsday prediction was optimistic. By early afternoon of June 7, Werner's non-Schnorchel U-boat group had barely made it into the Bay of Biscay before it came under heavy air attack. Five of the boats were never seen again, and Werner's U-boat was so badly damaged she could only submerge deep enough to escape a *coup de grâce* attack. Jury-rigging *U415*'s diesel engines and conserving electrical power, Werner and his wounded crew nursed their U-boat home to the pens at Brest in the middle of the night of June 8. Both the commander and the U-boat would return to front-line duty, but for Oblt zS Werner each new patrol seemed more perilous than the last. Within three days of D-Day, Allied aircrews had sunk six U-boats and damaged another six.[44] Prospects for the U-Bootwaffe were not improving.

In early June, electrical engineer Walter Schmietenknop and his *U767* crew had just found safe waters in which to hunt, off the coast of Nova Scotia. This was the nineteen-year-old's first operational tour, searching for targets outside Halifax Harbour, but his U-boat soon received news of the Allied invasion and orders to rush back to the Biscay ports. *U767* had the advantage of a recently installed Schnorchel to hasten her return undetected. But as the U-boat and crew approached the Biscay pens, they were refused entry. It was utter chaos. They couldn't dock. They couldn't resupply.

It was all *U767*'s commander, Oblt Walter Dankleff, could do to load as many Zaunkönig torpedoes as he could. Then he was ordered back to the English Channel to attack the Allied invasion fleet.[45] Submerged at periscope depth on the afternoon of June 15, Dankleff sighted a Royal Navy flotilla screening the Western Approaches to the English Channel. The U-boat captain prepared acoustic torpedoes for the frigate in his sights. Then, in rapid succession, Dankleff called for the firing of all five Zaunkönig torpedoes. Just as quickly, the torpedo crews opened ballast tanks to prevent the U-boat from shooting to the surface.

"Then, we waited," Schmietenknop wrote. "There was a huge bang and a thunderous rumble. A hit! The whole crew cheered."

At periscope depth, Oblt Dankleff reported that the first acoustic had scored a hit on HMS *Mourne* amidships. The second had struck and ignited the frigate's ammunition magazine, which tore the warship in two. Walter Schmietenknop, the young electrical engineer, had witnessed his first combat sinking. He wrote at the time that he hadn't considered those affected in *Mourne*. Of 138 aboard the stricken frigate, only twenty-seven crewmen survived. He noted he heard a third explosion, but they didn't wait around any longer. *U767* had emptied all her tubes and dived. RN escorts were rapidly closing on the U-boat's position.

At that location, the English Channel was only about 300 feet deep. Dankleff had sufficient experience not to dive deep immediately, so the first pattern of escort depth charges exploded far enough below *U767* to avoid any damage. Then Dankleff raced to the bottom and remained stopped and silent for four hours while the escorts dropped charges at various depths. When the danger seemed past, he returned to periscope depth, activated the U-boat's Schnorchel, and rushed to within the protective range of German batteries on the French coast. Three days later, however, the odds caught up with Dankleff's U-boat and her crew.

That Sunday afternoon, June 18, *U767* sailed into an ambush. RN destroyers *Fame*, *Havelock*, and *Inconstant* had set up a horseshoe configuration just off the island of Guernsey. Schmietenknop had just begun his watch when the alarm sounded. But before Oblt Dankleff could take evasive action, the destroyers' fire scored direct hits. Schmietenknop's station in the engine room was suddenly on fire. The U-boat rolled on her side and sank.

Schmietenknop could see a depth gauge as *U767* plummeted all the way to the bottom; it read more than 200 feet. With watertight hatches shut throughout the sub, there was no communication with outside the engine room. Water began pouring into the shattered hull. He managed to find his escape kit—a life jacket with a small oxygen tank attached. But sealed in the engine room, and with no apparent way out, he and seventeen other young submariners were waiting to die.

"*Singen*," a sergeant called to the others as a distraction, and he began to sing the national anthem. "*Deutschland, Deutschland über alles*!"

Schmietenknop was positioned closest to the top of the air pocket, near a wheel that would open an escape hatch upward to the outside of the U-boat. But when two shipmates tried to open it, it wouldn't budge; the water pressure outside was too great. One by one, the crewmen around Schmietenknop ran out of oxygen and fell unconscious. Then he noticed that a ring of water had formed around the hatch; it meant the pressure inside the U-boat had equalized to the pressure outside. Everybody else had passed out.

"I grabbed my breathing apparatus, made my way to the hatch, turned the [wheel] and opened it," he wrote later. "I got stuck in the hatch."

Then he remembered Lt Schuster and his training in Wilhelmshaven Harbour two years earlier. Just as he had practised in the simulation tank each day, Schmietenknop wriggled his way through the hatch, put his hands above his head, and began to swim upwards, toward water that appeared brighter. "That's where I have to go," he thought to himself. "There's life up there."

He nearly gave up, but the oxygen tank on his life jacket gave a few last breaths of air as he broke the surface. When he focused and looked around, he saw the RN destroyers moving away. He had been swimming for what felt like hours when he realized one of the destroyers was bearing down on him. He feared he'd be run over and killed. But the crew in HMS *Fame* spotted him and pulled him aboard. For Schmietenknop, the war was over. During the next three days, he stayed in a makeshift bunk near *Fame*'s depth-charge hold while the destroyer carried on her searches for other U-boats.

At some point, several RN sailors told him he was the sole survivor of the sunken *U767*. They brought Walter a magazine with Hitler's picture on it. They motioned they would cut Hitler's throat.

"No. No," the young German said and shook his head.

The sailors left the magazine. In it, Walter found a photo of Winston Churchill. When the sailors returned, he motioned he would cut Churchill's throat.

"They burst out laughing," Walter wrote, "and we all had a good laugh together."

Thus began Walter Schmietenknop's experience as a POW, first in England, then in Scotland, and eventually at an American POW camp in Georgia. He was repatriated to Germany in 1946, and in 1951 he emigrated to Canada for a new life in the countryside of a wartime enemy.

As late as January 1943, when David Hornell and his fiancée, Genevieve Noecker, decided to marry, the RCAF flight lieutenant figured the war had passed him by. He'd served in the Air Force for two years. Since Christmas 1942 he'd flown Canso flying boats with RCAF No. 120 (BR) Squadron, based at Coal Harbour on Vancouver Island. He'd consistently received high praise from his commanding officers, but at age thirty-three Hornell sensed the practice of sending younger pilots overseas would likely exclude him from operational service over Europe.[46]

Escalating losses from merchant convoys on the mid-

Atlantic in the fall of 1943, however, forced Allied air forces to deliver greater air cover more effectively. The RCAF transferred F/L Hornell to No. 162 (BR) Squadron on the Atlantic Coast, then in early 1944 to Reykjavík. His hundreds of hours of experience as a capable coastal patrol pilot, no matter his age, made him an instant asset—even more so when his Canso and crew were posted to the bomber reconnaissance station at Wick, in northern Scotland. Hornell commanded an all-Canadian crew: co-pilot F/O Bernard Denomy, navigator F/O Edward Matheson, engineers Sgt Donald Scott and Sgt Fernand St. Laurent, and wireless/air gunners F/O Graham Campbell, Sgt Joe Bodnoff, and Sgt Sydney Cole. All were younger men. All called their skipper "Pop" out of respect and their trust in him as their leader.

Patrols aboard the Canso involved up to twenty-three hours of continuous flying and as many as a thousand miles out to sea and back searching for U-boat targets. With June providing nearly twenty-four hours of daylight at that latitude, sightlines in good weather were excellent. The flying boat had a payload capacity of 4,000 pounds of bombs, depth charges, and/or torpedoes, with machine-gun armament at the nose and side blisters. But at best, carrying a full bomb load and eight crewmen, the Canso had a top speed of about 175 miles per hour. Hornell knew his aircraft was an excellent U-boat stalker, but painfully slow. Meanwhile, with beefed-up armament in 1944, U-boat commanders were under orders to remain on the surface in gun duels with Allied bombers. A Canso had been shot down on June 13 while sinking *U713*; three airmen had died. Another bomber, after sinking *U980* on June 11, had disappeared, presumably shot down, with all crew lost.

On June 24, ten hours into their patrol—for "Pop"

Hornell his sixtieth—an otherwise uneventful sortie changed for Canso P/162. The flying-boat bomber was 120 miles north of the Shetland Islands.

"Do you see that sub, Dave?" Joe Bodnoff called into the intercom.

"Sure do," Hornell answered, looking off the port beam.[47] He alerted the rest of the crew and began an attack from the stern. He knew full well that such an approach exposed the Canso to the U-boat's heaviest anti-aircraft armament.[48]

U1225 gave no indication of crash-diving. Her commander, Oblt Ekkehard Scherraus, had served in several U-boats, including *U506* during the infamous sinking of the troopship *Laconia* off Africa in 1942.[49] Scherraus ordered his gunners on the 20mm cannon to open fire on the Canso.

Aft of the Canso cockpit, gunner Syd Cole was at the radio right then. He felt the aircraft shudder with the flak hits from the U-boat as the range closed. "I tucked my head between my knees to make as little a target as possible, and started sending SOS for all it was worth," to alert Coastal Command of their exact location.[50] But flak had already disabled the radio transmitter. No distress call was ever received.

The Canso's .50-calibre Browning machine guns would not be effective until the bomber had closed to within 1,200 yards of the U-boat. Meantime, the U-boat's cannon and machine gunners continued to land fire on their target. They'd hit the Canso's starboard engine—it burst into flames—and ripped the aluminum skin on that wing to shreds. In the cockpit, Hornell and Denomy struggled to keep the Canso on its attack path.

"We coasted to within thirty or forty feet above the enemy sub," Denomy reported, "and loosed our depth charges."[51]

The Canso's four 250-pound charges straddled *U1225* perfectly.[52] The explosions actually lifted the U-boat out of the water. When she crashed back to the surface, the boat soon disappeared and sank. Some submariners had survived the explosion, but most went down with the boat.

Hornell then tried to gain altitude, but when the starboard engine fell from its mounts, he turned the aircraft into the wind, deliberately stalled it, and brought the burning and crippled Canso down safely on the surface. Most of the crew escaped through the port blister, while Hornell and Denomy crawled through hatches above the cockpit. All eight had survived, along with a couple of dinghies, a cylinder of water, and a can of emergency rations. But within twenty minutes Canso P/162 had sunk.[53]

Six of the crew managed to crowd into one dinghy, a seventh hanging on in the water. The six manoeuvred their dinghy toward the second one, with St. Laurent in it, to tie the lifeboats together. But St. Laurent's dinghy suddenly exploded and sank, leaving eight men trying to survive in sea water that was forty-four degrees Fahrenheit.[54]

With so little space in the dinghy, the Canso crewmen alternated, each man taking a turn in the frigid water, kicking and stroking to keep limbs from freezing; then, back in the dinghy, getting his arms and legs rubbed by the others to restore circulation. Eventually the group decided to discard rations and anything else aboard to squeeze all the men into the dinghy. If all that weren't dispiriting enough, the weather turned. Winds picked up to sixty knots and waves to fifty feet. They capsized several times. About midnight, five hours after they'd ditched the Canso, a Catalina flying boat approached and Graham Campbell fired flares to catch the eye of the pilot.[55] Heavy seas prevented the Catalina from landing, but Lt C.F. Kraaft kept circling to guide rescuers to the spot.[56]

"Courage," Kraaft flashed on his signal lamp to Hornell and his crew. "HSL [High Speed Launch] on way. Help coming."[57] The Catalina crew also signalled Hornell's crew that they had seen a huge oil slick nearby and many bodies floating, evidence that their Canso had sunk *U1225*.

After sixteen hours, Hornell's crew was losing to the elements. St. Laurent fell into unconsciousness and couldn't be resuscitated. The survivors put him overboard. Then Scott died. Hornell had lost his vision by this time, but kept encouraging his comrades with words of comfort and prayer. After twenty-one hours, the HSL rescue boat arrived and found the dinghy.

"It was an emotional moment," wrote Charles Deverell, crewman aboard HSL 2507. The rescue crew lowered a scramble net into the dinghy and Deverell began winching the Canso crew up into the HSL, one by one. Hornell's crew directed attention to their skipper. The rescuers tried to combat Hornell's hypothermia the best they could. "Finally, we just lay down close either side of him to give him our warmth. But I think he had died by then."[58]

The five surviving crew—F/O Denomy, F/O Matheson, F/O Campbell, and Sgts Bodnoff and Cole—aboard the HSL (its fuel tanks nearly empty) received an escort into the Shetland Islands. Next morning, the boat continued on to Lerwick with the survivors. F/L David "Pop" Hornell was buried in a cemetery overlooking the sea. A month later, a telegram arrived in Coal Harbour. Genevieve Hornell learned that her husband would be awarded the Victoria Cross—the first of only three RCAF members to receive the decoration for valour in the Second World War.[59]

"In the circumstances," Genevieve told a reporter the next day, "I feel it is about the most wonderful thing that could happen."[60]

Days after the announcement of Hornell's posthumous decoration, combatants in the Battle of the Atlantic witnessed another milestone. On July 20, 1944, 167 merchant navy ships merged into a massive eastbound convoy off Cape Race, Newfoundland. They covered an area of the sea four miles long and nineteen miles wide (a sailor in a crow's nest at one side of the convoy, even with clear skies, could not see the other side). Their passage to scores of United Kingdom ports of call would establish a record, in part thanks to the sacrifices made by David Hornell, his aircrew comrades, and thousands of naval escort crews and sailors of the merchant navy.

That midsummer day, tankers and cargo ships from New York City, Halifax, Sydney, and St. John's assembled as Convoy HXS 300, the largest trade convoy of the war. Escorted first by the Western Local Escort Force and then by the C-5 Mid-Ocean Escort Force into the Western Approaches—primarily ships of the RCN—all 167 ships arrived at their destinations safely two weeks later. They delivered a million tons of cargo—grain, sugar, molasses, foodstuffs, lumber, iron and steel, oil, tanks, Jeeps, half-tracks, locomotives, and other war munitions—to the UK.[61]

"[It] was unremarkable," noted Bob MacIntosh, RCN corvette stoker, "except to say it was the largest convoy crossing of the entire war—167 ships delivered unmolested."[62]

Through the first half of 1944, operations off the east coast of Canada and Newfoundland, as well as in the open Atlantic, had largely forced the Kriegsmarine to withdraw its U-boats from anti-convoy patrols. And even though the modernization of RCN ships continued to lag behind their navy allies and RCN manpower always seemed to be stretched paper-thin, merchant ships assigned to Canadian escort groups nearly all arrived at their destinations incident free. But the unglamorous work of escorting convoys safely across the North Atlantic took a toll. In the final year of the war, RCN escorts did not sink any U-boats in the western Atlantic, but they still sustained the loss of five warships.[63]

ONE nautical casualty within Canadian coastal waters, not initially counted by Allied statisticians, came to light during the interrogation of a captured U-boat crew in 1944. The first indication of trouble came to RCNVR LCdr Anthony Griffin, formerly commanding officer of HMCS *Pictou* and senior escort officer for RAdm Leonard Murray in Halifax, then in St. John's. It began with a call from the port's defence officer.

"Sir, the clapper on the bell-buoy off Cape Spear is missing," the man said, and he warned that with inclement weather approaching and an escort group expected, this could threaten the escorts' safe passage into St. John's Harbour. "I suspect sabotage," the defence officer said finally.[64]

"I'll warn the incoming group about the buoy," Griffin said, and added that the clapper should be replaced immediately. Soon after, Griffin assisted the merchant ship SS *Kelmscott*—torpedoed off Cape Spear but not sunk—to return under tow to St. John's. A short time later, Canadian escorts with Escort Group 9 sank *U845* in the same waters and took prisoners. Their interrogation revealed the madcap details of this U-boat's one and only patrol.

U845 had departed her home port of Bergen, Norway, in January, for operational patrols off Newfoundland and Nova Scotia.

"The interrogation disclosed that the U-boat had surfaced close to Sydney," Griffin wrote. "Some of the crew said they had gone ashore to the movies [as] ticket stubs were found on one of the men!"

The crew explained to interrogators that, eventually, *U845* had arrived outside St. John's Harbour. Their unorthodox commander, KK Werner Weber, attempted to follow a destroyer through protective mines and the entry gap into the harbour. Instead he grounded the U-boat on shoals off Cape Race. Much manipulation and improvising managed to free the U-boat.

"Believing the damage to be serious," the POWs told interrogators, "KK Weber decided to abandon and scuttle [the U-boat]. He surfaced and after making a patriotic speech went to the bridge carrying a large German flag."[65]

U845's chief engineer managed to dissuade Weber from giving up the U-boat, and the commander eventually agreed to vacate the area. Before he did, however, the crew (perhaps directed by a now frustrated commander) chose not to leave without a final insult to the enemy.

"[*U845*] surfaced near bell buoy R4," the prisoners said. "An abortive attempt was made to steal the bell as a souvenir."[66] Griffin deduced that the clapper had had to suffice.

Not long afterward, the U-boat sighted SS *Kelmscott*, an 8,000-ton freighter, and fired a spread of three torpedoes. Two of them struck the merchant ship but didn't sink it. Again the

U-boat departed, and in an attempt to attack a subsequent convoy, *U845* was then pursued by the three Canadian escorts, forced to surface, and sunk. KK Weber died in the final battle on the surface. Forty-two German submariners were rescued from the sinking U-boat, but not the clapper from Cape Spear's bell buoy.

Chapter Twelve

"FOR US, THE WAR WAS OVER"

That the war might soon end, and that he might yet survive it, were thoughts Roy Harbin considered while at sea in December 1944. The circumstances were certainly out of the ordinary. Through most of the year, Harbin, an eighteen-year-old Torontonian, had served as torpedoman aboard HMCS *Montreal*. The frigate had completed a dozen transatlantic convoy escorts. And while most had passed uneventfully, that fall, *Montreal* raced to the sinking Norwegian freighter *Fjordheim* north of Ireland to pick up survivors.

"The merchant sailors we picked up were anywhere from sixteen to eighty years old," Harbin said. "The old-timer had been sunk five times."[1]

Then, just before Christmas, the Canadian frigate joined Escort Group 26, based in Londonderry. Harbin called the escort "a sub-fighting group" patrolling waters around the British Isles, looking for trouble and chasing U-boats to exhaustion. On December 17 they made ASDIC contact with *U1209*, which had just completed passage along the west coast of Ireland south to Land's End. There the

U-boat commander, Oblt Ewald Hülsenbeck, began stalking a lone steamship.

"An argument took place between [Hülsenbeck] and the Navigating Chief Petty Officer," one of *U1209*'s crew explained later. "The CPO argued the boat was heading straight for Wolf Rock, but Hülsenbeck was convinced they were well to the west of it."[2]

At the height of the argument, *U1209* struck bottom, scraped across the Wolf Rock shoals, and then got pushed free in the swell. But the damage was done. Water began pouring into stern compartments of the U-boat. By this time the lighthouse keeper at Wolf Rock, Charles Cherrett, had spotted the U-boat on the surface and reported it.[3] When HMCS *Montreal* and HMCS *Ribble* arrived, they found that *U1209* had sunk and her surviving crew was adrift in life rafts.

"We picked up eighteen survivors, and they gave me a .45 [pistol] and two guys in sick bay to guard," Harbin said. "I'd never shot a .45 in my life!"

The impromptu guard didn't have to worry. He gave the Germans cards and cigarettes, and because one of his *Montreal* shipmates spoke German fluently, Harbin was able to strike up a conversation with one of his prisoners. He learned that the submariners were happy that Canadian ships had rescued them; they said they'd heard how wonderful a place Canada was. When Harbin's prisoner shared some of his experiences, both captor and captive realized they had things in common. "If they were walking among our own people, you wouldn't know it," Harbin said finally. "They lived just like the rest of us."

As it had with frigate electrician Roy Harbin, survival had become a priority for U-boat engineer Werner Hirschmann too. It's quite likely their paths had crossed on and beneath the surface of the North Atlantic during the winter of 1944–45. However, unlike Harbin, who joined the RCN because of the war, Hirschmann had enlisted long before the war began. He chose to serve in the Kriegsmarine partly because his father had during the Great War, partly because, with chronic asthma, he was told to go to sea as therapy, but mostly because all his life he'd read tales of naval heroes.

"I devoured any book I could get hold of, reading about Nelson, Drake or de Ruyter," he said. "The decision was made. I wanted to join the navy!"[4]

By the time Hirschmann had completed basic training, service as a stoker, and a transfer to the U-Bootwaffe, he was eighteen and the war had started. He'd been promoted to chief engineer in *U612* for a tour to the Mediterranean, and he arrived at the front lines of the Battle of the Atlantic just when Grossadmiral Dönitz was withdrawing the wolf packs in 1943. U-boat passage through British waters had grown perilous. In March 1945, Allied escort groups had sunk fifteen U-boats off the UK—six in the English Channel alone.[5]

"The hunters had now become the hunted," Hirschmann said. "And our main purpose was . . . survival rather than attacking enemy shipping."[6]

During his next deployment, as chief engineer in *U190*, he and his shipmates patrolled waters off the west coast of Africa. They found no targets for months, and they returned to a very different atmosphere back at the U-boat pens in Lorient. Hirschmann was struck by the sight of the chief of the U-boat flotilla standing at the end of the pier as they tied up. Tears streamed down his face. In the entire four months they'd been at sea, not one other U-boat had returned to

Lorient safely. Then, with Allied invasion armies moving closer to the Bay of Biscay ports, *U190* had joined the remaining U-boats withdrawing to the safety of Bremen, Germany, to be outfitted with Schnorchels.

While his commander, Oblt Hans-Erwin Reith, saw the addition of the Schnorchel to *U190* as an additional weapon, Hirschmann considered the device a lifeline. It allowed the U-boat to suck air into her hull while remaining submerged, thus enabling the diesel engines to run full-time charging batteries while also helping the U-boat avoid visual detection by enemy aircraft. He called the addition a "device of survival."[7] Whether offensive or defensive, the Schnorchel had emboldened German High Command to redeploy the larger Type IX U-boats, back to hunting patrols in the northwestern Atlantic. In March and April 1945, even as the Third Reich was on the verge of capitulation, Dönitz dispatched eight Schnorchel-equipped Type IX U-boats, including *U190*, to submerged patrols off Nova Scotia and Newfoundland.

ABOUT that time, Allied intelligence had learned that the Kriegsmarine's long-anticipated advanced hybrid "Walther" boats, the Type XXIs, had begun work-ups, and that they might soon form the vanguard of a new U-boat offensive in the Atlantic. Some Admiralty experts even hypothesized that Dönitz's super-boats were armed with V-weapons, similar to those launched against London and Antwerp. In fact, hunter-killer escorts with the US Navy had already intercepted and destroyed five of the Type IXs en route to North America. The actual threat that U-boat patrols off the Canadian coast posed that spring was more of the hit-and-run variety. *U190*, one of the three remaining U-boats in the spring 1945 patrols, spent most of her time submerged and waiting for opportunities, not searching for them.

"When we approached the Canadian coast, we no longer surfaced during the night," Hirschmann wrote, "and thus we started a period of fifty days submerged, prowling around the approaches of Halifax."[8]

On the evening of April 15, two minesweepers of the Halifax Local Defence Force—HMCS *Sarnia* and *Esquimalt*—received new orders. Allied Intelligence had traced lone U-boats operating off the Nova Scotia coast. *Sarnia*, already at sea, and *Esquimalt*, emerging from Halifax Harbour, were to conduct ASDIC sweeps to flush out enemy boats. Then, at about nine o'clock the next morning, when the sweeps were completed, the two minesweepers were to rendezvous near the Sambro lightship, an anchored ship used as a floating lighthouse twenty miles out to sea.[9]

As the ship's writer, Terry Manuel had daytime duties attending to *Esquimalt*'s paperwork, but he also took regular watches. The morning of April 16 he was up at four, positioned astern on deck near the minesweeper's two-pounder gun and scanning the horizon through binoculars. The moonless night was clear enough that he could see the glow of some Halifax lights—in 1944 no longer in total blackout, but in dim-out—some twenty miles offshore. At 5:15 a.m. a shrill whistle in the voice pipe sent him to action stations. The twenty-four-year-old dashed to the starboard depth-charge thrower, helping to arm the charges. *Esquimalt* then passed the lightship off the starboard side.[10] The sweeper was not zigzagging and had not deployed either of her two CAT devices.

At six o'clock, action stations was cancelled. Manuel secured the charges and went off watch. Below decks, Jim McIntyre, the cook, gave him a cup of coffee. Manuel slipped off his heavy watchkeeping gear, made his way to the crew's mess, and, using his life jacket as a pillow, curled up on some box lockers to sleep until breakfast call, expected thirty minutes later.

Aboard *U190*, submerged to periscope depth, Werner Hirschmann and his shipmates could hear the strong ASDIC pings and propeller noise of a warship approaching from the stern. Oblt Reith immediately called for the launch of an acoustic torpedo from a stern tube.[11] Then he ordered a deep dive.[12]

"My head had barely touched the life jacket when I heard a muffled thud," Manuel wrote later. "Then a loud and shattering explosion threw me violently over the mess table to land on all fours. The lights dimmed, flickered and went out."[13]

Had Manuel still been at the starboard depth-charge thrower, he'd have been killed instantly. The U-boat's acoustic torpedo penetrated the hull and exploded just below the thrower, killing the engine-room crew and 1st Lt John Smart, in the cabin directly above. But Manuel was a deck below the boat deck. *Esquimalt* had already rolled on her starboard side and was sinking fast. Manuel and mates Carl Jacques and Chesley Shave tried desperately to open the hatch from the crew's mess. It wouldn't budge.

"I'm getting out another way," Manuel shouted. Jacques followed.

In the dark, the two men groped to a companionway, but instead of leading upward, it lay horizontally. A hatch ahead was open. Manuel could see some light, but sea water and oil "poured through with the force of Niagara Falls." Then, in one enormous gush of water, both he and Jacques were flung through the open hatchway. In a moment they were above the surface, but situated on *Esquimalt*'s rolling and sinking hull.

About the same time, ASDIC operator Joe Wilson had managed to escape the ASDIC hut near *Esquimalt*'s bridge and had tried crawling across her toppled funnel. He jumped into one of four Carley floats the crew had managed to cut loose from the boat deck, but the sweeper's mast flipped the float and pulled six sailors under.

"I had my life jacket on," Wilson said, "and I rolled from under the mast, shooting back to the surface. When I clambered back into the raft, there were friends all around trying to get into the float, or hanging onto the side ropes."[14]

"She's going!" Manuel heard shipmates calling from another float on his side of the minesweeper. Manuel couldn't swim, but again luck was with him. A life jacket, stencilled *1st Lt*, the one assigned to John Smart, floated in front of him. He grabbed hold.

"Hang on, Scribe!" Carl Jacques shouted from the Carley float.[15] Moments later Jacques had leapt back into the water and hauled Manuel to safety. Behind him, *Esquimalt* burst her bows and sank, taking twenty-eight men to their deaths. It had only been four minutes from the torpedo strike to when the minesweeper disappeared. That left forty-four men, including the captain, Lt Robert MacMillan, fighting to stay alive on open floats. The water temperature was just thirty-eight degrees Fahrenheit.

Terry Manuel watched helplessly as shipmates—wounded in the explosion or oil-soaked from escaping the sweeper—tried to fight off the effects of shock and hypothermia. Nine o'clock came and went without any sign of HMCS *Sarnia* at the rendezvous point. *Esquimalt*'s crew dwindled one by one. Even Manuel's saviour, Carl Jacques, passed out and couldn't be resuscitated. After seven hours, just five men were left on his float, including SLt Mike Kazakoff, who'd taken off his shirt, affixed it to a paddle, and was waving it continuously so they could be spotted.

After hours of paddling, the Carley float containing Joe Wilson managed to reach the Sambro lightship.[16] Rescue aircraft were scrambled from land, and HMCS *Sarnia* raced to the scene. When the sweeper arrived, however, Lt Robert Douty, *Sarnia*'s CO, followed the officially sanctioned course of action by attempting to find the U-boat. Of course, *U190* had long since vacated those waters. Its crew had calculated that there was so much sunken debris off the Nova Scotia coast, ASDIC equipment would never distinguish a U-boat from the debris.

"We went as far inshore as we could," Werner Hirschmann said, "and put ourselves on the bottom to switch off all our equipment . . . and simply wait it out."[17]

Having found no evidence of a U-boat near the Sambro lightship, Douty gave orders for *Sarnia*'s crew to commence rescue operations. But by that time, any of *Esquimalt*'s crewmen who were still alive couldn't lift themselves from the Carley floats, so *Sarnia*'s crew hooked each man by his life jacket to a hoist and lifted him aboard. There, volunteers such as PO Liam Dwyer and the *Sarnia*'s sick-bay team attended to the survivors, while others wrapped the dead in blankets and laid them on deck. There were twenty-three corpses.

"Capt [MacMillan] was gnashing his teeth together so hard," Dwyer said, "I thought he would break them into a thousand pieces. . . . The survivors were retching from the fuel oil they'd swallowed. We had to watch that they didn't choke."[18]

HMCS *Sarnia* steamed full speed to Halifax with twenty-seven comrades from her sister ship barely alive. *Sarnia* picked up nurses and doctors en route through the harbour, then reached the navy docks, where all berths had been cleared of warships. The jetty was jammed with medical personnel and ambulances ready to receive *Esquimalt*'s crew. Hundreds of curious onlookers had also gathered to witness the last act of the rescue.

"[*Sarnia*'s Lt Roland] Hurst put his cap and greatcoat on the surviving commanding officer [MacMillan] and he walked down the gangplank unassisted," Dwyer wrote. "When he was helped into the ambulance the crowd clapped and cheered."

Government of Canada censors prevented publication of the *Esquimalt* sinking or any survivors' stories for three full weeks, until May 7, 1945.

CANADIAN Navy Wren Margaret Los knew that a U-boat had torpedoed and sunk *Esquimalt* before the rest of the country did. Painful as it was to lose navy comrades, Margaret also had to keep the truth from her sister, who'd lost a close chum when the minesweeper went down. But PO Los learned an even more vital war secret that same first week of May 1945. Since her enlistment in the Women's Royal Canadian Naval Service, Los had worked as a Morse code radio operator at HMCS *St. Hyacinthe*, then at RCAF No. 8 Service Flying Training School in New Brunswick, and by early 1944 at a secret facility on a bog across the Petitcodiac River from Moncton.

HMCS *Coverdale* wasn't built on the bog to keep it secret. Its high-frequency direction-finder equipment actually worked better there; the damp ground of the bog provided a better ground plane for receiving radio signals. At *Coverdale* through the late winter and early spring of 1945, Margaret and the other Wren Huff-Duff operators worked day and night, wearing headsets, listening to Morse code transmissions and writing down their contents. They were known as "the listeners."

"We monitored all German submarine traffic," she said. "When they surfaced to pump in sterile air and recharge their batteries, they'd send messages."[19]

Even the U-boats equipped with Schnorchels often took advantage of time on the surface in the middle of the ocean to transmit back to U-boat headquarters in Berlin or Lorient. And occasionally U-boat commanders would dash off weather or location information they assumed Allied intelligence couldn't intercept or decipher.

"They didn't know or didn't believe our equipment could pick them up in the middle of the Atlantic, or even as far away as the Bay of Biscay," Margaret continued. "They also didn't know that [Bletchley Park] had broken their codes."

When a transmission ended and PO Los had finished recording it on paper, a runner took the coded message down the hall to a teletype operator, who relayed its contents to the codebreakers at Bletchley Park in England. On May 4, 1945, Margaret and the listeners at *Coverdale* heard extraordinary news.

"We intercepted [Grossadmiral] Dönitz's message," she said. "It was sent in plain German, informing all their warships that their dear führer had died a hero's death."

Karl Dönitz first received word he'd been chosen successor

to Adolf Hitler on April 30, the very day the führer and Eva Braun (his wife of just twenty-four hours) fulfilled their suicide compact in a bunker in Berlin. Only subsequently did the grand admiral learn that Hitler was dead. So, with details of the suicide in hand and in his new role as Reichpresident, Dönitz aggrandized the announcement of Hitler's "dedication to the struggle," his "battle against the Bolshevist stormflood," and his "hero's death."[20] And that was the transmission that Margaret Los heard in plain German on her Huff-Duff set at *Coverdale* on May 4.

By the end of April, the submariners aboard *U190*, including Werner Hirschmann, had nearly run out of supplies with which to continue operations in Canadian waters. About 300 miles southeast of Newfoundland, his commander, Oblt Hans-Erwin Reith, made the decision to abandon the patrol and head eastward in a bid to return to Bergen or any of the harbours still under German control in Norway, before they ran out of food and fuel. Then came new orders that changed everything.

"We received the [surrender] order by radio from the German High Command to surface," Hirschmann said.[21]

"My U-boat men!" Dönitz announced to his U-Bootwaffe crews in a radio transmission. "A crushing material superiority has forced us into a narrow area. A continuation of our fight is no longer possible. Undefeated and spotless you lay down your arms."[22]

"Our orders," Hirschmann continued, "were to tell the world in open language who we were, and where we were, and to throw our ammunition overboard. In other words, for us, the war was over."[23]

It took nearly a week for *U190* to meet up with Allied

warships off Newfoundland, and therefore to carry out the grand admiral's orders to surrender peacefully. Meantime, news of Hitler's demise had already changed the escort protocols that had governed convoy operations since 1939. For most of the winter in the North Atlantic, AB Bert Jolly had served below decks in the corvette HMCS *Rosthern* as a stoker. Jolly admitted that his eyesight was substandard when he enlisted in March 1944, but the RCN recruiter assessing his application told him, "Stokers don't have to be able to see."[24] Nevertheless, Jolly experienced a revelation that first week of May, when his escort group brought westbound Convoy ON 297 to its final destination.

"The war was nearly over," he said, "and ours was the first convoy going into New York [City] with all its lights on! It was an amazing thing!"

On the verge of VE (Victory in Europe) Day, and with their convoy safely docked in New York, *Rosthern*'s crew got shore leave. They took advantage by going to movies, dances, bars, and even a party on the twenty-first floor of a downtown Manhattan bank. While others attending festivities wore tuxedoes and gowns, Jolly and his four shipmates in their square rigs were readily welcomed as war heroes in the Big Apple.

"If you were in the Service, everything was free," he said. "I went ashore and I think I had five dollars in change on me. I think I still had three dollars when I got back onboard ship."

WHILE it seemed New Yorkers couldn't do enough for visiting Royal Canadian Navy veterans, as the war in Europe ended, the citizens of Halifax largely felt the opposite. After nearly six years of an overwhelming navy presence in their city, many of the 70,000 Haligonians resented the blackouts, rationing, and congestion the war had inflicted on everyday life.

There was no love lost going the other way either. Jim Hazlewood, a lieutenant on HMCS *Dunvegan*, criticized the shopkeepers' attitude toward the 55,000 navy servicemen stationed in their city. "The average guy off a ship, when he went to a store, they didn't treat him very well," he said. "The prices were higher for navy than for anyone else."[25]

Such an accusation would have surprised no one. Not Halifax City Hall. Not Admiralty House, the headquarters of merchant navy operations. Not HMCS *Stadacona*, the navy barracks. Not even the offices of Leonard Murray, Commander-in-Chief Canadian Northwest Atlantic. Even worse, with the end of the war in sight, rumours that navy personnel would "tear Halifax apart" ran rampant.[26] Anticipating the worst, a month before VE Day, Halifax police chief Judson Conrad recommended that the city close all liquor stores the moment victory was announced. In contrast, Mayor Allan Butler encouraged movie houses to remain open for both civilians and naval personnel. And RAdm Murray insisted that the 18,000 servicemen in his command had won the Battle of the Atlantic and had earned the right to celebrate.[27]

Navy officials didn't help matters. On May 7, when word of German capitulation was broadcast, *Stadacona* closed its wet canteen at 9 p.m. So, with "open gangway" in effect (giving sailors freedom to leave the barracks), the navy revellers joined civilian ones downtown. Business owners panicked. Not only did theatres close, so did liquor outlets, shops, and cafés; only sixteen of fifty-five restaurants stayed open. By midnight, more than 12,000 celebrants had flooded downtown Halifax. Some swarmed onto streetcars, taking over the operators' seats, and began crashing the trolleys into each other. The roar of the crowds reached Citadel Hill, where 15,000 community singers were "more decorously celebrating victory"; hundreds of them soon drifted down the hill to investigate the commotion.[28] Meanwhile, police assigned to protect liquor stores were quickly overwhelmed as rioters seized and dispensed more than a thousand cases of beer and wine to fuel the overnight partying.

Then came May 8, the day Winston Churchill had designated for Victory in Europe observances across the Commonwealth. But Halifax faced the same problem it had the day before—a city full of VE Day celebrants with no place to go and no means to celebrate. The navy received the "open gangway" signal yet again when the traditional "Splice the main brace" flags flew from the Admiral's yardarm on the waterfront. So at 1 p.m., when *Stadacona*'s wet canteen ran dry, thousands of sailors looked beyond their barracks to blow off steam again.

That afternoon, Wren signaller Beatrice Schreiber had completed her day's assignments and found herself being escorted by the shore patrol to the Wren barracks at *Stadacona*. There, navy staff had posted "off-limits" signs to prevent celebrants from crashing the Wren dormitories. But that didn't stop the Wrens from organizing a conga line that snaked throughout the barracks while rolls of toilet paper streamed from windows and the rooftop.

"From our top bunks," she wrote, "we watched the shore patrol ushering sailors through *Stadacona* gates, removing bottles from sailors' tunics, and emptying their contents at their feet. . . . The highlight of our VE Day was when a sailor appeared from nowhere, riding a horse through the front door of our Wren block."[29]

As large as the growing crowds became, things could have been worse. There were warships inbound to Halifax Harbour that day. Among them, LCdr Ted Briggs and the crew of HMCS *New Waterford* had just completed a transatlantic convoy, and all onboard anticipated well-deserved shore leave in the city. When Briggs learned about the chaos downtown, he promptly turned the frigate around and sailed her thirty miles out to sea, "cracked open the rum ration for his crew and kept them out there for a couple of days."[30] *New Waterford* was not alone; by mid-afternoon every ship that could move was ordered to sea.[31]

Downtown Halifax was a contrast in war-ending festivities. At the entrance to Keith's Brewery, a thousand civilian and service celebrants pushed in the main gates, ran past shore patrolmen, and plundered the facility's kegs and cases of beer. Within minutes, 140 Provost Corps and city police officers had arrived to reinforce the shore patrol. They jammed a six-ton army truck into the gateway, but rioters pushed the vehicle out of the way, rushed past the police, and "liberated" 120,000 quart-bottles of beer.[32]

Six blocks away, on Citadel Hill, Mayor Butler, RAdm Murray, and other dignitaries presided at a sedate VE Day ceremony that drew several thousand people giving thanks for the defeat of Nazi Germany. During the observance, the mayor learned the brewery was under siege and pleaded with Murray to act. At 2:30 p.m., as the Citadel Hill event ended, Murray organized a parade of 375 navy personnel to march through the centre of the city in an attempt to restore order.[33] The show of strength backfired. As paradesmen marched along Barrington Street, the rioters pushed, shoved, and intimidated them by waving bottles of liquor under their noses or showering them with the contents. Between the Citadel and *Stadacona*, nearly a third of the parade of sailors disappeared into the crowd.

David MacDonald, a Halifax teenager who habitually ran to the top of Citadel Hill to watch Atlantic convoys leave the harbour, ran downtown to see what was happening. He was offered liquor, watched storefront windows being smashed, and saw stolen mink coats and expensive shoes tossed in the gutter. "There was an animal loose down there," he said.[34]

Amid the violence downtown, PO Rodine Buckley-Beevers Egan completed her watch. After ensuring her clerical staff were safe and secure inside the Wrens' *Stadacona* barracks, she made her way crosstown to her matrimonial flat. Surprisingly, she found the Zellers store on Barrington still open. She entered, made a few purchases, and made her way back through the front door, where she came face to face with a drunken sailor holding a lit torch.

"What do you think you're doing?" she shouted at him.

"We're going to torch this place," he said.

Having once taken a fellow petty officer to task for misogynist remarks, PO Buckley-Beevers Egan said, "Oh no, you're not!" And she blocked the sailor's path in the doorway. There was a tense momentary standoff. Then, likely anticipating less resistance somewhere else, the sailor moved on.[35]

At 6 p.m., RAdm Murray resorted to personally touring the downtown area at the vanguard of a convoy of trucks bristling with shore patrolmen. He used a loudspeaker to entreat his "lads" to return to their barracks and for citizens to go home. Meantime, a thousand soldiers made their way from a base in Debert, Nova Scotia, to restore order and enforce a newly imposed civic curfew on the city.

"The Navy by its action this day has undone [its] good reputation in Halifax for the last six years," Murray scolded his fellow servicemen.[36]

WHEN the rioting ended, three people were dead, parts of downtown Halifax—pretty much unscathed by the war—lay in ruins, and an extraordinary navy man's career was in tatters. In the days immediately following the riots, scores of conscience-stricken citizens called police to come and collect loot they had "just found in the backyard."[37] The mayor spoke on the radio about "the great crime" that Haligonians would never forget.[38] On May 10, the *Halifax Herald* editorialized that "the day that should have brought vast rejoicing [instead] brought madness and terror and destruction."[39] RAdm Murray tried to deflect criticism with his claim that "civilians led the assault and encouraged service personnel to take part."[40] But by May 12, the Mackenzie King government had appointed Supreme Court judge Roy Kellock to investigate the disturbance and to answer two key questions: How could such a thing happen? And who was responsible?

Two months later, the government received Kellock's *Report on the Halifax Disorders*, which described in detail the roughly $5 million in property losses—564 businesses damaged, 2,624 windows broken, 55,392 quarts of spirits looted from the liquor commission, and 30,516 quarts of beer taken from Keith's Brewery. Charges resulting from arrests over two days included 152 service personnel for drunkenness and 117 civilians for disorder. Judge Kellock assigned blame to Naval

Command for its "passive conduct"; in other words, RAdm Murray's inability to restrain his sailors.

Not all Royal Canadian Navy veterans agreed with the royal commission's findings, among them LCdr Anthony Griffin, who'd served aboard escorts in and out of Halifax throughout the war. "A miscarriage of justice," Griffin wrote in a memoir. "The real culprit was the Government of Canada."[41]

Griffin listed some of the common grievances his own crews had registered throughout the war. He blamed federal authorities for not recognizing that Halifax had become a wartime city, that it had suffered hopelessly from overcrowding, that naval personnel had faced exploitation, gouging, and insufficient access to outlets for entertainment. He contended that Ottawa should have declared Halifax a closed city—with entry only by permit—with fixed rents, more plentiful living quarters, and barracks that catered realistically to the needs of warship crews ashore.

"To put the blame on Murray," Griffin wrote finally, "[was] political cowardice."

Within the year, Leonard Murray, who declined to implicate any subordinate officers in his command, accepted full responsibility for the disorder and resigned.[42] A career that began in 1911 in that very city at the Royal Naval College, that saw Murray rise to become the C-in-C Northwest Atlantic, that included victory over Grossadmiral Karl Dönitz and his U-boats in the Battle of the Atlantic, was dashed overnight by a celebration run amok. The champion of the perennially under-equipped but overachieving Canadian escorts was forever blamed for the Halifax VE Day riots—an event often dubbed "Murray's folly." At age fifty, Leonard Murray left his native Nova Scotia for good. He moved to England, where he was eventually called to the bar and practised law in Admiralty Courts. RAdm Leonard Warren Murray died in 1971, virtually forgotten by the country and the armed service to which he'd devoted most of his professional life.

His adversary, Grossadmiral Dönitz, was arrested at the Reich's ad hoc seat of government in Flensburg on May 23, 1945. He was tried for war crimes by the International Military Tribunal at Nuremberg in 1946. Guilty on two of three counts, he was sentenced to ten years in Spandau Prison. He was released in 1956 and died in 1980 at Aumühle.

By rights, the only Canadian to command an Allied theatre during the Second World War should have been savouring victory that spring of 1945. The same day that his navy servicemen chose to join rioting civilians in tearing Halifax apart, RAdm Leonard Murray's arch-enemies, the German submariners and their commanders, began surrendering their U-boats all over the Atlantic. A/PO Carman Eldridge and his HMCS *North Bay* shipmates were among the many Canadian crews to suddenly receive those surrendered U-boats. Several days out of St. John's, escorting Convoy SC 174, *North Bay* learned the war was over. The commanding officer of the corvette, LCdr Alexander Campbell, immediately ordered "Up Spirits," a tot of rum for the entire crew, even as the convoy neared its destination.

"As we approached Londonderry," Eldridge wrote, "German submarines were popping up to surrender, and [we] started herding them into port."[43] In early May, Allied warships warily escorted eight U-boats from the eastern Atlantic and fourteen from the Arctic into Londonderry.[44] In stark contrast to the green rolling fields, the whitewashed cottages, and the ruins of a centuries-old castle, the U-boats—gun-grey and each flying the black flag of surrender—glided to their final port of call. "Sailing up River Foyle," Eldridge continued, "we saw many more subs tied to buoys along the river. It was unbelievable!"[45]

By the end of the month, Allied warships had intercepted and escorted ninety U-boats into UK ports. Forty-seven were surrendered at German or Norwegian ports, while five arrived at American harbours, one in Newfoundland, and another one in Canada.[46] Just before dark on May 10, an American Liberator spotted *U889* surfacing about 250 miles southeast of Cape Race, Newfoundland. Several Canadian escorts accompanying Convoy SC 175 altered course and found the U-boat stopped on the surface, her crew displaying the mandated large black flag of surrender.

Aboard the corvette HMCS *Dunvegan*, Signals Officer Jim Hazlewood coded a message in German for *U889*'s commander, Kptlt Friedrich Braeucker, to accept Canadian crewmen aboard and to join an escort of warships to Bay Bulls, Newfoundland.

"We gave them a course and speed and told the captain that if they deviated more than two degrees we'd open fire," Hazlewood said.

HMCS *Dunvegan* and three other RCN warships were then positioned forward and aft the U-boat as it proceeded to Newfoundland. And all four Canadian crews remained at action stations for forty hours straight, all with armament at the ready, while the U-boat remained under escort.[47] Hazlewood stayed in communication with Kptlt Braeucker into the evening.

"At 7 o'clock that night," Hazlewood said, "the captain came up onto the conning tower and flashed the message across, 'And so to bed. Goodnight.' We learned later that he'd graduated from Oxford University and spoke better English than we did."

Overnight, the U-boat and her Canadian escorts received orders to proceed instead to Shelburne, Nova Scotia. The redirection likely resulted when Canadian authorities chose to take advantage of a ready-made propaganda opportunity. Both the King government and RCN brass recognized that *U889* was about to surrender to a North American port. The precedent, they calculated, might as well be a Canadian one. Ashore in Shelburne, the navy assembled an escort of corvettes, Fairmile launches, and a boarding party of navy patrolmen to race out to receive and record *U889*'s surrender, and then bring the U-boat into the harbour.

In early 1945, AB Martin Franchetto, previously an ASDIC operator aboard HMCS *Moncton*, had transferred to Motor Launch *Q118*, a Fairmile sub-chaser stationed in Nova Scotia. As *U889* made her way under escort toward Shelburne, Franchetto and his shipmates took navy patrolmen aboard their Fairmile, as well as some unexpected passengers, to the rendezvous point outside the harbour.

"Our job was to take the boarding party and a National Film Board camera crew out to accept the official surrender," Franchetto wrote.[48]

He was stationed at the Fairmile's 20mm Oerlikon guns, just in case any of the submariners suddenly became hostile during the surrender. To ensure Franchetto and his crew did not get carried away by pent-up animosity for the submariners, the navy had taken further precautions. Franchetto's

Oerlikon guns were purposely not loaded, his drum of ammunition sitting on the deck beside him. And an RCN officer stood next to Franchetto with a loaded 45-calibre Webley pistol at the ready.

"His orders were to shoot me if I attempted to fire on the Germans," Franchetto continued. "Our feelings against the Nazis were so bitter, that it wouldn't have taken much to shoot those SOBs."

As things turned out, the officer minding Franchetto almost needed to restrain the Oerlikon gunner from opening fire on fellow Canadians. When *Q118* and her sister Fairmile *Q117* arrived at the surrender position, Franchetto watched in frustration as the navy patrolmen boarded the U-boat to disarm the Germans. In hot pursuit, the NFB crew and a pack of reporters dashed aboard the sub to film and take notes while RCN LCdr Gus Miles accepted Kptlt Braeucker's surrender of *U889*. As cigarettes were passed to the smiling Germans and the filmmakers fussed over the defeated crew as if they were celebrities, Franchetto started a slow burn. An Italian-born immigrant to Canada, he'd initially not been allowed to enlist because the Royal Canadian Navy considered him an alien immigrant (his native Italy was originally an Axis ally). Finally accepted as a loyal Canadian, Franchetto worked his way up to service in the Battle of the Atlantic. He'd seen too many RCN comrades die at sea, including his good friend Alec Templeton, who went down in HMCS *Valleyfield* in 1944. And here were his enemies, finally surrendering but being treated like heroes by the Canadian reporters and movie crew.

"I'd like to have given them a burst [from the Oerlikon guns] for Alec," he told a Shelburne reporter later. "All I wanted was a crack at just one sub."

Ultimately, however, the only shots taken as *U889* surrendered were those by news and NFB cameras of the U-boat crew being frisked, Kptlt Braeucker officially surrendering, and the hoisting of the RCN White Ensign atop the U-boat's halyards. That gesture seemed to placate the patriotic Martin Franchetto.

Also off the Newfoundland coast, HMCS *Thorlock* and *Victoriaville* had intercepted *U190* at sea and taken the surrender from her commander, Oblt Hans-Erwin Reith, and fifty-four crewmen. The Canadian warships then escorted *U190* to the outport at Bay Bulls. Aboard that U-boat, thirty RCN patrolmen oversaw a handful of German submariners and engineer Werner Hirschmann as they manoeuvred the submarine into the Newfoundland port to surrender. As disheartening as the Kriegsmarine defeat felt, Hirschmann soon recognized that his survival meant more. He had always considered the U-boat crews Germany's elite force, and he was surprised to discover that many in the RCN offered him deference.

"The commanding officer of the Canadian frigate [*Victoriaville*] that took us to Halifax had his lunch with us," Hirschmann said. "The enormous respect shown us by our Canadian custodians was surprising and appreciated."[49]

At a POW camp near Gravenhurst, Ontario, Hirschmann felt he and his fellow prisoners were being treated like guests in the country. Conditions proved tolerable, and the available services—including access to the Eaton's catalogue to purchase clothing—amazed even the most jaded German POWs. The Canadian camp commander even insisted that German prisoners continue to wear their uniforms and service medals, because to him they were still German servicemen. Postwar, Hirschmann immigrated to Canada, and in his seventies he was invited by survivors of the HMCS *Esquimalt* sinking to the anniversary observance of the climax of the Battle of the Atlantic. He met Joe Wilson, one of the twenty-seven Canadians who'd survived the attack in April 1945. It was the first time Hirschmann had heard from a survivor about the suffering that *U190*'s acoustic torpedo had caused. The two men shook hands and embraced.

"We German submariners, like all other sailors in the war . . . were just ordinary human beings swept [up] by historical events," Hirschmann said.

"He did his duty, the same as I did mine," Wilson said at the time. "He was just lucky and I was not."

The two former enemies became friends for the rest of their lives. Joe Wilson died in 2012, just before his ninetieth birthday, and was buried at sea; in 2019, Werner Hirschmann died at ninety-six as a Canadian citizen.

In stark contrast to Hirschmann's long life, a catastrophic number of his U-boat comrades never made it home from the war, much less to old age. The U-Bootwaffe—what Hirshmann had called Germany's elite force—sent 40,900 sailors to sea in 830 operational U-boats (in fact, 1,162 were built) between 1939 and 1945. Of those U-boats, the Allies destroyed 696, an operational loss of 83.9 percent. Even more catastrophic were the submariner casualties—25,870 killed in their "iron coffins," and another 5,000 captured and imprisoned—76 percent of U-boat personnel lost. It was the largest service loss of the war.[50]

✪ ✪ ✪

MARTIN Franchetto, the man with his hands on the Oerlikon guns overseeing *U889*'s surrender in Shelburne Harbour, never realized his wish for a crack at a sub. But his comrades did. Once *U190* reached Bay Bulls and Oblt Reith had signed an unconditional surrender to the flag officer on May 19, 1945, the U-boat was commissioned into the Royal Canadian Navy. The RCN handed over *U190*'s Enigma machine to the Department of National Defence, and her periscope to the Crow's Nest Officers' Club in St. John's. Then, in the fall of 1947, RCN warships towed *U190* to the scene of her last action—the sinking of HMCS *Esquimalt* off Sambro lightship.

"She will be destroyed in an anti-submarine exercise," Brooke Claxton, Canada's minister of national defence, had announced in July 1947.[51]

And so an array of Canadian military executioners arrived off Halifax on October 21 to send *U190* to the bottom, avenging HMCS *Esquimalt*'s thirty-nine dead crewmen. Overhead, eight Seafire, eight Firefly, two Anson, and two Swordfish military aircraft circled with their rockets aimed, while a flotilla of RCN warships—HMCS *Nootka*, *Haida*, and *New Liskeard*—lined up to deliver the *coup de grâce* with naval guns and Hedgehog. Operation Scuttled was planned as a synchronized exercise.[52] However, moments after the aircraft launched their first rockets, *U190* pointed her bows into the air and slipped under.

The scuttling of *U190* exacted some revenge for members of the Royal Canadian Navy, who saw twenty-four of their warships sunk in the Atlantic campaign. Among them, *Fraser*, lost off Saint-Valery-en-Caux in 1940; *Athabaskan*, sunk while defending the western flank of Operation Neptune; and *Alberni*, *Regina*, and *Trentonian* sunk while guarding supply lines to the armies in Normandy. *Louisburg* and *Weyburn* were taken down during Operation Torch in the Mediterranean. Then *Bras d'Or*, *Charlottetown*, *Chedabucto*, *Clayoquot*, *Esquimalt*, *Otter*, *Raccoon*, and *Shawinigan* were destroyed in defence of North American coastal waters. *Guysborough*, *Lévis*, *Margaree*, *Ottawa*, *Skeena*, *St. Croix*, *Spikenard*, *Valleyfield*, and *Windflower* were lost during escort duties along convoy routes. And the human casualties in those warships: 2,024 Canadians dead, 319 wounded, and ninety-five captured and imprisoned.[53]

FATE or kismet or chance or luck spared Gordon Baines from becoming a wartime statistic. From the moment he joined the navy, the young rating from Montreal paid close attention to the things that mattered. He put in extra time at his communications training. He documented his service in black-and-white photographs. He stayed in touch with his parents. He wrote regularly to his girlfriend, whom he nicknamed "Bright Eyes." And Hazel Le Cras dutifully wrote back to her "Boy Blue." Meantime, telegraphist Baines moved from convoy duty aboard HMCS *Amherst* and *Medicine Hat* through additional training ashore in Halifax and St. John's. When their long-distance relationship flagged, Gordon made the extra effort to win Hazel back. And in 1942, when his mother suddenly fell ill, he sought compassionate leave from HMCS *Avalon* in St. John's to attend to her at home in Montreal.

"He took the train from St. John's to Port-aux-Basques, then crossed to Sydney on the ferry SS *Caribou*," his son Grant said. "Before he left Sydney, he bought a return ticket on the *Caribou* back to Newfoundland."[54]

Baines's mother was more ill than he realized. He needed

to stay on longer in Montreal and asked for an extension of his leave. The navy granted him an extra seven days. It meant he would not be using that return ticket on the ferry crossing Cabot Strait back to Newfoundland.

"Good thing," his son Grant Baines said. "The ticket was booked for October 14 [1942]. He should've been on board the ferry . . . the night the *Caribou* was torpedoed and sunk."

Good fortune continued to favour Gordon Baines. He survived the Battle of the Atlantic, got a sought-after promotion, and got the girl of his dreams. Hazel Le Cras, by 1944 a member of the Royal Canadian Women's Naval Service, and Probationary Sub-Lieutenant Gordon Baines were married in October 1944. Gordon used his RCNVR pension to continue his education at Toronto's Ryerson Institute of Technology after the war and tucked that unused *Caribou* ferry ticket away—perhaps as a good-luck charm, but very much a piece of history.

It took many more postwar years before Cliff Perry discovered his brush with death. The Canadian sub-lieutenant had actually defied the odds a number of times while serving in the Royal Navy during the Battle of the Atlantic. In 1943, as an ASDIC officer aboard HMS *Westcott*, he'd survived winter gales and U-boat attacks on perhaps the deadliest convoy route of the war, into the Arctic to Murmansk in the Soviet Union. And in December of that year, the *Scharnhorst* targeted his convoy in what turned out to be the German battleship's final patrol. In the summer of 1944, Perry moved to HMS *Stayner* under LCdr Harry Hall.

"Hall had become one of the best anti-submarine commanders in the British Navy," Perry wrote in his memoirs. "He had earned his spurs in the North Atlantic, the Mediterranean, and on the Russian convoys."

In August 1944, *Stayner* moved to the English Channel to keep any lone-wolf U-boats from interfering with supply traffic to the Mulberry harbour at Arromanches in France. While not expecting any trouble, on August 4 *Stayner* and her sister ship HMS *Wensleydale* made a contact off Beachy Head. The Admiralty told Hall it was probably a wreck and to move on, but he persisted and began a box-pattern search. For the next twenty-four hours, *Stayner* kept up the search; at one point, unessential crew stood down while SLt Perry and his captain continued tracking.

"Dropping depth charges . . . we made several passes, lost the echo and started all over again," Perry wrote. "As the waters settled, a circle of oil bubbled to the surface. . . . One-by-one survivors started to surface. Only twelve of the German crew made it."

Years later, civilian Cliff Perry attended an international news conference in Toronto. He was introduced to a German newspaperman. The two men, about the same age, discovered they were both veterans—the German a submariner, the Canadian a sub-chaser.

"Did you have any personal experience with U-boats?" the man asked Perry.

"Yes," Perry said, but felt reluctant to get into details.

The German insisted. Perry had little choice but to offer his account of the chase and destruction of the U-boat in the English Channel. He couldn't get past the man's piercing blue eyes, which were fixed on him throughout his telling. When he'd finished, the German asked for the date, place, and U-boat number.

"August 5, 1944, off Beachy Head," Perry said. "It was *U671*."

There was a brief pause before his acquaintance said, "You are lucky to be alive, Herr Perry. You thought that there was only one U-boat. But there were two. And I was in command of the second one. We had you in our sights, but we had to leave. We were out of torpedoes."

Nan Adair remembered only one close call at Bletchley Park. While the Blitz left the GC&CS unscathed—principally because German intelligence had no idea the location had any significance—decoding staff such as Nan still routinely experienced bombing alerts. Yet only one Luftwaffe bomb fell on GC&CS during the entire war.[55]

"It made a big hole in the ground next to intelligence Hut 4, but that was all," she said.[56] The prospect of being a target for German bombers never fazed Nan or any of her decoding co-workers. But the so-called Bletchley geese* were always reminded by navy lecturers how critical and secretive their service was. They had all signed the Official Secrets Act, but their allegiance was pretty much self-regulated. So, when the war ended and Bletchley officials asked Nan to stay on—trying to break Russian military codes—she still couldn't explain to her family what war work she'd been doing the past four years.

"It was tough for me living at home, because my father was an ex-military man," she said. "And having a daughter who wasn't in uniform didn't go down too well. He had no idea what I was doing. And he died before I could ever tell him."

* Winston Churchill dubbed the personnel at Bletchley Park "the geese who laid the golden egg and never cackled." (Marion Hill, *Bletchley Park People: Churchill's Geese That Never Cackled* [Stroud, UK: Sutton, 2004], prologue.)

In contrast to Cliff Perry's close call in the English Channel, Ken Davy only saw one U-boat while in the service. When the riots began in Halifax on May 7 and 8 and the navy decided to vacate the harbour, his long-endurance corvette, HMCS *Forest Hill*, left Halifax for Shelburne. He got there in time to see *U889* arrive and surrender.

"It was the first time I'd seen the enemy," he said. "There were Germans on the jetty. And I thought, 'They don't look like superman at all.'"[57]

Davy grew up with water all around him, along Hamilton Harbour at the west end of Lake Ontario. He volunteered late in the war, in 1944, when he was seventeen, and all they needed then were sick bay attendants (SBAs). Still, he took great pride in his work as an SBA, or Tiffy, aboard *Forest Hill* on the Triangle Run. He coped with all his shipmates' maladies, from appendicitis to seasickness to venereal disease. And since the RCN had grown to become the fourth-largest navy in the world (after the US, Britain, and the Soviet Union) by 1945[58]—to more than 400 fighting ships (900 vessels in all) and over 100,000 men and women in uniform—Davy hoped there'd be a future in the service. And right after VJ (Victory over Japan) Day in August 1945, he witnessed the navy's vision of the future.

"I was riding the streetcar past the foot of Wellington Street [in Hamilton]," he said. "And I thought I saw my ship. That Sunday I went down, and it was *Forest Hill*."

Allied shipyards—in the UK and Canada—had manufactured 269 corvettes for active service during the Second World War; 123 had come from shipbuilders in British Columbia, Ontario, Quebec, and the Maritimes. But the Royal Canadian Navy's acquisition of light aircraft carriers, cruisers, and destroyers in 1944 and 1945 signalled its transition from an escort navy of emergency-built ships to a balanced fleet of modern warships with advanced weapon systems. In addition, Mackenzie King's "Minister of Everything," C.D. Howe, did not see either Canadian shipping or homegrown shipbuilding as promising industries.*[59] That left RCN's aging and obsolete wartime fleet high and dry. Within several years of the end of the war, all the corvettes except HMCS *Sackville* had been acquired by other navies, sold into merchant service, or scrapped.

"I saw them all tied up at Stelco [Steel Company of Canada] and different parts of [Hamilton] Harbour. They were just chopping them up for scrap." SBA Ken Davy had made it through the war, but his ship hadn't.

THE Battle of the Atlantic lasted for five years, eight months, and five days. Between September 1939 and May 1945, merchant ships completed 25,343 voyages—delivering more than 165 million tons of cargo from North America to the United Kingdom—under Canadian escort. Securing that cargo bridge came with a toll. In addition to the 2,438 RCN casualties, the battle claimed 752 airmen of the Royal Canadian Air Force. Costlier still in that vital campaign, Allied merchant navies lost 2,233 ships[60] (fifty-eight of them Canadian[61]). Lives lost among Allied merchant navies exceeded 30,000. Of 12,000 Canadians who served in the merchant navy, 1,146 lost their lives—one seafarer in eight. Another 198 became POWs overseas.[62]

---

* During Howe's time as minister, Canada manufactured 600 ships; 12,000 aircraft; 85,000 heavy guns; and 500,000 vehicles—more military vehicles than Germany, Italy, and Japan combined.

For the navy dead, Canadians readily observed their Remembrance Days thereafter in silence and reverence. And for those navy wounded or POWs who survived long enough to recite "They shall grow not old" to their dead comrades on November 11, Canada's pension architects established a safety net of medical, financial, land grant, and educational compensation for the veterans or surviving spouses. However, at war's end, the thousands of Canadian Merchant Navy sailors—who'd run the U-boat gauntlet most often, with the least armament, on the slowest ships, and who'd gone off the payroll the moment their ship was sunk—were officially refused equal status with their navy brothers and sisters. The Department of Veterans Affairs questioned merchant mariners' "veteranhood," considered them civilian mercenaries, not front-line veterans, and denied them the benefits that navy servicemen and women began receiving in 1945.

That judgment made men such as Bob Rae feel like an outcast, even in his own family. His brother Jim had enlisted in the navy, and his brother John in the RCAF. At war's end they came home to Leaside, in Toronto, and were celebrated as veterans receiving all the benefits befitting their service. But Bob returned from continuous merchant navy service, from 1943 to 1945, as a chief radio operator in the Canadian Park ships, and all he got was a cold shoulder from federal bureaucrats.

"Hoping to accumulate all the requirements for deep-sea service, I applied for an education grant," Rae said. "And I got a letter back saying, 'You're already a skilled radio operator. We can't give you anything.'"[63]

At the start of the war, Rae had tried to get into the Air Force, and while he waited for word, he took a job handling nitroglycerine at a munitions plant in Nobel, Ontario. Just eighteen and impressionable, he'd read newspaper stories and seen photographs of merchant sailors rescued from sunken cargo ships and burning tankers, coming ashore in Halifax with nothing. Seemingly broken, homeless, and alone, they kept returning to the sea to continue their wartime service.

"I thought, 'That takes courage,'" he said. "I said to myself, 'I want to do my part in the Merchant Navy, where men are needed now.'"

While he continued his war work in northern Ontario, he studied radio operation and Morse code by correspondence and got his licence at the Electronics Institute of Canada in 1942. Then, with his release from essential work at the nitroglycerine plant, he raced to Montreal to get a job aboard a merchantman. His service took him to Australia, Fiji, New Zealand, and eventually aboard cargo ships on the North Atlantic run between Canada and Britain. As senior radio operator, Rae handled all radio communications; as well, if his vessel were torpedoed and sinking, he could not abandon ship until he'd fulfilled one final act of duty.

"We had these metal containers with British Admiralty Merchant Shipping Instructions—BAMSI—and the Canadian equivalent—CAMSI. These were the books of all our codes," he said, adding that if they were sinking, "it was my job to stow the code books in the boxes—all with big holes in them—and pitch them overboard so they wouldn't be captured. It was the last thing [I would have to do]. And then I'd hammer out an S.O.S."[64]

Rae's ships—SS *Green Gables Park* and SS *Portland Park*—faced their share of U-boats during North Atlantic convoys in 1944 and '45. But in all his trips he never had to heave those secret code books overboard or telegraph that final distress call. He'd successfully completed all his transatlantic sailings, delivering the cargo to the UK to help Britons survive and fuel the Allies' liberation drive deeper into Europe. And at the end of the war, the Mackenzie King government made it clear it wanted merchant sailors to stay with their shipping companies to keep Canadian seagoing commerce thriving. That's when Rae approached the Department of Veterans Affairs about assistance to upgrade his radio skills and to improve himself. That's when they told him he didn't qualify as a veteran.

"What's the use?" Rae said at the time. Even when he received his Battle of the Atlantic service awards, he thought, "These medals don't mean a thing. And I threw them in a box in the bottom of a drawer . . . for forty years."

Not until the 1980s, when merchant navy advocates organized themselves into such lobby groups as the Canadian Merchant Navy Association, did attitudes change. It would take nearly another decade of additional legal presentations, more Senate committee debate, compromises among diverse veterans' advocate groups, lobbying for public attention via media coverage, and even a hunger strike on the footsteps of Parliament Hill to push the federal government to deliver equality to merchant navy veterans. In June 1992, Ottawa finally recognized merchant sailors' service on a par with that of their wartime military comrades in the army, air force, and navy. They were officially "veterans." And in February 2000, fifty-five years after helping to deliver victory in the Battle of the Atlantic, merchant navy veterans began receiving some of the $50 million compensation allocated by Veterans Affairs.[65]

Achieving veteran status and receiving long overdue pensions felt like redemption for those merchant navy vets who'd survived that long. But veteran radio operator Bob Rae felt greater satisfaction on Remembrance Day 1994, when he and his comrades were invited to the Memorial Chamber inside the Peace Tower on Parliament Hill. At nine o'clock that morning, the first ever Merchant Navy Book of Remembrance—containing the names of merchant navy sailors killed in both the Great War and the Second World War—was officially unveiled. As he stood there, wearing his medals recovered from that discarded box in the drawer and reflecting in the minutes of silence, Rae remembered the horror of merchant ships having to scatter because U-boats had overrun their convoy. A comrade's goodbye still haunted him.

"A radio operator said the last he heard from his chum on another ship was, 'So long, Rod,' as his ship was going down. . . . I have nothing but the greatest admiration for my fellow merchant navy men. They paid an awful price."[66]

UNLIKE the siege at Hong Kong in 1941, Operation Jubilee at Dieppe in 1942, the Dam Buster raid by Bomber Command, and the Christmas battle for Ortona, Italy, in 1943, or the D-Day invasion of Normandy and the clearing of the Scheldt through 1944—all Second World War battles in which Canadians played significant roles—the Battle of the Atlantic did not happen on a single geographical battlefield. There was no assault up a single beach, no house-to-house combat in a fabled city, no clearing of a fortified seaport, no seizing of a pivotal ridge. The Battle of the Atlantic was waged across 4,000 miles of ocean. Nor was there a single hour or day when the clash to save or sink Atlantic shipping was won or lost.

The U-Bootwaffe of the Kriegsmarine enjoyed two so-called Happy Times, when its technology and tactics delivered significant victories over Allied convoys and their escorts. In response, when hunter escorts chased U-boats to exhaustion, when Ultra cracked Enigma, and when VLR aircraft bridged the Black Pit, Allied naval strategists tasted victory too. But these moments were countermeasures or counteroffensives, not knockout blows. And while remembrance observances after the war bring veterans and others to cenotaphs across Canada on the first Sunday of every May, the Battle of the Atlantic is more commonly recognized as the longest continuing battle of the war. Its principal recording historians—Marc Milner and Roger Sarty in Canada, Jürgen Rohwer in Germany, and Richard Holmes in Britain—generally agree it was a battle of peaks and valleys, and therefore occupies no single place or moment for commemoration in war history.

By remaining such a continuous, unresolved, and unrelenting struggle without resolution for five years, eight months, and five days, its significance is rooted in its combatants' achieved objectives and in those not achieved. The Germans' aim initially was to choke to nothing, if possible, the flow of goods into Britain. Grossadmiral Karl Dönitz calculated that 300 active combat U-boats in the North Atlantic and their "effective U-boat quotient," an average of 900 tons of shipping sunk per U-boat per day, were the keys to victory. His wolf packs delivered that at times in mid-1941 and early 1942. And since the U-Bootwaffe remained the most potent arm of the Reich for the longest, its U-boats posed the greatest threat to Britain's survival in the short run and to any Allied hope of turning the tide of the war in the long run.

For the Allies, then, the Battle of the Atlantic was the centre of gravity. Keeping the UK un-invaded initially, then alive with a lifeline of survival essentials, and, ultimately, reinforced enough to one day launch the greatest amphibious military assault in history against Hitler's Fortress Europe, were the objectives. The navies of Britain, Canada, and the United States therefore had to gain and maintain mastery over Britain's shipping routes. As historian Holmes contended, without ultimate victory over the U-boats and a sustained supply for the war effort in the UK and the USSR, there could have been no D-Day, nor a VE-Day. "You win at sea first," he said, "and having secured the sea, you may then hope to win on land."[67]

To that end, despite the odds against them, the Atlantic convoys delivered on average 90,000 tons of war supplies to Britain every day.[68] A single small merchantman could carry 2,000 tons of steel; gun carriers, trucks, and motorcycles enough to motorize an infantry battalion; bombs to fill 225 heavy bombers to capacity; and timber and plywood, wallboard, and nails to build ninety-four four-room houses; it also had space on an afterdeck for two bombers or in its hold for enough aluminum to build 310 medium bombers or 740 fighter aircraft.[69] A single American Liberty ship (comparable to a Canadian Park ship) carried the equivalent of 300 freight cars.[70]

But as well as the need to fuel and fortify Britain's war effort, Allied merchant carriers and the warships escorting them had to feed the forty-one million civilians of the British Isles with nearly everything they consumed. Among the convoy columns of fuel-oil tankers and war munitions freighters that ran the gauntlet of Atlantic gales and U-boat torpedoes, most eastbound convoys included merchant ships loaded with food staples for British citizens. Typical contents aboard a single 10,000-ton (Canadian) Park ship were impressive—enough flour, cheese, bacon, ham, and canned and dried goods to feed a quarter-million people in the UK for a week.[71] That kind of manifest proved as precious a cargo as bullets and aviation fuel.

And after 1941, convoys originating at Sydney and Halifax in Nova Scotia also included containers marked "Milk for Britain," thanks to members of the Kin Canada service club. Its founder, Hal Rogers, had organized the War Services Committee and challenged Kin Canada members to raise funds to ship milk to kids in Britain. Between 1941 and 1948 the club raised $3 million, which ensured that over fifty million quarts of powdered milk regularly arrived for British children.[72]

"Food rationing was the main bugbear," Nicholas Masheter wrote, "everyone issued with ration books . . . and individuals limited to meager weekly portions."[73]

As they had at the outbreak of the war, the Masheter family members—Alix and Ted and their young son, Nicholas—in the final stages of the war remained hunkered down at their home in Sutton, on the outskirts of Birmingham. Because of his expertise as a rubber technologist, Ted Masheter served during the war as a liaison officer between the British and American Raw Materials Commissions. He commuted between the UK and North America, and for a time the family moved to Canada, joining Alix's family in Fenelon Falls, Ontario. But as D-Day loomed in 1944, the family boarded a troopship in a slow convoy to Liverpool.

Back home, they coped with blackouts, ration books, mending, and making do. Nicholas, born in 1939, remembered that rationing meant one egg per person every two weeks, and that fresh foods such as milk, sugar, vegetables, and meat (unless they raised them themselves) were rarely on the family dinner table. So, reconstituted foods, such as dried eggs, dehydrated juice, and Kin Canada's powdered milk, became staples. If Nicholas hadn't learned for himself, his parents, the newspapers, and Britain's leadership certainly emphasized why his country had made it through the war, and how the war was won.

"Survival had very largely depended on the efforts and sacrifice of the merchant seamen who braved the Atlantic crossings," he said. "And I know we were perhaps more aware of the heroic efforts of the escort ships than some, due to my uncle [Shaw Harris, stoker aboard HMCS *Wetaskiwin*] tossing about in his corvette on the Atlantic for the whole of the war."

Notes

Abbreviations

BdU KTB: U-boat Command War Diary
LAC: Library and Archives Canada
NID: Naval Intelligence Division
NAC: National Archives of Canada; now Library and Archives Canada (LAC)
DHH: Department of National Defence, Directorate of History and Heritage

Chapter One: Calm Before the Storm

1. Norman Longmate, *How We Lived Then: A History of Everyday Life During the Second World War* (London: Hutchinson, 1971), 13.
2. "Chamberlain Announces Britain Is at War with Germany," History of the BBC, September 3, 1939, https://www.bbc.com/history-ofthebbc/anniversaries/september/war-announced.
3. Longmate, *How We Lived Then*, 49.
4. "The Evacuation of Children during the Second World War," History Press, n.d., https://www.thehistorypress.co.uk/articles/the-evacuation-of-children-during-the-second-world-war/.
5. "Evacuation of Children."
6. Alix Masheter, to her father, September 4, 1939. Courtesy Jane McAllister.
7. Libby-Jane Charleston, "UK Population Survey of 1939 Holds Secrets of Pre-War Life," *Huffington Post*, July 11, 2015, https://www.huffingtonpost.com.au/2015/11/07/history-world-war_n_8485272.html.

8. Longmate, *How We Lived Then*, 30.
9. Longmate, 141.
10. Longmate, 141.
11. Longmate, 145.
12. Longmate, 146.
13. Masheter to father.
14. John Boileau, "Canada's Merchant Navy: The Men That Saved the World," *Legion*, July 14, 2010.
15. Winston Churchill speech, British Broadcasting Corporation, April 27, 1941.
16. Marc Milner, *Battle of the Atlantic* (Stroud, UK: Tempus, 2005), 9.
17. "Canada and the War: The War Economy and Controls—Shipping and Shipbuilding," Canadian War Museum, https://www.warmuseum.ca/cwm/exhibitions/newspapers/canadawar/shipping_e.html.
18. James Pritchard, *A Bridge of Ships: Canadian Shipbuilding During the Second World War* (Montreal: McGill-Queen's University Press, 2011), 315.
19. Pritchard, 303.
20. Matthew Moore, in his master's thesis "The Kiss of Death Bestowed with Gratitude," offers WWII casualty ratios of the Canadian services: 1:8 Merchant Navy, 1:16 RCAF, 1:32 Canadian Army, and 1:47 RCN.
21. Karl Dönitz, *Memoirs: Ten Years and Twenty Days*, trans. R.H. Stevens with David Woodward (London: Weidenfeld & Nicolson, 1959), 10.
22. U-boat Command (BdU) War Diary (KTB), September 28, 1939.
23. John Terraine, *Business in Great Waters: The U-Boat Wars, 1916–1945* (Barnsley, UK: Leo Cooper, 1989), 767–69.
24. Winston Churchill, *The Second World War: Their Finest Hour* (Boston: Houghton Mifflin, 1949), 598.
25. Quoted in "Canada in the Second World War: The Merchant Navy of Canada," Juno Beach Centre, France, http://www.junobeach.org/canada-in-wwii/articles/the-merchant-navy-of-canada/.
26. Leonard Warren Murray, notes prepared for CBC interview, 1967, LAC, Ottawa, Admiral Murray papers, Collection MG30 E207.
27. Richard Gimblett and Tabitha Marshall, "Royal Canadian Navy," *Canadian Encyclopedia*, March 4, 2015.

28. "Miserable, Rotten, Hopeless Life," *Canada—A People's History*, CBC, 2000, https://www.cbc.ca/history/EPISCONTENTSE1EP14CH1PA2LE.html.
29. Frank Curry, "Royal Canadian Navy War Diary, 1940 to 1945," March 10, 1941, Veterans Affairs Canada, https://www.veterans.gc.ca/eng/remembrance/those-who-served/diaries-letters-stories/second-world-war/curry.
30. Curry, August 30, 1941.
31. Dan van der Vat, "Lothar-Günther Buchheim" (obituary), *The Guardian*, March 5, 2007.
32. Lothar-Günther Buchheim, *U-boat War: The Experience of Submarine War*, trans. Gudie Lawaetz (New York: Bantam Books, 1979), 125, 128.
33. Buchheim, 128.
34. Harold Pearson Bonner, *Stay Below Decks* (unpublished memoir), courtesy Allan Bonner. All quotations from Bonner in this section are taken from this source.
35. Donald Macintyre, *U-Boat Killer: Fighting the U-Boats in the Battle of the Atlantic* (London: Rigel, 2004), 175.
36. Longmate, *How We Lived Then*, 229.
37. Longmate, 236.
38. Vera Lynn, *We'll Meet Again: A Personal and Social History of World War Two* (London: Sidgwick and Jackson, 1989), 105.
39. Masheter, letter to father.

CHAPTER TWO: DEATH OF A CONVOY

1. David O'Brien, *HX 72, First Convoy to Die: The Wolfpack Attack That Woke Up the Admiralty* (Halifax: Nimbus, 1999), 12–13.
2. Correlli Barnett, "The Partnership between Canada and Britain in Winning the Battle of the Atlantic," *Canadian Military History* 13, no. 4 (2004): 5–14.
3. Winston Churchill, *The Second World War: The Grand Alliance* (Boston: Houghton Mifflin, 1950), 606.
4. O'Brien, *HX 72*, 18.
5. Ted White (brother of Jim White), interview by David O'Brien, October 19, 1991, Halifax. Interviews of former crewmen of *Frederick S. Fales* and their families were conducted between 1989 and 1991.
6. Art Silver, interview by David O'Brien, May 28, 1989, Halifax. All quotations from Silver in this chapter are taken from this interview.

7. Jack Baker, interview by David O'Brien, May 31, 1989, Halifax. All quotations from Baker in this chapter are taken from this interview.
8. Bert Myers, interview by David O'Brien, May 20, 1989, Halifax. All quotations from Myers in this chapter are taken from this interview.
9. Pat O'Brien, interview by David O'Brien, June 27, 1989, Halifax. All quotations from O'Brien in this chapter are taken from this interview.
10. *Halifax Chronicle*, August 26, 1940.
11. John Terraine, *Business in Great Waters: The U-Boat Wars, 1916-1945* (Barnsley, UK: Leo Cooper, 1989), 205.
12. Peter Padfield, *Dönitz, the Last Führer: Portrait of a Nazi War Leader* (London: Victor Gollancz, 1984), 123–24.
13. Terraine, *Business in Great Waters*, 222.
14. Alexander Zakrzewski, "U-47 Commander Günther Prien Earned a Lasting Place in the Annals of Naval History for His Daring Raid on Scapa Flow," *Military Heritage*, Summer 2020, 23.
15. Zakrzewski, 24.
16. Quoted in Desmond Flower and James Reeves, eds., *The War, 1939–1945* (London: Cassell, 1960), 28–29.
17. Christopher J. Chlon, "Wolf of the Atlantic," *WWII History*, December 2017, 62.
18. Bernard Edwards, *The Wolf Packs Gather: Mayhem in the Western Approaches 1940* (Barnsley, UK: Pen & Sword Books, 2011).
19. Churchill, *Grand Alliance*, 111–12.
20. O'Brien, *HX 72*, 54.
21. Larry Milberry and Hugh Halliday, *The Royal Canadian Air Force at War 1939–1945* (Toronto: CANAV Books, 1990), 102–4.
22. O'Brien, *HX 72*, 61.
23. O'Brien, 69.
24. Terence Robertson, *The Golden Horseshoe: The Story of Otto Kretschmer, Germany's Top U-Boat Ace* (London: Evans Brothers, 1955), 114.
25. Terraine, *Business in Great Waters*, 257.
26. Ed Dawn, interview by David O'Brien, November 4, 1989, Halifax. All quotations from Dawn in this chapter are taken from this interview.
27. David O'Brien, correspondence with author, May 20, 2021.
28. Trevor Allen, *The Storm Passed By: Ireland and the Battle of the Atlantic* (Newbridge: Irish Academic Press, 1996), 33.

29. Joachim Schepke, *U-Boot Fahrer von heute* (Berlin: Deutscher Verlag, 1940).
30. Morris Beckman, *Atlantic Roulette: A Merchantman at War, June* 1940*: Running the Gauntlet of U-Boat Alley, E-Boat Alley, and the Luftwaffe* (Brighton, UK.: Tom Donovan, 1996), 108–9.
31. Harl Morris, interview by David O'Brien, December 15, 1989, Halifax. All quotations from Morris in this chapter are taken from this interview.
32. Schepke, *U-Boot Fahrer von heute.*
33. Beckman, *Atlantic Roulette*, 115–16.
34. R.W. Keymer, "F.S. La Malouine—Report of Attack on Convoy HX. 72" (The Commanding Officer, F.S. La Malouine, dated 15th October 1940), Western Approaches Command Convoy Journal, Public Record Office, Admiralty, UK, 9.
35. Winston Churchill, *The Second World War: Their Finest Hour* (Boston: Houghton Mifflin, 1949), 600.
36. Terraine, *Business in Great Waters,* 270.
37. Schepke, *U-Boot Fahrer von heute.*
38. Denis Richards, *Royal Air Force, 1939–1945,* vol. 1, *The Fight at Odds* (London: Her Majesty's Stationary Office, 1953), 186.

CHAPTER THREE: "WHAT THE FATES HELD IN STORE"

1. "Survivors of Frederick S. Fales Arrive," *Halifax Daily Star*, November 27, 1940.
2. Art Silver, interview by David O'Brien, May 28, 1989, Halifax. With permission.
3. Quoted in David O'Brien, *HX 72, First Convoy to Die: The Wolfpack Attack That Woke Up the Admiralty* (Halifax: Nimbus, 1999), 150.
4. Robert Fisher, "Canadian Merchant Ship Losses of the Second World War, 1939–1945," http://www.familyheritage.ca/Articles/merchant1.html.
5. John Terraine, *Business in Great Waters: The U-Boat Wars, 1916–1945* (Barnsley, UK: Leo Cooper, 1989), 767–69.
6. J.E. Michaud, "Canada's Merchant Navy," *Ottawa Citizen*, January 13, 1945.
7. John Boileau, "Merchant Navy of Canada," *Canadian Encyclopedia*, 2017, https://www.thecanadianencyclopedia.ca/en/article/merchant-navy-of-canada.

8. "The Merchant Navy," Veterans Affairs Canada, November 27, 2011, https://www.veterans.gc.ca/eng/remembrance/history/historical-sheets/merchant.
9. J.B. Dougall to Rachel Dougall, September 23, 1939. Courtesy Jane Hutchison.
10. Dougall to Rachel Dougall, November 20, 1939. Courtesy Jane Hutchison.
11. Dougall to Rachel Dougall, September 23, 1939. Courtesy Jane Hutchison.
12. Dougall to James Dougall, April 25, 1940. Courtesy Jane Hutchison.
13. Tony German, *The Sea Is at Our Gates: The History of the Canadian Navy* (Toronto: McClelland & Stewart, 1990), 71.
14. Marc Milner, *Canada's Navy: The First Century* (Toronto: University of Toronto Press, 1999), 74.
15. Jeffry V. Brock, *The Dark Broad Seas: Memoirs of a Sailor* (Toronto: McClelland & Stewart, 1981), 19.
16. Brock, 20.
17. Brock, 23.
18. Margaret Haliburton (née Los), interview by Alex Barris and author, 1992, Toronto, ON. All quotations from Haliburton in this section are taken from this interview.
19. "HMCS St-Hyacinthe," For Posterity's Sake: The Royal Canadian Navy History Project, n.d., http://www.forposterityssake.ca/SE/SE0010.htm.
20. Leonard Warren Murray, lecture notes, 1932, LAC, Admiral Murray papers, Collection MG30 E207.
21. Marc Milner, "The Rise of Leonard Murray: Navy, Part 30," *Legion*, December 2008.
22. Quoted in Milner, "Rise of Leonard Murray."
23. W.A.B. Douglas, Roger Sarty, Michael Whitby, Robert H. Caldwell, William Johnston, and William G.P. Rawling, *No Higher Purpose*, vol. 2, pt. 1 of *The Official Operational History of the Royal Canadian Navy, 1939–1945* (St. Catharines, ON: Vanwell), 32.
24. Quoted in Milner, "Rise of Leonard Murray."
25. Jack Fitzgerald, *Battlefront Newfoundland: Britain's Oldest Colony at War, 1939–1945* (St. John's, NL: Creative, 2010), 63.
26. Fitzgerald, 63.

27. "Memorandum for Commission, 23 March 1940," Public Archives of Newfoundland and Labrador, GN38, S4-1-4, File 5: J12-40.
28. W.A.B. Douglas, *The Creation of a National Air Force: The Official History of the Royal Canadian Air Force*, vol. 2 (Toronto: University of Toronto Press, 1986), 466.
29. Kenneth M. Molson, *Pioneering in Canadian Air Transport* (Winnipeg: James Richardson & Sons, 1986), 208.
30. Darrell Hillier, "No Small Feat: The Wartime Exploits of Squadron Leader N.E. 'Molly' Small, DFC, AFC," Bob's Gander History, http://bobsganderhistory.com.
31. Carl A. Christie, *Ocean Bridge: The History of RAF Ferry Command* (Toronto: University of Toronto Press, 1995), 106.
32. Bill Shead Jr., interview by Claire McCaffrey, June 14, 2013, https://redrivernorthheritage.com/bill-shead-interview-transcript/.
33. Fred Gaffen, *Forgotten Soldiers* (Penticton, BC: Theytus Books, 1985), 64.
34. Janice Summerby, "Native Soldiers—Foreign Battlefields," Veterans Affairs Canada, Queen's Printer, 2005, Cat. No. V32-56/2005.
35. Gaffen, *Forgotten Soldiers*, 29.
36. "Aboriginal Veteran Bio—Royal Canadian Navy, CPO Ted Jamieson," Aboriginal Veterans Tribute, 2014, http://www.vcn.bc.ca/~jeffrey1/rcn.html.
37. Harold Mills, *Frank Mills R.C.N.V.R.* Bk. 1, *Frank's Navy Service in Canada* (unpublished manuscript), 76. With permission. All quotations from Mills in this chapter are taken from this source.
38. Walter Schmietenknop, *Saved* (self-published manuscript). With permission from Schmietenknop family. All quotations from Schmietenknop in this chapter are taken from this source.
39. Nicholas Rankin, *Ian Fleming's Commandos: The Story of 30 Assault Unit in WWII* (London: Faber and Faber, 2011), 21.
40. John H. Godfrey, "The Naval Memoirs of Admiral J.H. Godfrey," vol. 5, *1947–1950*, NID, pt. 2, National Maritime Museum, GOD/171, 271. All quotations from Godfrey in this section are taken from this source.
41. Anthony Roland Wells, "Studies in British Naval Intelligence, 1880–1945" (thesis, King's College London), 125–27.
42. David O'Keefe, *One Day in August: The Untold Story Behind Canada's Tragedy at Dieppe* (Toronto: Knopf Canada, 2013), 27.
43. Rankin, *Ian Fleming's Commandos*, 29.

44. Quoted in Wells, "Studies in British Naval Intelligence," 127.
45. Patrick Beesly, *Very Special Intelligence: The Story of the Admiralty's Operational Intelligence Centre, 1939–1945* (New York: Ballantine Books, 1981), 58.
46. Quoted in Wells, "Studies in British Naval Intelligence," 155, 156.
47. Michael Bliss, *Right Honourable Men: The Descent of Canadian Politics from Macdonald to Chrétien* (Toronto: HarperCollins, 2004), 165.
48. James Pritchard, *A Bridge of Ships: Canadian Shipbuilding During the Second World War* (Montreal: McGill-Queen's University Press, 2011), 22.
49. Robert Bothwell and William Kilbourn, *C.D. Howe: A Biography* (Toronto: McClelland & Stewart, 1979).
50. Ken Cuthbertson, *1945: The Year That Made Modern Canada* (Toronto: HarperCollins, 2020), 71.
51. Quoted in John Harbron, *C.D. Howe* (Toronto: Fitzhenry and Whiteside, 1980), 44, 45.
52. Mark Bourrie, *The Fog of War: Censorship of Canada's Media in World War Two* (Vancouver: Douglas and McIntyre, 2011), 86.

Chapter Four: Cemetery of Shipping

1. Fraser McKee and Robert Darlington, *The Canadian Naval Chronicle, 1939–1945: The Successes and Losses of the Canadian Navy in World War II* (St. Catharines, ON: Vanwell, 1998), 18.
2. Desmond W. "Debby" Piers, Royal Canadian Navy interview, 1995, YouTube video, 2:24, https://www.youtube.com/watch?v=7wJvb_xv2FQ.
3. Desmond Piers, interview by author, May 17, 1997, Burlington, ON. All quotations from Piers in remainder of this chapter are taken from this interview.
4. Piers, Royal Canadian Navy interview.
5. Winston Churchill, *The Second World War: Their Finest Hour* (Boston: Houghton Mifflin, 1949), 402.
6. *Canada Carries On*, "Atlantic Patrol," produced by John Grierson, written and directed by Stuart Legg, narrated by Lorne Greene, National Film Board of Canada, released June 1940, https://en.wikipedia.org/wiki/Atlantic_Patrol.
7. Quoted in Graham Chandler, "Managing Canada's Wartime Image," *Legion*, November/December 2019, 60.

8. "Atlantic Patrol."
9. Chandler, "Managing Canada's Wartime Image," 61.
10. John Terraine, *Business in Great Waters: The U-Boat Wars, 1916–1945* (Barnsley, UK: Leo Cooper, 1989), 767.
11. Michael Kennedy, "Men That Came in with the Sea," *History Ireland* 3, no. 16 (May/June 2008).
12. Ian Hawkins, ed., *Destroyer: An Anthology of First-hand Accounts of the War at Sea, 1939–1945* (London: Anova Books, 2008), 137.
13. Joseph Schull, *Far Distant Ships: An Official Account of Canadian Naval Operations in World War II* (Toronto: Stoddart, 1950), 48.
14. François Lafitte, *The Internment of Aliens* (Harmondsworth, UK: Penguin, 1940).
15. "British Evacuee Ship Torpedoed. Children All Saved. Ordeal Was a Great Adventure," *Gourock Times*, September 6, 1940.
16. Bernard Atkins, "S.S. Nerissa: Wartime Evacuation and the Children's Overseas Reception Board," *Victoria Times-Colonist*, November 28, 2009.
17. Quoted in Stephen Moss, "Benares Tragedy: 'All I Can Remember Were the Screams and Cries for Help,'" *The Guardian*, September 15, 2010.
18. Ellin Bessner, *Double Threat: Canadian Jews, the Military, and World War II* (Toronto: New Jewish Press, 2018), 100.
19. Churchill, *Their Finest Hour*, 646.
20. Leland Stowe, "The Atlantic 1940: How Britain's Wealth Went West," SUBM.001.0323-0329, http://www.defence.gov.au/sydneyii/SUBM/SUBM.001.0323.pdf.
21. Chris Tindal, "Operation Fish: The Secret Plan to Hide Britain's Gold in Canada," January 18, 2017, https://acresofsnow.ca/operation-fish/.
22. Stowe, "Atlantic 1940."
23. Quoted in Stowe, "Atlantic 1940."
24. Stowe.
25. Roosevelt quoted in Churchill, *Their Finest Hour*, 568.
26. David O'Brien, *HX 72, First Convoy to Die: The Wolfpack Attack That Woke Up the Admiralty* (Halifax: Nimbus, 1999), 52.
27. Churchill, *Their Finest Hour*, 594.
28. Churchill, 598.
29. Churchill, 598.

30. Terraine, *Business in Great Waters*, 266.
31. Terence Robertson, *The Golden Horseshoe: The Story of Otto Kretschmer, Germany's Top U-Boat Ace* (London: Evans Brothers, 1955).
32. Terraine, *Business in Great Waters*, 270–71.
33. Nan Adair, interview by author, June 9, 2006, Milton Keynes, UK. All quotations from Adair in this section are taken from this interview.
34. F. Birch, "A History of British Sigint 1914–1945" (Bletchley Park, UK; unpublished GCHQ typescript, vol. 1), 17, 18.
35. Hugh Sebag-Montefiore, *Enigma: The Battle for the Code* (London: Weidenfeld & Nicolson, 2017), 69.
36. Lawrence Paterson, *Second U-Boat Flotilla* (Barnsley, UK: Leo Cooper, 2003), 34.
37. Sebag-Montefiore, *Enigma*, 77.
38. Nicholas Rankin, *Ian Fleming's Commandos: The Story of 30 Assault Unit in WWII* (London: Faber and Faber, 2011), 60.
39. David Kenyon, *Bletchley Park and D-Day: The Untold Story of How the Battle for Normandy Was Won* (London: Yale University Press, 2019), 46.
40. George Pollock, *The* Jervis Bay (London: William Kimber, 1958), 20.
41. Pollock, 205.
42. W.A.B. Douglas, Roger Sarty, Michael Whitby, Robert H. Caldwell, William Johnston, and William G.P. Rawling, *No Higher Purpose*, vol. 2, pt. 1 of *The Official Operational History of the Royal Canadian Navy, 1939–1945* (St. Catharines, ON: Vanwell), 120.
43. Arnold Hague, "Voyage Record: January 1940 to November 1940—D/S Bruse," http://www.warsailors.com/singleships/bruse.html.
44. Louis Audette, "Une Mer Cruelle," in Mack Lynch, ed., *Salty Dips: And All Our Joints Were Limber*, vol. 2. (Ottawa: Naval Officers' Associations of Canada, 1985), 60, 61. All quotations from Audette in this section are taken from this source.
45. Quoted in Douglas et al., *No Higher Purpose,* 120.
46. "Report and Minutes of a Board of Inquiry Held into the Action, Damage Sustained by HMCS *Saguenay* on 1 Dec. 1940," and LCdr Gus Miles "ROP of HMCS *Saguenay*, 30 Nov. to 5 Dec., 1940," 6 Dec., NAC (now LAC), RG 24, 6790, NSS 8340-353/26; DNC Department, Adm, Bath, "HMCS *Saguenay*: Torpedo Damage. 1-12-40," Department of National Defence, DHH, 81/520 Saguenay I 8000 pt 1.

47. "Report and Minutes."
48. Marc Milner, *Battle of the Atlantic* (Stroud, UK: Tempus, 2005), 43.
49. Milner, 43.
50. Milner, 43.
51. Anthony Cave Brown, *Bodyguard of Lies: The Extraordinary, True Story of the Clandestine War of Deception That Hid the Secrets of D-Day from Hitler and Sealed the Allied Victory* (New York: Harper & Row, 1975), 253.

Chapter Five: Sea Wolves and Sheepdogs

1. Gordon Baines, personal papers. Courtesy Grant Baines, Uxbridge, ON.
2. Gordon Baines to Hazel Le Cras, November 21, 1940. Courtesy Grant Baines, Uxbridge, ON.
3. Hazel Le Cras to Gordon Baines, November 25, 1940. Courtesy Grant Baines, Uxbridge, ON.
4. Hugh O'Hare to Gordon Baines, November 26, 1940. Courtesy Grant Baines, Uxbridge, ON.
5. Ken Macpherson and Marc Milner, *Corvettes of the Royal Canadian Navy, 1939–1945* (St. Catharines, ON: Vanwell, 1993), 91.
6. Terence Robertson, "Epitaph on a Small Fleet: The Brave Corvettes," *Maclean's*, October 22, 1960.
7. Macpherson and Milner, *Corvettes*, 18.
8. Quoted in Mac Johnston, *Corvettes Canada: Convoy Veterans of World War II Tell Their True Stories* (Whitby, ON: McGraw-Hill Ryerson, 1994), 106.
9. Macpherson and Milner, *Corvettes*, 18.
10. Robertson, "Epitaph on a Small Fleet."
11. Cdr J.D. Prentice to Capt (D), November 4, 1941, NAC, RG 24, 11929, NS 220-3-6.
12. Robertson, "Epitaph on a Small Fleet," 52.
13. W.A.B. Douglas, Roger Sarty, Michael Whitby, Robert H. Caldwell, William Johnston, and William G.P. Rawling, *No Higher Purpose*, vol. 2, pt. 1 of *The Official Operational History of the Royal Canadian Navy, 1939–1945* (St. Catharines, ON: Vanwell, 2007) 86–88.
14. Leonard Murray to Cdr Knight, November 23, 1939, quoted in William Glover, "Officer Training and the Quest for Operational Efficiency in the Royal Canadian Navy, 1939–45" (PhD diss., King's College, London, 1999), 30, 32, 59.

15. James B. Lamb, *The Corvette Navy: True Stories from Canada's Atlantic War* (Toronto: Macmillan Canada, 1977), 13.
16. Lamb, 13.
17. Marc Milner, *North Atlantic Run: The Royal Canadian Navy and the Battle for the Convoys* (Toronto: University of Toronto Press, 1985), 46.
18. Marc Milner, "Newfoundland Escort Force," *Legion*, September/October 2008, 40–41.
19. Milner, "The Newfoundland Escort Force," 41.
20. James Pritchard, *A Bridge of Ships: Canadian Shipbuilding During the Second World War* (Montreal: McGill-Queen's University Press, 2011), 29.
21. Pritchard, 34, 293.
22. Leslie Roberts, *C.D.: The Life and Times of Clarence Decatur Howe* (Toronto: Clarke, Irwin, 1957), 120.
23. Winston Churchill, *The Second World War: The Grand Alliance* (Boston: Houghton Mifflin, 1950), 119, 122, and 123.
24. Jerry Thornton, interview by Alex Barris, August 31, 1993, Toronto, ON. All quotations from Thornton in this chapter are taken from this interview.
25. Donald Macintyre, *U-Boat Killer: Fighting the U-Boats in the Battle of the Atlantic* (London: Rigel Publications, 2004), 28.
26. Macintyre, 29.
27. Macintyre, 33.
28. John Terraine, *Business in Great Waters: The U-Boat Wars, 1916-1945* (Barnsley, UK: Leo Cooper, 1989), 314–15.
29. Karl Dönitz, *Memoirs: Ten Years and Twenty Days*, trans. R.H. Stevens with David Woodward (London: Weidenfeld & Nicolson, 1959), 175.
30. Naval History, "Campaign Summaries of World War II, German U-boats at War, Part 2, 1940–41," https://www.naval-history.net/WW2CampaignsUboats2.htm.
31. Herbert A. Werner, *Iron Coffins: A Personal Account of the German U-boat Battles of World War II* (New York: Holt, Rinehart and Winston, 1969), 22–23.
32. Terraine, *Business in Great Waters*, 315.
33. Peter Padfield, *Dönitz, the Last Führer: Portrait of a Nazi War Leader* (London: Victor Gollancz, 1984), 215.

34. Milner, "Newfoundland Escort Force," 41.
35. Paul W. Collins, *The Newfyjohn Solution: St. John's Newfoundland as a Case Study of Second World War Allied Naval Base Development During the Battle of the Atlantic* (Alberta: WriteAdvice, 2014), 35.
36. Milner, "Newfoundland Escort Force," 42.
37. A.F. Pickard diary, 21–5 May 1941, A.F. Pickard papers, DHH 80/125, 7.
38. Donald Breslow, "Two World Leaders, Their Boats and One Giant Coverup," *BoatUS*, August/September 2012.
39. Churchill, *Grand Alliance*, 428.
40. Churchill, 429.
41. Andrew Caddell and Peter Russell, "A Secret Encounter That Shaped World History," *Globe and Mail*, August 13, 2014.
42. Lamb, *Corvette Navy*, 119.
43. Lamb, 121.
44. Lamb, 122.
45. Churchill, *Grand Alliance*, 444.
46. Lawrence Paterson, *Second U-Boat Flotilla* (Barnsley, UK: Leo Cooper, 2003), 97.
47. "U 501" Interrogation of Survivors, October 1941, C.B. 4051 (30), Naval Intelligence Division, Admiralty, S.W.1., N.I.D. 08409/43.
48. Paterson, *Second U-Boat Flotilla*, 101.
49. U-boat commanders' biographical sketches and statistics sourced from "The Men of the U-Boats," https://uboat.net/men/.
50. Robertson, "Epitaph on a Small Fleet."
51. Fraser McKee and Robert Darlington, *The Canadian Naval Chronicle, 1939–1945: The Successes and Losses of the Canadian Navy in World War II* (St. Catharines, ON: Vanwell, 1998), 34.
52. J.C. Hibbard to C-in-C Western Approaches, "Report of Proceedings S.C. 42," 18 September 1941, DHH 81/520/8280-SC42.
53. Hibbard.
54. Robertson, "Epitaph on a Small Fleet," 53.
55. Fritz Weinrich, quoted in Paterson, *Second U-Boat Flotilla*, 102–3.
56. Frederick R. Grubb to Captain (D) Newfoundland, 6 November 1941, file 8280-SC 42 NAC, RG 24, vol. 11334.
57. Quoted in Paterson, *Second U-Boat Flotilla*, 103.
58. Quoted in Robertson, "Epitaph on a Small Fleet," 53.
59. McKee and Darlington, *Canadian Naval Chronicle*, 34.

60. Quoted in Bernard Edwards, *Attack and Sink! The Battle for Convoy SC42* (Dorset, UK: New Era Writer's Guild, 1995), 174.
61. McKee and Darlington, *Canadian Naval Chronicle*, 36.

CHAPTER SIX: "BLOOD BROTHERS TO A CORK"

1. Vera Lynn, *We'll Meet Again: A Personal and Social History of World War Two* (London: Sidgwick and Jackson, 1989), 108.
2. J.B. Dougall to Rachel Dougall, May 9 and 16, 1941. Courtesy Jane Hutchinson.
3. Dougall to Rachel Dougall, October 20, 1940. Courtesy Jane Hutchinson.
4. Dougall to Rachel Dougall, June 14, 1941. Courtesy Jane Hutchinson.
5. John Rae to Rachel Dougall, March 6, 1941. Courtesy Jane Hutchinson.
6. Dougall to Rachel Dougall, August 10, 1940. Courtesy Jane Hutchinson.
7. Dougall to Rachel Dougall, February 28, 1940. Courtesy Jane Hutchinson.
8. Franklin Delano Roosevelt, "Fireside Chat 18: On the Greer Incident, September 11, 1941," Miller Center, University of Virginia, https://millercenter.org/the-presidency/presidential-speeches/september-11-1941-fireside-chat-18-greer-incident.
9. Frankie Witzenburg, "This Day in History: The Sinking of the USS Reuben James," U.S. Naval Institute, 2019, https://www.navalhistory.org/2019/10/31/this-day-in-history-the-sinking-of-the-uss-reuben-james-dd-245.
10. Roger Sarty, *Canada and the Battle of the Atlantic* (Montreal: Art Global, 1998), 76.
11. Quoted in Marc Milner, *North Atlantic Run: The Royal Canadian Navy and the Battle for the Convoys* (Toronto: University of Toronto Press, 1985), 57.
12. Marc Milner, *Battle of the Atlantic* (Stroud, UK: Tempus Publishing, 2005), 74.
13. Anthony Griffin, *Footfalls in Memory* (self-published, 1998). All quotations from Griffin in this section are taken from this source (see pages 92, 93, 342, 94). With permission.
14. Dale Elley Bristow, correspondence with author, April 30, 2021.

15. Louis Audette, "Une Mer Cruelle," in Mack Lynch, ed., *Salty Dips: And All Our Joints Were Limber*, vol. 2. (Ottawa: Naval Officers' Associations of Canada, 1985), 64.
16. Quoted in Lynch, *Salty Dips*, 65.
17. W.A.B. Douglas, Roger Sarty, Michael Whitby, Robert H. Caldwell, William Johnston, and William G.P. Rawling, *No Higher Purpose*, vol. 2, pt. 1 of *The Official Operational History of the Royal Canadian Navy, 1939–1945* (St. Catharines, ON: Vanwell), 86.
18. Quoted in Mac Johnston, *Corvettes Canada: Convoy Veterans of WWII Tell Their True* Stories (Whitby, ON: McGraw-Hill Ryerson, 1994), 70.
19. Desmond Piers, interview by Hal Lawrence, January 7, 1982, biographical files, DHH, 96–99.
20. Piers interview.
21. Quoted in Paul Kemp, *Convoy! Drama in Arctic Waters* (London: Castle Books, 2004), 11.
22. Winston Churchill, *The Second World War: The Grand Alliance* (Boston: Houghton Mifflin, 1950), 453.
23. Kemp, *Convoy!*, 23.
24. Kemp, 91.
25. German Naval War Diary, July 6, 1942, quoted in Kemp, 94.
26. Kemp, 127.
27. Howard Hazzard, interview by author, August 3, 2019, London, ON. All quotations from Hazzard in this section are taken from this interview.
28. Cliff Perry, interview by Alex Barris, June 21, 1993, Agincourt, ON, and Perry's unpublished memoir *My War Years* (2011), with permission from Dorothy and Judy Perry. All quotations and references from Perry in this section are taken from these two sources.
29. Kemp, *Convoy!*, 235.
30. B.B. Schofield, *The Russian Convoys* (London: Pan Books, 1984), 218.
31. E. Léderrey, *Germany's Defeat in the East: The Soviet Armies at War, 1941–1945* (London: War Office, 1955).
32. John Terraine, *Business in Great Waters: The U-Boat Wars, 1916-1945* (Barnsley, UK: Leo Cooper, 1989), 767.
33. Milner, *Battle of the Atlantic*, 77.
34. Hugh Sebag-Montefiore, *Enigma: The Battle for the Code* (London: Weidenfeld & Nicolson, 2017), 359, 360, 361.

35. Quoted in Terraine, *Business in Great Waters*, 400.
36. Joseph Schull, *Far Distant Ships: An Official Account of Canadian Naval Operations in WWII* (Toronto: Stoddart, 1987), 98.
37. Harrison Smith, "Reinhard Hardegen, U-boat commander Who Menaced American Shores, Dies at 105," *Washington Post*, June 18, 2018.
38. Lawrence Paterson, *Second U-Boat Flotilla* (Barnsley, UK: Leo Cooper, 2003), 118.
39. Sarty, *Canada and the Battle*, 94.
40. Stephen J. Thorne, "Reinhard Hardegen: Last of the U-boat Aces," *Legion*, July 11, 2018.
41. Thorne.
42. Thorne.
43. Hardegen's account of the conversation with Hitler appears first in an interview the U-boat captain gave to the *Atlanta Journal-Constitution* in 1999, and was reproduced by Harrison Smith in the *Washington Post* on June 18, 2018.
44. Terraine, *Business in Great Waters*, 409.
45. James Prentice to Captain (D) Newfoundland, 4 November 1941, "Strain on personnel in ships of the Newfoundland Escort Force," file 00-220-3-6, NAC, RG 24, vol. 11929.
46. Bill Bint, unpublished diary, Naval Museum of Alberta, Calgary, AB. With permission.
47. Prentice to Captain (D) Newfoundland.
48. Bint diary.
49. Bint diary.
50. Terraine, *Business in Great Waters*, 768.
51. Jürgen Rohwer and Hans Adolf Jacobsen, eds., *Decisive Battles of World War II: The German View* (New York: Putnam, 1965), 272.
52. Patrick Beesly, *Very Special Intelligence: The Story of the Admiralty's Operational Intelligence Centre, 1939–1945* (New York: Ballantine, 1981), 112.
53. Beesly, 112.
54. Quoted in Beesly, 113, 114.
55. Douglas et al., *No Higher Purpose*, 491, 492.
56. J.B. McDiarmid to VAdm Peter Gretton, RN (Ret'd), 23 July 1982, 1; Notes from M. Whitby interview by J.B. McDiarmid, Jan. 1999. Both DHH 2000/5.

57. Leonard Philbrook, interview by George MacNabb and Jim Curran, ca. 1990s, Toronto, ON. With permission. All quotations from Philbrook in this section are taken from this interview.
58. Sandy Gow, "Pusser Grub? My God But It Was Awful: Feeding the Fleet During the Second World War," *Canadian Military History* 25, no. 2 (2016): 2–3.
59. Gow, 6.
60. Gow, 31.
61. Audette, "Mer Cruelle," 64.

CHAPTER SEVEN: SWIM MEET IN THE GULF

1. *U553* log, 15 October 1941, DHH. Translation by Jan Drent.
2. Lothar-Günther Buchheim, *U-boat War: The Experience of Submarine War*, trans. Gudie Lawaetz (New York: Bantam Books, 1979), 217.
3. Peter Padfield, *Dönitz, the Last Führer: Portrait of a Nazi War Leader* (London: Victor Gollancz, 1984), 238.
4. Padfield, 239.
5. Murray Westgate, interview by Alex Barris, July 2, 1993, Toronto, ON. All quotations from Westgate in this chapter are taken from this interview.
6. William Lyon Mackenzie King, *Canada and the Fight for Freedom* (New York: Duell, Sloan and Pearce, 1944; Freeport, NY: Books for Libraries Press, 1972), 124.
7. James W. Essex, *Victory in the St. Lawrence: Canada's Unknown War* (Erin, ON: Boston Mills, 1984), 63.
8. J.B. Lamb, "The Battle of the Gulf: It's the Faux Pas, Much More than the Classic Success, That the Sailor Loves to Reminisce About," *Mayfair*, November 1946.
9. Elsa-Ann Pickard (daughter of Hans Sachau), interview by author, April 18, 2020, King City, ON. All quotations from Pickard in this section are taken from this interview.
10. Spud Roscoe, "The Fairmiles: Canada's Little Ships," radio research paper, ed. Jerry Proc, http://jproc.ca/rrp/fairmile2.html.
11. James Pritchard, *A Bridge of Ships: Canadian Shipbuilding During the Second World War* (Montreal: McGill-Queen's University Press, 2011), 271.
12. Roscoe, "Fairmiles."

13. W.A.B. Douglas, Roger Sarty, Michael Whitby, Robert H. Caldwell, William Johnston, and William G.P. Rawling, *No Higher Purpose*, vol. 2, pt. 1 of *The Official Operational History of the Royal Canadian Navy, 1939–1945* (St. Catharines, ON: Vanwell), 433.
14. Douglas et al., *No Higher Purpose*, 433.
15. Essex, *Victory in the St. Lawrence*, 68.
16. John D. Harbron, *The Longest Battle: The RCN in the Atlantic 1939–1945* (St. Catharines, ON: Vanwell, 1995), 69.
17. Essex, *Victory in the St. Lawrence*, 70.
18. W.A.B. Douglas, *The Creation of a National Air Force: The Official History of the Royal Canadian Air Force*, vol. 2 (Ottawa: University of Toronto Press, 1986), 496.
19. "U-boat Sinks Ship in St. Lawrence: Freighter Survivors Drift to River Bank," *Globe and Mail*, May 13, 1942.
20. "Macdonald Doesn't Disclose Point at Which U-Boat Fired," *Globe and Mail*, May 13, 1942.
21. "Ship Sunk in St. Lawrence on Mercy Trip: Carried Survivors From Vessel Attacked Earlier," *Ottawa Evening Journal*, May 13, 1942.
22. *U553* log, 11 May 1942.
23. Ernst Vogelsang, *U553*, BdU KTB, July 6, 1942, Stuttgart, Germany.
24. James Philip Fraser, in "ROP Convoy QS 15," 11 July 1942, NAC, RG 24, 12009, G018-1, V 1.
25. Ken Macpherson and Marc Milner, *Corvettes of the Royal Canadian Navy 1939–1945* (St. Catharines, ON: Vanwell, 1993), 17.
26. Martin Franchetto, *Lifejackets, Duffel Coats and Rubber Boots* (unpublished memoir, 2004). Courtesy Elaine Thorpe.
27. Essex, *Victory in the St. Lawrence*, 63.
28. Hansard, Canadian House of Commons, July 10, 1942.
29. Hugh A. Halliday, "Eastern Air Command: Air Force, Part 14," *Legion*, March 1, 2006.
30. Norville Small, quoted in Halliday.
31. "Eastern Air Command Anti-Submarine Report," July 1942, DHH, 181.003 (D25).
32. Darrell Hillier, "No Small Feat: The Wartime Exploits of Squadron Leader N.E. 'Molly' Small, DFC, AFC," Bob's Gander History, http://bobsganderhistory.com.
33. Marc Milner, "Predators in the St. Lawrence: Navy, Part 50," *Legion*, March 29, 2012.

34. George Hall, quoted in "HMCS *Trail*," ROP, Convoy LN-6, n.d., DHH, 89/34 mfm, reel 16, NSS 8280 LS 6.
35. "Little Bell Island in Newfoundland and Labrador's Conception Bay Was the Victim of Enemy Fire During the Second World War," notes from files of Bell Island Community Museum, April 1, 2016.
36. Log *U513*, September 5, 1942, Doc. 1. U-Boot Archiv, Cuxhaven-Altenbruch, DE.
37. Log *U513*.
38. Ross Creaser, quoted in Steve Neary, *The Enemy on Our Doorstep: The German Attacks at Bell Island, Newfoundland, 1942* (St. John's: Jesperson Press, 1994), 32.
39. Quoted in Neary, 32, 33.
40. John Terraine, *Business in Great Waters: The U-Boat Wars, 1916-1945* (Barnsley, UK: Leo Cooper, 1989), 768.
41. Quoted in Douglas, *Creation of a National Air Force*, 504.
42. Quoted in Douglas, 505.
43. Quoted in Michael Hadley, *U-boats Against Canada: German Submarines in Canadian Waters* (Montreal: McGill-Queen's University Press, 1985), 115, 116.
44. Douglas How, *Night of the Caribou* (Hantsport, NS: Lancelot Press, 1988), 61.
45. Margaret Brooke, quoted in Fred Langan, "Margaret Brooke, the Only Nursing Sister to Have Been Named a Member of the Order of the British Empire During the Second World War for Her Heroic Acts Following the Sinking of the SS Caribou," *Globe and Mail*, January 31, 2016.
46. Quoted in Langan.
47. Quoted in Langan.
48. Quoted in Langan.
49. Mark Richardson (son of Charles Richardson), email correspondence with author, May 15, 2020.
50. How, *Night of the Caribou*, 108–9.
51. William Lundrigan, quoted in How, 34, 111.
52. How, 112.
53. Stephen J. Thorne, "Frontlines: The 1942 Sinking of the Ferry Caribou," podcast, *Legion* magazine, October 15, 2019.
54. *Globe and Mail*, op-ed, October 19, 1942.

55. Angus L. Macdonald, quoted in Pat Devenish, "Key events of the Battle of the Atlantic: October," *Trident*, Nov. 2, 2020.
56. Eugène L'Heureux, quoted in Mark Bourrie, *The Fog of War: Censorship of Canada's Media in World War Two* (Vancouver: Douglas & McIntyre, 2011), 100.
57. James Cuthbert, quoted in How, *Night of the Caribou*, 147.
58. Marc Milner, "Hidden Victory in the St. Lawrence," *Legion*, September 22, 2021.
59. Essex, *Victory in the St. Lawrence*, 140.
60. DND for Air, 21 December 1942, S.15-24-20, Public Archives of Canada, RG 24, vol. 5200.
61. Terraine, *Business in Great Waters*, 768.
62. Padfield, *Dönitz*, 261.

CHAPTER EIGHT: "A YEAR ASTERN"

1. Nicholas Rankin, *Ian Fleming's Commandos: The Story of 30 Assault Unit in WWII* (London: Faber and Faber, 2011), 143.
2. W.A.B. Douglas, Roger Sarty, Michael Whitby, Robert H. Caldwell, William Johnston, and William G.P. Rawling, *No Higher Purpose*, vol. 2, pt. 1 of *The Official Operational History of the Royal Canadian Navy, 1939–1945* (St. Catharines, ON: Vanwell), 394.
3. Douglas et al., 395.
4. John Terraine, *Business in Great Waters: The U-Boat Wars, 1916–1945* (Barnsley, UK: Leo Cooper, 1989), 438, 439.
5. Marc Milner, "The Wolf Pack Attacks: The Battle for One World War Two Convoy," *Legion*, September 8, 2013.
6. Tony German, "Preserving the Atlantic Lifeline," *Legion*, May/June 1998, 12.
7. Terraine, *Business in Great Waters*, 768.
8. Patrick Beesly, *Very Special Intelligence: The Story of the Admiralty's Operational Intelligence Centre, 1939–1945* (New York: Ballantine, 1981), 191.
9. Arnold Hague Convoy Database, http://www.convoyweb.org.uk/hx/index.html; http://www.convoyweb.org.uk/on/index.html; http://www.convoyweb.org.uk/sc/index.html.
10. Mac Johnston, *Corvettes Canada: Convoy Veterans of WWII Tell Their True Stories* (Whitby, ON: McGraw-Hill Ryerson, 1994), 148.

11. Marc Milner, *North Atlantic Run: The Royal Canadian Navy and the Battle for the Convoys* (Toronto: University of Toronto Press, 1985), 97.
12. Tony German, *The Sea Is at Our Gates: The History of the Canadian Navy* (Toronto: McClelland & Stewart, 1990), 123.
13. Joseph Schull, *Far Distant Ships: An Official Account of Canadian Naval Operations in WWII* (Toronto: Stoddart, 1987), 173, 174.
14. Roger Sarty, *Canada and the Battle of the Atlantic* (Montreal: Art Global, 1998), 119.
15. German, "Preserving the Atlantic Lifeline," 13.
16. Douglas et al., *No Higher Purpose*, 478.
17. Fraser McKee and Robert Darlington, *The Canadian Naval Chronicle, 1939–1945: The Successes and Losses of the Canadian Navy in World War II* (St. Catharines, ON: Vanwell, 1996), 47, 48.
18. Douglas et al., *No Higher Purpose*, 484.
19. Robert C. Fisher, "Tactics, Training, Technology: The RCN's Summer of Success, July–September 1942," *Canadian Military History* 6, no. 2 (January 20, 2012): 8, 9.
20. Quoted in Schull, *Far Distant Ships*, 131.
21. John Caldecott Littler, *Sea Fever* (Victoria: Kiwi Publications, 1995), 189.
22. Littler, 189.
23. James B. Lamb, *The Corvette Navy: True Stories from Canada's Atlantic War* (Toronto: Macmillan Canada, 1977), 161.
24. Quoted in Schull, *Far Distant Ships*, 133.
25. Terraine, *Business in Great Waters*, 768.
26. Carl Anderson, "The Summer of '42: A Story of HMCS *Sackville*," *Action Stations!* 35, no. 1 (Spring 2016): 11, 12.
27. Minutes by Cdr. C.D. Howard-Johnston, RN, 18 Sept. 1942, Public Record Office (United Kingdom), Admiralty, 237/88.
28. *Sackville* radar officer, quoted in Milner, *North Atlantic Run*, 140.
29. "Final Report on the Interrogation of Survivors from U-210, Sunk by H.M.C.S. Assiniboine on August 6, 1942," Navy Department Office of the Chief of Naval Operations, Washington, OP-16-Z, October 2, 1942, 7, 8, 10, http://www.uboatarchive.net/U-210A/U-210INT.htm.
30. Lothar-Günther Buchheim, *U-Boat War: The Experience of Submarine War*, trans. Gudie Lawaetz (New York: Bantam Books, 1979), 44, 80.

31. "Final Report on the Interrogation," 26.
32. G.N. Tucker, "Shot Range Was Feature of Sea Battle," DHH, PRF HMCS *Assiniboine*.
33. J.H. Stubbs, Commanding Officer, HMCS Assiniboine, SC 94—Reports of Proceedings of HMCS Assiniboine, Section I—5th August, 1942, DHH, 1650-U-210.
34. Fred Addy service records, courtesy of Dorothy Addy and Helen G. Storms, correspondence, March 2020.
35. Harry B. Barrett, *The Navy & Me* (Port Dover, ON: Patterson's Creek Press, 2003), 106.
36. Quoted in correspondence between author and Gordon Laco, May 9, 2021.
37. Marc Milner, "Fire and Fog: The Assiniboine Rams U-210," *Legion*, July/August 2014, 55.
38. "Final Report on the Interrogation," 26.
39. DSO citation, quoted in Len Burrow and Emile Beaudoin, *Unlucky Lady: The Life & Death of HMCS Athabaskan* (Toronto: McClelland & Stewart, 1989), 58.
40. Denis Richards and Hilary St. George Saunders, *The Fight Avails*, vol. 2 of *Royal Air Force 1939–1945* (London: HMSO, 1954), 101.
41. Richards and Saunders, 103.
42. David J. Bercuson and Holger H. Herwig, *Long Night of the Tankers: Hitler's War Against Caribbean Oil* (Calgary: University of Calgary Press, 2014), 218.
43. Hal Lawrence, *A Bloody War: One Man's Memories of the Canadian Navy, 1939–45* (Toronto: Macmillan Canada, 1979), 97.
44. Sean E. Livingston, *Oakville's Flower: The History of HMCS* Oakville (Toronto: Dundurn, 2014), 55.
45. Livingston, 55.
46. Lawrence, *Bloody War*, 98.
47. Marc Milner, "Bullets, Bombs and Coke Bottles: Battling a U-boat in the Caribbean," *Legion*, December 2014, 72.
48. "Final Report on the Interrogation," 26.
49. Livingston, *Oakville's Flower*, 57.
50. Quoted in Lawrence, *Bloody War*, 99.
51. Lawrence, 102.
52. Lawrence, 103.

53. Livingston, *Oakville's Flower*, 68.
54. Royal Canadian Navy press release, Naval Headquarters (Information Section), Ottawa, November 10, 1942, 1.
55. Terraine, *Business in Great Waters*, 768.
56. T.C. Pullen, "Convoy O.N. 127 & the Loss of HMCS Ottawa, 13 September, 1942: A Personal Reminiscence," *Northern Mariner* 2, no. 2 (April 1992): 13.
57. Pullen, 14.
58. Quoted in James Goodwin, *"Our Gallant Doctor"—Enigma and Tragedy: Surgeon Lieutenant George Hendry and HMCS* Ottawa, 1942 (Toronto: Dundurn Press, 2007), 152.
59. Marc Milner, "Attack on Convoy SC-107," *Legion*, November/December 2015, 47.
60. Douglas et al., *No Higher Purpose*, 550.
61. Milner, "Attack on Convoy SC-107," 48.
62. Desmond Piers, interview by author, May 17, 1997, Burlington, ON.
63. Milner, "Attack on Convoy SC-107," 48.
64. Douglas et al., *No Higher Purpose*, 553.
65. Winston Churchill to Mackenzie King, DSec to SSEA, tg 264, 17 December 1942, in John F. Hilliker, ed., *Documents on Canadian External Relations,* vol. 11, *1942–1943* (Ottawa: Department of External Affairs and International Trade, 1980), 355.
66. McKee and Darlington, *Canadian Naval Chronicle*, 78.
67. German, *Sea Is at Our Gates*, 131.
68. Lawrence, *Bloody War,* 113.
69. Quoted in Hans J. Röll, *Korvettenkapitän Werner Hartenstein: Mit* U156 *auf Feindfahrt und der Fall "Laconia"* (Germany: Würzburg Flechsig, 2009), 89.
70. Peter Padfield, *Dönitz, the Last Führer: Portrait of a Nazi War Leader* (London: Victor Gollancz, 1984), 253.
71. Quoted in G.H. Bennett, "The 1942 Laconia Order, the Murder of Shipwrecked Survivors and the Allied Pursuit of Justice 1945–46," *Law, Crime and History* 1, no. 1 (2011): 16–34.
72. Quoted in F/Vorträge, Commander-in-Chief, Kriegsmarine, reports/discussions with the Führer, Sept. 28, 1942, Public Records Office, UK, PG (captured naval records) 32187.

Chapter Nine: "Tough-Looking Bunch of Bastards"

1. Cyril Rickers to McKinnon Industries, Port Dalhousie, ON, January 20, 1943. Courtesy Don Rickers.
2. Don Rickers, "Peril on the North Atlantic," *The Voice* (Pelham, ON), November 6, 2019.
3. James B. Lamb, *The Corvette Navy: True Stories from Canada's Atlantic War* (Toronto: Macmillan Canada, 1977), 136.
4. Notes by Alan Fairley, son of Fred Fairley (master of *Empire Sailor*), https://uboat.net/allies/merchants/ship/2454.html.
5. Leonard Warren Murray, quoted in "Canada in the Second World War: The Merchant Navy of Canada," Juno Beach Centre, France, http://www.junobeach.org/canada-in-wwii/articles/the-merchant-navy-of-canada/.
6. Warren F. Kimball, ed., *Churchill and Roosevelt: The Complete Correspondence*, vol. 1, *Alliance Emerging, October* 1933–*November* 1942 (Princeton, NJ: Princeton University Press, 1984), 648–49.
7. Marc Milner, *North Atlantic Run: The Royal Canadian Navy and the Battle for the Convoys* (Toronto: University of Toronto Press, 1985), 195.
8. W.A.B. Douglas, Roger Sarty, Michael Whitby, Robert H. Caldwell, William Johnston, and William G.P. Rawling, *No Higher Purpose*, vol. 2, pt. 1 of *The Official Operational History of the Royal Canadian Navy, 1939–1945* (St. Catharines, ON: Vanwell), 592.
9. Monthly Anti-Submarine Report (January 1943), quoted in Milner, *North Atlantic Run*, 213.
10. Ken Macpherson and Marc Milner, *Corvettes of the Royal Canadian Navy 1939–1945* (St. Catharines, ON: Vanwell Publishing, 1993), 127.
11. Quoted in Mac Johnston, *Corvettes Canada: Convoy Veterans of WW II Tell Their True Stories* (Whitby, ON: McGraw-Hill Ryerson, 1994), 175.
12. Tony German, *The Sea Is at Our Gates: The History of the Canadian Navy* (Toronto: McClelland & Stewart, 1990), 133.
13. John Marshall, "John Mitchell Tells of Sinking Submarine," *Leamington Post & News*, May 13, 1943.
14. Raymond Hatrick, quoted in Marshall.
15. Louis Mountbatten, quoted in Fraser McKee and Robert Darlington, *The Canadian Naval Chronicle 1939–1945: The Successes and Losses of the Canadian Navy in World War II* (St. Catharines, ON: Vanwell Publishing, 1996), 82.

16. Douglas et al., *No Higher Purpose*, 614.
17. Jimmy Brown, "Let 'Em Learn: The Rigorous Training of the Western Approaches Command," http://www.harry-tates.org.uk/Terror%20of%20Tobermory.htm.
18. Richard Baker, *The Terror of Tobermory: An Informal Biography of Vice-Admiral Sir Gilbert Stephenson, KBE, CB, GMB* (London: W.H. Allen, 1972), foreword.
19. The exchange is recounted in numerous published histories, including German, *Sea Is at Our Gates*, 137.
20. German, 137.
21. Quoted in Douglas et al., *No Higher Purpose*, 163.
22. Winston Churchill, *The Second World War: The Hinge of Fate* (Boston: Houghton Mifflin, 1950), 675.
23. Winston Churchill, *The Second World War: Closing the Ring* (Boston: Houghton Mifflin, 1951), 4–6.
24. "On the Water—Answering the Call, 1917–1945: Building Ships for Victory," Smithsonian National Museum of American History, https://americanhistory.si.edu/onthewater/exhibition/6_2.html.
25. "Canada and the War: The War Economy and Controls—Shipping and Shipbuilding," Canadian War Museum, https://www.warmuseum.ca/cwm/exhibitions/newspapers/canadawar/shipping_e.html.
26. James Pritchard, *A Bridge of Ships: Canadian Shipbuilding During the Second World War* (Montreal: McGill-Queen's University Press, 2011), 126, 131.
27. Pritchard, 135.
28. Jean Bruce, *Back the Attack! Canadian Women During the Second World War—at Home and Abroad* (Toronto: Macmillan, 1985), 69.
29. Quoted in "Woman Welder Says Union Demands She Quit Job: Vancouver Labor Men Indignant at Report," *Vancouver Sun*, May 6, 1942.
30. Rosamond Greer, *The Girls of the King's Navy* (Victoria: Sono Nis Press, 1983), 32.
31. Barbara Winters, "The Wrens of the Second World War: Their Place in the History of Canadian Servicewomen," in *A Nation's Navy: In Quest of Canadian Naval Identity*, ed. Michael L. Hadley, Rob Huebert, and Fred W. Crickard (Montreal: McGill-Queen's University Press, 1996), 296.

32. Winters, 284.
33. Rodine "Ronnie" Buckley-Beevers (Egan), interview by author, 1993, Uxbridge, ON. All quotations from Buckley-Beevers in this section are taken from this interview.
34. Roy Harbin, interview by Alex Barris, June 17, 1993, Agincourt, ON.
35. Willis, quoted by Buckley-Beevers, interview by author.
36. BdU KTB, November 30, 1942.
37. BdU KTB, September 28, 1939.
38. German, *Sea Is at Our Gates*, 136.
39. Karl Dönitz, quoted in Peter Padfield, *Dönitz, the Last Führer: Portrait of a Nazi War Leader* (London: Victor Gollancz Ltd., 1984), 267.
40. Hugh Sebag-Montefiore, *Enigma: The Battle for the Code* (London: Weidenfeld & Nicolson, 2017), 263.
41. German, *Sea Is at Our Gates*, 136.
42. Carl A. Christie, *Truly Royal: The History of the Canadian Air Force* (Toronto: University of Toronto Press, forthcoming), ch. 12, 6.
43. Roger Sarty, *Canada and the Battle of the Atlantic* (Montreal: Art Global, 1998), 129.
44. "Chapter VII. Fourth Patrol of U-604," US Navy Department Office of the Chief of Naval Operations, Washington, Op-16-Z, Final Report—G/Serial 26, Report of Survivors from U-604 and U-185 sunk 11 August 1943 and 24 August 1943, 22.
45. Johnston, *Corvettes Canada*, 149.
46. "Chapter VII. Fourth Patrol," 22.
47. Dennis, quoted in Johnston, *Corvettes Canada*, 200.
48. Fred Colborne, RCAF HQ file 28-2-46, "RCAF aircraft attacks on U-boats," DHH 181.003 (D1338). All quotations from Colborne, Thomson, Duncan, Elden, Watson, Irving, and Blain in this section are taken from this source.
49. Colborne.
50. Chief of the Air Staff to Chief of the Naval Staff, May 4, 1943, S.28-1-6, in Colborne.
51. "Chapter VII. Fourth Patrol," 22.
52. BdU KTB, February 26, 1943.
53. Paul R. Heineman to Commander Task Force Twenty-Four, "Report of Escort of Convoy ON-166," 28 February 1943, file A14-1(2), pt. 3 National Archives and Records Administration, RG 313, CTF 24, Red, 1943 Confidential, box 8745.

54. Harry Mann, quoted in Heineman, 150.
55. Milner, *North Atlantic Run*, 156.
56. John Terraine, *Business in Great Waters: The U-Boat Wars, 1916–1945* (Barnsley, UK: Leo Cooper, 1989), 768.
57. Quoted in Atlantic Convoy Conference Minutes, DHH, 181.009 (D268).
58. Victor Brodeur to Leonard Murray, 5 Feb. 1943, NAC, RG 24, 11928, NSS 8740-102/1, pt. 1.
59. Quoted in Atlantic Convoy Conference Minutes.
60. W.A.B. Douglas, Roger Sarty, Michael Whitby, Robert H. Caldwell, William Johnston, and William G.P Rawling, *A Blue Water Navy*, vol. 2, pt. 2 of *The Official Operational History of the Royal Canadian Navy in the Second World War, 1939–1943* (St. Catharines, ON: Vanwell, 2007), 72.
61. Christie, *Truly Royal*, ch. 13, 5.
62. Douglas et al., *No Higher Purpose*, 630.

Chapter Ten: Hunter-Killers

1. Robert G. Halford, *The Unknown Navy: Canada's World War II Merchant Navy* (St. Catharines, ON: Vanwell Publishing, 1995), 140.
2. Jan Drent, "Labour and the Unions in a Wartime Essential Industry: Shipyard Workers in BC, 1939–1945," *Northern Mariner* 6, no. 4 (October 1996): 52.
3. Dave Broadfoot, interview by Alex Barris and author, August 16, 1993, Toronto, ON.
4. Broadfoot interview.
5. "A History of HMS Biter," Royal Navy Research Archive, http://www.royalnavyresearcharchive.org.uk/ESCORT/BITER.htm#.X9bAhi3b3GI.
6. Broadfoot interview.
7. Marc Milner, *North Atlantic Run: The Royal Canadian Navy and the Battle for the Convoys* (Toronto: University of Toronto Press, 1985), 157, 158.
8. W.A.B. Douglas, *The Creation of a National Air Force: The Official History of the Royal Canadian Air Force*, vol. 2 (Toronto: University of Toronto Press, 1986), 551.
9. Douglas, 566.
10. Milner, *North Atlantic Run*, 155.

11. Tony German, *The Sea Is at Our Gates: The History of the Canadian Navy* (Toronto: McClelland & Stewart, 1990), 139.
12. Hugh Sebag-Montefiore, *Enigma: The Battle for the Code* (London: Weidenfeld & Nicolson, 2017), 246.
13. Nan Adair, interview by author, June 9, 2006, Milton Keynes, UK. All quotations from Adair in this section are taken from this interview.
14. Glyn Howell, "The Deadly Perils of U-boat Alley," *Pembrokeshire Life*, ca. 2003. All quotations from Howell in this section are taken from this source.
15. Mike Parker, *Running the Gauntlet: An Oral History of Canadian Merchant Seamen in World War II* (Halifax: Nimbus, 1994), 181.
16. RCAF attack report, 4 May 1943, DHH 181.003 (DI341). All quotations from Moffit in this section are taken from this source.
17. Roy Gill, quoted in "Commodore's Narrative," Convoy HX 237 report, War Sailors.com, https://www.warsailors.com/convoys/hx237.html.
18. Fraser McKee and Robert Darlington, *The Canadian Naval Chronicle, 1939–1945: The Successes and Losses of the Canadian Navy in World War II* (St. Catharines, ON: Vanwell, 1998), 180, 181.
19. Quoted in "Commodore's Narrative."
20. David J. Bercuson and Holger H. Herwig, *Deadly Seas: The Duel Between the St Croix and the U305 in the Battle of the Atlantic* (Toronto: Random House, 1997), 237, 238.
21. BdU KTB, May 24, 1943.
22. Karl Dönitz, *Mein wechselvolles Leben* (Göttingen: Musteerschmidt Verlag, 1968), 190.
23. Matthew Cooper, *The German Army, 1939–1945* (New York: Stein and Day, 1978), 451.
24. John Terraine, *Business in Great Waters: The U-Boat Wars, 1916–1945* (Barnsley, UK: Leo Cooper, 1989), 768.
25. "The U-boat Shipyards," Uboat.net, n.d., https://uboat.net/technical/shipyards/.
26. BdU KTB, May 14, 1943.
27. Lawrence Paterson, *First U-Boat Flotilla* (Barnsley, UK: Leo Cooper, 2002), 186.
28. W.A.B. Douglas, Roger Sarty, Michael Whitby, Robert H. Caldwell, William Johnston, and William G.P Rawling, *A Blue Water Navy*: vol. 2, pt. 2 of *The Official Operational History of*

the Royal Canadian Navy in the Second World War, 1939–1943 (St. Catharines, ON: Vanwell, 2007), 78.

29. Bercuson and Herwig, *Deadly Seas*, 193.
30. Douglas et al., *Blue Water Navy*, 78.
31. Bercuson and Herwig, *Deadly Seas*, 241.
32. "U-boat Types: The Walter U-boats," Uboat.net, n.d., https://uboat.net/types/walter_hist.htm.
33. Peter Padfield, *Dönitz, the Last Führer: Portrait of a Nazi War Leader* (London: Victor Gollancz, 1984), 309, 310.
34. Quoted in Padfield, 310.
35. Hilary St. George Saunders, *The Fight Is Won*, vol. 3 of *Royal Air Force, 1939–1945* (London: HMSO, 1954), 47.
36. Saunders, 48.
37. Terraine, *Business in Great Waters*, 583.
38. Douglas A. Rollins, "Danger Is My Opportunity: The Life and Times of Donald Edward Rollins, 1920–1972," unpublished biography, courtesy of the author.
39. W. Appleby Brown, S/L No. 3 Operational Training Unit, quoted in Certificates of Qualification document, Oct. 4, 1942, courtesy Doug Rollins.
40. Doug Rollins, "'Twas the Flight Before Christmas: F/O Don Rollins of 407 Squadron, RCAF, Survives a Nocturnal Mid-Air Collision," *CAHS Journal* 56, no. 3 (Fall 2018): 95.
41. Rollins, "Danger Is My Opportunity." All quotations from Rollins in this section are taken from this source.
42. Terraine, *Business in Great Waters*, 633.
43. Terraine, 633.
44. Paterson, *First U-Boat Flotilla*, 183.
45. Patrick Beesly, *Very Special Intelligence: The Story of the Admiralty's Operational Intelligence Centre, 1939–1945* (New York: Ballantine Books, 1981), 199.
46. Quoted in Beesly, 200.
47. William Fisher, "The End of HMCS St. Croix," *Canadian Military History* 8, no. 3 (January 24, 2012): 63–69.
48. Fisher, 63, 64.
49. "The Men—U-boat Commanders: Rudolf Bahr," Uboat.net, n.d., https://uboat.net/men/commanders/30.html.
50. Quoted in Bercuson and Herwig, *Deadly Seas*, 261.

51. Lawrence Paterson, *First U-Boat Flotilla* (Barnsley, UK: Leo Cooper Ltd., 2002), 207.
52. Fisher, "End of HMCS St. Croix." All quotations from Fisher in this section are taken from this source (see pp. 64, 65, 68, and 69).
53. Carl A. Christie, *Truly Royal: The History of the Canadian Air Force* (Toronto: University of Toronto Press, forthcoming), ch. 14, 15.
54. Quoted in F.H. Hinsley, *British Intelligence in the Second World War*, vol. 3 (London: HMSO, 1981), 225.
55. M.B. Evans, quoted in Douglas et al., *Blue Water Navy*, 93.
56. Douglas et al., 93.
57. Sharon Adams, "GNATs versus CATs," *Legion*, June 16, 2017.
58. A.L. Macdonald diary, 11 August 1943, A. L. Macdonald Papers F390, LAC.
59. Schmietenknop, *Saved* (self-published, 2007), ch. 5.
60. Schmietenknop, ch. 5.
61. Quoted in Robert Goralski, *World War II Almanac, 1931–1945: A Political and Military Record* (New York: Random House, 1981), 293.
62. Andrew Blum, "When the Nazis Came to Canada," *Toronto Star*, June 29, 2019, in Blum, *The Weather Machine* (New York: HarperCollins, 2019).
63. Douglas et al., *Blue Water Navy*, 97, 98.

Chapter Eleven: Hunted to Exhaustion

1. Peter Fritzsche, *Life and Death in the Third Reich* (Cambridge, MA: Harvard University Press, 2008), 284, 285.
2. Quoted in G.H. Bennett, "The 1942 Laconia Order, The Murder of Shipwrecked Survivors and the Allied Pursuit of Justice 1945–46," *Law, Crime and History* 1, no. 1 (2011): 16–34.
3. "The Men—U-boat Commanders: Heinz-Wilhelm Eck," Uboat.net., n.d., https://uboat.net/men/commanders/30.html.
4. Peter Padfield, *Dönitz, the Last Führer: Portrait of a Nazi War Leader* (London: Victor Gollancz, 1984), 355.
5. Edward D. Re, "War Crimes Trials; Vol. I—The 'Peleus' Trial" (book review), *St. John's Law Review* 23, no. 1 (November 1948): 205.
6. "Canadian Corvette Aids Blazing Tanker," *Winnipeg Free Press*, February 17, 1944.
7. George Doig Jr., email correspondence with author, November 26, 2020.

8. "Canadian Corvette Aids Blazing Tanker."
9. "Canadian Corvette Aids Blazing Tanker."
10. Barb Edy, email correspondence with author, June 27, 2013.
11. Harold Doig, interview by author, November 1977, Saskatoon, SK.
12. Bill Bint, diary, Naval Museum of Alberta, Calgary, AB. With permission.
13. Fraser McKee and Robert Darlington, *The Canadian Naval Chronicle, 1939–1945: The Successes and Losses of the Canadian Navy in World War II* (St. Catharines, ON: Vanwell, 1998), 143.
14. Bint diary.
15. Joseph Schull, *Far Distant Ships: An Official Account of Canadian Naval Operations in World War II* (Toronto: Stoddart, 1987), 255.
16. Bint diary.
17. McKee and Darlington, *Canadian Naval Chronicle*, 144.
18. William Sclater, *Haida: A Story of the Hard Fighting Tribal Class Destroyers of the Royal Canadian Navy* (Toronto: Oxford University Press, 1946), 98.
19. W.A.B. Douglas, Roger Sarty, Michael Whitby, Robert H. Caldwell, William Johnston, and William G.P Rawling, *A Blue Water Navy*, vol. 2, pt. 2 of *The Official Operational History of the Royal Canadian Navy in the Second World War, 1939–1943* (St. Catharines, ON: Vanwell, 2007), 41.
20. Ken Macpherson, *Frigates of the Royal Canadian Navy, 1943–1974* (St. Catharines, ON: Vanwell Publishing, 1988), foreword.
21. Quoted in MacPherson, foreword.
22. MacPherson, foreword.
23. Quoted in MacPherson, foreword.
24. MacPherson, introduction.
25. John M. Dyke, "Memories of My Life as a Professional Engineer in the Royal Canadian Navy and the Canadian Boiler Industry" (unpublished), 3. With permission from Colin and Suzanne Dyke.
26. Douglas et al., *Blue Water Navy*, 420.
27. McKee and Darlington, *Canadian Naval Chronicle*, 148.
28. "Ian Tate—Surviving a Torpedo Attack—Port Hope Veteran One of 38 Pulled from Frigid St. Lawrence [*sic*] after U-boat Strikes," *Northumberland News*, November 9, 2007.
29. Douglas et al., *A Blue Water Navy*, 422.
30. Quoted in McKee and Darlington, *Canadian Naval Chronicle*, 148.

31. "Sacrifice And Heroism of Valleyfield Crew Naval Epic," *Evening Telegram* (Toronto), May 20, 1944.
32. "Navy Tells of Courage of Valleyfield Crew," *Halifax Chronicle*, May 20, 1944.
33. "Last Message to Wife Given Toronto Survivor by Valleyfield Skipper," *Evening Telegram* (Toronto), May 20, 1944.
34. Rome, David, ed., *Canadian Jews in World War II:* pt. 1, *Decorations* (Montreal: Canadian Jewish Congress, 1947), 63.
35. John Morley Dyke, "Veteran Stories: John Morley Dyke, Navy," Memory Project, Historica Canada, https://www.thememoryproject.com/stories/492:john-morley-dyke/.
36. Dyke, "Memories of My Life." All quotations from Dyke in this section are taken from this source (see pp. 1, 4, 5, and 6).
37. Mac Johnston, *Corvettes Canada: Convoy Veterans of World War II Tell Their True Stories* (Whitby, ON: McGraw-Hill Ryerson, 1994), 241, 242.
38. John Terraine, *Business in Great Waters: The U-Boat Wars, 1916–1945* (Barnsley, UK: Leo Cooper, 1989), 768.
39. Tony German, "Preserving the Atlantic Lifeline," *Legion*, May/June 1998.
40. Herbert A. Werner, *Iron Coffins: A Personal Account of the German U-boat Battles of World War II* (New York: Holt, Rinehart and Winston, 1969), 230, 231.
41. Quoted in Werner. All remaining quotations from Werner and Rösing's exchange are taken from this source (see pp. 236–37).
42. "About Operation Overlord: Facts and Figures," *Seattle Times*, June 6, 2014.
43. Werner, *Iron Coffins*, 242.
44. Marc Milner, *Battle of the Atlantic* (Stroud, UK: Tempus, 2005), 219.
45. Walter Schmietenknop, *Saved* (self-published, 2007). Schmietenknop's recollections of this incident are all taken from this source (see ch. 5, 6, and 10). With permission.
46. Kevin Plummer, "From Sunday School Teacher to Victoria Cross Recipient: David E. Hornell of Mimico and His Flight Crew's Struggle to Survive Adrift in the North Atlantic," *Torontoist*, June 2014.
47. Quoted in Plummer.
48. Hugh Halliday, *Target U-boat* (unpublished), 133. With permission.
49. Lawrence Paterson, *Second U-Boat Flotilla* (Barnsley, UK: Leo

Cooper, 2003), 171.
50. Quoted in Plummer, "From Sunday School Teacher."
51. Quoted in Plummer.
52. Halliday, *Target U-boat*, 134.
53. Larry Milberry and Hugh Halliday, *The Royal Canadian Air Force at War 1939–1945* (Toronto: CANAV Books, 1990), 347.
54. Plummer, "From Sunday School Teacher."
55. Milberry and Halliday, *Royal Canadian Air Force*, 347.
56. Halliday, *Target U-boat*, 135.
57. Plummer, "From Sunday School Teacher."
58. Quoted in Milberry and Halliday, *Royal Canadian Air Force*, 348.
59. W.A.B. Douglas, *The Creation of a National Air Force: The Official History of the Royal Canadian Air Force*, vol. 2 (Toronto: University of Toronto Press, 1986), 594.
60. Quoted in "Proud of Dave for V.C. and Crew's Tribute," *Globe and Mail*, July 27, 1944.
61. Mike Parker, *Running the Gauntlet: An Oral History of Canadian Merchant Seamen in World War II* (Halifax: Nimbus, 1994), 154.
62. Quoted in Johnston, *Corvettes Canada*, 190.
63. Douglas et al., *Blue Water Navy*, 409.
64. Anthony Griffin, *Footfalls in Memory* (self-published, 1998), 131. With permission.
65. "U 845" Interrogation of Survivors, May 1944, C.B. 04051 (102), Naval Intelligence Division, Admiralty, S.W. 1. N.I.D. 03209/44, http://www.uboatarchive.net/Int/U-845INT.htm.
66. "U 845" Interrogation of Survivors.

Chapter Twelve: "For Us, the War Was Over"

1. Roy Harbin, interview by Alex Barris, June 17, 1993, Agincourt, ON. All quotations from Harbin in this section are taken from this interview.
2. "U413, U1209, U877 and U199" Interrogation of Survivors, Naval Intelligence Division, Admiralty, S.W.1., N.I.D. 1/PW/REP/17, IV. Last Patrol and Sinking of U1209, http://www.uboatarchive.net/Int/U-413INT.htm/.
3. Sally Corbet, ed., "On This Day 18th December 1944 *U*-1209 Hits Wolf Rock," Penwith Local History Group, Penzance, UK, http://www.penwithlocalhistorygroup.co.uk/on-this-day/?id=314.

4. Werner Hirschmann, speech to Royal Canadian Military Institute, Toronto, ON, May 27, 2010.
5. Marc Milner, *Battle of the Atlantic* (Stroud, UK: Tempus, 2005), 245.
6. Hirschmann speech.
7. Hirschmann speech.
8. Werner Hirschmann, "*U-190*: Life in the U-boats," in "A Double Look: The Esquimalt Sinking," in Thomas G. Lynch, ed., *Fading Memories: Canadian Sailors and the Battle of the Atlantic* (Halifax: Atlantic Chief and Petty Officers Association, 1993), 48.
9. R.V. Dexter, "The Sea-Breeze Hodograph at Halifax," *Bulletin of the American Meteorological Society* 39, no. 5 (May 1958): 245.
10. Terry Manuel, correspondence with author, June 20, 1994.
11. Tom Hawthorn, "HMCS Esquimalt's Final Survivor," *Globe and Mail*, July 22, 2009.
12. Hirschmann, "Double Look," 49.
13. Manuel correspondence. All quotations from Manuel in this section are taken from this source.
14. Joe Wilson, "Torpedoed!" in "A Double Look: The Esquimalt Sinking," in Lynch, *Fading Memories*, 43.
15. Quoted in Manuel correspondence.
16. Wilson, "Torpedoed!" 43.
17. Werner Hirschmann, "Veteran Stories: Werner Max Hirschmann, Navy," Memory Project, Historica Canada, http://www.thememoryproject.com/stories/1434:werner-max-hirschmann/.
18. Liam D. Dwyer, correspondence with author, October 1, 1993. Pompano Beach, FL.
19. Margaret Haliburton (née Los), interview by Alex Barris and author, 1992, Toronto, ON. All quotations from Los in this section are taken from this source.
20. Karl Dönitz, *40 Fragen an Karl Dönitz* (Munich: Bernard & Graef, 1980), 164.
21. Hirschmann, "Veteran Stories."
22. Quoted in Peter Padfield, *Dönitz, the Last Führer: Portrait of a Nazi War Leader* (London: Victor Gollancz, 1984), 419.
23. Hirschmann, "Veteran Stories."
24. Quoted in "The Jolly Sailor," Royal Aviation Museum of Western Canada, 2018, info@royalaviationmuseum.com. All quotations from Jolly in this section are taken from this source.

25. Jim Hazlewood, interview by Alex Barris, July 19, 1993, Agincourt, ON. All quotations from Hazlewood in this chapter are taken from this interview.
26. David MacDonald, interview by Alex Barris, June 23, 1993, Toronto, ON.
27. Franklin Russell, "The $3 Million Party That Wrecked Halifax," *Maclean's,* March 26, 1960.
28. Russell.
29. Beatrice Geary (née Schreiber), correspondence with Alex Barris and author, October 2, 1993.
30. MacDonald interview.
31. Martin Franchetto, *Lifejackets, Duffel Coats and Rubber Boots* (unpublished memoir, 2004). Courtesy Elaine Thorpe.
32. Russell, "$3 Million Party."
33. Alex Barris and Ted Barris, *Days of Victory: Canadians Remember 1939–1945* (Toronto: Macmillan, 1995), 222.
34. MacDonald interview.
35. Rodine "Ronnie" Buckley-Beevers (Egan), interview by author, 1993, Uxbridge, ON.
36. Quoted in "Says Civilians Were Largely Responsible," *Halifax Herald,* May 10, 1945.
37. Russell, "$3 Million Party."
38. Allan Butler, quoted in Rosamond Greer, *The Girls of the King's Navy* (Victoria: Sono Nis Press, 1983), 122.
39. "Citizens Call for Searching Inquiry," *Halifax Herald,* May 10, 1945; also Greer, *Girls of the King's Navy,* 122.
40. Leonard Murray, "An Incident: Says Civilians Were Largely Responsible" (editorial), *Halifax Herald,* May 10, 1945.
41. Anthony Griffin, *Footfalls in Memory* (self-published, 1998), 139. With permission.
42. Roger Sarty, "Rear-Admiral L.W. Murray and the Battle of the Atlantic: The Professional Who Led Canada's Citizen Sailors," in Bernd Horn and Stephen Harris, eds., *Warrior Chiefs: Perspectives on Senior Canadian Military Leaders* (Toronto: Dundurn Press, 2001), 185.
43. Carman Eldridge, correspondence with author, September 24, 1993.
44. Joseph Schull, *Far Distant Ships: An Official Account of Canadian Naval Operations in WWII* (Toronto: Stoddart, 1987), 405.

45. Eldridge correspondence.
46. Schull, *Far Distant Ships*, 405.
47. "Report of Surrender of Enemy Submarine U-889," submitted to Captain (D) Halifax by 1st Lt James C. Pratt (HMCS *Dunvegan*), May 14, 1945, DHH File OS.045-1.
48. Franchetto, *Lifejackets*. All quotations from Franchetto in this section are taken from this source.
49. Hirschmann speech. All quotations from Hirschmann and Wilson in this section are taken from this source.
50. Marc Milner, *Battle of the Atlantic* (Stroud, UK: Tempus, 2005), 249.
51. "Canadian Navy to Sink German Submarine," *Windsor Daily Star*, July 17, 1947.
52. Listing of U-boats, "U-190," Uboat.net, n.d., https://uboat.net/boats/u190.htm.
53. Schull, *Far Distant Ships*, 430, 431.
54. Grant Baines, interview by author, February 16, 2020, Uxbridge, ON.
55. Marion Hill, *Bletchley Park People: Churchill's Geese That Never Cackled* (Stroud, UK: Sutton, 2004), 56, 57.
56. Nan Adair, interview by author, June 9, 2006, Milton Keynes, UK. All quotations from Adair in this section are taken from this source.
57. Ken Davy, interview by author, July 9, 2019, Burlington, ON. All quotations from Davy in this chapter are taken from this interview.
58. Richard Gimblett and Tabitha Marshall, "Royal Canadian Navy," *Canadian Encyclopedia*, March 4, 2015.
59. James Pritchard, *A Bridge of Ships: Canadian Shipbuilding During the Second World War* (Montreal: McGill-Queen's University Press, 2011), 326, 330.
60. John Terraine, *Business in Great Waters: The U-Boat Wars, 1916–1945* (Barnsley, UK: Leo Cooper, 1989), 767–69.
61. Robert Fisher, "Canadian Merchant Ship Losses of the Second World War, 1939–1945," NavalHistory.ca, June 2001, http://www.familyheritage.ca/Articles/merchant1.html.
62. Patricia Giesler, *Valour at Sea: Canada's Merchant Navy* (Veterans' Affairs Canada, Ottawa: Queen's Printer: 2005), 29.
63. Bob Rae, interview by Valerie Pringle, *CTV News*, November 11, 1994.
64. Bob Rae, presentation to Smith-Ennismore Historical Society, Lakefield, ON, November 2001.

65. Matthew Moore, "The Kiss of Death Bestowed with Gratitude: The Postwar Treatment of Canada's Second World War Merchant Navy, Redress, and the Negotiation of Veteran Identity" (master's thesis, Carleton University, 2015), 115, 116, 140.
66. Bob Rae, interview by Mike Duffy, *CTV News*, December 13, 1994.
67. Richard Holmes, "Normandy 1944," lecture to Defence Electronics History Society, May 11, 2006, Shrivenham, UK.
68. Schull, *Far Distant Ships*, 430.
69. Thomas C. Steven, "Canadian Shipyards Notably Increase Production in 1942," *Canadian Shipping and Marine Engineering News*, January 1943.
70. Robert G. Halford, *The Unknown Navy: Canada's World War II Merchant Navy* (St. Catharines, ON: Vanwell, 1995), 107.
71. John Boileau, "Canada's Merchant Navy: The Men That Saved the World," *Legion*, July 14, 2010.
72. "The Milk for Britain Story: A Testament to Kin and Canada," Kin Canada, 2021, https://www.kincanada.ca/milk-for-britain.
73. Nicholas Masheter, correspondence with author, April 2, 2021.

Sources

UNPUBLISHED SOURCES

Author Interviews

All interviews conducted in the preparation of this book are included in the Notes section.

Unpublished Works

Bint, Bill, unpublished diary. Courtesy Naval Museum of Alberta.

Birch, F. "A History of British Sigint 1914–1945." GCHQ typescript, vol. 1.

Bonner, Harold Pearson. *Stay Below Decks*. Courtesy Allan Bonner.

Curry, Frank. "Royal Canadian Navy War Diary, 1940 to 1945," March 10, 1941. Veterans Affairs Canada.

Dyke, John M. "Memories of My Life as a Professional Engineer in the Royal Canadian Navy." Courtesy Colin and Suzanne Dyke.

Franchetto, Martin. *Lifejackets, Duffel Coats and Rubber Boots*, 2004. Courtesy of Elaine Thorpe.

Glover, William. "Officer Training and the Quest for Operational Efficiency in the Royal Canadian Navy, 1939–45." PhD diss., King's College, London, 1999.

Godfrey, John H. "The Naval Memoirs of Admiral J.H. Godfrey," Vol. 5, 1947–1950. Naval Intelligence Division (NID), Part II, National Maritime Museum.

Halliday, Hugh. "Target U-boat." With permission from author.

Mills, Harold. *Frank Mills R.C.N.V.R.* Bk. 1 and Bk. 2, *Frank's Navy Service in Canada and Overseas*. Courtesy of author.

Moore, Matthew. "The Kiss of Death Bestowed with Gratitude." MA thesis, Carleton University, Ottawa, 2015.

Murray, Leonard Warren. Notes prepared for CBC interview, 1967. Library and Archives Canada (LAC), Ottawa, Admiral Murray papers, Collection MG30 E207.

Pickard, A.F. Diary, 21–5 May 1941. A.F. Pickard papers, Department of National Defence, Directorate of History and Heritage (DHH).

Rollins, Douglas A. "Danger Is My Opportunity: The Life and Times of Donald Edward Rollins, 1920–1972." Courtesy of author.

Roscoe, Spud. "The Fairmiles: Canada's Little Ships." Radio research paper.

Wells, Anthony Roland. "Studies in British Naval Intelligence, 1880–1945." Thesis, King's College, London.

PUBLISHED SOURCES

Books

Allen, Trevor. *The Storm Passed By: Ireland and the Battle of the Atlantic.* Newbridge, IE: Irish Academic Press, 1996.

Badcock, T.C. *The Enigma: World War II Story about a German Submarine That Came to Newfoundland.* St. John's, NL: DRC Publishing, 2009.

Baker, Richard. *The Terror of Tobermory: An Informal Biography of Vice-Admiral Sir Gilbert Stephenson, KBE, CB, GMB.* London: W.H. Allen, 1972.

Barrett, Harry B. *The Navy & Me.* Port Dover, ON: Patterson's Creek Press, 2003.

Barris, Alex, and Ted Barris. *Days of Victory: Canadians Remember 1939–1945.* Toronto: Macmillan, 1995.

Beckman, Morris. *Atlantic Roulette: A Merchantman at War, June 1940: Running the Gauntlet of U-Boat Alley, E-Boat Alley, and the Luftwaffe.* Brighton, UK: Tom Donovan, 1996.

Beesly, Patrick. *Very Special Intelligence: The Story of the Admiralty's Operational Intelligence Centre, 1939–1945.* New York: Ballantine Books, 1981.

Bercuson, David J., and Holger H. Herwig. *Deadly Seas: The Duel Between the St Croix and the U305 in the Battle of the Atlantic.* Toronto: Random House, 1997.

———. *Long Night of the Tankers: Hitler's War Against Caribbean Oil.* Calgary: University of Calgary Press, 2014.

Bessner, Ellin. *Double Threat: Canadian Jews, the Military, and World War II.* Toronto: New Jewish Press, 2018.

Bishop, Arthur. *Our Bravest and Our Best: The Stories of Canada's Victoria Cross Winners.* Whitby, ON: McGraw-Hill Ryerson, 1995.

Blair, Clay. *Hitler's U-Boat War: The Hunters, 1939–1942.* New York: Random House, 1996.

Bliss, Michael. *Right Honourable Men: The Descent of Canadian Politics from Macdonald to Chrétien.* Toronto: HarperCollins, 2004.

Blum, Andrew. *The Weather Machine.* New York: HarperCollins, 2019.

Boileau, John, and Dan Black. *Too Young to Die: Canada's Boy Soldiers, Sailors and Airmen in the Second World War.* Toronto: James Lorimer & Co., 2016.

Bothwell, Robert, and William Kilbourn. *C.D. Howe: A Biography.* Toronto: McClelland & Stewart, 1979.

Bourrie, Mark. *The Fog of War: Censorship of Canada's Media in World War Two.* Vancouver: Douglas & McIntyre, 2011.

B.R. (CAN) 1503, Instructions to Sick Berth Staff of the Royal Canadian Navy. Ottawa: Edmond Cloutier, 1943.

Brock, Jeffry V. *The Dark Broad Seas: Memories of a Sailor.* Vol. 1, *With Many Voices.* Toronto: McClelland & Stewart, 1981.

Brookes, Ewart. *The Gates of Hell: The Terrible Story of the Arctic Convoys of the Second World War.* London: Arrow Books, 1960.

Broome, Jack. *Convoy Is to Scatter: The Story of PQ 17.* London: Futura Publications, 1974.

Brown, Anthony Cave. *Bodyguard of Lies: The Extraordinary, True Story of the Clandestine War of Deception That Hid the Secrets of D-Day from Hitler and Sealed the Allied Victory.* Toronto: Bantam Books, 1976.

Bruce, Jean. *Back the Attack!: Canadian Women During the Second World War—at Home and Abroad.* Toronto: Macmillan, 1985.

Buchheim, Lothar-Günther. *U-boat War: The Experience of Submarine War.* Translated by Gudie Lawaetz. New York: Bantam Books, 1979.

Burrow, Len, and Emile Beaudoin. *Unlucky Lady: The Life and Death of HMCS Athabaskan 1940–44.* Toronto: McClelland & Stewart, 1989.

Callison, Brian. *The Bone Collectors: A Novel of the Atlantic Convoys.* London: Collins, 1984.

Christie, Carl A. *Ocean Bridge: The History of RAF Ferry Command.* Toronto: University of Toronto Press, 1995.

———. *Truly Royal: The History of the Canadian Air Force.* Toronto: University of Toronto Press, forthcoming.

Churchill, Winston. *The Second World War: Their Finest Hour.* Boston: Houghton Mifflin, 1949.

———. *The Second World War: The Grand Alliance.* Boston: Houghton Mifflin, 1950.

———. *The Second World War: The Hinge of Fate.* Boston: Houghton Mifflin, 1950.

———. *The Second World War: Closing the Ring.* Boston: Houghton Mifflin, 1951.

Coles, Dudley. *Leap of Faith: A Reflection on Choices That Shaped an Extraordinary Life.* Ottawa: Library and Archives Canada, 2008.

Collins, Paul W. *The Newfyjohn Solution: St. John's Newfoundland as a Case Study of Second World War Allied Naval Base Development During the Battle of the Atlantic.* Alberta: WriteAdvice Press, 2014.

Cooper, Matthew. *The German Army, 1939–1945.* New York: Stein and Day, 1978.

Coulter, J.L.S. *The Royal Naval Medical Service.* Vol. 2, *Operations.* London: HMSO, 1956.

Crooks, Sylvia. *Homefront & Battlefront: Nelson BC in World War II.* Vancouver: Granville Island Publishing, 2007.

Cunningham, Cyril. *Beaulieu: The Finishing School for Secret Agents.* Barnsley, UK: Pen & Sword Books, 1998.

Cuthbertson, Ken. *1945: The Year That Made Modern Canada.* Toronto: HarperCollins, 2020.

Dönitz, Karl. *Ten Years and Twenty Days.* Translated by R.H. Stevens. London: Weidenfeld & Nicolson, 1959.

———. *40 Fragen an Karl Dönitz.* Munich: Bernard & Graef, 1980.

———. *Mein wechselvolles Leben.* Göttingen: Musteerschmidt Verlag, 1968.

Douglas, W.A.B. *The Creation of a National Air Force: The Official History of the Royal Canadian Air Force.* Vol. 2. Ottawa: University of Toronto Press, 1986.

Douglas, W.A.B., Roger Sarty, Michael Whitby, Robert H. Caldwell, William Johnston, and William G.P. Rawling. *No Higher Purpose.* Vol. 2, pt. 1, of *The Official Operational History of the Royal Canadian*

Navy in the Second World War, 1939–1943. St. Catharines, ON: Vanwell, 2002.

———. *A Blue Water Navy:* Vol. 2, pt. 2, of *The Official Operational History of the Royal Canadian Navy in the Second World War, 1939–1943*. St. Catharines, ON: Vanwell, 2007.

Dunmore, Spencer. *Above and Beyond: The Canadians' War in the Air, 1939–45*. Toronto: McClelland & Stewart, 1996.

———. *In Great Waters: The Epic Story of the Battle of the Atlantic, 1939–45*. Toronto: McClelland & Stewart, 1999.

Edwards, Bernard. *Attack and Sink! The Battle for Convoy SC42*. Dorset, UK: New Era Writer's Guild, 1995.

———. *The Wolf Packs Gather: Mayhem in the Western Approaches 1940*. Barnsley, UK: Pen & Sword Books, 2011.

Enver, Ted. *Britain's Best Kept Secret: Ultra's Base at Bletchley Park*. Stroud, UK: Sutton Publishing, 1994.

Essex, James W. *Victory in the St. Lawrence: Canada's Unknown War*. Erin, ON: Boston Mills Press, 1984.

Evans, George H. *Through the Corridors of Hell*. Antigonish, NS: Formac Publishing, 1980.

Fitzgerald, Jack. *Battlefront Newfoundland: Britain's Oldest Colony at War, 1939–1945*. St. John's: Creative, 2010.

Flower, Desmond, and James Reeves, eds. *The War 1939–45*. London: Cassell, 1960.

Fritzsche, Peter. *Life and Death in the Third Reich*. Cambridge, MA: Harvard University Press, 2008.

Gaffen, Fred. *Forgotten Soldiers*. Penticton, BC: Theytus Books, 1985.

Gafiuk, Anne. *Quietus: Last Flight; Accident Proneness in WWII: Wartime Aviation Stories on the Canadian Home Front*. Nanton, AB: Nanton Lancaster Society, 2017.

German, Tony. *The Sea Is at Our Gates: The History of the Canadian Navy*. Toronto: McClelland & Stewart, 1990.

Giesler, Patricia. *Valour at Sea: Canada's Merchant Navy*. Veterans Affairs Canada, Ottawa: Queen's Printer, 2005.

Goodwin, James. "*Our Gallant Doctor*"—*Enigma and Tragedy: Surgeon Lieutenant George Hendry and HMCS* Ottawa, *1942*. Toronto: Dundurn, 2007.

Goralski, Robert. *World War II Almanac, 1931–1945: A Political and Military Record*. New York: Random House, 1981.

Greenfield, Nathan M. *Battle of the St. Lawrence: The Second World War in Canada*. Toronto: HarperCollins, 2004.

Greer, Rosamond. *The Girls of the King's Navy*. Victoria, BC: Sono Nis Press, 1983.

Griffin, Anthony. *Footfalls in Memory*. Self-published, 1998.

Hadley, Michael L. *Count Not the Dead: The Popular Image of the German Submarine*. Montreal: McGill-Queen's University Press, 1995.

———. *U-boats Against Canada: German Submarines in Canadian Waters*. Montreal: McGill-Queen's University Press, 1985.

Hadley, Michael L., Rob Huebert, and Fred W. Crickard, eds. *A Nation's Navy: In Quest of Canadian Naval Identity*. Montreal: McGill-Queen's University Press, 1996.

Hague, Arnold. *The Allied Convoy System, 1939–1945: Its Organization, Defence and Operation*. St. Catharines, ON: Vanwell, 2000.

Halford, Robert G. *The Unknown Navy: Canada's World War II Merchant Navy*. St. Catharines, ON: Vanwell, 1995.

Harbron, John D. *C.D. Howe*. Toronto: Fitzhenry and Whiteside, 1980.

———. *The Longest Battle: The RCN in the Atlantic, 1939–1945*. St. Catharines, ON: Vanwell, 1995.

Hawkins, Ian, ed. *Destroyer: An Anthology of First-hand Accounts of the War at Sea, 1939–1945*, London: Anova Books, 2008.

Heiligman, Deborah. *Torpedoes: The True Story of the World War II Sinking of the Children's Ship*. New York: Henry Holt, 2019.

Hill, Marion. *Bletchley Park People: Churchill's Geese That Never Cackled*. Stroud, UK: Sutton, 2004.

Hinsley, F.H. *British Intelligence in the Second World War*. Vol. 3. London: HMSO, 1981.

Hirschfeld, Wolfgang. *The Secret Diary of a U-Boat*. Barnsley, UK: Leo Cooper, 1996.

Historica-Dominion Institute. *We Were Freedom: Canadian Stories of the Second World War*. Toronto: Key Porter, 2010.

Horn, Bernd, and Stephen Harris. *Warrior Chiefs: Perspectives on Senior Canadian Military Leaders*. Toronto: Dundurn, 2001.

How, Douglas. *Night of the Caribou*. Hantsport, NS: Lancelot Press, 1988.

Howarth, David. *The Shetland Bus: Memoir of Wartime Convoys*. London: Grafton Books, 1991.

Hutchison, Bruce. *The Incredible Canadian: A Candid Portrait of Mackenzie King*. Toronto: Longmans, Green, 1953.

Johnston, Mac. *Corvettes Canada: Convoy Veterans of WWII Tell Their True Stories*. Whitby, ON: McGraw-Hill Ryerson, 1994.
Jones, R.V. *Most Secret War: British Scientific Intelligence, 1939–1945*. London: Penguin, 1978.
Kemp, Paul. *Convoy! Drama in Arctic Waters*. London: Castle Books, 2004.
Kenyon, David. *Bletchley Park and D-Day: The Untold Story of How the Battle of Normandy Was Won*. London: Yale University Press, 2019.
Kimball, Warren F., ed. *Churchill and Roosevelt: The Complete Correspondence*. Vol. 1, *Alliance Emerging, October 1933–November 1942*. Princeton, NJ: Princeton University Press, 1984.
Lafitte, François. *The Internment of Aliens*. Harmondsworth, UK: Penguin, 1940.
Lamb, James B. *The Corvette Navy: True Stories from Canada's Atlantic War*. Toronto: Stoddart, 2000.
———. *On the Triangle Run*. Toronto: Macmillan Canada, 1986.
Lawrence, Hal. *A Bloody War: One Man's Memories of the Canadian Navy, 1939–45*. Toronto: Macmillan Canada, 1979.
———. *Tales of the North Atlantic*. Toronto: McClelland & Stewart, 1985.
Léderrey, E. *Germany's Defeat in the East: The Soviet Armies at War, 1941–1945*. London: War Office, 1955.
Littler, John Caldecott. *Sea Fever*. Victoria: Kiwi Publications, 1995.
Litwiller, Roger. *White Ensign Flying: Corvette HMCS* Trentonian. Toronto: Dundurn, 2014.
Livingston, Sean E. *Oakville's Flower: The History of HMCS* Oakville. Toronto: Dundurn, 2014.
Longmate, Norman. *How We Lived Then: A History of Everyday Life During the Second World War*. London: Hutchinson, 1971.
Lynch, Mack, ed. *Salty Dips: And All Our Joints Were Limber*. Vol. 2. Ottawa: Naval Officers' Associations of Canada, 1985.
Lynch, Thomas G. *Canada's Flowers: History of the Corvettes of Canada, 1939–1945*. Halifax: Nimbus, 1981.
———., ed. *Fading Memories: Canadian Sailors and the Battle of the Atlantic*. Halifax: Atlantic Chief and Petty Officers Association, 1993.
Lynn, Vera. *We'll Meet Again: A Personal and Social History of World War Two*. London: Sidgwick & Jackson, 1989.
MacBeth, Jack. *Ready, Aye, Ready: An Illustrated History of the Royal Canadian Navy*. Toronto: Key Porter Books, 1989.

Macintyre, Donald. *The Battle of the Atlantic*. London: Pan Books, 1969.
———. *U-Boat Killer: Fighting the U-Boats in the Battle of the Atlantic*. London: Rigel, 2004.
Macpherson, Ken. *Frigates of the Royal Canadian Navy, 1943–1974*. St. Catharines, ON: Vanwell, 1988.
———. *Minesweepers of the Royal Canadian Navy, 1938–1945*. St. Catharines, ON: Vanwell, 1990.
———. *The River Class Destroyers of the Royal Canadian Navy*. Toronto: Charles J. Musson, 1985.
Macpherson, Ken, and Marc Milner. *Corvettes of the Royal Canadian Navy, 1939–1945*. St. Catharines, ON: Vanwell, 1993.
McKee, Fraser. *The Armed Yachts of Canada*. Erin, ON: Boston Mills, 1983.
———. *Sink All the Shipping There: The Wartime Loss of Canada's Merchant Ships and Fishing Schooners*. St. Catharines, ON: Vanwell, 2004.
McKee, Fraser, and Robert Darlington. *The Canadian Naval Chronicle, 1939–1945: The Successes and Losses of the Canadian Navy in World War II*. St. Catharines, ON: Vanwell, 1996.
Melady, John. *Escape from Canada! The Untold Story of German POWs in Canada, 1939–1945*. Toronto: Macmillan Canada, 1981.
Metson, Graham. *An East Coast Port: Halifax at War, 1939–1945*. Toronto: McGraw-Hill Ryerson, 1981.
Middlebrook, Martin. *Convoy: The Battle for Convoys SC 122 and HX 229*. London: Penguin, 1978.
Middlebrook, Martin, and Chris Everitt. *The Bomber Command Diaries: An Operational Reference Book, 1939–1945*. New York: Viking, 1985.
Milberry, Larry, and Hugh Halliday. *The Royal Canadian Air Force at War, 1939–1945*. Toronto: CANAV Books, 1990.
Milner, Marc, *Battle of the Atlantic*. Stroud, UK: Tempus, 2005.
———. *Canada's Navy: The First Century*. Toronto: University of Toronto Press, 1999.
———. *North Atlantic Run: The Royal Canadian Navy and the Battle for the Convoys*. Toronto: University of Toronto Press, 1985.
Molson, Kenneth M. *Pioneering in Canadian Air Transport*. Winnipeg: James Richardson & Sons, 1986.
Mortin, Jenni. *A Prairie Town Goes to War*. Shelburne, ON: Battered Silicon Dispatch Box, 2003.
Navigation Dictionary. 2nd ed. U.S. Naval Oceanographic Office, Washington, DC: U.S. Government Printing Office, 1956.

Neary, Steve. *The Enemy on Our Doorstep: The German Attacks at Bell Island, Newfoundland, 1942*. St. John's: Jesperson Press, 1994.
Nicholson, G.W.L. *More Fighting Newfoundlanders: A History of Newfoundland's Fighting Forces in the Second World War*. St. John's: Government of Newfoundland, 1969.
O'Brien, David. *HX 72, First Convoy to Die: The Wolfpack Attack That Woke Up the Admiralty*. Halifax: Nimbus, 1999.
O'Keefe, David. *One Day in August: The Untold Story Behind Canada's Tragedy at Dieppe*. Toronto: Alfred A. Knopf, 2013.
Padfield, Peter. *Dönitz, the Last Führer: Portrait of a Nazi War Leader*. London: Victor Gollancz, 1984.
Parker, Mike. *Running the Gauntlet: An Oral History of Canadian Merchant Seamen in World War II*. Halifax: Nimbus, 1994.
Paterson, Lawrence. *First U-Boat Flotilla*. Barnsley, UK: Leo Cooper, 2002.
———. *Second U-Boat Flotilla*. Barnsley, UK: Leo Cooper, 2003.
Pollock, George. *The* Jervis Bay. London: William Kimber, 1958.
Portugal, Jean E. *We Were There: The Navy*. Vol. 1, *A Record for Canada*. Shelburne, ON: Battered Silicon Dispatch Box, 1998.
Preston, Antony, and Alan Raven. *Ensign 3: Flower Class Corvettes*. Norwich, UK: Bivouac Books, 1973.
Pritchard, James. *A Bridge of Ships: Canadian Shipbuilding During the Second World War*. Montreal: McGill-Queen's University Press, 2011.
Pugsley, William H. *Saints, Devils and Ordinary Seamen: Life on the Royal Canadian Navy's Lower Deck*. Toronto: Collins, 1945.
Quigley, Gene. *Voices of World War II: A Collection of Oral Histories*. St. John's: Jesperson, 2006. Transcripts courtesy of the author.
Rankin, Nicholas. *Ian Fleming's Commandos: The Story of 30 Assault Unit in WWII*. London: Faber and Faber, 2011.
Reid, Max. *DEMS at War! Defensively Equipped Merchant Ships and the Battle of the Atlantic, 1939–1945*. Ottawa: Commoners Publishing Society Inc., 1990.
Richards, Denis. *The Fight at Odds*. Vol. 1 of *Royal Air Force 1939–1945*. London: HMSO, 1953.
Richards, Denis, and Hilary St. George Saunders. *The Fight Avails*. Vol. 2 of *Royal Air Force 1939-1945*. London: HMSO, 1954.
Richards, Stanley T. *Operation Sick Bay: The Story of the Sick Berth and Medical Assistant Branch of the Royal Canadian Navy, 1910–1965*, West Vancouver: Cantaur, 1994.

Roberts, Leslie. *C.D.: The Life and Times of Clarence Decatur Howe*. Toronto: Clarke, Irwin, 1957.
Robertson, Terence. *The Golden Horseshoe: The Story of Otto Kretschmer, Germany's Top U-Boat Ace*. London: Evans Brothers, 1955.
Rohwer, Jürgen, and Hans Adolf Jacobsen, eds. *Decisive Battles of World War II: The German View*. New York: Putnam, 1965.
Röll, Hans J. *Korvettenkapitän Werner Hartenstein: Mit U156 auf Feindfahrt und der Fall "Laconia."* Germany: Würzburg Flechsig, 2009.
Rome, David, ed. *Canadian Jews in World War II*. Pt. I, *Decorations*. Montreal: Canadian Jewish Congress, 1947.
———. *Canadian Jews in World War II*. Pt. II, *Casualties*. Montreal: Canadian Jewish Congress, 1947.
Sarty, Roger. *Canada and the Battle of the Atlantic*. Montreal: Art Global, 1998.
Saunders, Hilary St. George. *Royal Air Force, 1939–1945*. Vol. 2, *The Fight Is Won*. London: HMSO, 1954.
Schepke, Joachim. *U-Boot Fahrer von heute*. Berlin: Deutscher Verlag, 1940.
Schmietenknop, Walter. *Saved*. Self-published, 2007.
Schneider, Werner. *12 Feindfahrten: Als Funker auf U-431, U-410 und U-371 im Atlantik und im Mittelmeer*. Weinheilm, DE: Germania-Verlag, 2006
Schull, Joseph. *Far Distant Ships: An Official Account of Canadian Naval Operations in WWII*. Toronto: Stoddart, 1987.
Sclater, William. *Haida: A Story of the Hard Fighting Tribal Class Destroyers of the Royal Canadian Navy*. Toronto: Oxford University Press, 1946.
Sebag-Montefiore, Hugh. *Enigma: The Battle for the Code*. London: Weidenfeld & Nicolson, 2017.
Sellers, Walter. *Hard Aground*. St. John's: Breakwater, 1992.
Shirer, William L. *The Rise and Fall of the Third Reich: A History of Nazi Germany*. New York: Simon and Schuster, 1959.
Schofield, B.B. *The Russian Convoys*. London: Pan Books, 1984.
Smith, Michael. *The Secrets of Station X: How Bletchley Park Helped Win the War*. London: Biteback, 2011.
Smith, Michael, and Ralph Erskine, eds. *Action This Day: Bletchley Park from the Breaking of the Enigma Code to the Birth of the Modern Computer*. London: Bantam Press, 2001.
Sugarman, Martin. *Full Ahead Both! Jewish Service in the British, Commonwealth and Israeli Merchant Navies in WW2—A Record of Honour*. London: AJEX Jewish Military Museum, 2016.

Tarrant, V.E. *The U-Boat Offensive, 1914–1945*. Annapolis, MD: Naval Institute Press, 1989.
Terraine, John. *Business in Great Waters: The U-Boat Wars, 1916–1945*. Barnsley, UK: Leo Cooper, 1989.
———. *The Right of the Line: The Royal Air Force in the European War, 1939–1945*. London: Hodder and Stoughton, 1985.
Tucker, Gilbert Norman. *Origins and Early Years*. Vol. 1 of *The Naval Service of Canada: Its Official History*. Ottawa: King's Printer, under authority of the Minister of National Defence, 1952.
———. *Activities on Shore During the Second World War*. Vol. 2 of *The Naval Service of Canada: Its Official History*. Ottawa: King's Printer, under authority of the Minister of National Defence, 1952.
Turing, Dermot. *Bletchley Park: Demystifying the Bombe*. Stroud, UK: Pitkin Publishing, 2015.
———. *The Bombe Breakthrough*. London: Pitkin Publishing, 2018.
Walker, Malcolm. *History of the Meteorological Office*. Cambridge: Cambridge University Press, 2011.
Watt, Frederick B. *In All Respects Ready: The Merchant Navy and the Battle of the Atlantic, 1940–1945*. Toronto: Totem, 1985.
Werner, Herbert. *Iron Coffins: A Personal Account of the German U-Boat Battles of World War II*. New York: Rinehart and Winston, 1969.
Windas, Cedric W. *Traditions of the Navy: A Collection of Naval Customs, Terms and Traditions*. Ottawa: Algrove, 2001.
Whinney, Bob. *The U-Boat Peril: A Fight for Survival*. London: Cassell, 1986.
Winterbotham, F.W. *The Ultra Secret*. New York: Dell, 1975.

NEWSPAPERS, PERIODICALS, BROADCASTERS, WEBLOGS
British Broadcasting Corporation
Bulletin of the American Meteorological Society
Canadian Broadcasting Corporation
Canadian Encyclopedia (online)
Canadian Military History
Familyheritage.ca
For Posterity's Sake: A Royal Canadian Navy Historical Project (www.forposterityssake.ca)
Globe and Mail
Gourock Times (Scotland)

Guardian
Halifax Chronicle
Halifax Daily Star
Halifax Herald
Harper's New Monthly Magazine
History Ireland
History of Second World War Magazine
History Press (www.thehistorypress.co.uk)
Huffington Post
Leamington Post and News
Legion Magazine
Maclean's
Military Heritage Magazine
News-Herald (Franklin, PA)
Northern Mariner
Northumberland News
Ottawa Citizen
Ottawa Evening Journal
Pembrokeshire Life (UK)
Red River North Heritage: Bill Shead Interview Transcript (https://redrivernorthheritage.com/bill-shead-interview-transcript/)
Seattle Times
Toronto (Evening) Telegram
Vancouver Community Network (http://www.vcn.bc.ca)
Veterans Affairs Canada (www.veterans.gc.ca)
Victoria Times-Colonist
Voice of Pelham (Ontario)
Washington Post
Windsor Daily Star

Photo Credits

FIRST PHOTO SECTION

Page 1

Portrait Alix Masheter: courtesy Nicholas Masheter; convoy in Bedford Basin April 1942 (PA-112993) and convoy conference at Admiralty House in Halifax (PA-105297): Library and Archives Canada (LAC); portrait U-boat commander Joachim Schepke, *Halifax Daily Star* clipping: courtesy David O'Brien.

Page 2

Portraits of John Birnie Dougall and Rachel Dougall: courtesy Jane Hutchison; Margaret Los: courtesy Margaret Los Haliburton family; George Edward Jamieson: courtesy Deanna Sky and Six Nations of the Grand River; Wren operating direction-finding device at HMCS *Coverdale* (PA-142540), North Atlantic convoy aerial (WRN-445), and Norville "Molly" Small (PL-12610): LAC.

Page 3

U190 crew in Nazi salute (CWM 19870078-002): Canadian War Museum; Karl Dönitz (146-1976-127-06A): Bundesarchiv Bilddatenbank; Franklin D. Roosevelt and Winston Churchill at Atlantic Charter meetings (80-G-26850): National Museum of the U.S. Navy; lend-lease destroyers at Halifax (PA-104338): LAC; HMCS *Orillia* launched at Collingwood, Ontario, 1940 (1985.0242.0003), photographer A.R. Turner: Marine Museum of the Great Lakes at Kingston; C.D. Howe: biographi.ca.

PAGE 4

Newfoundland Escort Force (PA-115350) and James Prentice on bridge (PA-204284): LAC; Hazel Le Cras and Gordon Baines, and Gordon Baines in HMCS *Amherst* radio shack: Gordon Baines photo collection, courtesy Grant Baines; Nan Adair, bombe bay, Alan Turing: Nan Adair Wright photo collection.

PAGE 5

Anthony Griffin: courtesy Griffin family; U-boat commanders Günther Prien: uboat.net; Otto Kretschmer: medium.com; Desmond "Debby" Piers (PA-204363) and women shipbuilders lunching in lifeboat (WRM-5201): LAC.

PAGE 6

Murray Westgate, Ian Tate with Paul Bélanger on steps, HMCS *Fort Ramsay* official opening, and survivors of torpedoed SS *Nicoya* ashore in Gaspé: all from Ian Tate photo collection, courtesy Davidson Tate; Fairmile *Q*056 launched at Humber Bay, Hans Sachau at helm: courtesy Elsa-Ann Pickard.

PAGE 7

Torpedo ashore in Gaspé: Ian Tate photo collection, courtesy Davidson Tate; survivor from sunken USS *Chatham* (PA-200327): LAC; James Lamb aboard HMCS *Camrose*: James Lamb photo collection, courtesy Jaimie Lamb; St. John's *Evening Telegram* front page (VA 40-16.1): The Rooms (Newfoundland and Labrador) Provincial Archives Division.

PAGE 8

Percy Nelles and Angus Macdonald at corvette model (PA-134335), HMCS *Battleford* at sea (PA-115381), securing depth charges (PA-134326): LAC; crew mess deck aboard HMCS *Amherst*, "Up Spirits" doling out day's rum tot: Gordon Baines photo collection, courtesy Grant Baines; portrait of Leonard Philbrook: courtesy Lee Philbrook.

SECOND PHOTO SECTION

PAGE 1

Portrait of Frank Mills, courtesy Harold Mills; ice-clearing duty, portrait of Cliff Perry: Cliff Perry photo collection, courtesy Perry family; corvette K165 HMCS *Battleford* (PA-115381), refuelling at sea (PA-116335): LAC.

PAGE 2

Hedgehog loading (PA-114737), Hedgehog deployed (PA-204584), ASDIC room and crew (PA-134330): LAC; Canadian Anti-Acoustic Torpedo (CAT) device on deck, John Dyke: John Dyke photo collection, courtesy Dyke family.

PAGE 3

Ken Rickers: courtesy Don Rickers; George and Harold Doig: courtesy George Doig Jr.; *Toronto Daily Star* front page: forposteritysake.ca; TNT loaded into merchant ship (PA-106527), survivors from sunken HMCS *Clayoquot* (PA-134342): LAC; Walter Schmietenknop: courtesy Schmietenknop family.

PAGE 4

HMCS *Assiniboine* versus *U*210 battle (DND E50834); John Stubbs, Royal Canadian Navy: Department of National Defence, Directorate of History and Heritage; sketch of battle from the *Halifax Mail*: forposteritysake.ca; Leonard Murray congratulates crew (PA-037456), Clarence King on bridge (PA-191029), Hal Lawrence and Arthur Powell (PA-106527): LAC; "Men of Valor" poster (CWM 19750317): Canadian War Museum.

PAGE 5

Depth charges astern (DHH O8521) (PA-116840), *U*165 under attack (DHH PMR83-1618), HMCS *Regina* show their gun-shield logo (PMR87-101): Department of National Defence, Directorate of History and Heritage; HMCS *Chilliwack* crew board *U*744 (CWM 19910001-029): Canadian War Museum; collecting human remains (PA-204344): LAC.

PAGE 6

Ian Tate and his HMCS *Valleyfield* anti-sub weapons team: Ian Tate photo collection, courtesy Davidson Tate; Don Rollins aircrew and Wellington bomber: courtesy Doug Rollins; David Hornell crew (DND PL30826), Catalina drops depth charges (DND RE64-1044): Department of National Defence, Directorate of History and Heritage; U-boat periscope and Schnorchel (PA-134331), VLR Liberator over convoy (PA-107907): LAC.

PAGE 7

HMCS *Esquimalt*, Terry Manual and crew mates: courtesy Terry Manual; portrait of Werner Hirschmann, forposterityssake.ca; Martin Franchetto at his gun position, NFB crew films surrender: courtesy Franchetto family; surrender of *U*190 (PA-145584): LAC.

PAGE 8

Portrait of Roy Harbin, courtesy Harbin family; German sailor POW being escorted: Cliff Perry photo collection, courtesy Perry family; Rodine Egan: courtesy Egan family; Halifax rioting: Justice Kellock collection, Halifax Municipal Archives; Bob Rae registration card, portrait of Bob Rae with medals: courtesy Steve Rae; portrait of Ken Davy: courtesy Ken Davy.

Index

Page numbers in italic followed by *n* refer to footnotes.

INDEX OF SHIP NAMES

HMC Ships

USN Ships

Merchant, Passenger, and Troop Ships

GENERAL INDEX